Fashion Patternmaking Techniques
for **Accessories**

Fashion Patternmaking Techniques for **Accessories**

Shoes
Bags
Hats
Gloves
Ties
Buttons

It Includes
Clothing for Dogs

Antonio Donnanno

HOAKI

HOAKI

Hoaki Books, S.L.
C/ Ausiàs March, 128
08013 Barcelona, Spain
T. 0034 935 952 283
F. 0034 932 654 883
info@hoaki.com
www.hoaki.com
hoaki_books

Fashion Patternmaking Techniques for Accessories
Shoes, Bags, Hats, Gloves, Ties and Buttons. It Includes Clothing for Dogs.

Reprint: 2021, 2019

Copyright © 2019 Hoaki Books, S.L
ISBN: 978-84-16851-61-4
Imprint: Promopress
Copyright © 2016 Ikon Editrice srl
Original title: *Accessori moda. La tecnica dei modelli*

Translation: Katherine Kirby
Drawings: Tiziana Universi
Cover design: spread

D.L.: B 23781-2018
Printed in Turkey

PREFACE

Fashion accessories are the objects which accompany and complete any type of clothing or outfit, for both men and women.

They have taken on an important role in fashion, craftsmanship and manufacturing, both economically and in terms of employment, closely related to the export of "Made in Italy" goods in general.

This book will illustrate bags, footwear, belts, gloves, ties, walking sticks and umbrellas. Today's accessories even include the following: - Eyewear - Fancy Buttons - Ribbons and Trimmings - Braces - Rings, Bracelets, Necklaces and Earrings - Pins - Silk Flowers.

A few accessories, both for men and women, have fallen out of favour and are no longer part of fashion, such as:

- The *cane*, an object generally used by men - not just the elderly, but rather often used as a weapon of self defence.

In the 18th century, fashion placed exquisite walking sticks in the hands of dames and knights, often with porcelain or ivory handles. Nobles often walked with a dagger cane, featuring a small dagger hidden within them. Today, walking sticks are no longer part of commonly-found fashion accessories. - The *handkerchief*, an ancient, versatile accessory. Handkerchiefs appear as far back as a portrait of a Chinese emperor who lived a thousand years before Christ.

The Romans used to carry two of them: the "orarium", tied to the left wrist, and the "sudarium", kept threaded under the belt.

The handkerchief even became part of the Eucharist, appearing as the strip of fabric that priests wear on their left wrist when celebrating Mass. Women's dowries included a certain number of handkerchiefs with their embroidered initials.

Today, aside from a few rare occasions and circumstances, the handkerchief is no longer considered a useful accessory.

- The *Hand Muff*, in the past, was an accessory for men and women. In the 17th century, the Sun King wore hand muffs made of extremely rare fur. In the 18th century, the hand muff became quite voluminous (especially the men's version), made of prized fur or with the addition of feathers. In the 19th century, this accessory was exclusively for women, exquisitely decorated with bows, fringe and tassels.

- *Jewellery*: this accessory could be the subject of its own chapter, requiring its own special handling due to the immense variety offered by creative jewellery making. The description of the techniques and general design principles must be accompanied by extensive instructions and guiding data sheets to create objects in an ancient or contemporary style.

For more than half a century, the industry's specialists have been engaged in a verification of the values, techniques and traditions of the past, both through individual work and through comparison and discussion. It is no longer possible to define jewellery in terms of the materials used, by the association to specific social categories or their decorative role. Fixed rules and restrictive limitations no longer exist. The generally accepted criteria today is that a jewel must be worn.

- Other accessories we no longer use: - Bands, gaiters, veils, hat/hairpins and hair grips; Perfume jars, tobacco tins, etc.

Today's youths use new accessories, not so much as fashion complements, but as high-tech or capricious items, such as mobile phone cases, bum bags, object cases with shoulder straps, piercings, etc.

I've covered the various themes listed in this volume by referring in particular to ancient and modern artisan techniques as well as those used in large-scape industrial manufacturing.

A few highly-specialised manual processes are carried out today only by a few old-school craftsmen or amateurs.

In order to reduce labour costs, professionals usually have to work quickly to meet very short turnaround times, and they often do not dedicate the time required for a few special manual techniques.

ACKNOWLEDGEMENTS

It isn't easy to write a technically complex book such such as this one, which deals with topics, arguments and techniques that vary for every type of accessory covered, without hearing from the various operators in the fields described, their technicians and their workers, who for years have been successful, overcoming the various problems they come across each day, inventing new techniques, new tools and new machines to create the products of undeniably high quality that have made the "Made in Italy" label famous.

The author of this text is the General Director of the Euromode School - The European Fashion Institute, which facilitated the creation of the book, especially in terms of the collaboration with teachers in the footwear and leather-working industries, to whom I owe the greatest and most sincere thank you for their contributions.

In a similar vein, for the information, expert advice and precious technical collaboration, I would like to thank all the owners of businesses consulted who, with their quick and unconditional availability, have made it possible to write this text, opening the doors to their companies and making their specialists available to demonstrate different working phases.

In particular, a thank you goes out to: Valleverde s.p.a. and the Company President, Mr Armando Arcangeli for the notable contribution made to the chapter on footwear; Soli Gerardo s.r.l. and the business's owner of the same name, for the contribution made to the chapter on gloves; the Cristianini hat factory and its owner Alberto Cristianini, for the contribution made on straw hats; the Cervo hat factory and its owner Giorgio Borrione, for their men's hats; Lemie s.p.a. and its owner Fulvio Rovaris, for bags and belts; Roberto Giovanardi and his tie factory, for the information about ties; the Ombrellificio Silvia s.n.c. umbrella factory and its owner Riccardo Riccardi; the Bottonificio Miban s.n.c. button manufacturer and its owner Romano Goni for the insight on buttons.

In addition, the author would like to express his gratitude to:
- Cappelleria Melegari in Milan;
- Museo del Cappello Borsalino in Alessandria;
- Museo della Paglia e dell'Intreccio in Signa (FI);
- Museo della calzatura "Pietro Bertolini" in Vigevano;
- Museo dell'Arte del cappello in Ghiffa (VB);
- The website on walking sticks: www.bastoni.it;
- Museo dell'ombrello e del parasole in Gignese (VB).

TABLE OF CONTENTS

Chapter 1
PAGE 9 LEATHER

Chapter 2
PAGE 17 FOOTWEAR

Chapter 3
PAGE 67 BAGS, RUCKSACKS, LUGGAGE AND BELTS

Chapter 4
PAGE 117 HATS AND BEANIES

Chapter 5
PAGE 161 GLOVES

Chapter 6
PAGE 181 NECK TIES

Chapter 7
PAGE 197 UMBRELLAS AND WALKING STICKS

Chapter 8
PAGE 211 BUTTONS

Chapter 9
PAGE 219 DOG APPAREL

LEATHER

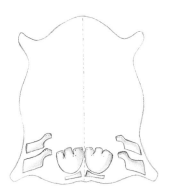

About leather 10
Leather processing 11
Tanning 12
Finishing 13
Types of leather and their uses 14
Natural and imitation leather 15
Leather processing 16

ABOUT LEATHER

Used for accessories such as wallets, belts and footwear, leather is a product made by tanning the hides of farmed or wild animals. A material that was first used in ancient times, today it is still a product of irreplaceable, notably complex characteristics, both chemically and technologically speaking. Nearly 80% of all leather produced around the world is used to make shoes, the rest for leather goods and clothing.

ANIMAL SOURCES OF LEATHER

Hides used for this purpose are generally taken from the following animals:
- **Hides from farm-raised mammals**, such as: bovines (bulls, cows and calves); equines (horses, donkeys, mules, zebras, etc.); ovines (sheep, rams, lambs); caprines (goats, billy goats, kids); suidae (pigs, sows, boar, peccary); camelids (camels, dromedaries, llamas, guanacos, alpacas, vigognas).
- **Leather from wild animals**, such as: buffalo, bison, elephants, rhinoceroses, hippopotamuses, reindeer, chamois, deer, roe deer, fallow deer, gazelles, boar, kangaroos, seals, walruses, ostriches.
- **Hides from reptiles and amphibians**, such as: crocodiles, caymans or alligators, snakes (boas, pythons, cobras, etc.), large lizards, giant frogs, sharks (dogfish, swordfish, hammerhead sharks, etc.), rajiformes, etc.

Each of these animals produces a wide variety of hides and leathers, each different from the next, not just because they are from different species, but also due to different feeding systems, environments and breeding, in addition to the type of body covering they have. The leather made from a wild animal is different than that made from a domesticated meat or dairy animal. In addition, animals raised in a cold, humid climate produce better leather than those living in hot, dry environments; animals with dense fur such as sheep and goats produce hides of a lower quality than animals with sparse fur, such as calves and horses.

HIDE CONSERVATION

Hides are collected by skinning animals that have been hunted or slaughtered. Immediately after, if a certain lapse of time before tanning is required, to avoid their putrefaction and allow for the temporary storage of the skins while awaiting transport to the tannery, they undergo:
- Salt curing, covering the inner part (that nearest the meat) of the hide with salt, just after skinning.
- Pickling, immersing the hides in a solution of diluted NaCl (sodium chloride) and HC1 or H2SO4 (acid), keeping them in a salt bath afterwards to encourage the subsequent absorption of the tanning materials that they'll be treated with.
- Drying, carried out by exposing well-tensioned hides to the air (and not the sun).

Skins processed in this way are sold as rawhide, dry hides or salted (cured) hides.

If, on the other hand, the skins go directly from slaughter to the tannery, there is no need to dry them or treat them in any other way. These skins are called fresh hides.

The largest suppliers of leather are the United States and Argentina, followed, in order of importance, by Europe, Asia, Australia and Africa. Italy is a significant producer of bovine, ovine, caprine, equine and suidae leather. However, it does not produce enough to meet the demand of the country, thus it imports hides and leather from other nations.

ANIMALS USED TO MAKE LEATHER		
REPTILES AND AMPHIBIANS	**WILD ANIMALS**	**FARMED ANIMALS**
CROCODILES CAYMANS (OR ALLIGATORS) SNAKES LARGE LIZARDS GIANT FROGS SKARKS SKATES RAYS	BISON FALLOW DEER BUFFALO GAZELLES RHINOCEROSES BOAR ELEPHANTS KANGAROOS REINDEERS SEALS CHAMOIS WALRUSES DEER OSTRICHES ROE DEER	BOVINES OVINES CAPRINES EQUINES SUIDAE CAMELS DROMEDARIES LLAMAS

Leather processing

Dried and salted hides are sent to the tanneries where, to reach the consistency and quality desired for the pre-established final production, they undergo a few processes divided into three phases: beamhouse operations, tanning, and finishing.

Beamhouse operations
There are basically four tanning preparation (beamhouse) phases: Soaking; fleshing, scudding and unhairing; liming and splitting; deliming and pickling:
- **Soaking:** is a process done in a special drum or tub, with water and chemical agents based on soda and potassium, to soften the dry hide and remove the salt and other curing substances used for preservation, to bring softness and elasticity to the hide.
- **Fleshing, scudding and Unhairing:** is the process carried out with calcium sulphide or fermented substances to remove the bits of muscle and fat which have remained attached on one side, and the hair from the other side of the skin.
- **Liming and Splitting:** liming, immersing the hide in a solution of lime and sodium sulphide, is necessary to soften the epidermis, while splitting consists of dividing the thickest hides into one or more layers to make them thinner, in a thickness adaptable for uppers, soles or for leather goods, as needed.
- **Deliming and Pickling:** an operation carried out by immersion in ammonium salt solutions to eliminate processing residues, grease and dirt.

After having carried out these operations, leather will be in a state called *"fleshed hide"* or a *"pelt"*, that is, in a soft state, ready for the next phase.

Tanning
With this operation, leather undergoes chemical and mechanical processing to preserve it indefinitely and to ensure its conservation over time. Tanning also gives the fibres a solid structure and compact quality in addition to elasticity and softness that varies according to the use its destined for.

A liquid containing tanning substances is put into drums, devices where all the operations of staking, tanning and dying take place The drum is essentially a barrel-shaped container with rods, which rotates around its central axis. As it rotates, the hides are held by the rods, then allowed to fall in the liquid. The drum is also used to stake and clean the hides. In this case, it's made up of two reels: the first, which contains sawdust, tumbles the hides; the second frees the hides from the sawdust.

Tanning materials
To carry out the tanning process and make the hides durable and elastic, vegetable tannins were used with oak and spruce bark, chestnut wood, tanner's sumac (also called Sicilian sumac) leaves and gallnuts up until the 19th century. In ancient Egypt, in addition to the vegetable tanning process, a mineral tanning process was also used, mostly made of common table salt and alum.

The materials used for tanning today can be divided into:
Vegetable tannins, oil-based tannins, mineral tannins and synthetic tannins.

Soaking in drums

Fleshing and unhairing

Splitting

Deliming and bating

Vegetable tannins
These tannins are substances with acidic properties, therefore also called tannic acids, characterised by their ability to tan hides. From a chemical point of view, tannins can be divided into two groups:
- The first creates aromatic oxides and sugars by hidrosis. It is formed by sugar molecules (generally glucose) esterified with acids, usually gallic acid and/or acids deriving from its condensation, such as m-digallic acid; the number of units of gallic acid monomer present in each tannin molecule may then exceed that of the esterifiable hydroxides present, which may vary from 9 to 1 for Chinese tannins and from 5 to 1 for Turkish tannins.
- The second type of tannin does not contain sugar, but gallic acid and esterified derivatives of ellagic acid, which in turn derives from the double condensation of two gallic acid molecules. The chemical composition of the tannin is usually represented by the formula $C_{76}H_{52}O_{46}$, even if the tannins do not correspond to a single type of chemical but rather a mixture. They usually are about 10% water.

Different types of tannins are found in gallnuts (excretions found on oaks and other plants, provoked by parasites), in the bark of many plants, in different fruits (chestnuts, horse chestnuts), and in certain leaves (tea).

TANNING

Tannins look like powders of different colours which range from whitish-yellow to brown, amorphous, with a weak yet characteristic odour and a strong, astringent flavour. They decompose when heated to about 210° C, creating pyrogallol and carbon dioxide. The tanning action of tannins is due to their acidic properties, so that, with acidic compounds of a similar nature, one gets the same results.

Oil tanning

These are usually fish oils (generally cod). Tanning takes place thanks to the bond which is created between the fatty acid esters which absorb oxygen. When tanning, the hides are coated multiple times with the oil and then fulled. They are then left for some time to air out, fermented in warm spaces and, lastly, pressed or washed with sodium carbonate solutions with the aim of eliminating the excess oil. This tanning process is used especially for suede, lamb, deer and kid leather.

Mineral tannins

Mineral tannins are used for the following types of tanning:
1) Chrome tanning, which requires a preliminary process, called "pickling", in which a drum of hides is filled with water and sea salt followed by acidification, preferably with sulphuric acid. The hides are then processed in tubs or vats with water-based solutions containing basic chrome sulphates. Now called "wet blue", the hides are then pressed, washed and neutralised with sodium bicarbonate solutions, dyes, fatliquored at 70-80° C with emulsified oils and shined. During this tanning process, scraps are created, used to prepare regenerated leather.
2) Alum tanning: carried out with water-based solutions of aluminium sulphate containing sodium chloride also. This procedure is similar to chrome tanning.
Mineral tanned leathers are grey-green in colour, easily absorb finishes, are quite durable, lightweight and tend not to fade.

Synthetic tannins

These tannins are composed of organic substances which can link to the proteins in the leather, making them imputrescible. They include:
1) formaldehyde (or formic aldehyde CH2 O);
2) quinones;
3) synthetic tannins, composed of phenols with formaldehyde, with acetone or with acidic compounds. These tannins are used as adjuvants for the tanning action of the vegetable tannins, with fungicidal, non-fermentative and antiseptic qualities.

Duration of the tanning process

Vegetable tanning can be carried out through four procedures, each one of a different duration and with different scopes:
1) Slow tanning, which is the oldest method of tanning with tannins, lasting from 12 to 18 months. Every two months, the hides are removed from the drums and undergo further processing with new vegetables and fresh water.
2) Mixed tanning, which is carried out in 4-6 months, consisting of a modification of the traditional method, adding treatment in drums with concentrated solutions of tannic extracts to speed up the tanning process.
3) Quick tanning, which is carried out in about 20 days, completing the operations with tannin extracts, in increasing concentrations, in different tubs.

4) Ultra-quick tanning, completed in 6-7 days, done by working in drums with warm tannin extracts. This type of tanning produces products which aren't very prized as the leather ends up weak and fragile due to the forced absorption of tanning materials and the heat it is exposed to.

Pit tanning

Pit tanning is used for leather destined for all the lower parts of men's and women's footwear - footbeds, soles, midsoles, heel pads, heels and welts - to make them resistant and ensure durability.
Unlike the leather used on the footwear uppers and leather goods, which are rotated constantly within the tanning drum, this method must not be used for the leather for footwear lowers as the rotation and the stress it causes would weaken the collagen which makes the hide durable and inalterable.
To avoid this, the ancient method of pit tanning is still used today. Three or more pits are required for this type of tanning, following the below procedure:
1) The first pit contains a limited amount of tanning agents. Cleaned and prepared hides are put in this pit to soak for about six weeks.
2) The second pit contains a higher concentration of tanning agents. Hides are placed in this pit to soak for another six weeks.
3) In the third pit, the tanner places the hides alternated with tanning materials, then, once the pit is full, he covers it completely with tanning materials and lets them soak for another eleven months.
Thanks to this process, raw animal hides become leather for soles that are robust, easy to clean, and heat and water resistant.

FINISHING

After the tanning process, the hides, often called 'crusts', undergo other finishing processes, based on production needs and quality. They are:

- **Mechanical Dewatering**, the process by which all the water absorbed is eliminated via adjustable rollers and presses for initial drying.
- **Drying**, through special systems within which warm air circulates to get rid of any remaining moisture.
- **Sanding, rolling, pressing**, to eliminate inconsistencies, especially on the flesh side, making the hides compact and the surfaces even and smooth.
- **Dying**, to add the colour requested by the manufacturer or according to fashion trends.

The hides can be dyed in different ways:
1) Vat dying, with the use of aniline dyes;
2) Brush dying, with which the dye is applied only on the grain side;
3) Spray dying, used to create a stain effect.

- **Fatliquoring**, with the application of oil, often in an emulsion, to soften the hides;
- **Drying**, to dry the skins again after dying. This phase can happen in different ways:
1) Via a mechanical method, with which the skins are passed through a 20 meter tunnel, heated and ventilated;
2) Via the more traditional method, which consists of laying the grain side of the hides on a piece of glass, passing over them repeatedly with a blunt blade to straighten out the folds, then letting them dry at a temperature of 40-60°C for 24-48 hours;
3) With the oldest, yet most practical method, which is that of stretching and affixing the dyed skins on wood frames, letting them dry at a temperature of 40-60°C for 24-48 hours.

- **Staking**, a treatment that's a bit more vigorous than ironing in which the hide, held under tension, is hit with curved blades, rubbed and massaged to add softness to certain kinds of skins.
- **Wheeling, sanding or napping**, through which the suede effect of split hides is obtained.
- **Buffing**, an operation similar to wheeling, but with a more delicate, fine effect.
- **Ironing and coating**, with the former, the flesh side is smoothed with a large iron or through the pressure of a mechanical roller at a temperature of 80-90° C; the latter is the application of a topcoat of glaze or paint.
- **Graining or embossing**, to imprint streaks, points, veining, scales in relief for imitation effects or to create various designs.
- **Printing**, to reproduce letters on the leather or designs in colours, gold, silver or in relief.
- **Waxing**, carried out on the grain side of the hide, treating it with wax and making it semi-glossy.

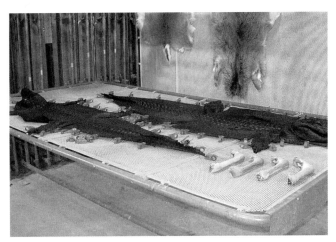

A few phases of the leather finishing process

Types of leather and their uses

Leathers have two distinct, different sides: one external, covered in hair, bristles, scales, quills, etc., called the *grain*, the other side, which adheres to the body of the animal, called the *flesh side*.

The entire layer which forms the true skin, thus the leather of the animal between these two parts, is called the *dermis*.

The dermis is made of long, fibrous cells, arranged in a irregular fashion, but firmly linked to one another to form a compact, durable body.

From the top grain layer, soft, smooth nappa leather is obtained; the nappa can also be brushed to create nubuck, which has an even finer surface. The flesh side of the leather is rougher, and can be buffed to become suede.

Hides that have been tanned and finished, which are ready to be sold, generally under the name of "leathers" (even if they often have different names according to their future uses or the animals that they come from).

Thick skins are divided into two or more layers according to the type of leather and the needs. Adult ox hides usually are split into three parts, while calfskins are split in two.

Eighty percent of commercial leathers are from bovine hides and cover a wide range of use: from footwear to leather goods to belts.

Names and uses of different types of leather

- **Sole leather:** thick, dense, waterproof and slightly flexible, this leather is used in its natural colour (reddish yellow) or in black; it's best use is as soles for footwear or as industrial seals; it is generally made from ox, cow, bull or buffalo hides.
- **Upper leather:** thinner, softer leather than that for the sole; it's soft, pliable and shiny on one or both sides; it is used mainly for footwear, luggage, bags, pouches, jackets and upholstery; it is made from calf or vacchetta (cow) hides.
- **Saddle and belt leather:** this type of leather comes from the part of the hide called the bend, the back and sides of the animal, and is quite traction-resistant, flexible and compact.
- **Glove leather:** very soft, thin and flexible types of leather; they can be shiny, brushed or textured; glove leather is usually made from kid or lamb hides.
- **Suede:** made from the splitting of two thick hides, or from the degraining of normal hides; it is used for footwear, casual clothing and for bags.
- **Coated leather:** thin, flexible leather that, with the application of top coatings, is given a shiny look. This leather is used for footwear and bags; generally from calfskin.
- **Textured leather:** during the finishing stage, the surface of this leather is imprinted with designs by special machinery and equipment. They often feature granulated surfaces with dots, stripes, etc. Generally made of donkey or mule hide, this leather is rough and not very flexible, often used for linings, footwear and leather goods.
- **Morocco leather:** a type of fine, soft leather that is sometimes shiny or dyed, made from goat or sheep skins, generally manufactured in Morocco, Iraq and Turkey. It's used for belts, bags, upholstery and slippers.
- **Russia leather:** leather made of goat, calf or horse skins, generally red or black in colour, tanned with birch leaves. It is solid and waterproof.

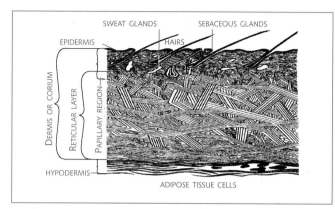

Animal skins are soft, slimy, stretchy, fold-able and full of water (65%). Only one of the three layers is used for leather production: the dermis or corium, made of the papillary layer and of the reticular layer that, due to its structure in random yet solidly connected strips, ensures the density and elasticity of the leather.

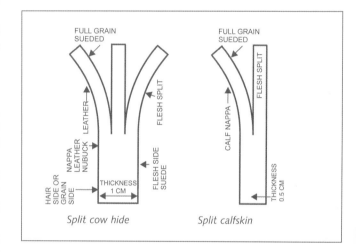

Split cow hide   *Split calfskin*

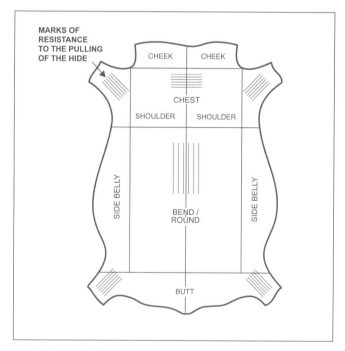

Merchandising subdivision of calfskins, indicating the main marks of resistance to pulling.

Natural and imitation leather

- **Cowhide**: a type of leather from cows. Thick and dense, waterproof and lightly pliable. The grain side shows irregularly-placed pores; it is used mainly for soles, but also for uppers, after appropriate splitting. Cowhide suede can be used for clothing as well.
- **Calfskin**: a highly prized type of leather, with a porous structure distributed uniformly across the entire surface. It's thinner than cowhide, soft, pliable and shiny. It is used mostly for uppers, footwear, bags, clothing and furniture.
Calfskin suede is a high-quality hide for its elegant surface and silky hand, often used for fine items of clothing.
- **Goatskin**: this type of leather has coarse pores and is often used for gloves, bags, slippers, hat bands and for prized garments. Goatskin suede is elegant and always holds its shape. It is soft and silky to the touch.
- **Lambskin**: has a fine, porous structure, a reduced weight and is soft to the touch. Lambskin is considered a prized, elegant leather, use in various ways in high quality clothing and leather goods. Dried and well stretched on frames, ironed and shined, lambskin can be transformed into parchment.
- **Pig or boar skin**: the leather made from the hides of these animals is durable, sufficiently soft and pliable. It is characterised by a surface with a fine grain, with small holes in groups of three, visible with a magnifying glass.
- **Shark and seal skin**: these animals provide thick, rigid leather, and therefore they must always be split; they are characterised by a rather fine grain and are used for bags, luggage, belts and various other leather goods.
- **Ostrich leather**: characterised by small raised points due to the feathers, this leather is sought-after especially for women's footwear and bags.
- **Llama leather**: this leather has a soft, supple surface and is used for casual, suede jackets for men and women and for various leather goods.
- **Crocodile or alligator leather**: characterised by scales of different shapes and sizes, this leather is very costly and quite rare. It is used for footwear and for bags, exclusively made from the belly of the animal as the skin on the back is too tough and scaly.
- **Snakes, lizards and giant frogs**: These animals also have scales, but they're smaller, finer and have greater pliability. They are used to make women's footwear, bags, various high-quality leather goods, belts and ties.

Limitations
- **Regenerated leather**: made from scraps coming from the shaving of chrome-tanned leather. Those scraps are shredded in special machines so as to create a mixture that is treated with a sodium bicarbonate solution then vegetable tanned, with the addition of natural rubber and sodium chloride as a coagulant and transformed into sheets that are pressed and dried between rollers heated to a temperature lower than 70° C.
The product obtained can be used as such, coated, or worked in a way that gives it the look of leather obtained from various types of hides. Regenerated leather is used to create leather goods at a low price point (such as heel pads, insoles, etc.).
- **Bonded leather**: is made from the scraps and powders of natural leather processing, then treating it with gluten and compressing it.

- **Fibroleum or coriolum**: is obtained from the shredding of leather scraps, reduced down to wads, then processed with gluten and pressed with various fibres.
- **Linoleum**: is a product made of a mixture of particles from leather, wood, casein, cork and minerals, combined with linseed oil, cooked and pressed.
- **Pegamoid**: is a product made of canvas combined with all the ingredients used for linoleum except linseed oil, which is replaced by synthetic resins.
- **Pleather, leatherette or artificial leather**: is a product made from synthetic polyvinyl plastics.
- **Vulcanised fibre**: a mixture of cellulose processed with zinc chloride and transformed into an amyloid substance through heat and pressure, resulting in a strong, durable mass similar to cardboard, that is rigid and waterproof, finished with various grain textures. This product is mainly used to produce office folders and durable suitcases.
- **Natural rubber**: a product obtained from the latex of a few tropical plants, which is then heated and mixed with sulphur and other chemicals. It's often used for both casual and more elegant footwear soles.
- **Synthetic rubber**: is a category of polymers synthesized from various products, including butadiene, isobutine, chloroprene, etc. It is used to make soles, uppers and many types of waterproof garments and accessories.

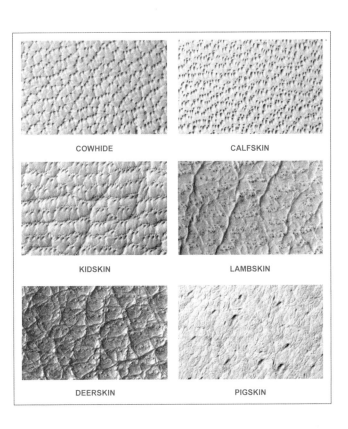

COWHIDE

CALFSKIN

KIDSKIN

LAMBSKIN

DEERSKIN

PIGSKIN

LEATHER PROCESSING
BEAMHOUSE OPERATIONS - WORKING HIDES

Hides

2. Liming and unhairing

3. Fleshing

1. Soaking

4. Deliming

TANNING - FLESHED HIDE

5. Tanning in vats

6. Tanning in drums

TANNED - FINISHING

7. Pressing - splitting - shaving

8. Re-tanning

9. Air-drying - semi-drying

10. Softening

11. Final drying

12. Staking

13. Final inspection and measuring thickness

14. Leather and finished hides in the warehouse

FOOTWEAR

A short history 18
Main footwear forms and lines 20
Tools and equipment 22
Shoe-making terminology 24
The basics of footwear patterns 25
Anatomy of the foot 26
Conformation of the foot 27
Shoe measurements 28
Lasts 29
Measurements and outline of the foot 30
Patternmaking techniques 31
The classic men's derby 32
Classic men's footwear 33
Moccasin or loafer 34
Tubular construction 35
Women's loafers and ballerina flats 36
Derby shoe and high heels 37
Court shoes 38
Desert boots and men's ankle boots 40
Men's boots 41
Women's boots 42
Heels 43

Open shoes and sandals 44
Mules, platforms and clogs 45
Sports and causal shoes 46
Children's footwear 47
Artisan working phases 48
Sewing the upper and lining 50
The lower parts of the shoe 51
Reinforcements and lasting the upper 52
Welts and rands 53
Outsoles 54
Heels on men's footwear 55
Finishing the shoe 56
The shoemaking industry 58
Industrial production 59
Industrial manufacturing processes 60
Industrial working processes 61
Cutting 62
Preparing the uppers 63
The binding room 64
Stitching machinery 65
Injected footwear 66

A SHORT HISTORY

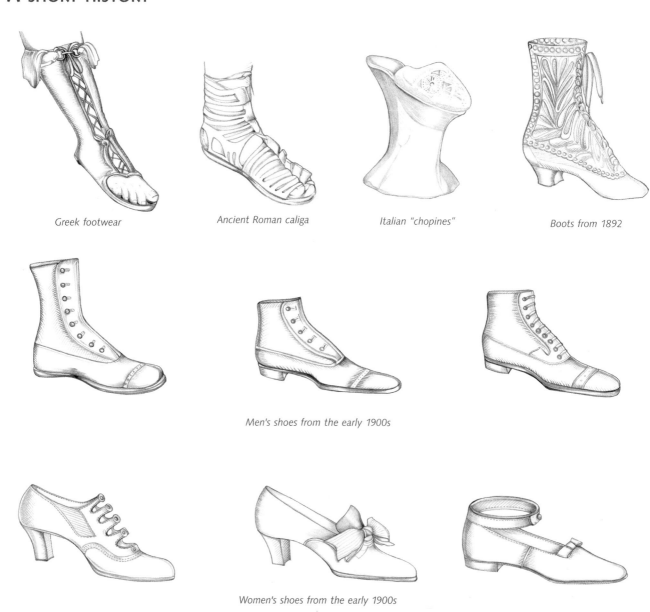

Greek footwear

Ancient Roman caliga

Italian "chopines"

Boots from 1892

Men's shoes from the early 1900s

Women's shoes from the early 1900s

Shoes are comfortable footwear made of an upper plus a sole, together covering the top and bottom of the foot. The upper used on wide variety of models can be in leather, fabric or other materials. The sole can be in leather, rubber, such as para rubber or another type, with various shapes and heel sizes.

The first shoes date back to ancient Egypt and were not unlike Greek and (later) Roman models. The most ancient footwear model that we know the shape of is the "carabatina", a leather-soled sandal tied to the foot with interlaced strips of leather. Roman footwear was unisex and differentiated between right and left foot shapes. For walking, they wore "calceus", similar to their "carabatina", while out in the countryside they wore "perones", boots high to the calf, laced with hobnailed soles. When hunting or horseback riding, on the other hand, they wore lace-up thin leather boots enriched with ornamentation, medals and caste indications.

Senators wore black and white "calceus" and emperors wore "mulleus" with red leather laces. The army used a hobnailed shoe called a "caliga", which eventually evolved into the nickname of one emperor: Caligula.

In the 11th century, kings and dignitaries worn soft ankle boots, with long rows of buttons. In the 12th century, at the English court, shoes with a sharp point like the tail of a snake began to appear, remaining in fashion for the following three centuries. They grew ever longer, until having to be laced at the ankle, with a sock-shoe called "poulaine" (or Crakow).

In the 13th century "espadrillas" (canvas shoes with cord soles) appeared in Naples, originating from Catalonia and the Basque Country, still worn today. In the same period in Ciociaria, near Rome, people wore "cioce", while in Friuli they made velvet slippers with a fabric sole.

By the 1400s, Italian footwear was already of a high quality: cut of nearly just one piece of material, shoes had a fine sole and wrapped the foot like a glove.

In the 1500s, shoes were flat and rose to the ankle, with a square shape and various seams over the upper, giving them a bulging look.

In the early 1600s, footwear became more robust, with a rounded, long or square toes and high heels.

Shoes 1930 - 35

Shoes 1940 - 50

Shoes 1950 - 65

Shoes 1970 - 80

Shoes 1990 - 2004

In Venice, "ciapine" (or chopine or copine) came into fashion: dangerously high (some were up to 1 meter/3.28') and uncomfortable footwear worn by women to appear taller, made of wood and covered in leather of various colours and, at times, painted and personalised.

Ciapine were adopted in other countries such as Syria, where they were called "Kubkab".

In the 1700s, shoes were embellished with accessories and applications. It was the era of buckles, simple or with precious stones, crystals, pearls, silver and enamel, with which one boasted or showed of one's wealth.

In the 1800s, during the Imperial period, women wore low, comfortable shoes while men wore boots. In the late 1800s, men's shoes took on exaggerated, ridiculous shapes with pointed, sharp, raised toes "a la poulaine", and with wide, flattened heels, while women's shoes had heels once again.

Men (as well as women and children) wore gaiters and, from America, practical "walkovers" arrived, a model with a rounded toe. In the early 1900s, both men and women wore ankle boots with gaiters with incorporated elastic over them, while formal men's shoes were two-tone.

After WWII, women preferred to wear comfortable "ballerina" flats and "stiletto heels", while the proletariat and the poor wore "tennis shoes". Young intellectuals preferred desert boots worn under blue jeans.

In the Sixties, when skirts rose above the knee, shoes took on new importance in relation to the body. Boots began to be worn, in softer leather as it touched the leg.

It was the start of a new attempt to redefine footwear, with shoes that eventually came to resemble stockings as they rose above the knee.

The shoe and how it fit gained importance and stylists began playing with proportions and materials.

Today there are footwear designers, such as Pollini, Fratelli Rossetti, Sergio Rossi, Bruno Magli, Diego della Valle, Tanino Crisci, Claudio Viola, Osvaldo Martino and many others who offer innovative colour and material combinations, who come up with new proportions between heel and upper, accenting or softening the curve of the instep.

Main footwear forms and lines

Monk strap shoe

Oxford brogues with wingtips

Semi-brogue Oxford with a straight toe-cap

Men's derby

Semi-brogue derby with a straight toe-cap

Two-tone Budapest brogue derby

Moccasin or loafer

Boat shoe

Women's penny loafer

Loafer with elastic

Straight-cut loafer

Moccasin

Oxford

Buckle loafer

Penny loafer

Women's heeled derby

Ballerina flat

Every season, the lines and the shapes of footwear, like clothing, undergo changes and updates by manufacturers and designers. The models considered classic today, worn by stylish men and women, are the same ones that were created at the end of the 19th century, are defined mainly by their shape, their closure method (open or closed lacing systems, buckle fastenings or slip-ons), by the number of pieces that make up the upper and by the presence or lack of decorative openwork (brogueings) on the upper.

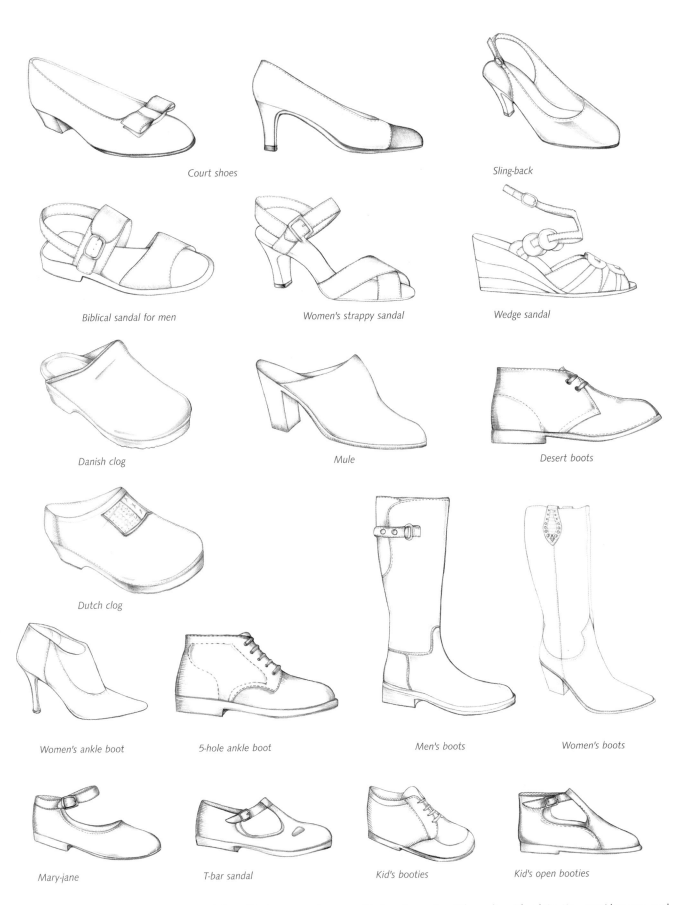

Court shoes

Sling-back

Biblical sandal for men

Women's strappy sandal

Wedge sandal

Danish clog

Mule

Desert boots

Dutch clog

Women's ankle boot

5-hole ankle boot

Men's boots

Women's boots

Mary-jane

T-bar sandal

Kid's booties

Kid's open booties

There are about a dozen classic men's models and just as many for women as well. Of those, many variants are derived from the production of other models, especially in the working of the upper, where designers have infinite creativity. The main footwear models are:
- Oxfords, with plain tip, semi-brogue and brogue versions;
- Derby shoes (or Gibsons), with plain tip, semi-brogue and brogue versions;
- Norwegians (weejuns), Monkstraps, Moccasins, Sandals, Court shoes, Penny Loafers, Mary Janes, Ballerina flats, Slingbacks, Platforms, Mules, Clogs, Desert Boots, Chukkas, Ankle Boots, T-bars, Booties, Slippers.

Tools and equipment

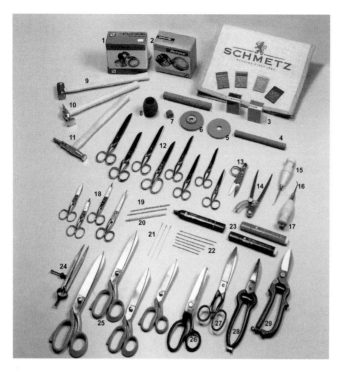

1. Putsch cup blade
2. Fortuna cup blade
3. Schmetz needles
4. Dressing sticks for New Rimca wheels
5. Fleshing grinder without a bearing
6. Fleshing grinder with a bearing
7. Mini emery hone
8. Conveyor roller
9. Vigevano edging hammer
10. Chromed edging hammer
11. Magnet-tip modeller hammer
12. Stainless steel edging scissors
13. 12 cm weaver scissors
14. 15 cm/5.91" drawing compass

15-17. Awl
18. Stainless steel curved scissors from 12 to 17 cm/4.72-6.69"
19. Refills
20. Mini biro
21. Moccasin brush n. 3-4-5-6
22. Saddler's needle n. 1-2-2/0-4/0-6/0
23. Tratto® marker
24. 15 cm/5.91" spring compass
25. Tailor's shears
26. Sample cutting shears
27. Curved blade shears, rubberised
28. Black-handled leather shears

29. Extra-large green-handle leather shears
1. Automatic carding wheel,140 ø
2. 160 ø steel wheel (hole of 40)
3. Automatic carding wheel, 75 ø
4. 120 ø steel wheel (hole of 40)
5. 1-Layer pinholder tray
6. Large brass spirit lamp
7. 25 cm/9.84" fixed workstand
8. Discs in canvas - military wool - Wales and Scotland wool 150 ø
9. Gold-silver-bronze-copper-black rolls
10. Oval electric iron
11. Heating plate for the iron
12. Paraffin wax

13. Chrome-plated tool sharpener
14. Slim taper file
15. Mercur cutter blade
16. Leone shoemaker's knife
17-18-19. Denifl shoemaker's knife
20-23. Metwar needles
24. Mozart blades
25. Olfa AB 50 box cutter
26. Olfa AB 50 blades
27. Pelteko 58 blades
28. Sharpening stone
29. Mozart cutter
30. Blade-holder/cutter
31. Pelteko knife

Pattern paper. Smooth; medium thickness. In sheets or rolls, but it must be quite durable to be used without ripping.

Manila paper. To trace the base patterns in all their components. The outlines made are placed on the leather to be cut.

Carbon paper. Used to "duplicate" parts of the entire pattern, taken up from the form.

Paper scissors. To cut out the patterns without using the leather scissors (which would get dull).

Pencil and a rubber. To trace the patterns.

French curves. Helpful when drawing the curves of a pattern.

Compasses. Used to draw the arcs and circles of patterns on paper and paperboard, in addition to on leather.

Wheatpaste glue. A paste made from the starch of wheat and water with pieces of chestnuts or potato. The resulting glue is used to hold two pieces together so they can be glued, but also to make them more robust.

Thread for sewing. Thread made of cotton, silk, or durable linen. Twisted yarn is used on the upper part of the shoes, composed of 3 to 9 individual threads. Silk thread, which is thinner, is used to sew the different parts of the uppers.

Pitch. Prepared by heating the resin along with the beeswax and paraffin. The resulting soft "dough", create ready-to-use pieces. Cobbler's thread is rubbed over the pitch multiple times, making the thread more robust, compact and water-resistant.

Welt needles. 8 cm/3.15" long curved needles. Two needles, inserted in opposite directions, are needed to sew the welt.

Awl. A sort of awl used by shoemakers to create holes in the sole.

There are two types of awls: a shorter one, to create holes for the toggles to insert in the rand; and a longer, slightly curved one to add the holes for the seams on the welts.

Stitch marker wheel. A metal tool with a wood handle with a point formed by two rounded teeth, connected by a concave curve. It's used to mark the position of the stitching on the welts and to pass over the stitches after they've been sewn to make them more regular and decorative.

Measuring tape. A measuring tape with metric measurements on one side and imperial measurements on the other.

Clicking knife. A sharp, flexible steel tool, similar to a scalpel, used to cut the upper, following the paperboard outlines. The central part of the shoemaker's knife is covered by a layer of leather, to protect the hand.

Shoemaker's knife. This knife has a slightly angled steel blade, used to cut tough leather on the lower part of the shoe, with a thickness ranging from 6 cm to 8 cm/1.36-3.15".

The central part of this tool is also covered by a layer of leather to protect the hand, as it is necessary to apply quite a lot of pressure when cutting the leather of the sole.

Bone knife. A knife-shaped piece of bone with a point made by the shoemaker. This tool is used to smooth the channel (a fissure into which the seam of the sole is inserted).

Hone. A piece of stone that is used to hone the shoemaker's knife and the cutter. Blades should be honed after cutting every single piece.

Hollow punch. A tool with ridges in tempered steel, used to make holes on the upper, both decorative and functional (eyelets for laces). The hollow punch may have a point with a diameter fro 1.3 to 5mm/0.05-0.20".

Sleeking bone. Used to eliminate and smooth the marks left by the hammer and forceps when hammering to smooth out the welt.

Pin dispenser. Used to quickly disburse tacks and pins used to assemble the shoes.

Groover. Tool used to create crevices/splits of various types and to mark stitch points.

Work table. A wood or iron structure with a working surface in tempered masonite; with measurements varying from 1.3 m to 1.8 m/4.27-5.91', it can be fitted with a piece to place objects, tools and a lamp.

A zinc plate and a plastic plate. Used to cut leather without ruining the top of the table.

Calibre. Tool used to check the number and the measurement of the length of the foot.

Leveller. A tool that, sharpened like a planer, is used to level the edges. Equipped with a guide channel, it removes protruding surfaces on the edges of the sole and heel with precision down to the millimetre, ensuring equal sizes.

Smoother or anvil. Used, after having been heated over a flame, to iron the surface of the leather of the finished, still-wet shoe, pressing out residual folds or creases.

Glue gun. Container filled with glue or mastic, complete with a spout to pour out the liquid and a brush to spread the liquid on the pieces to be glued. It is used to make new shoes or repair old ones.

Cobbler's hammer. Looks and is shaped like a normal hammer, weighing about 500g, but is used with different functions in different points. One part of the hammer is made of a flat, disc-shaped surface, used to hammer the tip of the heel pads, to soften the joints between the two parts of leather, or the side parts of the shoes to remove the small folds in the leather. The other part of the hammer is composed of a blunted tip used to flatten the folds that form between one nail and another.

Cobbler's plane. A tempered steel tool that's slightly curved and very sharp, used to thin the leather to the right and left of the markings for the welt stitching.

Leather pliers or lasting pliers. Tool with two uses:
1) Grab onto and pull the edges of the upper resting on the last; 2) Hit the nails used to affix the upper on the wood of the last, using the special flat surface of the pincer end.

Pincers. Used to extract nails and other various uses.

Rasp. There are two types of rasps: the classic half-moon rasp, used to level the lower parts of the shoe and shape the curves of the edges; and special rasps for the inner parts, rounded or long and thin, used to level the inserts within the shoe.

Glass shard. A normal piece of glass used to remove any irregularities that are created on the sole during the production process. The glass is used to remove thin layers of leather from the sole, making it permanently smooth.

Ornamental embroidery wheels. These are tempered steel wheels that are used to create different types of edging, running them along the surface to create a sort of decoration, after having heated them to a suitable temperature by holding them over a flame. The decorations may be added to various points such as: the upper edge of the heel, the edge of the welt, the line of the sole demarcating, between the dyed leather and natural leather, the upside-down edge of the welt that is attached to the upper.

Sewing machine. Sewing machines used to make footwear are robust and designed to create the stitching used in the assembly phase. They're equipped with rotating prong feed dogs, a controlled wheel presser foot, accompanying needle and a separately-controlled trimmer.

Notching machine. Used to cut the corners of leather, creating zig-zag, curved or straight motifs.

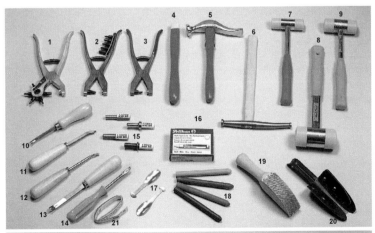

1. 6-size leather punch
2. 5-size leather punch
3. 1-size leather punch
4. Handle for a cobbler's hammer
5. Cobbler's hammer
6. Wood heel hammer
7. 28 mm/1.10" nylon mallet
8. 45 mm/1.77" nylon mallet
9. 35 mm/1.38" nylon mallet
10. Planer for women's heels
11. Staple remover
12. Wood handled tack remover
13. Planing tool
14. Plastic handled tack remover
15. 40 cm/15.75" steel pin for the workstand
16. Wax marking crayon
17. Tongue for the hammer head
18. Wax retouching crayon
19. Roughener
20. Men's and women's form
21. Shoemaker's tape measure
22-26. Different pliers/pincers
27-30. Different side nippers

At right: A heavy-duty leather sewing machine

SHOE-MAKING TERMINOLOGY

3-D pattern: the entire pattern of a shoe, created by applying special pattern paper on the outside of the last.

Alloy: a mixture of different metals.

Ankle boots: a type of footwear that rises to the ankle.

Appliques: applied decorative elements.

Apron: the upper part of the upper of a moccasin, marked by external stitching

Ballerina shoes: light, flexible shoes without a heel or with a very low heel.

Basketball shoes: sporty footwear with a high, reinforced, padded ankle.

Bend: the part of a hide corresponding to the back of the animal.

Binding: the stitching which joins the sole to the upper.

Blake construction: a method of joining the upper to the sole with stitching.

Bonded leather: a material made of regenerated leather.

Bonding margin: part of the upper affixed to the insole.

Cementing: union of the upper to the sole with glue.

Chukkas: a type of shoe made with ideal-stitched construction in different materials: suede, unlined in smooth leather, etc.

Counter: A reinforcement added to the inside part of the shoe at the heel.

Court shoe: also called pumps, generally for women, with a low-cut upper.

Cowboy boots: traditional pointed-toe boots with a heel.

Culatta or butt: leather from the rump of a calf.

Derby: type of shoe with ideal-stitched construction, generally worn in the winter, with quarters sewn on top of the vamp.

Dewatering: removing the water from tanned hides with presses and rolls covered in felt.

Drum: a rotating machine in the shape of a drum used to tan hides.

Drummed or tumbled: refers to hides tumbled in empty drums.

Drying: operation by which the moisture of the leather is reduced through the use of warm air.

Embossed: a technique where heat is used to give a bas-relief to leather.

EVA: material used for heels or wedges that are to be wrapped in a different material.

Exposed edges: raw cut edges of leather.

Guttaperca: a material used to make leather alternatives.

Half 3-D pattern: half of the 3-D pattern of a last, created by resting it on pattern paper.

Heel: a piece added to the back of the shoe's sole formed of lifting layers or a single block, generally covered in a different material.

Heel band: a template for the heel.

Heel breast: the inner curve of the heel.

Invisible stitching: A stitching method in which both sides of the seam are covered by a strip of leather.

Ideal: a traditional hand-working technique in which the upper is sewn to the insole via external stitching.

Lasting machine: a machine that pulls the shoe over the last.

Lasting margin: the excess part of the upper, folded over and used for construction/attaching to the insole.

Lubrication: when leather is softened with oil.

Machine lasted: a type of construction that, once the footbed has been attached, lasts the shoe on a special machine.

Mary Janes: classic children's footwear, often for formal occasions, with a low ankle, a rounded toe and a single strap, marking the transition from child to adult.

Microporous rubber: a type of porous, lightweight, flexible rubber used for soles.

Moccasins or loafers: classic, low-heeled, slip-on footwear for men and women, worn in both summer and winter, with or without a top strap. Extremely comfortable and generally made of soft leather.

Moccasin construction: A special type of processing in which the upper passes under the last, wrapping around it to be joined at the top of the foot.

Multi-layer: a composition of two or more layers of various materials joined together, used to create heels for men's footwear.

Orthodic insole: an anatomically correct insole.

Oxford: a type of shoe closed by a lacing system that is attached under the vamp.

Penny loafers: lightweight, rounded and comfortable slip-on shoe with a medium heel.

Piping: a strip of leather rolled into a tube shape.

Polishing: an operation which brings out a shiny surface through a special treatment.

Quarter: the rear part of the upper.

Ridge: the part of the sole that extends out from the upper.

San Crispino: a type of construction similar to that of ideal, except that the upper is folded around the insole.

Sandal: summer footwear composed of a sole and a strappy upper in leather or other materials.

Sealing: operation in which the parts are covered with mastic.

Seam margin: the excess part of the upper that is folded under when the parts of the upper are joined.

Seat: where the heel is applied to an open, very soft upper.

Shank: a sheet of metal inserted in the sole to reinforce the back part of the shoe.

Shoemaker's knife: another name for the clickers knife.

Shot peening: process by which the fibres of the leather are made soft and stretchy through ironing and folding.

Shoulder: front part of a calf that goes from the shoulder to the head.

Size: the measurements of the shoe last.

Skiving/fleshing: the removal of connective tissue and meat from the hide, done by hand with knives or with a special machine.

Slippers: typical house shoes for men or women, in soft leather, velvet or cloth, generally with a flexible leather or rubber sole, with or without a heel.

Split: type of leather used for fine linings.

Square feet: measurement system for hides.

Sole leather thick, not very pliable leather that's durable and waterproof.

Sole template: the pattern of the shape of the shoe's sole.

Strap: strips of leather or other materials that pass across the top of loafers.

Suede: the effect obtained by buffing the flesh side of a piece of leather.

Strobel construction: a method of sewing the upper without lasting margins (force-lasted).

T-bar (sandal): a sandal with ideal-stitched construction, generally for kids, comfortable and with two holes on the upper.

Tanning: the process by which hides absorb the tanning materials that they're soaked in inside the drums. The liquid penetrates the spaces between the protein fibres and turns them into leather.

Textured leather: leather with motifs in relief, created with presses.

Thunit: a synthetic material that looks like leather.

Toe box: the very front part of the upper.

Trainers: soft athletic shoes with lots of give.

Tunnel stitching: a seam done by hand passing the thread through half the thickness of the leather.

Upper: the top part of the shoe that wraps around the foot.

Velours: a term referring to peached leather.

Waist: the narrow part of the last between the ball of the foot and the heel.

Walking shoes: a casual type of shoe designed for functionality and comfort, often at the expense of aesthetics.

Waxed: a surface that has been polished with wax.

Waxing: the surface of the grain side of the leather is treated with wax to make it semi-glossy.

Welt: a strip of leather which joins the sole to the upper.

Wingtip: a type of brogue decoration on the toe cap.

THE BASICS OF FOOTWEAR PATTERNS

Footwear patterns, as we've seen, are determined according to the characteristics of their construction method.

There are a few shoe models that are considered classic, as they've become famous and commonly found over the years. They're defined, first and foremost, by the way in which they're fastened: 1) Shoes with laces (with closed or open lacing systems); 2) Shoes that slip on or have a buckle.

Shoes with closed lacing systems, such as Oxfords, have quarters (the two pieces of leather where the eyelets are) that are stitched under the vamp but over the tongue. Shoes with open open lacing systems, such as Derbys, have quarters positioned over the vamp, laced together over the tongue. Depending on the type of shoe, the upper can vary in shape and number of pieces. Simple moccasins are composed of one piece of leather, while other models, such as the Derby or Budapest, are composed of multiple pieces: quarters, external heel counters and a vamp which may in turn be composed of a smooth toe box or with wingtips or other types of decorative stitching/openwork.

Brogueing (decorative openwork), is another distinctive quality of various types of shoes, especially for men's footwear, which characterised fashion from the last century onward.

In addition, there are many types of variations in the construction of single models which, along with the designer's creativity, define the style.

Shoe components.

- **Shank:** a piece of flat steel, usually about 10 cm/3.94" long and 1.5 cm/0.59" wide, inserted in the cavity between the insole and outsole, at the centre of the shoe, from the halfway point of the heel forward. The shank adds stability to the shoe.
- **Heel counter:** the external piece which covers the seam of the side pieces of the upper (quarters), made of a thin strip or a broader piece. The inner counter is a layer of leather that reinforces the centre-rear point, where the two sides of the upper meet.
- **Lining:** an inner part made of soft suede that lines the upper.
- **Sock lining:** The layer of soft leather that covers the insole, in direct contact with the bottom of the foot.
- **Interlining:** a very thin reinforcing layer, placed between the outer leather of the upper and the lining, and between the outer and inner counters.

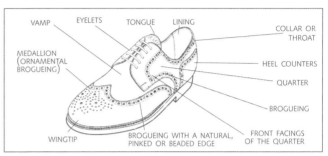

Outer parts of a men's shoe

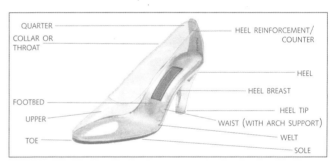

Outer parts of a women's shoe

- **Welt:** a strip of leather 2 cm/0.79" wide and about 60 cm/23.62" long, about 3 mm/0.12" thick, that acts as a structural part of the shoe as it helps hold the sole, footbed and upper together.
- **Rand:** a strip of leather 3 cm/1.18" wide and 3 mm/0.12" thick that makes up the base for the sole and heel, completing the welt.
- **Cork filler or insert:** fills the void that is created once the welt is stitched and adds a certain amount of give and stability to the sole.
- **Heel tip or heel quarter:** a layer of no-slip rubber about 6 mm/0.24" thick that is applied to the heel.
- **Upper leather:** is generally chrome-tanned leather.
- **Toe-cap:** a layer of 2 mm/0.08" thick leather, inserted between the outer leather of the upper and the lining to stop the upper part of the shoe from becoming deformed in addition to protecting the toes and creating a specific shape for that part of the upper.
- **Sole:** the part of the shoe that is in direct contact with the ground. The sole can range from 0.5 cm/0.20" thick for formal footwear to a few cm for more robust models.
- **Heel sole:** the sole of the heel that is in direct contact with the ground.
- **Heel lifts:** ranging from two up to four, according to the desired height.
- **Insole or footbed:** the layer of leather that the shoe is attached to. The insole can be 2-3.5 cm/0.79-1.38" thick depending on the type of shoe.

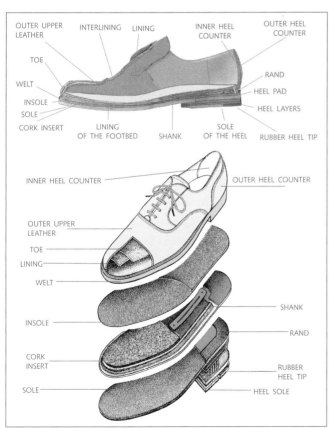

Inner parts of a men's shoe

Anatomy of the Foot

Without wanting to turn shoemaking into a science lesson, to properly make footwear it is helpful to have a firm grasp of the main anatomy of the foot (the structure of the foot) and of physiology of the foot (how the inner organs work), to fully understand the part of the body that this trade is based on.
In addition, the measurement of the foot is the starting point for planning and designing shoes. As such, all the anatomical references of the foot must be kept in mind in order to create comfortable shoes that are suitable for their destined use.
Bones, joints, muscles and tendons of the foot and the way they work together is the most complex mechanical apparatus of the human body.
With a surface of just 25-30 cm/9.84-11.81", the bottom of the foot must bear all the weight of the body and, when walking, it flexibly adapts to all the irregularities and incline of the ground.

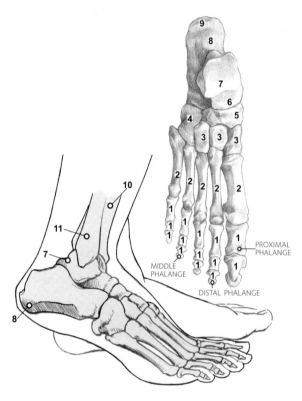

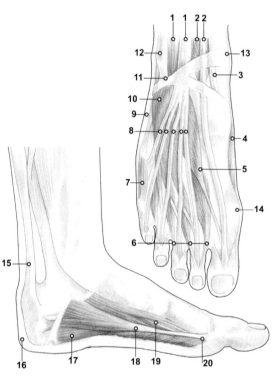

The skeleton

There are 26 bones in the foot, divided into three groups: *Tarsals* (astragalus or talus, calcaneus, navicular, three cuneiforms, and the cuboid), *Metatarsals* (five in total) and *Phalanges*:
1. Phalanges (14 in total);
2. Metatarsals (5 in total);
3. Cuneiforms (3 in total);
4. Cuboid (1 in total);
5. Navicular (1 in total);
6 - 7. Astralagus or Talus (1 in total);
8. Calcaneus (1 in total);
9. Tuberosity of the calcaneus.

The bones of the foot are articulated between them, forming different joints.
The talus is joined with the tibia (10), whose lower end forms the internal malleolus, while the exterior is formed by the end of the fibula (11), articulated on the side of the talus.
The overall bone, capsular and ligamentary structure of the foot makes up a vaulted form, characterised by two longitudinal arches and one front transversal arch.
This architectural structure corresponds to the static and dynamic needs of the foot. It's integrity is essential for the distribution of the body's weight equally on all parts of the foot.

Muscles

Plantar muscles are divided into three groups: 1) Medial, relating to the big toe; 2) Lateral, relating to the baby toe; and 3) Central. The layer of muscles on the foot is rather thin on the top, except for the area where the foot connects to the leg and where, growing thicker, it forms a few ligaments.
1. Muscle extensor along the toes;
2. Muscle extensor along the big toe (hallux);
3. Tendon on the front tibia;
4. Big toe abductor;
5. Muscle extensor along the big toe (hallux);
6. Dorsal interossei;
7. Small toe abductor;
8. Tendons of the extensor along the toes;
9. Third peroneus tendons;
10. Extensor digitorum brevis muscle;
11. Inferior peroneal retinaculum;
12. Lateral malleolus;
13. Medial malleolus;
14. Metatarsophalangeal joint (MTP joint)
15. Achilles tendon;
16. Calcaneus;
17. Short toe flexor;
18. Big toe (hallux) abductor;
19. Short flexor of the big toe (hallux);
20. Flexor tendons.

CONFORMATION OF THE FOOT

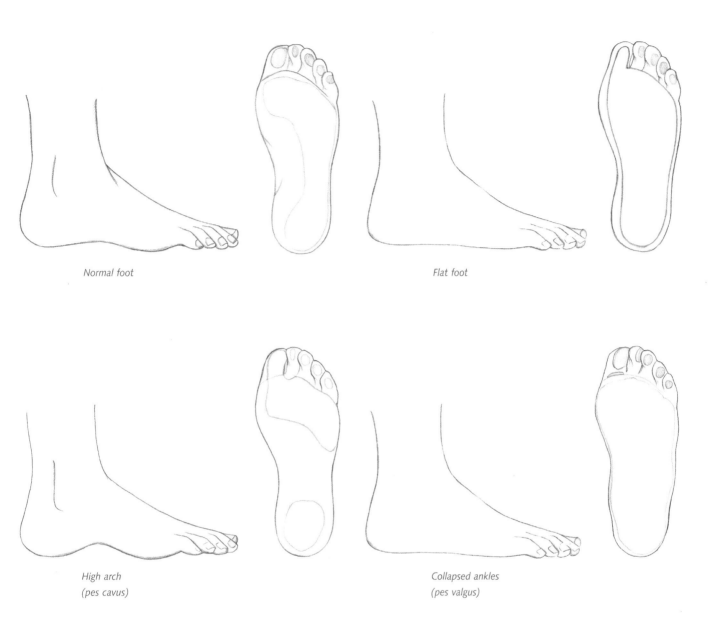

Normal foot

Flat foot

*High arch
(pes cavus)*

*Collapsed ankles
(pes valgus)*

A normally shaped foot, even if completely resting on the ground, will touch the floor only with the heel, the outer edge and the tissue that covers the metatarsal heads.

A regular foot is proportional to the person's height; it has a smooth plantar surface, functional muscles and a sole with the necessary padding.

The feet of thin people are generally thinner as well, while those of robust people are heavier and wider. The latter also usually have higher insteps.

When walking, the sole of the foot lowers by about 5 mm/0.20" and tends to be elongated when under the weight of the body. As soon as the foot is freed from the body's weight, it returns to its normal shape. The sole of the foot thus acts as a shock absorber, relieving the stress on·the spine and head.

Unsuitable footwear, especially for children, can block the foot from moving naturally and, if the foot is consistently in a poor position, it can cause serious damage to the ability to maintain an upright position and walk.

Irregular conformations

The most common irregular conformations are those that involve the flattening of the arch of the foot, i.e. flat foot, often due to an overloading of the tendons and the muscles. With this type of conformation, the body's weight is borne by the heel and also all of the forefoot.

Other irregular conformations are: pes cavus (high arches), pes valgus (ankles falling inwards), pes varus (ankles falling outwards), talipes calcaneovalgus (which tends to rest on the calcaneus), talipes equinovarus (which rests on the metatarsal heads), etc.

Among external affects, that is, of the membranes, there are calluses, corns, bunions (evidenced by the big toe pointing outwards), ingrown toenails, warts, excessive sweating, etc.

SHOE MEASUREMENTS

In the global market of footwear, last numbering is expressed in different ways.

1) *Paris measurements* - the numbering system used in all of Europe, except Great Britain. 1 Paris point = about 6.8 mm/0.27".

2) *Metric system* - 28 (cm) corresponds to "42" using French points.

3) *English measurements* - the numbering system used in Great Britain and its English-speaking former colonies. One English point is equal to about 8 mm/0.31"; size 8 in the English system corresponds to 42 in Paris points.

4) *American measurements* - the numbering system used in the USA. One American point is equal to the English measurement (about 8 mm/0.31"). The difference is in the starting point for the numbers: 9.5 corresponds to the British 8 and the Paris 42.

Instep

A shoe's instep varies according to the collar of each model, so it isn't possible to provide precise measurements. For that reason, it is necessary to closely study the instep when executing the model and carefully try the shoe on before starting production. A few companies will used more than one instep for each size.

TABLE OF DIFFERENT MEASUREMENT SYSTEMS

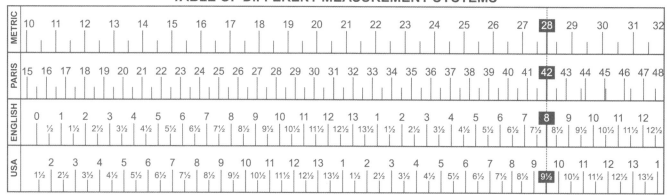

WIDTH TABLE

Depending on different bone structures, people may have feet of the same length but different widths (circumference).

Companies working in the industry found it was necessary to affix and describe these different widths with a special numbering system.

The number 5 (E) in this scale indicates a narrow foot; the number 6 (F) a medium foot; the number 7 (G) a regular foot, and 8 (H) is the widest measurement. In the tables, based on the shoe size, the width of the ball, the arch, the instep and the ankle are calculated.

Length in English points	Ball of the foot in cm/in									
	A 1	B 2	C 3	D 4	E 5	F 6	G 7	H 8	I 9	
5	19.5/7.68	20.00/7.87	20.50/8.07	21.00/8.27	21.50/8.46	22.00/8.66	22.50/8.86	23.00/9.06	23.50/9.25	increase of 0.5 points in width
6	20.10/7.91	20.60/8.11	21.10/8.31	21.60/8.50	22.10/8.70	22.60/8.90	23.10/9.09	23.60/9.29	24.10/9.49	
7	20.65/8.13	21.15/8.33	21.65/8.52	22.15/8.72	22.65/8.92	23.15/9.11	23.65/9.31	24.15/9.50	24.65/9.70	
8	21.20/8.34"	21.70/8.54	22.20/8.74	22.70/8.94	23.20/9.13	23.70/9.33	24.20/9.53	24.70/9.72	25.20/9.92	
9	21.70/8.54"	22.20/8.74	22.70/8.94	23.20/9.13	23.70/9.33	24.20/9.53	24.70/9.72	25.20/9.92	25.70/10.12	
10	22.25/8.76	22.75/8.96	23.25/9.15	23.75/9.35	24.25/9.55	24.75/9.74	25.25/9.94	25.75/10.14	26.25/10.33	
11	22.75/8.96	23.25/9.15	23.75/9.35	24.25/9.55	24.75/9.74	25.25/9.94	25.75/10.14	26.25/10.33	26.75/10.53	
12	23.30/9.17	23.80/9.37	24.30/9.57	24.80/9.76	25.30/9.96	25.80/10.16	26.30/10.35	26.80/10.55	27.30/10.75	

Shoe size in Paris points	Size	Ball of the foot	Arch	Instep	Width at the ankle
	Measurement in cm/in				
39	26/10.24	22.5/8.86	23.3/9.17	32/12.60	22/8.66
40	26.7/10.51	23/9.06	24/9.45	32.7/12.87	22.5/8.86
41	27.3/10.75	23.5/9.25	24.5/9.65	33.3/13.11	23/9.06
42	28/11.02	24/9.45	25/9.84	34/13.39	23.5/9.25
43	28.7/11.30	24.5/9.65	25.5/10.04	34.7/13.66	24/9.45
44	29.3/11.54	25/9.84	26/10.24	35.3/13.90	24.5/9.65
45	30/11.81	25.5/10.04	26.5/10.43	36/14.17	25/9.84

With the help of these tables, you can infer the shoe size, based on the measurements of the average length foot and a width from column F.

LASTS

The "last" is a sort of anatomical model of the foot made of treated oak, beech or hornbeam wood, or even in moulded plastic, used to construct the shoe.

The last, which determines the internal measurements and the external outline of the shoe, is prepared according to special tables if it's for a shoe to be mass produced, or based on the client's foot, if its a made-to-measure item. In this case, the measurements are to be taken for both shoes, as the right foot is always a bit bigger than the left.

In addition, the last also serves to meet the needs of fashion, precisely representing the newly-designed models.

Wood lasts, once made by hand with special cutting tools and taking a lot of time to make, today are made on automatic copying lathes that, following the outlines drawn, can create a form in a little over five minutes. They can create the right and left last at the same time, reaching such precision that they can reflect differences of mere millimetres.

After having checked and smoothed the last, the manufacturer will create a horizontal hole on the upper third, then cut a rounded wedge shape and create a vertical hole, used to attach the wedge to the rest of the last with a pin. This is so that, after using the last, it will be easy to extract it from the shoe.

Custom shapes

Custom lasts can be made by using the raw ones off the lathe, with the "filing" method or the "addition" system.

With the filing method, the excess portions are filed away with a rasp and then with sandpaper of different gauges.

With the addition method, the last is brought to the desired size by gluing different types of suitably thick leather pieces to the points that need to be altered. This method may create a number of inconveniences as, over time, the leather may detach or become deformed. For this reason, it is always best to create a definitive last using the glued form as an model.

Testing the shoe

Many made-to-measure footwear laboratories, especially those working for repeat customers or those with special anatomical characteristics, prepare test shoes after they've completed and fine-tuned the lasts. When testing the shoe, the shoemaker will create a sample garment with inexpensive leather, making the general, though well-defined shape of the footwear. If the shoes have a few problem points, their form is then updated. Once everything is perfect, the definitive shoes are made.

This job, although it may seem time consuming, eradicates the risk of manufacturing shoes that are incorrect and avoids wasting time and precious materials.

For heeled shoes, it is necessary to determine the height at which the collar or opening will be placed. In this case, the appropriate height must be deducted from the quarter, which must be neither too high, as it would rub against the tendons, nor to low, as it wouldn't stay on the foot.

Raw form on the lathe

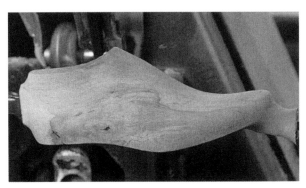
Shaped last

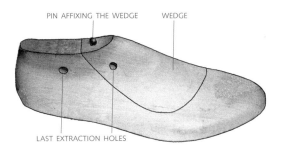

PIN AFFIXING THE WEDGE WEDGE

LAST EXTRACTION HOLES

Last with the wedge cut and affixed

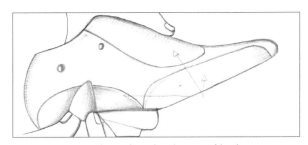
Custom last, adapted with strips of leather

Women's shoe lasts with different types of toe shapes

MEASUREMENTS AND OUTLINE OF THE FOOT

The length of the foot corresponds to 1/8 of the height of the body, thus it should be equal to that of the head.

The shape of the foot is quite similar to that of its skeleton and has three surfaces: dorsal, plantar and medial.

The dorsal surface is curvilinear transversally and longitudinally and has the maximum height medially, gradually sloping down on the sides and towards the toes.

The plantar surface is flat at the rear, the side and the forefoot, but is arched in the centre.

The medial surface has a triangular shape: it starts at the calcaneus, it's longest under the malleolus, is reduced to a margin towards the forefoot and is a bit hollowed out towards the edge that turns into the plantar surface.

Measuring the foot

To create a custom shoe, it is necessary to measure the length, height and circumference of the feet in two different positions: with and without the weight of the body.

Measurements should be taken with a centimetre measuring tape with different notches on each side: on one side is the point scale, used to measure the length of the foot (for example, the Paris point scale, in which each division is 2/3 cm long, that is 6.667 mm/0.26"); on the other side of the tape, the smallest units of the metric system are marked, used to measure the circumference and width of the foot.

Measurements can be checked with a *calibre*, which is an indispensable tools for shoemakers. The calibre is used by placing the foot within it, to then detect the length and width on the tool's measurement scale. There are various types of calibres: the most commonly seen one is the Brannock device.

It's a good practice to "inspect" the feet to check for and note their shape and any anomalies.

Circumference measurements

To take the measurement of the *ball of the foot* (on the metatarsophalangeal joint), pass the measuring tape under the sole and around the foot, keeping it slightly oblique.

About 6 cm/2.36" from the ball of the foot towards the ankle, measure the circumference of the instep (dorsal side of the foot). Then measure the *heel* (circumference of the calcaneus), passing the tape over the malleolus and around the calcaneus. For boots, measuring the ankle circumference is also necessary.

Foot length

After having measured the foot, 1.5 cm/0.59" will have to be added to the measurement as the foot elongates by 1.5cm/0.59" when walking. This means the shoemaker must make sure that the toes won't hit the toe box when walking, giving the foot a minimum amount of freedom of movement within the shoe (e.g. if the size measured is 42, the shoes must be made with the measurements of a 43.5).

Outlining the feet

To trace the outline of the feet (it's always best to take the outline of both the feet as they're almost never perfectly identical), hold the pencil perfectly perpendicular to the floor, thereby ensuring the outline is neither too tight or too wide. In addition, the toes should be pressed downwards so that they are at their maximum width.

Foot profile

When measuring the foot's profile, it's best to use a heel of the same height as that to be used for the shoe. So, place a piece of drawing paper next to the foot, then mark the profile with a pencil (previously affixed to a bracket) along the dorsal side of the foot.

Footprint

The footprint, especially for custom shoes, is important to getting a precise picture of the plantar surface and thus for solving any problems with the use of insole lifts.

After having covered the sole of the foot with ink, have the customer rest his/her foot on a piece of white paper while seated, applying a light amount of pressure for a few seconds.

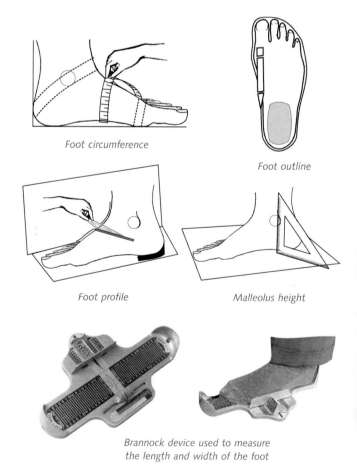

Foot circumference

Foot outline

Foot profile

Malleolus height

Brannock device used to measure the length and width of the foot

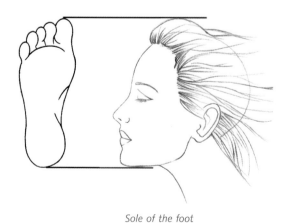

Sole of the foot

Patternmaking techniques

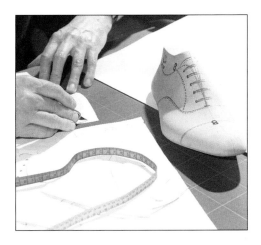

Creating the pattern

When making new models, the stylist makes use of the *last*, drawing the various parts of the upper, including the decorations, so as to get an idea of the results on the three-dimensional structure in its exact proportions.

Paper pattern of the upper

To create the pattern of the upper or *the 3-D pattern*, proceed as follows:

- On the form, draw the median line, which goes from the toe to the lowest part of the heel. This line divides the last in two equal halves.
- From the external side, rest the last over a piece of paper and trace around it. After having added a few centimetres to the entire outline, cut out the outlined shape.
- Create a few triangle shaped cuts along the entire median to adapt it to the last.
- Bring the cut outline to another sheet of paper and add 1.5-2 cm/0.59-0.79" to make it easier to work with.
- Place the cut outline on the last and, after having affixed the paper with a small nail, transfer the outlines of the form and the measurements: the lines, curves, decorative elements, etc.

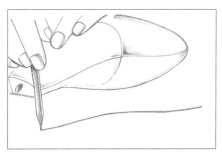

Tracing the outlines

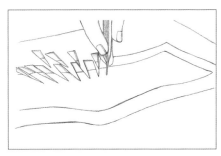

Carrying out the triangular cuts

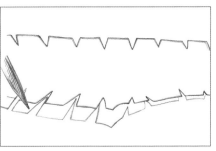

Adding the 1.5-2 cm/0.59-0.79" margin

Positioning on the last

The "half 3-D pattern" taken from the outer part of the last. Points A and B are the lasting margins, to be calculated between inside and outside.

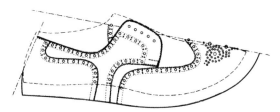

Paper Derby brogue pattern

31

THE CLASSIC MEN'S DERBY

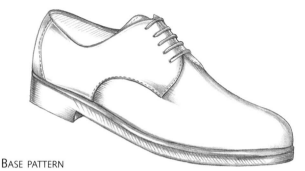

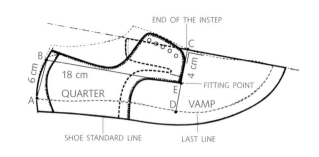

BASE PATTERN

After having traced the rough paper pattern from the last, without removing it, draw the base pattern on the *half 3-D pattern*, as well as a few precise measurements:

- Draw the line A-B from the centre of the heel upwards by 6 cm/2.36", until crossing the curved line of the last.
- From the end point of the instep, draw C-D, perpendicular to the bottom part of the instep.
- 4 cm/1.57" from C, draw B-E. THE FITTING POINT.
- Draw the *quarter*, carefully calculating the resting point of the malleolus, which must not touch the edge of the quarter. Outline the shape as shown in the figure.
- Take up all the parts of the model again: quarter and vamp.
- Add the necessary lasting margins (the extra part of the upper that will be folded over) and the seam margins (the extra part of the vamp or quarter that will be folded under when joining the pieces of the upper).

In the collar, the folding margins must be present in the meeting point between the quarter and the vamp; on the back the margins must be added for the heel counter, starting from 0 at the top and enlarging to 2 mm/0.08" at the bottom.

The half of the vamp that has been drawn should be repeated on another piece of paper. Add the necessary cuts to the opened vamp to create the desired moulding on the top of the instep.

Because the types of leather used for uppers have some give, the upper will take on the moulding on its own once mounted on the last.

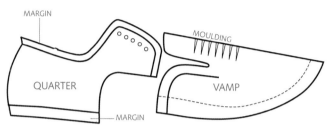

THE LINING

The lining of the vamp should be cut according to the vamp pattern while the lining of the quarter should be as shown in the figure.

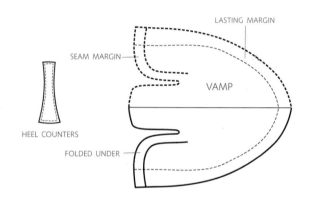

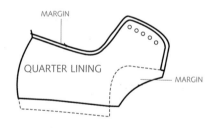

Laying out the patterns on leather

Adding the toe cap between the upper and the lining

CLASSIC MEN'S FOOTWEAR

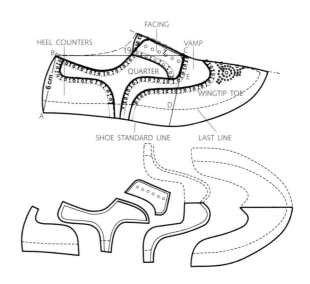

Oxfords typically have a closed lacing system, with laces threaded through five pairs of eyelets. They are suitable for narrow feet with a low instep. To create the pattern for classic Oxfords, follow the same steps as for the derby, keeping the arrival point of the B-C line in mind, where the vamp and the quarter meet. This indication is used to determine if the instep obtained is high or low. Oxfords, like derby shoes, can be: plain, with a toe cap or with wingtips.

Wingtip Oxford pattern

Semi-brogue Oxford with a plain toe

Oxford

Semi-brogue derby with a toe-cap

Derby brogues with wingtips

Monk strap shoe

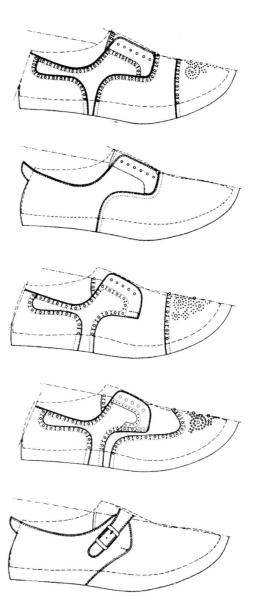

MOCCASIN OR LOAFER

Moccasins, slip-ons, slippers or loafers are the present-day heirs to the footwear of Native Americans. Their vamp, quarters and tongue are fashioned from the same piece of leather, without laces or buckles.

The sole of moccasins is made of a thin, flexible piece of leather, while the other parts of the shoe are relatively similar to other classic footwear models. The strap over the top of the loafer or moccasin must never be too tight, ensuring they are easy to put on. Characteristic decorative elements of loafers and slippers are the stitching on the vamp (often done by hand) and the eyelets on the tongue, embellished with tassels or metal clasps that, however, must be loosen-able so as not to press on the front rise.

CREATING THE PATTERN

To trace a pattern for loafers, proceed as with the other models:
- On a piece of paper, draw the half 3-D pattern, completing both the front and back of the shoe.
- Draw the heel height A-B of 6 cm/2.36".

- D-E 4.5-5 cm/1.77-1.97".
- B-E 15 cm/5.91". 9.5-10 cm/3.74-3.94" opening.
- Draw the outlines of the model as desired.

Moccasin soles

For this type of footwear, the soles must be handled differently depending on the season - summer or winter.

For summer models, the sole should be closed, or, even better, with a welt to create the appearance of thickness, playing with the type of milling (flat, round or waxed).

Heels for summer models are generally low, with a rubber pad as a heel guard, trimmed with Greek frets. It may be lined in canvas or in split leather, or left unlined.

The winter model, on the other hand, should be in leather with an open welt, finished with Greek frets or a faux rapid stitch or visible top-stitching. The sole may be in leather, rubber or para rubber; the heels should be closed for casual/elegant models, while for decisively casual or sportswear models, they should be open with the welt, which follows along the heel band of the shoe.

Loafer with vamp, quarters and tongue in one single piece

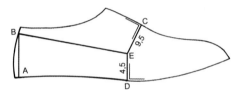

Two-tone loafers

Penny loafer

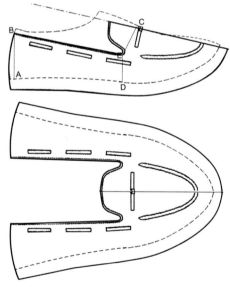

Pattern with vamp, quarters and tongue in one single piece

Bit loafer

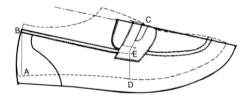

TUBULAR CONSTRUCTION

There are three types of tubular construction shoes: laced, with elastic or plain. They can be created in two different ways:
1. Moccasin construction, mounted and sewn upwards on the last;
2. Bologna construction, punctured and sewn off the last, then lasted.

These patterns are rather difficult to create, especially those "a sacchetto" (meaning "bag" construction), because they are created with the *upper in one piece*: one must, then, cover the entire last.

Moccasin construction

To complete the first category, proceed as follows:
- Place two strips of paper at the height of the vamp (upper part of the shoe delimited by the outer seams), pushing them under the last until the opposite side. Then, adjust the vamp.
- After having covered the last, draw the pattern, including the inner part. Then draw the lines on the front portion to be used as cutting guides.
- Lay the pattern flat on a piece of cardboard after having cut the marked parts and after having drawn the apron.
- Take up the vamp, adding the margins (necessary for the seam). According to the pattern to be carried out, there are three types of stitching methods: *invisible*, *tunnel* and *inserted*.
- "Invisible" stitching requires a margin of at least 8 mm/0.31", because the upper is also taken up when sewing it.
- "Tunnel" stitch construction is done along the cut edge without a margin, with the awl (a tool to make holes) passing through the grain and the flesh sides.
- Inserted construction is similar to tunnel stitch construction, plus the insertion of piping between the apron and the vamp.

Hand-crafted working phases

A few of the tubular construction processes are sewn by hand. Figure A shows how the cut is flush with the end of the shank (reinforcement material) to ensure it adheres well to the waist (inner hollowing of the last), with a zig-zag seam.

Drawings B and C show the manual lasting to extend the underside until it adheres perfectly to the last. In addition, it should be noted that the leather midsole is combined with para rubber and sewn together with the upper, to be neatly attached. The sole is also in para rubber.

Tubular footwear of this type generally has a tacked-on seat (where the heel is applied), which is why it is possible to use a special machine just for this operation: the heel seat and side lasting machine.

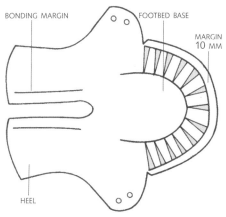

Open 3-D pattern

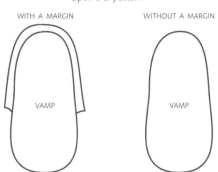

"Invisible" construction   Tunnel stitch and inserted construction

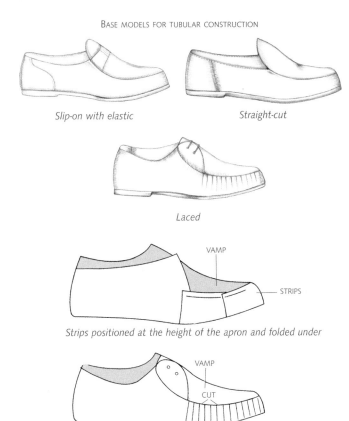

BASE MODELS FOR TUBULAR CONSTRUCTION

Slip-on with elastic   *Straight-cut*

Laced

Strips positioned at the height of the apron and folded under

Drawn 3-D pattern

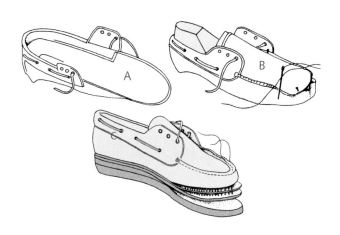

WOMEN'S LOAFERS AND BALLERINA FLATS

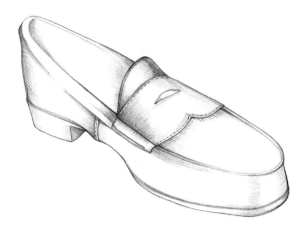

Creating the pattern on the last

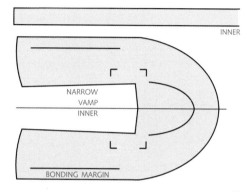

PENNY LOAFERS

Penny loafers are a style of women's shoes similar to moccasins, easy to put on and take off and quite comfortable to walk and drive in.

The penny loafer pattern is created, as usual, by drawing the half 3-D pattern on the pre-selected last. The 3-D pattern is then cut twice (ie, doubled), adding the necessary margin and marking the resting points of the strap.

So, everything is drawn and cut in two: the tongue, the strap and the heel counters.

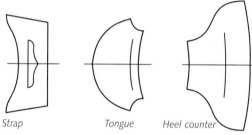

Strap   Tongue   Heel counter

BALLERINA FLATS

Ballerina flats are a type of lightweight, flexible, low-heel shoe (from 0 to 25 mm/0.98) with an open, soft upper and an oval-shaped collar.

This type of shoe is attached to a very thin insole, then glued to the footbed. The heel, if any, is in very thin leather. The pattern, which can be made for straights (i.e. without a right or left), is drawn on the last, as usual. Then proceed to cutting the paperboard into two. Add the margins along the external edge of the upper and, if elastic is to be used, on the perimeter of the throat opening.

Creating the pattern on the last

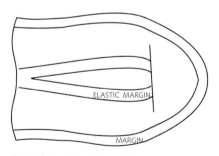

Ballerina flat made with straights

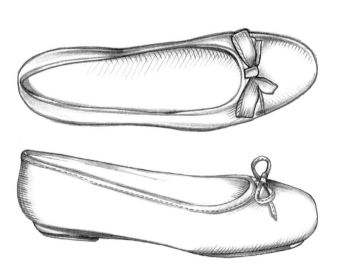

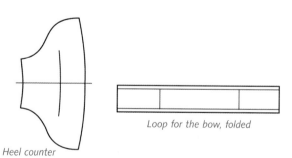

Heel counter   *Loop for the bow, folded*

Derby shoes and high heels

Derby shoes with a heel

The pattern shown here includes the vamp and the heel. It can also be made in a combination of suede and leather, or in a two-tone version.

The pattern is drawn on the last and then traced on paper, as done before. It must be traced accurately and precisely, especially the wingtips, which must be symmetrical and perfect, so as not to compromise the beauty of the shoe.

The lining should be created without too many seams, which would add thickness; the sole can be rubber detached from the heel, while the heel and the welt must be in leather.

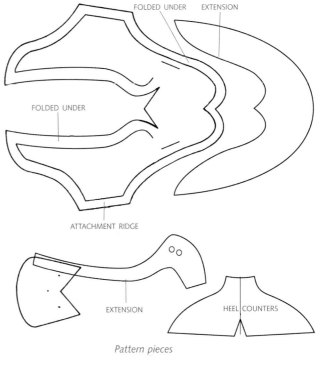

FOLDED UNDER   EXTENSION

FOLDED UNDER

ATTACHMENT RIDGE

EXTENSION   HEEL COUNTERS

Pattern pieces

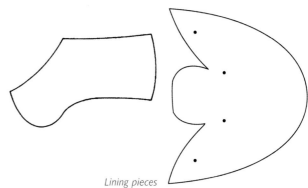

Lining pieces

High heels

High heels, also called pumps, are those with a classic cut, casual or formal, with a 5-7 cm/1.97-2.76" heel.

The heel may be in leather for more casual versions or covered in the same material as the upper for the formal versions. The sole continues down the interior face of the heel.

To create the pattern, proceed as with the other models, drawing the half 3-D pattern on the paper on the last, adding the necessary margins.

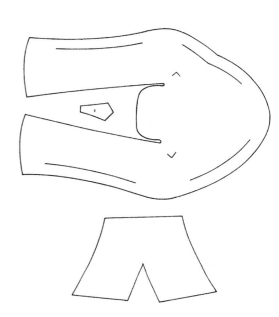

COURT SHOES

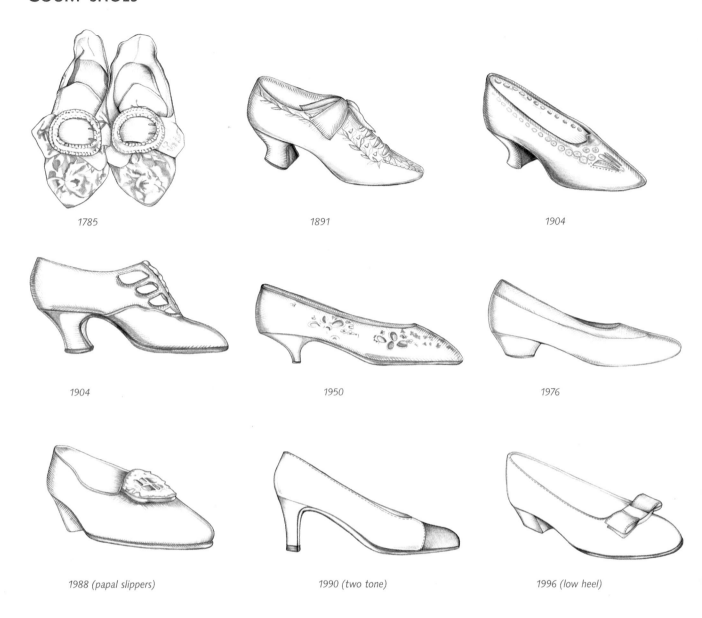

1785

1891

1904

1904

1950

1976

1988 (papal slippers)

1990 (two tone)

1996 (low heel)

The court shoe is one of the most common items of women's footwear thanks to its simple, easy-to-make shape that can be adapted easily to many stylistic requirements.

Always on trend, court shoes can be compared to an elegant dress for the feet. They have an essential, serious, practical, refined, distinct, classic and austere form. This type of shoe, today typically feminine, has distant origins as footwear for men.

From the early 16th century, a sort of flat, thin, open slipper which could be held on to the foot with the strength of the muscles and tendons of the toes, was part of the uniform of infantry soldiers.

Only around the 17th century did European women begin to wear this type of shoe, but without heels, as walking footwear, replacing the uncomfortable slippers and restrictive lace-up ankle boots. Towards the end of the 17th century, these shoes spread like wildfire, especially as dancing shoes for both men and women.

After the shoes became definitively feminine, starting around 1830, court shoes gained heels, embellishment accessories such as bows, buckles, etc. and other elements conferring elegance and refinement.

The new models were the opposite of the closed dancing shoes of the time, having a V-shaped collar on the upper that grazed the toes and cut-outs on the sides that revealed the arch of the foot.

The court shoes from Dorsay, found in the wardrobes of the dames of the late 1800s, in black or light brown kidskin, with a comfortable heel of about 6 cm/2.36" (still even today) and similar characteristics, are among the most classic models of women's footwear.

In 1950, at a time when fashion dictated stiletto heels of 12 cm/4.72", Coco Chanel and Raymond Massaro launched two-tone court shoes with a beige body and heel and a black toe to make the foot seem smaller, a low heel and a strap at the ankle.

In the 1960s in America, Jacqueline Kennedy adopted and imposed her own style, characterised by custom court shoes made just for her by the world's best shoemakers.

In the 1980s-1990s, with the arrival of working women and female managers, this type of comfortable shoe, with a heel lower than 5 cm/1.97" and a wide range of cuts, was widespread.

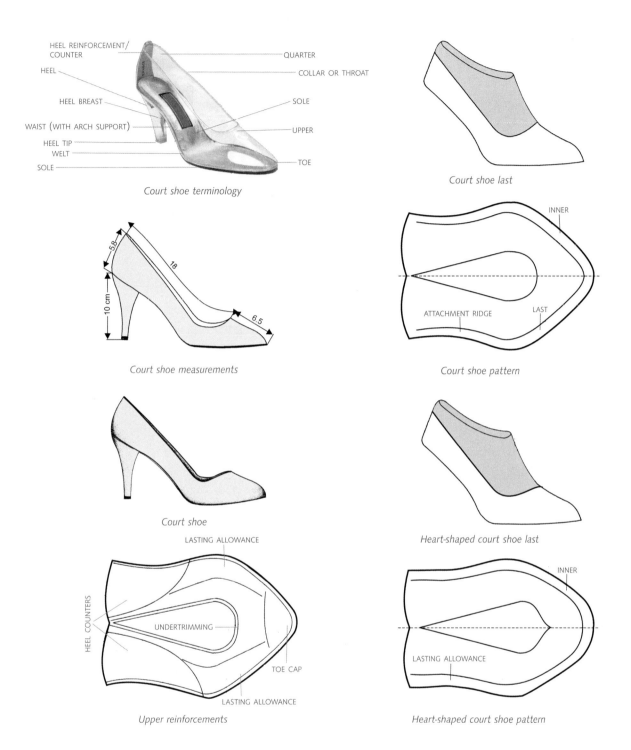

Court shoe terminology

Court shoe last

Court shoe measurements

Court shoe pattern

Court shoe

Heart-shaped court shoe last

Upper reinforcements

Heart-shaped court shoe pattern

The measurements shown in the figure are the average for a classic court shoe, but each footwear model may have its own characteristics and special measurements.

Indeed, court shoes may have throats and cuts of different shapes: heart-shaped, square, pointed, etc. throat openings, even if it is indispensable for them to maintain a pure, stylised line. A good pattern should wrap the foot perfectly and not bulge, which is why detecting the shape on the last is so important.

After having drawn the desired outline on the last, preferably with the full throat opening, trace the pattern, wrapping the last with transparent paper, then copy the pattern to flat paper. If you draw the opening halfway and then copy it on the pa-

perboard, you'll need to drop the throat down by 1.5 mm/ 0.06" on the inside (the side nearest the other leg) as that part tends to ride up.

For shoes with heels over 10 cm/3.94", since the upper is made of softer, highly-prized leathers such as suede, kidskin, etc., it must be reinforced in various points, with different materials. For example, apply the *guttaperca gum* (a thin strip of fabric that binds the to the leather when heated by a hot iron); add a special trimming strip along the throat; lasting allowances are added to the sides, thereby creating a core between the lining and the upper, which will maintain the shoe's lines over time.

DESERT BOOTS AND MEN'S ANKLE BOOTS

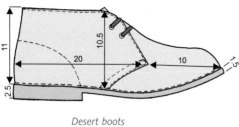

Desert boots

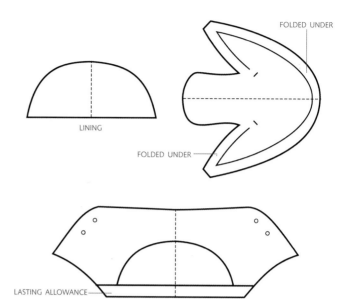

LINING

FOLDED UNDER

FOLDED UNDER

LASTING ALLOWANCE

DESERT BOOTS

In the desert boot pattern, the footbed serves the purpose of supporting the shoe, as the upper is mounted externally and the sole is usually in para rubber.

As usual, after having drawn the outlines on the last, trace the 3-D pattern with paper and then carry it over to a flat sheet of paperboard after having added the necessary margins. Trace the rear reinforcement to line the heel.

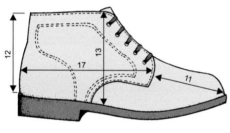

5-hole ankle boot

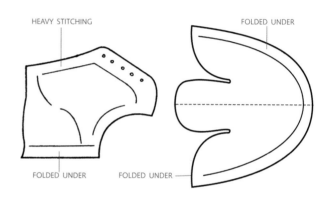

HEAVY STITCHING

FOLDED UNDER

FOLDED UNDER   FOLDED UNDER

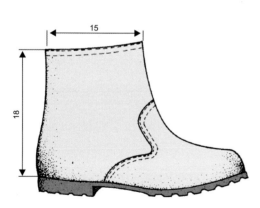

Ankle boot with inner zip

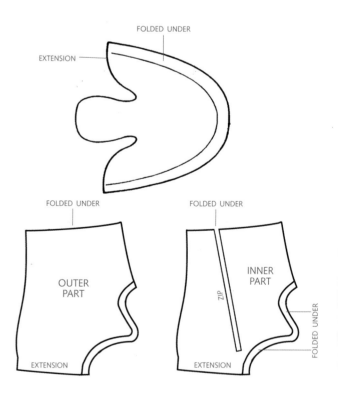

FOLDED UNDER

EXTENSION

FOLDED UNDER   FOLDED UNDER

OUTER PART   INNER PART

ZIP   FOLDED UNDER

EXTENSION   EXTENSION

Men's boots

Riding-style boots

FOLDED UNDER

STRIP

INNER LEG SEAM   CENTRE BACK   CENTRE FRONT   INNER LEG SEAM

FOLDED UNDER

CENTRE BACK

BACK LEG

MARGIN

FOLDED UNDER

CENTRE FRONT

FOLDED UNDER   FRONT LEG   FOLDED UNDER

MARGIN

UPPER

MARGIN

Shoe drawn on the 3-D pattern

STRIP 20 + 20

ASYMMETRICAL BAND UNDER THE KNEE

40

4

2

Riding-style boots

Shape in 3 pieces

The last of the boot is generally divided into three pieces to make it easier for it to be removed from the finished product. To remove the last, first the central part of the boot is removed, then the back and then the front (which includes the last of the foot, the most difficult to remove).

The boot pattern is then traced in the same way as with the shoes, applying paper on the last to draw the cuts and seams, creating the 3-D pattern with the following procedure:

- Determine the under-knee band by folding it in two, making sure that the seam is on the inside of the leg.
- Determine the front leg by keeping the paper folded in two, so that it is whole on the centre front.
- Determine the upper as usual, creating it in double from the drawing on the last.
- Determine the rear part of the leg, keeping the paper folded in two.
- Add the margins and the parts to be folded under when sewing.

WOMEN'S BOOTS

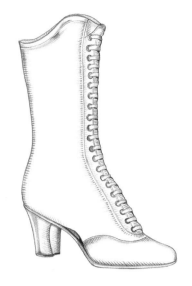

Woman's boot from the late 19th century

Women's ankle boot from the early 20th century

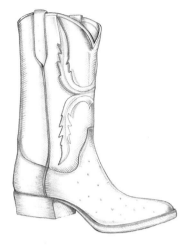

Woman's cowboy boot 1995

Riding-style boots

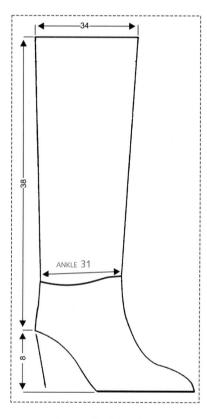

Drawing the 3-D pattern

Classic woman's boot

Always a symbol of strength, boots were generally worn by men, with a few exceptions (such as that of riding boots). It was only around 1830 that aristocratic and bourgeois women began wearing boots regularly.

To soften the appearance of the foot, new ankle boots were created with a very tight fit, always worn laced tightly or buttoned all the way up. Later on, boots lost their role as a status symbol and were transformed into a symbol of equality between the sexes, making their entry into the world of fashion.

PATTERNS

Like those for men, patterns for women's boots are created by using the half 3-D pattern, with a full ankle for tube boots and a normal ankle for those with a zip.

Start by attaching the lower portion of the 3-D pattern with the mastic, then continue into the desired height, creating the cut lines, generally bare and essential.

The measurements illustrated in the figure are for a classic tube boot with an 8 cm/3.15" heel, while the menswear inspired riding boot has a 3 cm/1.18" heel.

HEELS

Common heel slightly asymmetrical

Casual heel trapezoid shaped wider at the base

Casual heel trapezoid shaped narrower at the base

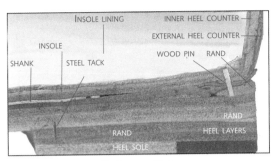

Heel composition

WOMEN'S HEELS

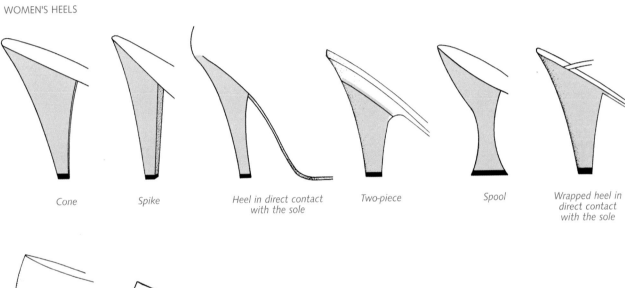

Cone — *Spike* — *Heel in direct contact with the sole* — *Two-piece* — *Spool* — *Wrapped heel in direct contact with the sole*

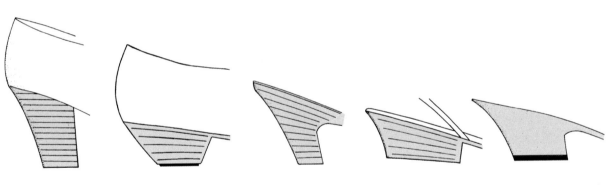

Leather heel in direct contact with the sole — *Leather oval* — *Leather heel with the sole in-line with the breast* — *Low leather heel* — *Wrapped heel with the sole in-line with the breast*

The heel is the most representative and important part of both men's and women's footwear.

The origins of the heel are unclear, but they surely date back to pre-Christian eras. The first evidence of a heeled shoe is from 1533, when Catherine de' Medici, being rather short, chose a pair of shoes with a heel to marry the duke of Orleans in Paris. It thereafter became fashionable. Heels can be made of a single block, generally covered, or of separate lifting layers. There are a few heel shapes and sizes. The include:

- *Cone:* a common type of heel that extends under the shoe in a conical shape.
- *Spike:* a type of very high heel that grows thinner towards the base.

- *Spool:* wider at the top and bottom, its shape looks like a spool for yarn.
- *Normal heel:* a heel that finishes in direct contact with the sole of the shoe.
- *Sole in one with the breast:* when the outsole connects to and extends down the heel breast (as seen, for example on Louis/French heels).
- *Cuban:* a type of heel with straight sides.
- *Louis heel:* a type of flared heel, wider at the top and bottom, in which the sole extends down the heel breast.

In men's shoes, the ideal heel is 2.5 cm/0.98" but, of course, this height can vary. The most comfortable heel for this type of shoe is a symmetrical one in a U-shape, placed on the median line and cut ever so diagonally towards the outside.

Open shoes and sandals

Sling-backs

Open-work shoe

Women's peep toe heels with a button t-strap

Women's strappy sandal

Open shoes for women

There are two types of open shoes for women:

1) open at the sides or back (like the slingback) but closed at the toe. They are made with a normal last, following the procedures already described.

2) Open at the toe, which is made on a shorter last, cut in a different way. Gradually as the opening gets bigger, it must adapt more and more to the shape of the foot.

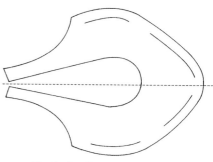

Sling-back pattern

Note: To complete the sling-back pattern, after having created the 3-D pattern, you will have to cut the mirrored paperboard, remembering that the throat of the shoe should always be shifted more towards the inside instead of the foot than towards the outside.

Sandals

Like shoes, sandals are drawn on the last.

For sandals that have a two-strap upper and a stand in the back, the only difficulty is that the straps are to be drawn by marking the individual position at the right point.

To place them correctly, it's helpful to try the sandal on a medium-sized foot.

In addition, to better contain the foot, the upper should be slightly tapered.

Sandal with a buckle

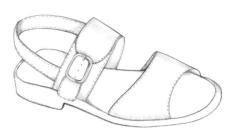

Biblical sandal for men

Mules, platforms and clogs

Mules

Mules are a type of slipper that covers the instep, closed at the toe. They can have different height heels and various shapes: with the sole extending over the heel breast, with the heel applied to the sole, with an orthopaedic heel, etc.

The pattern for this type of footwear is made from a half 3-D pattern, then traced on flat paper. Having a high-rising instep and a long upper, to give this shoe the right shape, the upper must be shaped or *pre-formed*, using a special preforming machine which sets the shape without it being lost during construction/lasting.

Wedges

This type of footwear, existing also in an orthopaedic version, appeared in the 1930s. It is composed of a wedge-shaped insert which ends at the end of the calcaneus, inserted between the insole and the outsole, raising the heel. In the 1970s this type of sole experienced a boom, often very flashy, colourful, in wood, leather, straw and synthetics, reaching heights of 15 cm/5.91". In the 1990s, wedge heels were also used for youthful, casual items.

The shape of this type of sole can vary greatly and be quite creative. Starting with open or closed sandals, those closed with buckles or buttons, etc.

The pattern requires a very simple line that's perfectly centred, both for the upper and for the back.

Clogs and platforms

For centuries (up until 1915), wooden clogs were the most common type of footwear in northern Europe.

Dutch clogs, hand-painted with floral motifs, were worn during festivities and holidays.

Today, cooks and healthcare workers in Europe and America wear well-padded Danish-style clogs with leather uppers and expanded polyurethane soles that are inspired by the wooden originals. They are lightweight, comfortable and anti-slip.

To make this type of clog, the outline of the leather upper is created through different types of processes, which range from artisanal to industrial methods, often involving wetting the upper, heat moulding or softening the leather and letting it soak for a certain amount of time.

Women's clogs, an item that is always on-trend, especially in summer, are created by shaping the wood to create a lower support base, while the upper is made of strips of different types of materials in various colours.

Women's mule

Wedge sandal

Women's heels

Women's platform

Dutch clog

Danish clog

SPORTS AND CASUAL SHOES

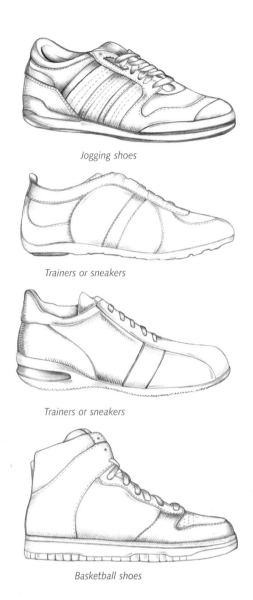

Jogging shoes

Trainers or sneakers

Trainers or sneakers

Basketball shoes

CREATING THE PATTERN

For the shape of this type of footwear, all the notions illustrated previously apply, remembering, however, that sports shoes must be functional and comfortable, also considering the fact that they are often worn over bulky wool socks and thus require a slightly larger footprint. The pattern thus starts with a half 3-D pattern, drawing the desired lines and shapes. As far as the fastening system is concerned, they generally have at least 5-6 eyelets, to allow the shoe to open wider.

For these shoes, the most suitable pattern is that of a long Oxford or derby with a quarter, or even *cycling* shoe models.

The two edges of the lacing system should be about 14-16 mm/0.55-0.63" apart to allow the shoe to adapt to the foot and needs of each wearer. The margins are calculated in consideration of the thickness of the padding. However, it should be noted that this type of footwear has no set of a priori, precise measurements as each pattern should consider all the variables that characterise it, including: padding, material used, etc. To increase the comfort and functionality of the shoe, add a foam rubber insert, attached to the insole.

Casual footwear

Casual shoes *or trainers* are designed while keeping comfort and functionality in mind. That is obtained by carrying out a careful study of the shape and the base of the shoe. The latter should be properly designed, with a rounded toe and heel and a coffered sole to ensure the shoe has enough grip on any type of terrain and on the parts of the foot that need it most.

In addition, these types of shoes should be: reinforced in the points most exposed to strain and abrasion; given an anatomically correct, padded footbed covered in fabric, generally in bright colours; equipped with long laces to ensure a snug fit on the foot; reinforced in the points of greatest tension and wear.

Jogging shoes

Jogging shoes are used for long walks or for running, in the city or on countryside trails. For this reason, the upper must be very soft and padded with foam rubber, to facilitate the movement of the foot as much as possible.

This type of shoe is similar to a long *derby*, with various partitions, both for reinforcement and for decoration, with the purpose of giving them a progressive shape. The bottom and the sole of the shoe is generally in a soft yet durable material such as TR and PVC, polyurethane or synthetic rubber.

Basketball shoes

This type of footwear must have a high ankle to help the athlete's foot withstand the force its subjected to when playing sports, controlling its movement. It must thus be quite padded and reinforced, especially in the points that are subject to the most tension, adhesion and strain.

In addition, the bottom of this type of shoe, as with tennis shoes, must be flat so as not to ruin the court, as established by the sports discipline.

Soles

All these types of shoes, especially if only for casual, non-professional uses, can have the same sole, thereby making its generally expensive production more economical.

All the materials used to make a sample - the transparency, adherence, gumminess, durability, the design on the outsole and of the brand, etc. - should be studied and tested before being sent to production, so as to avoid any issues.

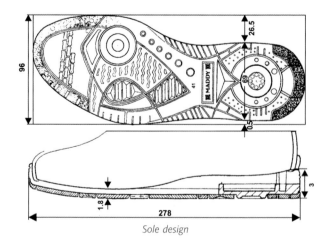

Sole design

CHILDREN'S FOOTWEAR

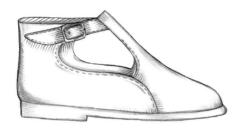

Kid's open booties

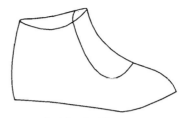

Last for size 23

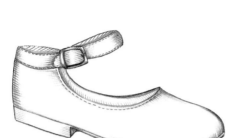

Mary-jane

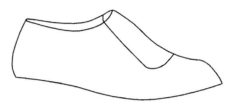

Last for size 31

T-bar sandal

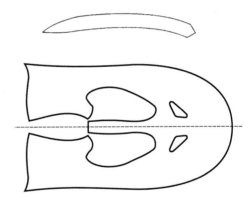

T-bar children's shoes

Kid's booties

The main element to consider for children's footwear is the last, which must be properly defined in all its details and which must absolutely respect the anatomy of children's feet, remembering that they are always growing and must be protected from all possible defects.

To that end, always use a last that's hollowed out in the throat as they make it possible to insert anatomical insoles in the shoes.

MODELS

The models most suitable for small children are ankle boots, anatomically adapted inside so that the feet will not be damaged as the child grows.

The first models of footwear indicated for babies are the classic *Mary Janes*, low-cut shoes with a strap at the ankle.

The classic, always on-trend models for larger children are *two-hole* sandals called *T-bar shoes*, which can be low-cut or reach the ankle.

To make children's footwear half 3-D patterns, proceed as you would for adult footwear. For girls from seven to twelve years old, who generally have long, thin feet, it may be necessary to study special designs with straps and fastenings to ensure the shoe adheres to the foot while allowing regular movements.

ARTISAN WORKING PHASES

Artisan shoe working phases can be summarised in the following points:

1) Cutting the upper and the lining;
2) Preparing the upper for assembly;
3) Sewing the pieces of the upper;
4) Applying the lining and finishing the upper;
5) Cutting and preparing the lower part of the shoes;
6) Applying reinforcements, counters and interlinings;
7) Lasting and hammering the prepared upper;
8) Preparing, sewing and finishing the welt;
9) Applying the rand;
10) Applying the shank;
11) Preparing and applying the midsole and outsole;
12) Preparing, applying and finishing the heel;
13) Finishing the interior of the shoe;
14) Finishing the shoe.

Cutting the upper and the lining

Cow or horse leather of excellent quality, selected to be used for uppers (also called box-calf), is entrusted to artisan cutters called "clickers" to create the pieces of the upper.

The clicker, after having closely examined the hide to ensure there are no imperfections, will mark any points not to be used, and position the patterns of the uppers, playing close attention to the direction the leather stretches and its degree of elasticity.

The patterns should be placed so that the right and left sides of the shoe are cut out symmetrically from the same piece of leather, in order to have identical characteristics, in addition to following a precise order. Thus: the vamp is positioned on the best part (near the spine), then the quarters right next to it and then the other parts.

To complete the cut, the leather is placed on a special cutting table complete with a 6-7 cm/2.36-2.76" thick piece of rubber, making it possible to cut without leaving marks underneath.

The cut of the leather should be neat and precise, making use of an effective, sharp clicker's knife.

As the cuts are made, each piece must be marked with an identifying number corresponding to the side and the shoe it belongs to.

The lining of the upper part of the shoe covers the reinforcements and increases the comfort of the shoe.

Due to its quality, the leather used for the lining is usually calfskin, vegetable tanned to allow the foot to breathe.

The lining should be made of the fewest number of pieces possible. In addition, the seams of the upper must not overlap those of the lining. Therefore, the lining pieces must be of different heights than the upper.

The reinforcements and supports are additional, complementary pieces, some cut from the same material as the upper or strips of linen which are applied, between the upper and the lining, to the upper edges of the quarter, as supports for the areas where the eyelets are and on other parts at risk of becoming deformed.

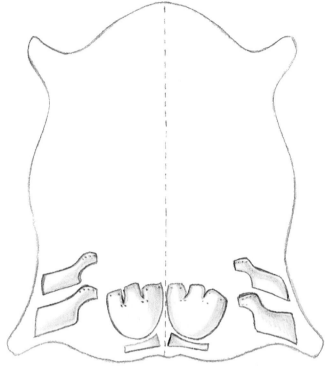

Placing and cutting the pieces

Thinning the edges

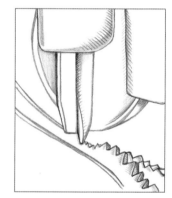

Notching the edges

Preparing the upper for assembly

Before sewing the pieces of the upper with the quilting machine, a few preliminary steps need to be completed first. They are:
- Marking the points where the various pieces are to be joined, drawing a line with a point a few millimetres from the edge.
- Marking the decorations and the eyelets with an awl.
- Using the shoemaker's knife to thin the edges of the cut pieces where necessary, so as to avoid a double thickness at the seams. The operation of joining the pieces is done with different procedures, some to bring out the edge being overlapped, such as the procedure in which the cut edge is turned inwards, overlapped and then sewn with the other piece.
- Inking the outer edges.
- Notching or pinking with a machine or a reinforcing edge.

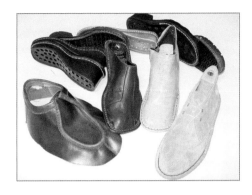

In addition to a smooth version, many types of shoes have a perforated version, with decorative openwork, called "broguing". There are two types of footwear models that have broguings:
1) Semi-brogues, that have perforations and serrations on the seam of the toe cap, which is straight (i.e. not wingtips). They may also have perforations on the toe itself.
2) Full brogues, which have perforations and serrations on the seam of the wingtip toe cap. They may also have perforations on the toe itself.
The perforations along the seam line form a sequential motif while those on the toes or the quarter create a geometric or other sort of creative motif.
The decorative perforations are made with a 3 mm/0.12" hollow punch or die at a distance of 5 mm/0.20" between them. In addition, two smaller, 1 mm/0.04" holes can be punched between them.
The perforations are far enough from the edge so as to leave room for the seam.

Broguing on the toe

This type of broguing is ornamental and decorative (for summer footwear, they may also help the feet breathe). The holes are arranged in various geometric designs or motifs, created by alternating different-size holes (from 1 to 5 mm/0.04-0.20") in a harmonious interplay of lines and shapes.
The broguing designs are first studied and created on a piece of cardboard that is then placed on the upper and used as a template.
To avoid being able to see the leather or the lining underneath the holes, glue a small leather insert in the same colour of the upper.

Upper reinforcements

To give greater stability to the upper and ensure it doesn't become deformed, use a gummy rubber solution dissolved in petrol to apply reinforcements to a few set places. They are:
- The upper edges of the quarter, where a 3-4 cm/1.18-1.57" ribbon of durable fabric is applied;
- Between the leather of the vamp and the lining, where strips of durable linen are applied;
- Between the leather of the quarter and the lining, where strips of durable linen are applied;

- The toe of the upper is reinforced with leather supports cut into strips from the same material as the upper;
- The part that surrounds the eyelets is reinforced, gluing 2-2.5 cm/0.79-0.98" leather strips, thinned along the edge;
- The upper edge of the quarter, to ensure it doesn't tear with use, is reinforced with the application of a strip of the same leather as the upper measuring 1.8 cm/0.71", folded in two. After sewing, the edgings will extend about 1 mm/0.04" from the edge.

1

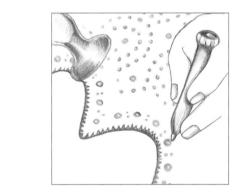

2

BROGUINGS ALONG THE EDGES OF THE WINGTIPS

BROGUINGS

BROGUINGS ON THE QUARTER

Smooth toe

Simple toe

3

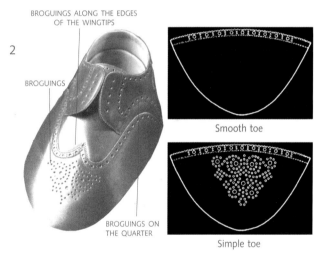

REINFORCEMENT ON THE UPPER EDGE OF THE QUARTER

REINFORCEMENT ALONG THE EYELETS

RIBBON

REINFORCEMENT ON THE TOE

STRIP OF FABRIC

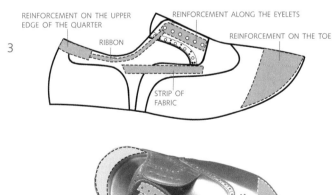

1. Creating the decorative perforations with a hand-held punch;
2. Upper with broguings, ready for use;
3. Upper reinforcements.

SEWING THE UPPER AND LINING

Sewing the pieces of the upper

Assembling the toe with the vamp

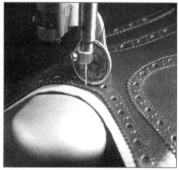

Sewing the lining

Sewing the upper

All the parts that make up the upper should be joined and hemmed. Before proceeding to the sewing phase, mark the point where the seam is to be placed with a line, then apply a strip of glue along the line and join the two pieces to be sewn. This trick makes sure the parts won't move when being sewn. As they are functional and also decorative and aesthetic, the seams must be completed with a robust, durable thread and a straight, regular movement.

The assembly seams on the upper are to be completed in one or two steps on the upper edge of the quarter, while on the seams, where the upper is subjected to stress and wear from the foot, complete two, three or even four seams.

The hem of the upper is to be done with twisted linen thread in the thicker parts, with cotton thread in the thinner parts, and with silk thread in the extra thin, delicate parts. In addition, to highlight the decorative aspect of the stitching (in addition to using different thread for different seams), you can use larger needles, put three stitches in a centimetre, combine rows of seams of different widths, one next to the other, etc.

The thickness of the twisted thread used for the seams may composed of three up to nine pieces, with a 80/4 ratio (80 meters/262.47' with a weight of 4 grams/0.14 oz).

The colour of the top thread is generally darker than the upper; the lower thread should be in the same tone as the top thread.

Sewing the lining

After having sewn all the pieces of the upper and the lining, the two parts need to be joined, sewing them exclusively on the edge of the quarter to ensure the other reinforcements can be inserted between the two layers.

The lining is joined to the upper with the grain turned towards the foot, on the inside of the shoe. It can be done with various procedures depending on the type of shoe, in addition to being composed of a number of different pieces. In particular:

1) For derby shoes, the tongue and vamp, made of one single piece, must be lined together;

2) For Oxfords, the tongue (which is a separate piece) is lined before being sewn to the vamp;

3) For moccasins, the lining is made up of four parts: the vamp, two short quarters and another, separate piece which joins the two quarters on the heel. In this case, the stitching with the upper is done by holding the leather lining with the flesh side towards the foot within the shoe because, being coarse, it stops the foot from slipping forward.

Finishing touches

After having sewn the lining, finish the shoe by:

- Cutting the lining that extends from the edges of the quarters, done cautiously and precisely, without ruining the seams and in such a way that can't be seen from the outside.

- The punching of the eyelet holes should be done with a 2-3 mm/0.08-0.12" hole punch, spaced about 1.5 cm/0.06" apart.

- Use an awl to push the trailing thread of the seams within the upper, tie it in a knot with the trailing end of the inner thread and trim the excess.

THE LOWER PARTS OF THE SHOE

Cutting the lower parts of the shoe

The lower parts of the shoe are the welt, the footbed, the sole and the layers of the heel, in addition to the heel pad and the toe support, are made of vegetable tanned calfskin.

In particular, the belly and shoulders of the calfskin (or box calf), where the hide is about 2.5-3.5 mm/0.10-0.14" thick, are used for the inserts, heel pads, toe support and welts. The soles, heels and rand are cut from the back, where the average thickness is about 6 mm/0.24". The midsoles and intermediary layers of the heel are cut from the chest.

All the various sections of the calfskin are subdivided directly by the tanneries according to the thickness and to the piece which they are destined for. They arrive to the clickers already separated and wrapped in packages to make it easier to choose the leather according to its future use. To cut the lower parts of the shoe, proceed as follows:

- Draw the contours of the various pieces of the lower part of the shoe (or lay out the patterns) on the box calf, in the positions suitable to the necessary thickness.
- Cut the outline of the footbed/insole (2.5-3.5 mm/0.10-0.14" thick), leaving a margin along the edges. The footbed is the most important part of the shoe because it is attached to the welt and the upper, creating the inner base.
- Thin the footbed on the edges from the grain side, with a glass shard or another type of cutting tool.
- Soften the footbed and affix it to the wood last with nails or staples, making sure it adheres perfectly.
- Trim the leather of the footbed with the special knife, adapting it to the wood last it's attached to.
- On the bottom of the footbed, mark the shape of the heel and the edging, which is to be done about 6 mm/0.24" from the edge.
- Carve out the edge along the drawn line with the special cobbler's plane or another special machine, about 2 mm/0.08" deep and 6 mm/0.24" wide.

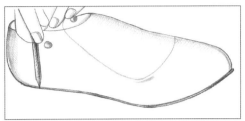
Drawing the outline

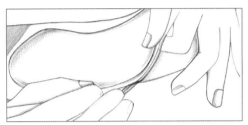
Manually cutting the sole

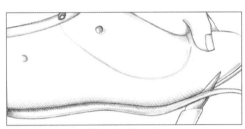
Trimming the sole

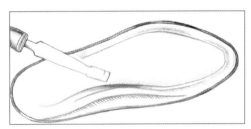
Edge for sewing the welt

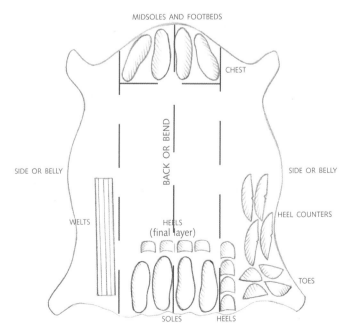
Tanned calfskin for the lower parts of the shoe

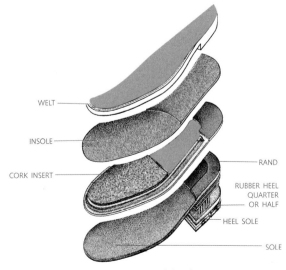
The lower parts of the shoe

REINFORCEMENTS AND LASTING THE UPPER

TOE   HEEL COUNTERS

Toe cap and heel counter

The toe cap, straight or wingtip, is the reinforcement on the toe, while the heel counter is the reinforcement on the heel. Both are cut from the flank of the calfskin, thinned adequately (the part of the toe cap that is towards the centre of the foot should be rasped until it is 0.5 mm/0.02" thick, while the toe box should be left in its full thickness to protect the toes, and the heel counter should be gradually rasped starting from the edge of the shoe), covered with wheatpaste on both sides and shaped on the last.

The toe box and the heel counter are thus inserted and glued between the outer leather of the upper and the lining.

Interlining

The interlining is the set of reinforcement strips taken from the cut outs of the external leather used for the upper, positioned on the inside of the upper, below the lining. These pieces are used to strengthen the sides, preventing rips and folds.

Lasting the upper

Lasting is the process by which the assembled upper is combined with the insole (also called the footbed), through the following steps:

- Sprinkle a bit of talcum powder on the inside of the upper to make it easier to eventually remove the last (after the shoe is completed);
- Rest the upper on the last with the insole below, making sure it adheres perfectly;
- Pull the upper over the last and affix it, keeping it extended with the special lasting pliers, with eight suitable tacks (1.2-1.4 mm/0.05-0.06" in diameter and 25 mm/0.98" long). Place two on each side, three on the toe and one on the heel, hammering them with the pliers each time, making sure they pierce the layers of leather and go about 5 mm/0.20" into the wood.
- Affix the upper turned towards the footbed with additional nails, keeping it taut and making sure that the upper doesn't move from the central axis.
- Use the cutter to trim off the excess leather of the upper and its inserts along the entire edge, up to the groove of the footbed, where the welt will be sewn.
- Use the hammer to fold all the nails over towards the centre of the shoe, until they touch the footbed.
- Hammer the upper with the cobbler's hammer to flatten all the folds and to make it perfectly cover the last.

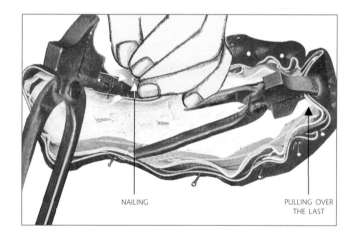

NAILING   PULLING OVER THE LAST

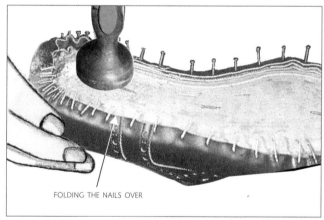

FOLDING THE NAILS OVER

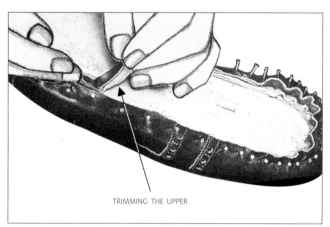

TRIMMING THE UPPER

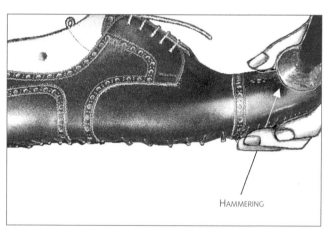

HAMMERING

WELTS AND RANDS

The welt

The welt is the supporting structure of the shoe which holds the upper, insole and outsole together. It is made of a leather strip cut from the sides of the calf hide, about 18-20 mm x 60 cm and 3 mm thick (0.71-0.79 x 2.36 x 0.12"). After having wet them to make them softer and easier to work, the leather strips are smoothed over at a 45-degree angle so they adhere perfectly to the edge and can be sewn on. To do so, carve out a channel about 1 mm/0.04" deep for the seams. The welt can be simple or reversed.

Sewing a simple welt

Simple welts are sewn with long stitches, generally 6 mm/0.24", in the following way:
- Position the welt on the nailed-down upper, with the smooth side along the canal of the footbed.
- Start from the heel and puncture the footbed, upper and welt with an awl, making the holes in the canal of the footbed and the welt.
- After having made the first knot, pass both threads through the same hole, entering with one needle on one side, and the other needle on the other side.
- After each double-stitch, pull firmly on the threads to make sure they are affixed and adhere to the leather.
- Gradually, as the stitches are created, remove the nails that are holding down the upper.
- Once done sewing, near the heel, the two threads are firmly knotted and trimmed.
- Cut the welt in excess with respect to the established limit, near the heel.
- Trim the upper right along the welt and footbed with the cutter.
- Smooth out the stitching with the hammer.
- Smooth and adjust the welt with the lasting pliers and sleeking bone.

The rand

The rand is the strip of welt found at the heel, in the same width as the welt. For footwear with a simply-sewn welt, the rand should be trimmed to the proper length. It is then nailed with birch wood nails called *pegs*, creating a hole with the short awl, smaller in diameter than the pegs, inserting a bit of glue as well. The pegs are placed 7-8 mm/0.28-0.31" apart. To wrap the rand more easily around the heel, you'll need to add small slits to the inner edge. After having inserted all of them, the pegs should be levelled flush with the shoemaker's knife and rasp.

The Shank

The shank is a metal support that's about 15 x 11 mm/0.59 x 0.43", affixed to the centre of the footbed, in the cavity formed by the thickness of the welt, starting at the front half of the heel, to give greater stability and durability to the lower parts of the shoe. When walking, the back of the shoe should stay still. Only the front of the shoe should be able to fold, thereby ensuring the food has a sturdier support below it. The shank is covered and affixed with a layer of leather, inserted in the cavity just beyond the length of the iron, clued and nailed down with the wood pins.

Cork inserts

These are strips that are inserted in the cavity that remains between the leather that covers the shank and the edge of the welt. The cork midsole is glued and levelled off with a rasp, without touching the stitching.

Simple welt

Reverse welt

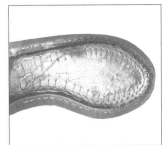
Sewing the welt

Trimming the welt

Smoothing the welt

Wood pins/pegs: beech wood pegs, about 3-3.5 mm/0.12-0.14" thick and about 15 mm/0.59" long, used to affix the rands.

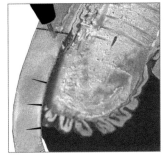
Positioning the rand

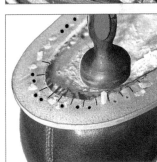
Affixing the rand with pegs

Positioning the shank

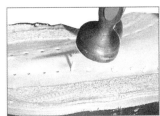
Affixing the shank

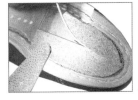
Adding the cork strips

Outsoles

The outsole is the lower piece of the shoe that comes in direct contact with the ground. There are shoes with simple soles, those that have single or double soles, and those that have a midsole. The sole is glued and sewn to the lower part of the shoe. Before being sewn, the sole should be sliced with a shard of glass, creating a channel on the part that goes towards the sole, about 6 mm/0.24" from the edge, around the entire contour. The incision should be made at a 45 degree angle up to the middle of the sole with a special scraper with a 90-degree angle point, thus leaving a lip that will cover the seam. So, using the point of the bone knife, lift the lip of the incision to make sewing the sole easier.

The seam on the shoes with a simple welt will be visible only on the upper part of the shoe and heel, while the part underneath will be covered by the aforementioned lip.

Marking and hand-sewing the sole
The procedure to sew the simple welt is:
- Mark the stitch points on the welt with a stitch marker to make sure they are evenly spaced.
- Use the awl to puncture all layers of the sole, from the marked points to the incision of the last layer.
- In opposite directions, pass two curved needles with waxed thread coated in resin (to make it waterproof) through the hole, without damaging the lip of the incision, which is needed to cover the thread.
- Pull the two threads, trying to always exert the same amount of pressure on each, to create even stitches.
- At the last stitch, tie the ends of the two pieces of thread into a sturdy knot.
- Adjust and even out the visible stitches on the welt, pressing on each stitch with equal pressure with the points of the stitch marker.
- Spread the glue over the stitching in the incision, close the lip over the stitches, using the claw of the hammer, then hammer the lip to flatten the surfaces of the sole and smooth it with the handle to make it definitively compact and flush.

Seam with a reverse welt
Reverse welt seams are used generally for sports shoes, where the seams are highlighted especially for a decorative as well as structural purpose.
- Position the welt on the nailed-down upper, with the smoothed side against the upper, angled upwards.
- Use the awl to perforate the welt, upper and footbed and pass the curved needles and threads through them in opposite directions, making a stitch every 10 mm/0.39".
- Gradually, as the stitches are created, remove the nails that are holding down the upper.
- When the welt reaches the other end, the excess part should be trimmed.
- Complete the seam and knot the two pieces of thread.
- Fold the welt 90°, placing one side in line with the part under the shoe.
- Insert the shank, the leather to cover it and the cork pieces.
- Apply the midsole, if any, with a layer of glue and a second row of stitching.
- Apply the outsole, creating the incision and sewing the three layers of leather together, creating a third row of stitching, running parallel to the second row and symmetrical to the first.

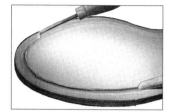
Incision on the sole

Reverse welt

Mark the seams with the stitch marker

Perforate the soles with the awl

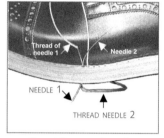
Thread the curved needles

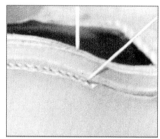
Pull forcefully on the thread

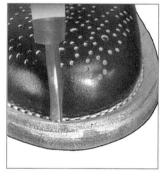
Make the seams uniform with the stitch marker

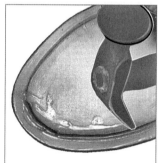
Glue and close the incision

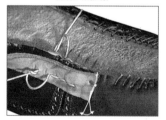
Position the welt

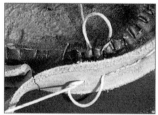
Cut and fold the welt

Heels on men's footwear

In ancient times, the heels of men's footwear were applied to riding boots to make them safer as they stood up in the stirrups to charge the enemy.

In the 17th century, heels made of wood wedges were placed inside shoes, between the heel and the sole, to make the wearer seem taller.

In the Baroque era, court dignitaries wore shoes with heels, often in exaggerated dimensions.

In subsequent centuries, heels for men's footwear have fluctuated in popularity, always linked to the dictates of fashion.

Today, heels on men's shoes are made to create a proper resting spot for the foot, encouraging the uniform distribution of the weight of the body between the toe and the heel.

Sizes and shapes of men's heels

Regular heels for classic men's footwear are 2.5 cm/0.98" high and ¼ of the sole + 1 cm/0.39" (E.g.: 29/4 = 7.2 + 1 = 8.2 cm/3.23") and the width equal to that of the back sole.

The heel is composed of multiple layers of leather about 5-6 mm/0.20-0.24" thick, mounted on the second rand and affixed in turn to the sole with glue and wood nails. The last layer, called *the sole of the heel*, is composed of a half heel in leather and half in rubber. The latter, positioned just above the halfway mark of the heel, is placed in the point that first comes into contact with the ground when walking. It is that most subject to wear and thus frequently replaced.

The layers of the heels on the two shoes must all have the same thickness and, for greater safety, after having mounted the heels, it is necessary to carry out one last inspection, comparing the left and right shoes, making sure that the heels are of the exact same height.

The classic forms of the most commonly-used men's heels are symmetrical and U-shaped, or slightly asymmetrical with a slight protuberance towards the internal side of the shoe.

Sports and casual shoes, on the other hand, usually have trapezoid shaped heels in which the base is wider, if they are a wide heel; or in the shape of a trapezoid with a narrower base, if they are a narrow heel.

Heel construction phases

To create and assemble the heels, you'll need to pay plenty of attention and be precise, especially when creating the curves and the thickness of each layer, which must be identical on both heels.

The construction phases for heels are:

- Hammer and leave the heel leather pieces to soak in water, then keep them in a damp place to make them denser.
- Measure the thickness of the sole of the two heels and, if they are different, even them out with the rasp or by hammering the thicker layers with the hammer.
- Using a pattern, mark the outline and the length of the heel on the shoe.
- Use a glass shard to rasp and smooth the surface of the marked shoe to make it flat and even.
- Spread glue on the edges of the sanded surface.
- Place and glue the second rand, prepared in advance, giving it the right curvature by cutting a few small triangles out of its internal border.
- Make a line of holes with the awl in the middle of the rand, add a drop of glue and hammer in all the wood pegs (long enough to pass through the sole, the first rand and the overturned heel counter.
- Use the cutter to trim the surface of the rand, levelling it and evening out the heads of the wood pins.
- Cut the layers of the heel and hit them with the hammer on a basalt stone to flatten out any folds and make them more compact.
- Roughen the leather of the first layer of the heel with the rasp, apply the glue, glue it and affix with wood pins. Use the same procedure to create the other layers, checking the measurements of the two heels each time.
- Apply the last layer of the heel, composed half of leather and half of no-slip rubber, gluing them and affixing them with small nails.
- Use the shoemaker's knife to even out the outer edge of the heel (or seat), hit it with the the hammer to flatten it, wetting it continuously to keep it soft and, lastly, eliminate any last traces with the rasp.

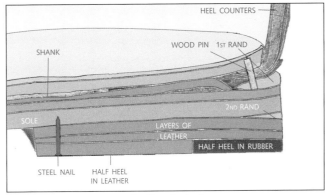

Section of a heel

Classic men's heels

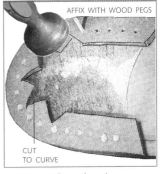

Second rand

Completed heel

Finishing the shoe

Finishing the welt edge and the heel seat

The *edge* (that of the welt, midsole and outsole as a unit) and the *seat* (surface of the lateral edge of the heel), are finished as follows:
- Dampen the leather and further thin the edge with the metal cutting disc.
- Shape the curves with the rasp, compacting the entire surface.
- Eliminate all the microsurfaces protruding from the edge, using the special tool for levelling in the shape of a cutting plane, equipped with a guide groove.
- Finely smooth the edges with a glass shard.
- Colour the edge and the seat using different systems, according to the type of shoe, including:
a) White or light coloured summer footwear, where the edge and the seat are left in the natural colour of the leather, or dyed/painted the same colour as the upper.
b) Winter footwear with simple welt seams, where the edge and the seat are treated, soaking them with the desired colour and then with a layer of wax, using the iron (a metal tool heated over a flame, compressing the paint and the wax to obtain a smooth, shiny surface).
- Apply the yellow mordant to the visible seams on the welt, to bring them out and make them waterproof, or dye them the same colour of the upper or the edge and the seat.

Finishing the outside sole

The outer sole is to be finished to make it waterproof and to make it look its best:
- First, remove all irregularities from the surface of the outer sole, smoothing it perfectly with a glass shard.
- Apply multiple layers of neutral shoe shine on the outsole and the heel sole, using a warm cutting iron to melt the shoe shine. Leave enough time for it to be absorbed.
- If part of the design, paint the heel and the junction of the footwear in the same colour as the edge, which may have different designs and decorations.

Decorations on the lower part and edges

Decorations on artisan shoes, made by hand or with special machines, almost always embody exclusivity and the signature of the craftsman that made them. The decorations are made with "fudge wheels", a wheel of serrated metal that, after being headed over a flame, is run over the part to be decorated or edged, or with machines equipped with incised rollers heated to the right temperature.
The parts that generally are subject to decoration or edging are:
1) The reverse welt that adheres to and flanks the upper, which is decorated with a serrated wheel at 45°.
2) The curved line demarcating the division of the sole and that painted along the entire edge of the sole, which are decorated with a wheel incised with a custom design (lines, triangles, Greek frets, etc.).
3) The upper edges and the corners of the heels.

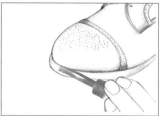

Trim the dampened edge.

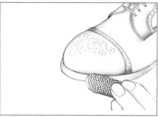

Shape the curves with the rasp.

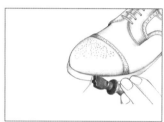

Eliminate any protruding surfaces.

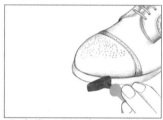

Apply the paint and wax with heat.

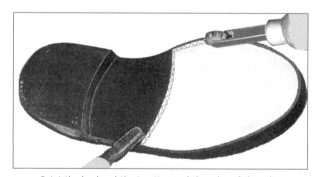

Paint the heel and the junction and the edge of the sole. Decorate along the line of the junction and the sole.

Decorate the reverse welt close to the upper.

Manually finishing the inner shoe

After having finished the outer part of the sole and heel, remove the wood last, helped by the use of a special iron hook with a strap, which is inserted in the hole of the last and pulled with the help of the foot, holding the shoe firm with the hands. Once the wood last has been extracted, use your hands to check to make sure that the inner footbed has no protruding parts, wood pins or metal nails.

If so, you'll need to use pliers to remove the metal nails and carefully smooth the surface of the footbed with special rasps for shoe interiors and thick and fine sandpaper, making it perfectly smooth.

Inserts and foot pads

Orthopaedic inserts are pieces of cork shaped according to the conformation of the bottom of the foot, about 8 mm/0.31" thick and in the appropriate length.

For custom shoes, the conformation of the foot and the measurements are to be noted when measuring the foot. The inserts, in the correct thickness and length, must be placed correctly in the shoe.

In addition, before definitively gluing them, it's essential to have the customer try on the shoe and walk around a bit. Foot pads are cork disks about 2 cm/0.79" in diameter with a thickness of about 2 mm/0.08", positioned at the centre of the heel for better cushioning.

Even the measurements and the thickness of the inserts, for custom shoes, must be suitable to the needs and shape of the foot that has been measured.

Sock lining

The sock lining is the lining that is applied above the smoothed footbed, in direct contact with the foot, cut out of the same leather used for the interior of the upper.

The sock lining can be whole (the full length of the footbed), or three quarters, half or one quarter (just for the heel).

It should be evenly covered with glue, positioned within the shoe above the footbed and the orthopaedic inserts and foot pads and glued carefully, avoiding folds or creases.

Finishing the upper

1) Ironing: The surface of the still-damp external upper should be ironed one last time to eliminate all the wrinkles and folds that formed during the various processes.

To do so, use the smoother or iron that, once heated, should be pressed forcefully passing it over the entire surface carefully. This step, when done correctly, makes the upper perfectly ironed and shiny.

2) Shining: For the final shining, apply three to four layers of shoe shine on the upper, letting it absorb for about 15 minutes. Then shine the upper with a soft-bristle brush and a cloth. For Brogues, which have decorative holes, colour all the light parts of the perforations in the same hue as the upper before going on to the external shining.

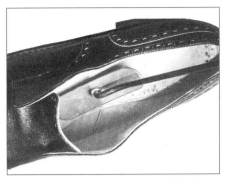
Smooth the inner surface with a rasp and sandpaper.

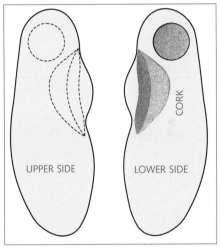
Footbed with anatomical pads.

Iron and shine the outer upper with a smoother.

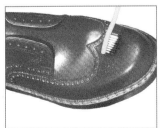
Dying the inside of the holes.

Shine with a cloth until reflective.

THE SHOEMAKING INDUSTRY

The Italian shoemaking industry reached its height in recent years, even if its "birthday" goes back a few decades.

Advanced technology and computer systems have also been introduced to this industry, allowing for rapid developments to take place in production, administration and sales.

To compete in the global market, modern companies must have efficient, effective departments in every area of its structure. In particular, they make use of the following organisational services:

1) Research department;
2) Timeline and procedures department;
3) Planning office (for programming the launch).

- The research department:

1) Selects the hides and various materials;
2) Creates the forms and prototypes;
3) Creates the paper patterns;
4) Draws up the working documentation;
5) Defines the quality level;
6) Outlines working allowances.

- The timeline and procedures department:

1) Chooses the manufacturing methods (by hand or machine);
2) Decides on the type of processing/treatment;
3) Coordinates the other departments;
4) Manages the work spaces;
5) Establishes the layout of the machinery;
6) Researches equipment;
7) Creates good working conditions (safety, temperature/air quality, lighting, etc.);
8) Defines working methodologies;
9) Analyses the tasks to complete;
10) Studies the movements of workers;
11) Defines time lines;
12) Studies the right balance in work distribution.

- The planning department:

Programming

1) Allocates the machines to the departments;
2) Compiles the worker knowledge/skill table;
3) Organises the succession of orders;
4) Calculates working times; establishes due dates;
5) Decides to extend or reduce working hours;
6) Makes decisions on supplies according to the production needs and availability of liquidity;
7) Studies the prices of expenses (raw materials, machine depreciation, labour, energy expenses, etc.);
8) Issues exit vouchers;
9) Schedules employee training;
10) Checks the progress of orders.

Launch

The launch ensures the coordination of the programming and the units, while it's purpose is to ensure the programme is followed, starting the work in each department.

1) Distribution of the materials necessary for the job;
2) Launch of the operations of each department;
3) Check in on the execution of the job, daily;
4) Quality and quantity control.

The work environment and automation

Automation is the automatic coordination of all jobs relating to fabrication, transfer of pieces from one station to another, and their presentation in the correct position in front of the machinery tools.

The movement of raw materials and pieces that are part of a job is launched by a switch or button. Workers no longer need to check the machines, as that is done by servo mechanisms as well (computers).

Inspectors are replaced by inspection machines that check the product automatically.

Development

The rules of automatic development are programmed in the computer's memory and thus the different sizes are developed automatically.

The selection overhead conveyor

This device makes it possible to select the items to be used and supply the work stations.

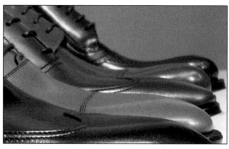

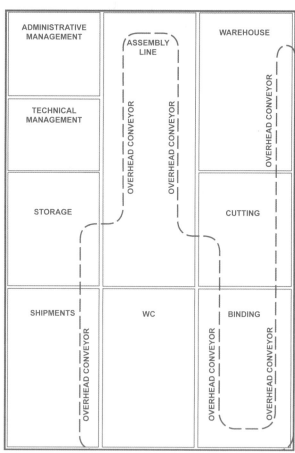

Potential work space with an overhead conveyor

Industrial production

Storage and inspection

In the shoemaking industry, the inspection and storage of leather, soles and accessories takes on an important role. Warehousing, carefully studied in a functional sense, can drastically help the finances of the management. To achieve this, all the information regarding materials, from their arrival to the warehouse to their storage, must circulate quickly and precisely in the hands of individuals in charge.

The precise location of various articles makes them easy to group, with the related picking of orders to be sent to the punching and cutting room. For this reason, it can be said that the first step in optimised cutting starts in the leather storage room. The inspection records, like the warehousing itself, change notably from company to company, both for the different arrangement of the rooms and for the different types of organisation.

Inspection and registration

When the hides arrive, they should be viewed, that is, passed over inspection tables where their length, thickness and colour are closely examined, referring to the samples. Lastly, any defects should be marked with appropriate signalling so that operators in the cutting room will be able to see them immediately and eliminate them. The recording of the hides, accessories and their movement is generally done with the help of a computer.

Fashion design with CAD

The work done by patternmakers is both a creative and concrete one. Thus, it is also very important for every company to have a group of technicians expert in patterns and their development.

After having analysed fashion trends, the stylist and creator will follow his or her creative intuition and draw a collection for the following season. The patternmaker should then study the most concrete patterns that can be made industrially.

Computer-assisted processing

New CAD-CAM technology is available to help study and make the samples, to then go directly to production. Start with the size module to create the desired last, which can be generated visually in all its dimensions and be made through a cutter controlled directly from the CAD program. You can draw it directly on the screen, or on the pattern paper laying flat, with the possibility to correct it.

Once the pattern is drawn, separate it from the last or the 3-D pattern, giving it the chosen colour palette.

The image of the shoe pattern is similar to a picture and can be presented as a picture of the prototype, discussing it in the first few sample meetings.

These drafts can also be used on the work orders to display the sample.

The CAD module for footwear makes it possible, with simple operations that do not require any particular computer training, to:

1) Define and create a last;
2) Draw the style lines;
3) Give colour to the model with a realistic effect;
4) Lay the 3-D pattern flat.

Defining the last

The operator can make use of a series of shaping features through which s/he can change a given form or replace its parts with already saved parts belonging to different lasts, until getting the new, desired last.

The procedure is quite similar to the system of creating a new lasts manually. Often it is the result of manipulating an already-existing last, using plaster to add or a tool to take away.

Creating the last

The new last, created from the modifications applied to a pre-existing one, can be made physically with a 5-axis milling machine, suitable for the production of a sample.

Drawing style lines

Using the movement of the mouse or the computer stylus, you can freely draw the desired shape, with the chance to correct the lines, take measurements, affix points of reference or rotate the insert to access any point.

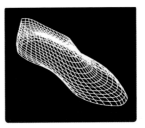

Defining the last

Creating the last

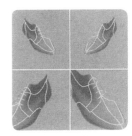

Drawing style lines

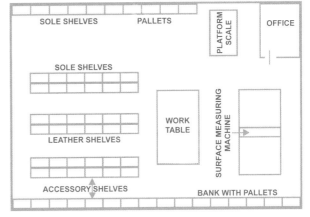

Warehouse

Realistic colouring and rendering

After you have drawn the style lines, the shoe pattern should be separated from the last. Render it on the computer screen with the colours you prefer, freely chosen from a palette that offers 400 options.

The pattern can be completed by drawing the accessories and the desired ornamentation so as to get an overall view of the whole.

The image obtained can be moved as you'd like and, when a light source is positioned, it can be seen in terms of a realistic light output, with all the chiaroscuro of the given illumination. The resulting effect is similar to a photograph.

Patternmaking techniques

Pattern CAD makes it possible to work on a flat surface, going from drawing on the 3-D pattern to detecting the broken-up pattern, adding the appropriate margins, parts to be folded under, holes, embroidery, etc.

The various designs, like wingtips, a toe cap, a heel, etc., can be saved in a computer folder and, if necessary, used for other models.

Flattening

The pattern created is automatically flattened, with methods similar to those used manually, when separating the tape from the last. It is possible to modify the result of the flattened pattern and obtain the base, which is still valid on the same last.

Using the features included in the CAD program, which do not require special computer training, you can carry out the following operations:

1) Digitize a 3-D pattern.
2) Separate the various parts.
3) Industrialise the model, introducing edges, stitching, resting points, etc.
4) Develop the cuts for all parts of the pattern.
5) Add notes to the project.
6) Execute the semi-automatic or automatic nesting of the pieces.
7) Manage the cutting system.

Digitizing the 3-D pattern

The first operation carried out to get to the cutting phase is the digitization of the 3-D pattern, which may be:

1) the result of the creation of a previously-made pattern and brought up on the screen from the archive;
2) The result of the digitization of the base pattern drawn on paper, using the special digitizing tablet;
3) A new, hand-made pattern.

When digitizing, the external and internal outlines of the shoe pattern are introduced, positioning all the axes necessary to develop the piece.

The resulting 3-D pattern should be saved as such, so as to be used subsequently to create new patterns, implementing the required modifications.

Separating the various parts

In this phase, each piece is selected, changed as needed, separated from the rest of the 3-D pattern, oriented according to the direction of the upper and then saved and archived, ready to be brought up for any changes or a new use.

Industrialization of the pattern

In the pattern industrialization phase, using simple operations, it is possible to take measurements, add margins, discard excess parts, extend and join lines.

Developing sizes

The development of sizes is carried out through the commonly used rules with the values referring to the Parisian, English, American or other custom rules, inserted directly into the program, carrying them over to the digitized base pattern.

Realistic colouring and rendering

Digitizing the 3-D pattern   *Industrialization of the pattern*

 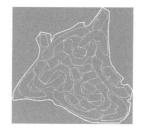

Developing sizes   *Nesting*

Working notes

With this program, each project can be connected to working notes, legends/keys and all that may be useful to highlight or signal something to workers in subsequent phases, or to facilitate the job and prevent errors.

Automatic nesting

Laying out is the last phase of the program before cutting. It can be done in three ways:

1) Laying out order.
2) Automatic nesting.
3) Assisted nesting.

- The laying out order should contain all the instructions relative to the type, size and number of pieces to be nested.

- Automatic nesting, partially reducing waste, is highly recommended for inexpensive materials.
- Assisted nesting, including the chance to intervene to assign the pieces a different location if you don't think they're well placed, further reduces the percentage of waste, thereby best using the material.

Once the nesting has been set, all pieces are there to evaluate the cost of the garment, considering, of course, what type of material is being used.
At this point, after having optimised the nesting, the material can be cut to create the bases.

Industrial working processes

Technical card and the work order
The head of the die-cutting department, having received the work order and the technical card, will gather the materials required from the warehouse: leather, linings, etc. and deliver them to each clicker, along with the work order.

Technical card
The technical card is used to check all the work phases from how many strokes of the die cutter it takes to cut a pair of shoes to the work times required by the stitching depart-

ment, to the products needed to assemble the shoe on the work order.
So, the card makes it possible for the head of the department to schedule the work and provide the worker with everything s/he needs to carry out the work. In addition, the card makes it possible to know how much all the working operations will cost, item by item and in total, in order to evaluate the costs.

The work order
The work order follows the piece to be worked, starting from the programming office, signed by the office heads of each sector, detaching a stub from it to demonstrate the completed work, then signing in the special box of reference. By doing so, it is possible to determine who worked on the product if there are any issues.
Once all the work is done, the order is returned to the office for invoicing and, then, registration and archiving.

TECHNICAL CARD		N°............
DERBY		

DESCRIPTION	CONSUMABLES
UPPER	
QUARTER	
STAND	
TONGUE	
LINING	
FOOTBED	
FOOTPRINT	
HEEL	
HEEL BAND	
BINDING OPER. Time	
FLESHING	
SEW STAND	
FOLD QUARTER	
APPLY LINING	
ADD TONGUE	
APPLY UP LINING	
CLOSE DERBY	
APPLIED PIECES	
DYED YARN	
EYELETS	
WAXED LACES	

PROCESSES
LAST: ....

UPPER	5	ASSEMBLY STEPS
TOE	7	SOLE
LINING	2	FINISH:
SEAM	3	VAR

WORK ORDER			N°..............		
		SIGNATURE	OPER.	VAR.	ORDER N PAIR
Mr/Ms .... Item .... Pair					
Leather .... Colour					
Print .... Colour					
Lining .... Process .... Last					
Footbed .... Counter .... Cover					
Undersole .... Sole					
Heel .... 1/2 Heel .... Top piece					
Base .... Heel .... Finishes					
Brand .... Delivery					
Leather					
Lining					

17	18	19	20	21	22	23	24	25	26	27	28	29	30	31
10	11	34	35	36	37	38	39	40	41	42	43	44	45	46
2.1/2	3	3.1/2	4	4.1/2	5	5.1/2	6	6.1/2	7					
7.1/2	8	8.1/2	9	9.1/2	10	10.1/2	11	11.1/2	12					

Notes

CUTTING

Cutting department

In addition to manual cutting methods, used for samples or for sets of just a few pairs, cutting can be done with the following methods:
1) With die cutters or punching machines; 2) With a knife; 3) With a concentrated jet of water; 4) With a laser.

Cutting

The die cutting system makes use of steel punches with the outlines of the footwear affixed on surfaces of the die cutter/ punch machine. The machine cuts out the form on the leather, placed under the die.

The die which creates the derby pattern is one of the easiest to manoeuvre and position, as it lines up quite well when laid out. Tubular-construction shoes, being a whole pattern, it is one of the most complicated, both for the consumption of materials and for the positioning of the leather. For this reason, the die cutter operator may work more slowly and, as a consequence, the work times are extended, in addition to wasting more material.

Today's die cutters are quite technologically advanced, productive and offer the maximum possible use of the material. There are automatic single-tool die cutters (which can produce 70 blows per minute); automatic multi-tool die cutters; computerised and automated punch cutters, with a mobile trolley with dies that can be programmed and managed by a CAD/CAM system to lay out the outlines to be cut and for the flexible programming of production.

Cutting with a blade

This system can be used for leather and woven fabric or synthetics. It is composed of a work table with a rotating transport for the fabric and two mechanical arms for the hides. One of the arms is needed to place the hide under the blade and the other, with suction, carried the cut piece, passing it on to the next table. With this type of cutting method, it is possible to cut up to 8 squared stacked hides at a time, or different layers of fabric, with savings on production costs and on execution times.

Cutting with a waterjet

With this technique, the cut is made with a small jet of water (0.10 mm/0.003937" diameter) propelled at a speed ranging from 600 to 900 meters per second - that's 2 to 3 times the speed of sound.

The waterjet stream is produced by a high pressure generator, which compresses the water at about 4,500 bar of pressure, shooting it through a tiny 0.10 to 0.30 mm/0.003937-0.011811" diameter hole. This stream, loaded with kinetic energy, is directed towards the outline, creating a clean cut in various centimetres of thickness. This system can be used to cut leather uppers, synthetic materials, non-woven fabric, leather soles or plastic soles.

Automatic die cutter

Hole punching machine

Two-thread sole stitching machine

Glue machine

Round knife cutter and band saw

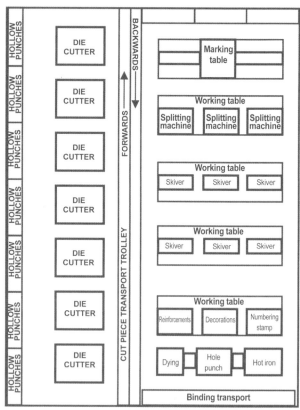
Cutting dept

PREPARING THE UPPER

Before sending the cut pieces to the stitching department, a few other steps are necessary. They are:
1) Marking the joining points; 2) Equalising;
3) Stamping and boring holes; 4) Skiving; 5) Bevelling;
6) Applying reinforcements and bands.

Marking the joining points: marking, done on a special work surface where marking and numbering machines are installed, is the first operation that is done. It consists of creating joining points and numbering, where not already done during die cutting.

Equalising: is necessary to further even out the thickness of the cut pieces, even if you are using already-equalised hides. Cut uppers are passed under the equalizer to bring them to the desired thickness, varying them for a few parts of the model which must be even thinner, such as: the tongue, the stitching, padding, the stand, etc. The equaliser makes it possible to carry out other steps, such as composite skiving, inlays, etc.

Stamping and hole boring: manual or automatic hydraulic presses can be used to stamp or create holes in leather. Heat presses can also create various designs, decorative seams, braids, outlines, etc.

The planes can be used to create different types of holes, both for braiding/weaving and for broguings on the vamp; application of micro-spirals that create floral designs, etc.

Skiving: skiving involves removing part of the inner sole to make a few operations possible, such as:

1) Skiving for folding is done by considering the thickness, which must neither be too thin, as the leather would have angles that are too sharp, nor too thick, for the opposite reason. Considering, for example, a 4 mm/0.16" fold-over, a groove or skiving of 8 mm/0.31" is necessary to make the parts match up perfectly.

2) The seam margin that's folded under is to be skived below the hide, for half of its thickness, 5 mm/0.20" deep, while the papillary layer is skived 2 mm/0.09", necessary to even out the thickness and hide the joinery.

3) The overlapping parts are skived by half their thickness (4 mm/0.16") and then cauterised, to give them a tidy edge.

Bevelling: this operation is done with manual or automatic/computerised bevelling machines. These machines may be controlled electronically through microprocessors, which make it possible for their data cards to receive essential data or programs related to 800 different types of bevelling operations. In addition, special software makes it possible to save the thickness and the width of the bevelling, the angling of the presser foot and the speed at which the material is fed into the machine.

Rienforcements and bands: these pieces are used to reinforce the upper in various points, such as the quarters of a derby, under the eyelets, for women's court shoes, etc.
If the leather is thin, a guttaperca gum facing is applied (the material needs no additional adhesive), using a heated plate. Padding should be glued to the upper before being stitched because it is more precise and quickens the task. Reinforcement ribbons in various sizes and thicknesses are to be placed where necessary. Such as:
1) The lacing system of a derby, so that it doesn't rip or disintegrate; 2) The collar of a court shoe, so it holds its shape and doesn't cede to the stress placed on it during the binding, acting as a reinforcement, extending the life of the shoe; 3) On the tongues of moccasins so they keep their shape, without unflattering side recesses. Reinforcements and ribbons should be applied with a special automatically operated pneumatic machine, applying bands and reinforcements that are anywhere from 3 to 20 mm/0.12-0.79" wide, automatically cut.

Automatic hydraulic press

Skiving machine with a microprocessor

Sole bevelling machine

Automatic seam opening and ribbon applying machine

THE BINDING ROOM

The main issues faced in the binding or stitching room are the same as in other departments of commercial production: a good layout that creates maximum efficiency for the workers. The layout is closely linked to the manufacturing system used by the company which, in turn, is related to the company's managerial policies.

The most frequently used systems in the shoemaking industry are:

1) An assembly line (or conveyor belt).

With this system (which is the simplest), shoes are generally worked one by one. The passage from one operation to the next may be carried out via slides, with a regular-interval conveyor belt or a simple manual transfer.

2) A progressive line system (or synchronised system);

3) A bundle assembly system.

Each of these systems has its drawbacks and advantages, but each company must decide on one, considering a few base principles, such as:

- Elasticity, meaning the ability to pass quickly from the production of one item to the next.

- Specialisation on the production line.

- The minimum course principle, meaning the study of a layout that, compatible with the company's various commercial needs, tends to reduce the course to a minimum.

- Principle of producing with minimum delivery terms.

This principle is fundamental for the sales department, especially to know the speed with which the work order can be delivered from the factory.

Processing department

In many companies around the globe, 'work stations' or 'rink systems' are used to assemble footwear. In these systems, the footwear goes from one operation to the next without stopping, carrying out the complete work cycle which starts with the application of the footbed and finishes with the removal of the last.

Using this system, which involves about 5 to 7 workers, about 900 to 1,100 pairs of shoes can be made in 8 hours. This system can be used to make all types of footwear, especially those with gluing techniques and pre-defined soles, for men, women and kids. However, it can also be used for blake and ideal construction to great results.

Operation sequence

- Worker 1

1) Applies the footbed using traditional systems.

2) Loads the rotary machine to smooth the seat of the upper.

- Worker 2

3 - 4) In a single step: Assembly of the toe, the heel seat and the side.

- Worker 3

5) Heal seating; insertion in the shoe oven.

- Worker 4

6 - 7) Roughing and gluing.

- Worker 5

8) Applying the sole.

- Worker 6

9-10) Pressing the sole with a traditional machine.

- Worker 7

11) Last extraction; application of the heel with an automated machine, with positioning for the subsequent operation of ironing the finished shoe with hot and cold ovens, loaded manually or automatically with grips.

The finishing operations vary according to the quality and type of footwear produced.

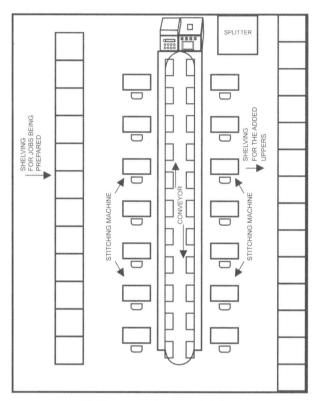

Stitching room and conveyor belt layout

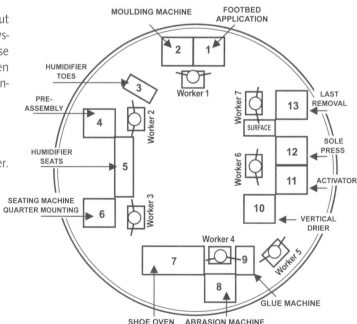

Number of workers: 5 -Number of operations = 900 pairs in 8 hours
Number of workers: 7 -Number of operations = 1100 pairs in 8 hours

Work station

STITCHING MACHINERY

The department with the highest costs is the stitching department. Unfortunately, it is also the department where the fewest innovations have been made.

Already-existing machines have been perfected, with options to programme stitching and automatic thread trimming, but the production process has not seen any real technological revolutions, even if there are computerised stitching systems.

These systems, found in companies all over the world, consist of a numeric control that manages a two-axis trolley. Uppers closed in an aluminium containing case are hung in this trolley and moved according to the program, thereby completing the stitches with precision.

These programs are created in the CAD centre when the pattern is made, using these computerised stitching systems as needed:
1) with upper assembly machines,
2) with decorative stitching machines.

The assembly of the upper via a computerised system ranges from classic men's and women's footwear to casual and sports shoes and even work and military footwear, etc.

These systems have notable advantages, both in terms of productivity and in the standardisation of the quality and production costs, using workers that only have to feed the machine with pieces to be assembled.

Overlock machine, 1 thread and plate transport, for applying the footbed to leather uppers, with PVC and PV soles.

Post-bed machine, 1 needle, overcast, normal hook and vertical axes. Upper and lower wheel transport. Recommended for all operations that require seams with a needle and trimmings.

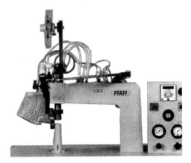

Lightweight soldering machine with continuous feed, with hot-air functioning, to apply seam-covering ribbons with continuous soldering, used for waterproof walking footwear (after-skiing footwear, inner layers for hiking boots, etc.).

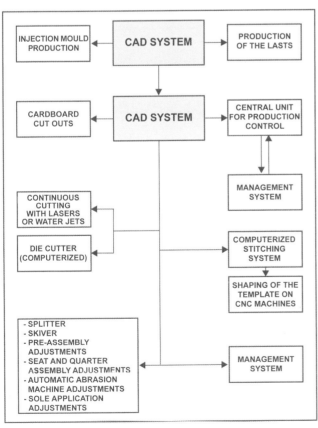

Complete production cycle with CAD

Eyelet machine to apply eyelets that have a shaft from 3 to 12 mm/0.12-0.47".
This machine is loaded by a magnetic vibration apparatus that, suitably regulated, conveys the eyelets into the driving channel, that transports them to the riveting punch. The punch and the mould that drive the eyelets can be changed according to the size of the eyelet. The punch is also used for perforation.

Upper lacing machine.

INJECTED FOOTWEAR

The injection process is one by which bag-constructed uppers sewn to the footbed/sock lining with a Strobel machine, then mounted on aluminium lasts. Those lasts proceed on carousels that, at necessary stages, inject TR (thermoplastic rubber) and PVC, polyurethane or rubber between the upper and the mould of the bottom, creating the sole in one or more colours.

TR soles

This type of plastic sole, being injected directly in the mould, is quite suited for production in different colours. Moulds have a hive-like structure, where it is possible to inject the different colours.

These soles are used for sports footwear in particular, from trainers to basketball shoes, casual shoes, footwear worn after skiing, etc, in addition to all the box soles that have the insertion of various welts, including in leather.

This material is quite suited for imitation crepe para rubber, making it possible to create soles composed of leather and para rubber.

PVC and leather soles

PVC is used to fill leather-wrapped soles.

To create them, load the mould with the leather sole and the outer strip of the heel, then inject PVC to fill the empty spaces, i.e., the welt and the inside of the heel, thereby creating a highly durable, inexpensive and attractive sole.

With the same mould, it is possible to produce an inexpensive black all-PVC sole, suitable for work shoes.

Synthetic rubber soles

Synthetic rubber is a product created from polycondensation or polyaddition (polymerization). It can be used to create products with characteristics unlike and superior to natural rubber.

In general, synthetic rubber is mixed with other products: rubber, fillers, activating agents, anti-decay agents, dyes, accelerators, sulphur, etc. to create a compound that is then added to a special machine, called a closed mixer. With the addition of heat, all the components are thoroughly mixed.

This creates a plastic mass that is then transferred to an open mixer, where it is homogenised. Once the 'dough' is ready, it is immediately rolled and placed in a die plate to create pieces with specific weights and dimensions.

The mixture is then ready to be poured in the sole mould, which should be cleared of overflowing materials.

Rubber soles may have special characteristics: no-slip, anti-oil, no-wear, solvent resistant, heat resistant, etc.

Rotary rubber injection machines

The machines used for the injection of elastomers are based on a high closing force press, which is used in the mould injection phase while, for the other phases, the mould holder sees to the closing and movement of the mould.

Rotary machines, compared to linear injection machines, make it easier for the operator to get the product directly in the working position, and for finishing and overflow removal processes.

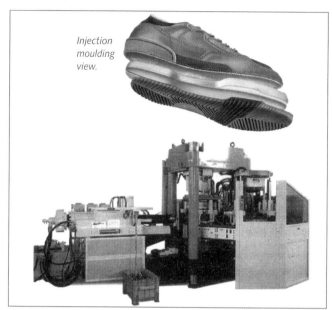

Injection moulding view.

Injection moulding machine

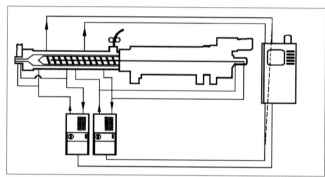

Diagram of the adjustable deposit injection system

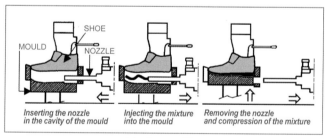

SHOE

MOULD NOZZLE

Inserting the nozzle in the cavity of the mould

Injecting the mixture into the mould

Removing the nozzle and compression of the mixture

Injection moulding

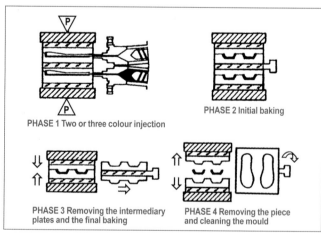

PHASE 1 Two or three colour injection

PHASE 2 Initial baking

PHASE 3 Removing the intermediary plates and the final baking

PHASE 4 Removing the piece and cleaning the mould

Production process

BAGS, RUCKSACKS, LUGGAGE AND BELTS

Bags. 68
Main bag shapes 70
Luggage. 71
Bag terminology. 72
Seams and stitching 73
Classic bag with a semi-stiff flap. 74
Classic bag with a soft flap. 75
Shaped bag 76
Small soft bag with a zip 77
Soft bag with a zip closure 78
Baguette bag 79
Small hobo bag 80
Trapezoid hobo bag 81
Small soft rectangular bag 82
Small bag with a handle 83
Semi-structured bag 1 84
Young girl's purse. 85
Semi-structured bag 2 86
Structured purse. 87
Soft bag. 88
Satchel bag 89
Semi-structured shopper. 90
Shopping bag. 91
Structured shopping bag. 92
Zip-fastened bowling bag 93
Flat shopper. 94
Bucket bag. 95
Elegant bag 96
Plain seam briefcase. 97
Bag with bellows pockets 98
Hard shell suitcase 99
Small suitcase with a wooden frame 100
Leather 24-hour bag. 102
Bag with a motif and gathering. 104
Shoulder pouch bag 105
Pouch bag base 106
Rucksack with a pocket 107
Rucksack with two pockets. 107
Mountain rucksack. 108
Stitched sporty bag 110
Gym bag 110
Volleyball bag. 111
Round sack 111
Belts. 112
Belt production steps 114
Finishing touches 116

Bags

Medieval   Renaissance   French Directory   Restoration   1835

1840   1870   1880   1885   1890

1895   1900   1920   1930

Bags are an important accessory, an essential item for today's industry and economy in Italy and beyond. They are connected to fashions in clothing and footwear and thus subject to seasonal changes, often part of the offerings of famous stylists.

Bags go back to the birth of money and coins in general. Ancient Greek records mention a *byrsa* (oxhide), meaning a sack hung from the belt within which money was kept. Ancient Romans used the *bursa*, which is where modern-day purses derive from, serving the same purpose. Only starting in the Middle Ages did the first representations of shoulder bags begin to appear.

In the 12th and 14th centuries, men's bags were quite roomy, connected to the belt and used as game bags by hunters.

In Italy, *scarselle* were used to carry money, closed by metal hinges in various shapes, often with reproductions of castle towers.

In the 15th century, the nobility's *scarselle* had a triangular shape with a rounded flap, made by highly-qualified craftsmen, while the masses wore pendant sacks, tied to the belt with long laces.

In the 1600s and 1700s, men's and women's fashions began to introduce roomy pockets to every garment: jackets, trousers, capes for men and skirts, overskirts and underskirts for women, leading to the abandonment of bags.

Bags made a comeback as a necessary accessory after the French revolution, when long skirts disappeared and fashion dictated lightweight dresses with a columnar line, thus without the ability to add the voluminous pockets which previously were used as carry-alls.

In this period, women placed all the items they had to carry in a container shaped like an ancient urn or netting, called *reticules*, *ridicules* or *indispensables*, or in other models shaped like flowers or shells. Men, on the other hand, moved on to the coin purse and wallet, often embroidered.

Towards the end of the 1800s, small purses became a must-have, inseparable accessory for women.

In England, women adored the vanity case: silver mesh with a chain shoulder strap.

Small purses truly came into their own in the early 20th century, especially in the 1920s, when small, sombre rectangular shapes began to appear, destined to last over time, wrapped in prized leather with equally exquisite linings on the inside.

1935

1940

1950

1960

1970

1975

1980

1985

1990

1995

2000

2005

2007

2009

In this era, the great stylists such as Chanel began to appear, making highly-prized bags (Chanel's small envelope-like bag in nappa leather and satin, entirely quilted on the outside in a diamond pattern with a golden chain handle is one famous example); Gucci, Gherardini, Hermes with his designs inspired by saddlery and the famous Kelly bag from 1935, named so because Grace Kelly herself liked it.

In 1936 the cylindrical bucket bag with a long shoulder strap appeared thanks to Elsa Schiaparelli, re-worked by Gucci in boar hide in 1937 with a green and red fabric strip, which has become a classic today.

After WWII, shoulder bags continued to be an indispensable accessory for women, while men began to carry a more masculine version, a model inspired by the bags used by officials during the war, complete with external pockets and a shoulder strap.

In the 1960s, bags gained importance as the accessory connected to fashion and current themes: from vanity case styles in patent leather to clutch bags in nappa leather, from shoulder sacks or hippie bags and frayed, colourful saddzle bags seen in 1968.

From the 1970s onwards, with the establishment of Italian ready-to-wear lines, classic luxury bags were joined by models made with

hides that underwent fanciful tanning processes, imitating crocodile, lizard and other hides, with a wide range of colours and patterns. Italian craftsmanship was on the forefront of the processing and use of leather in accessories, footwear, bags and luggage.

While Ferragamo was an inexhaustible inventor of the paradigms of footwear and an innovator in terms of materials, Gucci focused on a limited number of structures, repeating the same bag models for years with growing success, or coming up with others that stood alongside the classic versions.

The classic lines of Nazareno Gabrielli, Gherardini, Roberta di Camerino, of the Rossetti leather goods shops and the emerging Bottega Veneta took root. Even Trussardi can be placed entirely within classic, stable lines, with balanced shapes and materials that evolved slowly yet also tended to characterise a specific time in Italian fashion.

On the other hand, Mario Valentino, Carrano, Albanese and the fashion creators such as Coveri, Ferrè, Pancaldi, etc. stood out for their versatility and continuous ability to change. All of them used leather, in addition to fabric, for their products.

Main bag shapes

As we've seen, bags were once used exclusively for galas. They were quite small, being mainly ornamental. During the other hours of the day, bags weren't necessary, as clothing was loose and flowing with roomy, deep pockets. Today bags come in every shape and size, with versions for every occasion: classic bags, day bags, evening bags, beach bags, shopping bags, gym bags, work bags, and luggage.

Classic bags and day bags have to combine their decorative and utilitarian functions. They must be used to carry house keys, car keys, a wallet, ID holder, make up, an agenda, a few other small items, and so on.

To meet these needs and for the sake of practicality and comfort, these bags must be designed with simple, linear forms in abundant proportions, featuring inner compartments and outer bellows. According to the needs and the occasion, they may have a long shoulder strap, mid-length handles (like a shopper) or shorter handles (those of a handbag). Practical day bags can be in any type of leather, including matt calfskin, treated or printed hides, dyed in various colours according to the dictates of fashion, in addition to new materials such as printed plastic and faux leather, rubber, printed waterproof canvas, etc.

For urban wear in general, light, softer leather is preferred, or even fabric, straw, raffia or wicker. In addition to the classic forms, there are bucket, tote and sack shaped bags.

To take to the beach, bags are generally larger and made of different materials, such as: fabric, straw, wicker, chintz, clear or printed PVC, rubber, etc. These bags also have varied accessories, such as large wooden rings, rope handles, hemp cords, large studs in wood or other varnished materials, buttons and buckles in metal or colourful plastic, to name just a few of the most imaginative.

For formal wear or other fancy occasions, bags take on a different status in the overall look. In fact, the materials used change and, in the winter one can choose from fine, delicate calfskin, suede, buckskin, crocodile, snake, coated leather and ostrich, while the forms get thinner, rounder, elongated vertically or horizontally, large or small in size, with two handles or a shoulder strap, depending on fashion at the time. They are characterised by motifs or special leather processes, such as horizontal or diagonal shirring, the insertion of contrast leather motifs or thin edgings that create interplays of colour and design. Natural and coated leather can be combined, etc. Bags are then fastened with zips and ornamental studs, clasps, gold-plated clips, tortoise shell buckles, etc.

The inside should be lined with deerskin or prized satin, usually with a woven motif representing the brand's logo.

For formal autumn and spring bags, the shapes don't change too much, while the materials do, becoming lighter and more vivacious in the colour palette.

For elegant summer bags, the material generally matches one's shoes or sandals, either in a vibrant or soothing tone, though always bright and luminous, possibly also matching the clothing being worn.

For cocktail attire or important parties, bags are replaced by envelope bags, clutches and other small purses, made in prized hides such as crocodile, python, black patent leather, tortoise, smooth or embroidered satin, or in the same fabric as the dress being worn or with fabric appliqués. The shape may be a flat envelope or a rectangle/square.

Luggage

The luggage sector can be grouped with the leather goods industry as they both use the same materials, share the same tools and the same special machinery and create products with similar and, at times, even identical techniques.

Luggage pieces vary greatly, but the most important ones are found just about everywhere: suitcases.

Luggage is a category of containers that meet the criteria of utility and functionality. Today, we are able to make objects that unite utility with elegance and quality.

There are two main types of luggage: hard and soft shell.

Variants of these two types of bases can be divided into travel luggage, professional accessories, athletic bags, small suitcases for representatives and officials, etc.

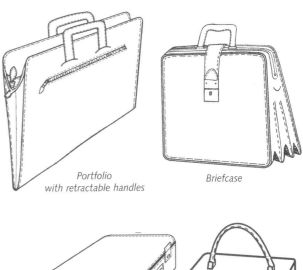

*Portfolio
with retractable handles*

Briefcase

Luggage materials

The materials used for luggage are more or less the same as those used for other leather goods.
- External hides: vacchetta, calfskin, horse, sheep, boar, buckskin, crocodile, snake, etc.
- Lining hides: split calfskin, sheepskin, kid, suede and smooth leathers, split hides reinforced with a gum facing or canvas, etc.
- Imitation leather, such as: pegamoid, fibre, plastic, vulcanised fibre, etc.
- External fabric: damask, Ottoman (a textured fabric with horizontal stripes), brocade, carpet, hemp, glen plaids, etc.
- Lining fabric: quilting, summer wool, velvet, suede lining, cotton moire, grosgrain, polished cotton, etc.
- Paper and cardboard: cardboard that's like wood or leather, for suitcases; packaging paper, leather paper, etc.
- Glues and mastics: animal-derived glue (bone glue), vinyl adhesives (very flexible), natural rubber mastics.
- Wood: poplar for the forms, plywood.
- Yarn and cord: cotton yarn with a gauge from 1 to 8 for exteriors and under 1 for interiors, cords of different gauges used as fillers.
- Fillers and reinforcement materials: batting, wadding, cork, plastic trim, foam rubber, tube-shaped metal or metal wires.
- Accessories: wood clasps, snap fastenings, rivets, locks, rings, buckles.

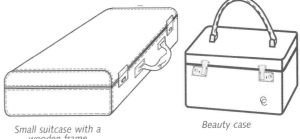

*Small suitcase with a
wooden frame*

Beauty case

Equipment and machinery

The equipment and machinery used to create luggage is essentially the same as for other leather goods.

The main luggage products

The following items are considered luggage:
- Suitcases: soft shell; hard or structured shell; semi-hard or partially structured; on a wood shaft, 48-hour bags that are semi-hard or on a wood shaft; 24-hour bags that are semi-hard or on a wood frame; attaché cases (briefcases); wardrobe suitcases, semi-hard or on a wood frame.
- Bags: travel bags, portfolios; professional bags, sports bags.
- Athletic sacks.
- Pencil cases.
- Beauty cases.
- Hat boxes.

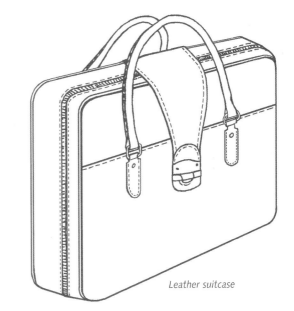

Leather suitcase

Travel carry-all

Rucksack with a pocket

BAG TERMINOLOGY

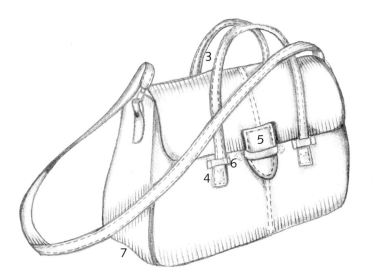

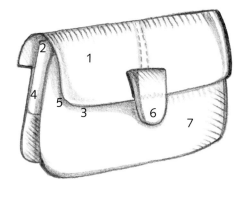

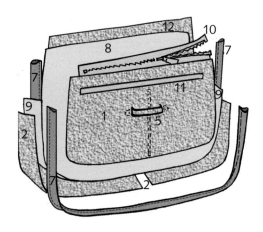

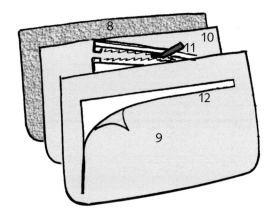

Satchel bag with a removable shoulder strap
1) Front panel;
2) Bottom and side;
3) Handles;
4) Chap;
5) Closure tab;
6) Keeper loop;
7) Welted piping;
8) Front pocket lining;
9) Side lining;
10) Zip;
11) Front zip pocket;
12) Back panel.

Flap closure purse
1) Flap;
2) Backing;
3) Underflap;
4) Flap reinforcement gusset;
5) Front reinforcement;
6) Closure tab;
7) Front panel;
8) Back panel;
9) Back lining;
10) Intermediary back lining;
11) Zip;
12) Zip pocket.

Seams and stitching

A seam is the union of two or more layers of fabric or leather, while stitching can be defined as a series of stitches used for decoration or to finish an edge, or to cover the edge itself.
Seams are divided into four categories:
1) Superimposed Seams (SS);
2) Lapped Seams (LS);
3) Bound Seams (BS);
4) Flat Seams (FS);
Stitching is divided into two categories:
1) Edge Finishing (EF);
2) Ornamental or Decorative Stitching (OS).
Each category includes different types of seams, each of which has its own application for a determined use.
For leather goods, seams take on different names than they do with fabric.

The main types of seams are:
1) Plain (blind) seam;
2) Closed seam;
3) Welt seam;
4) Seam for inside-out construction;
5) Cut edge seam and border;
6) French seam;
7) Piped seam;
8) Seam with edging for a bag border stitching machine;
9) Extendible assembly for bellows.

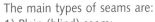

An example of a bound seam (BS)   An example of a lapped seam (LS)   An example of a superimposed seam (SS)

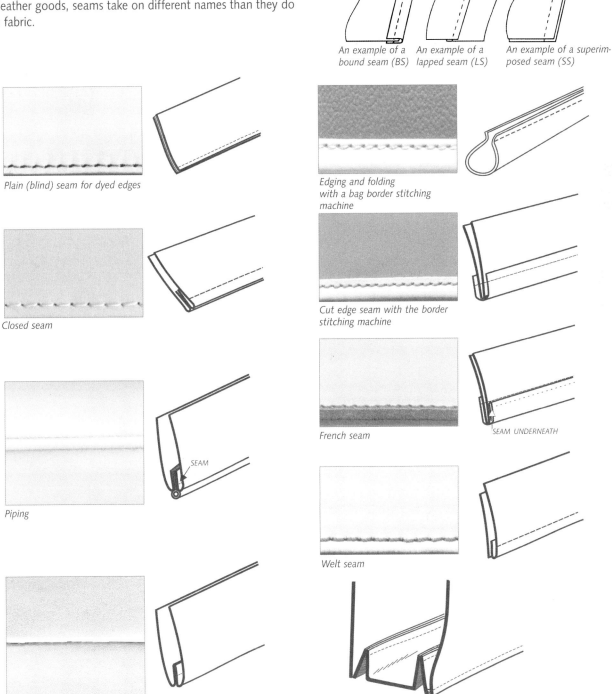

Plain (blind) seam for dyed edges

Closed seam

Piping — SEAM

Inside-out assembly

Edging and folding with a bag border stitching machine

Cut edge seam with the border stitching machine

French seam   SEAM UNDERNEATH

Welt seam

Extendible assembly for bellows

CLASSIC BAG WITH A SEMI-STIFF FLAP

EDGED WITH A BAG BORDER STITCHING MACHINE

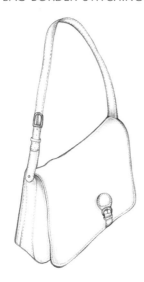

The classic flap bag is generally 23-30 cm/9.1-11.8" wide, 16-20 cm/6.3-7.9" high and 5-9 cm/2.0-3.5" deep. It can have a shorter or longer flap on the front, closed with a magnet placed on the underside, or via other means. It may be carried with a small, stiff handle or worn via a cross-body or shoulder strap.

Pattern for the back+flap quadrant:

- Draw a rectangle whose height is equal to the bag (18 cm/7.1") + the depth (7 cm/2.8") + the desired length of the flap (15 cm/5.9"); in the desired width (24 cm/9.4"). Round out the corners.

Pattern for the back of the flap and the lining:

- Draw a rectangle as above, but with height reduced by 0.5 cm/0.2". Draw the opening for the zip in the desired position.

Pattern for the front quadrant and lining:

- Draw a rectangle in the same the height and width of the bag (18 cm/7.09" and 24 cm/9.45" respectively). Round out the lower corners.

Pattern for the side/bottom and lining:

- Draw a rectangle with the same height and depth of the bag (e.g 7 cm/2.8"); for the length, use that of the outside of the front quadrant (e.g. 57 cm/22.4").

Pattern for the chap or leather anchors for the ring of the shoulder strap:

- As shown in the figure.

Pattern for the inner zip pocket lining:

- Draw a rectangle with the same height and length as the back+flap quadrant (40 cm/15.7). For the width, use the width of the same quadrant minus 3 cm/1.2" (21 cm/8.3").

Shoulder strap: in the measurements desired.

Edging: width 2 cm/0.8"; thickness 0.6 mm/0.02".

Flap fastening: as illustrated or as desired.

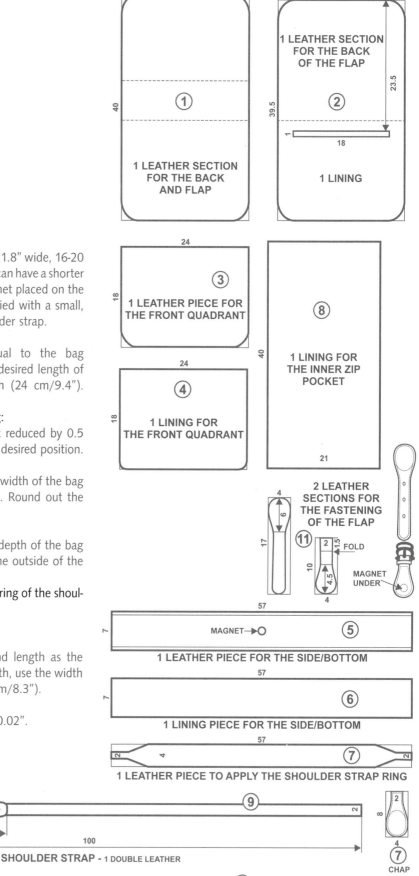

74

Classic bag with a soft flap

INSIDE-OUT ASSEMBLY

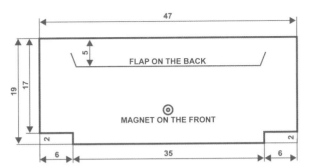

2 LEATHER PIECES FOR THE FRONT AND BACK QUADRANTS

47
19
17
5
FLAP ON THE BACK
MAGNET ON THE FRONT
2
6
35
6
2

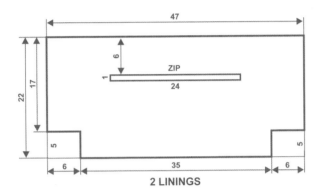

2 LININGS

47
22
17
6
ZIP
1
24
5
6
35
6
5

1 DOUBLE PIECE OF LEATHER FOR THE FLAP

2
30
2
HOLES FOR THE HANDLE
5
3
22
24
34

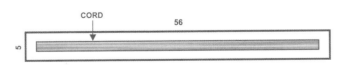

1 LEATHER PIECE FOR THE BOTTOM

35
7

CORD
56
5

1 STRIPS OF LEATHER FOR THE TUBULAR HANDLES AND CORDS 52 CM LONG

Bag measurements:
- Width 34 cm/13.39";
- Height 18 cm/7.09";
- Depth 12 cm/4.72".

Pattern for the front and back quadrants:
- Draw a rectangle whose height is equal to the height of the purse +1 cm/0/39" (19 cm/7.478") and whose width is equal to the width of the purse +13 cm/5.12" for the sides (47 cm/18.50").
- Trace the outline as shown in the figure.

Pattern for the flap:
- Draw a rectangle that's 24 cm/9.45" high and 34 cm/13.39" wide. Trace and draw the holes for the handles as shown.

Pattern for the lining with a zip:
- Draw a rectangle that has the height of the quadrant +3 cm/1.18" for the bottom (22 cm/8.66") and whose width is equal to that of the quadrant (47 cm/18.50").
- Shape as in the figure.

Bottom pattern:
- Draw a rectangle whose height is equal to the depth of the purse -5 cm/1.97" (7 cm/2.76") and whose length is equal to the width of the purse (34 cm/13.39").

Pattern for the zip pocket lining:
- 18 x 34 cm (7.09 x 13.39") rectangle.

Pattern for the handles:
- As illustrated.

Shaped bag

WITH BRAIDED HANDLES

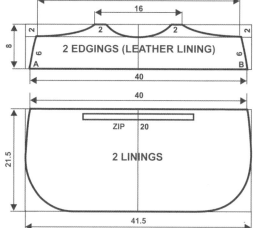

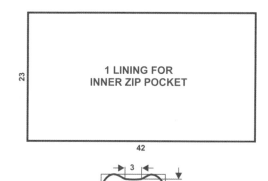

Bag measurements:
- Width 41.5 cm/16.34";
- Height 26.5 cm/10.43";
- Depth 8 cm/3.15".

Pattern for the front and back quadrants:
- Draw a rectangle whose height is equal to the height of the purse (26.5 cm/10.43") and whose width is equal to the width of the purse (37 cm/14.57").
- Trace the outline as shown in the figure.

Pattern for the facing:
- On a piece of tracing paper, take up the upper part of the pattern of the quadrant, until line A-B for a total height of 8 cm/3.15".

Pattern for the lining with a zip:
- Take up the lower part of the quadrant pattern, until line A-B.
- Draw the position of the zip.

Bottom/side pattern:
- Draw a rectangle whose height is equal to the depth of the purse (8 cm/3.15") and whose length is equal to the length of the external border of the quadrant (81.5 cm/32.09").

Pattern for the zip pocket lining:
- 23 x 42 cm (9.06 x 16.54") rectangle.

Pattern for the chap, handle attachment and braided handle:
- As illustrated.

1 LINING FOR INNER ZIP POCKET

4 DOUBLE LEATHER PIECES

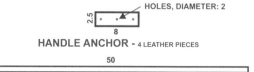

HOLES, DIAMETER: 2

HANDLE ANCHOR - 4 LEATHER PIECES

BOTTOM AND SIDES - 1 LEATHER PIECE 1 LINING

Small soft bag with a zip

AND PIPING

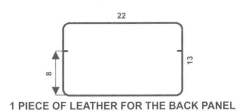

1 PIECE OF LEATHER FOR THE BACK PANEL

1 PIECE OF LEATHER FOR THE BOTTOM - 1 LINING

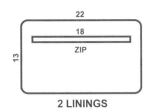

2 LININGS

**2 LEATHER PIECES
FOR THE ZIP PULL TABS**

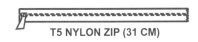

T5 NYLON ZIP (31 CM)

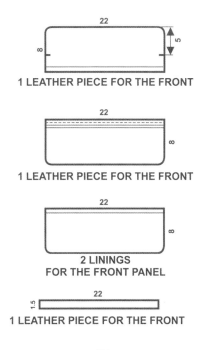

1 LEATHER PIECE FOR THE FRONT

1 LEATHER PIECE FOR THE FRONT

**2 LININGS
FOR THE FRONT PANEL**

1 LEATHER PIECE FOR THE FRONT

ZIP

- 2 LEATHER PIECES - 2 LININGS WITH ZIPS

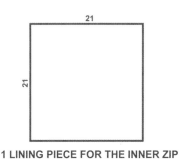

1 LINING PIECE FOR THE INNER ZIP

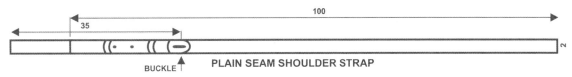

PLAIN SEAM SHOULDER STRAP

BUCKLE

Bag measurements:
Length: 22 cm/8.66", Height: 13 cm/5.12", Depth: 5 cm/1.97".
This bag is composed of:
Leather pieces:
- 1 leather back panel;
- 2 leather pieces for the front panels;
- 1 decorative strip for the front panel;
- 2 leather strips for the outer top zip;
- 1 leather strip for the bottom;
- 2 leather pieces for the zip pull tabs;
Lining pieces:
- 2 pieces of lining for the pocket on the back panel;
- 2 pieces of lining for the pocket on the front panel;
- Complete lining for the inner;
- Plain seam shoulder strap in the desired length/width.
Draw the pattern following the indications and the measurements shown in the figures.

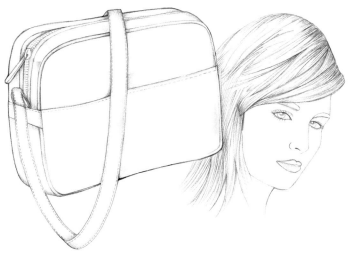

SOFT BAG WITH A ZIP CLOSURE

WITH THE BOTTOM ASSEMBLED INSIDE-OUT

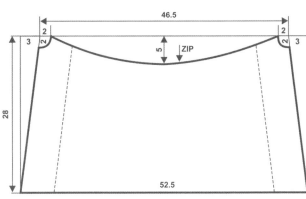

2 PIECES OF LEATHER FOR THE QUADRANT

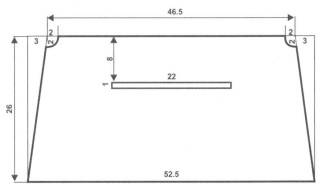

2 LININGS

Bag measurements:
- Width 32 cm/12.60".
- Height 26 cm/10.24".
- Depth 12 cm/4.72".

Pattern for the front and back quadrants:
- Draw a rectangle whose height is equal to the height of the purse +2 cm/0.79" (28 cm/11.02") and whose width is equal to the width of the purse + that of the sides + seams (52.5 cm/20.67").
- Trace the outline as shown in the figure.

Pattern for the lining with a zip:
- The same measurements as the leather quadrant -2 cm/0.79" for the height (26 x 52.5).
- Draw the position of the zip.

Pattern for the zip pocket lining:
- Draw a rectangle that's 25 cm/9.84" high and 35 cm/13.78" wide.

Bottom pattern:
- Draw a rectangle whose height is equal to the depth of the purse (12 cm/4.72") and whose length is equal to the width of the purse (32 cm/12.60").

Patterns for the shoulder strap:
- As illustrated.

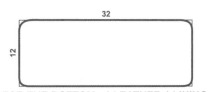

FOR THE BOTTOM - 1 LEATHER 1 LINING

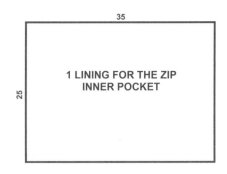

1 LINING FOR THE ZIP INNER POCKET

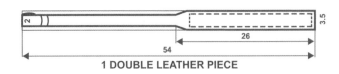

1 DOUBLE LEATHER PIECE

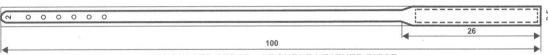

SHOULDER STRAP - 1 DOUBLE LEATHER PIECE

Baguette bag

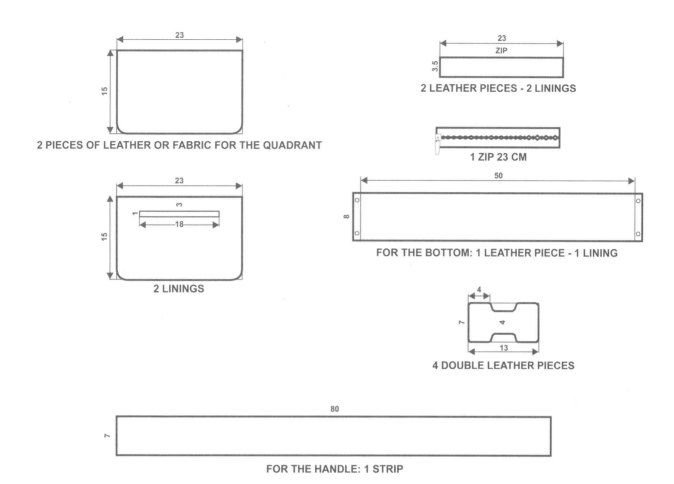

23
15
2 PIECES OF LEATHER OR FABRIC FOR THE QUADRANT

23
ZIP
3.5
2 LEATHER PIECES - 2 LININGS

1 ZIP 23 CM

23
3
1
18
15
2 LININGS

50
8
FOR THE BOTTOM: 1 LEATHER PIECE - 1 LINING

4
7
4
13
4 DOUBLE LEATHER PIECES

80
7
FOR THE HANDLE: 1 STRIP

Bag measurements:
- Width 22.5 cm/8.86".
- Height 14 cm/5.51".
- Depth 8 cm/3.15".

Pattern for the front and back quadrants:
- Draw a rectangle whose height is equal to the height of the purse +1 cm/0.39" (15 cm/5.91") and whose width is equal to the width of the purse +0.5 cm/0.20" (23 cm/9.06").
- Trace the outline as shown in the figure.

Pattern for the lining with a zip:
- The same measurements as the leather quadrant (23 x 15 cm/9.06 x 5.91").
- Draw the position of the zip.

Bottom/side pattern:
- Draw a rectangle whose height is equal to the depth of the purse (8 cm/3.15") and whose length is equal to the length of the external border of the quadrant + 3 cm/1.18" to affix the chap for the rings of the shoulder strap (50 cm/19.69").

Pattern for the chap for the rings and shoulder straps:
- As illustrated.

D-rings:
- 2 rings, with a pitch of 4 cm/1.57".

Snap hook:
- 2 rings, with a pitch of 4 cm/1.57".

Small hobo bag

INSIDE-OUT ASSEMBLY

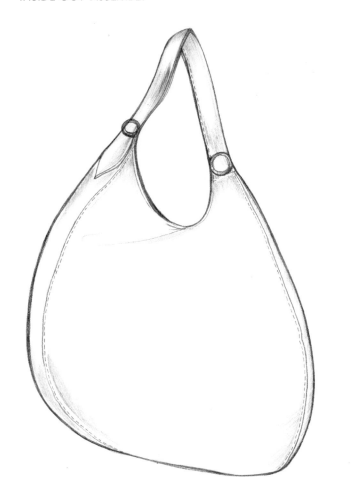

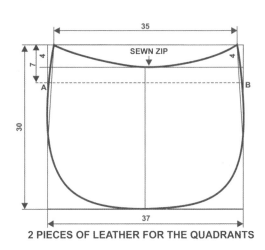

2 PIECES OF LEATHER FOR THE QUADRANTS

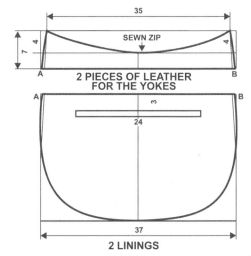

2 PIECES OF LEATHER FOR THE YOKES

2 LININGS

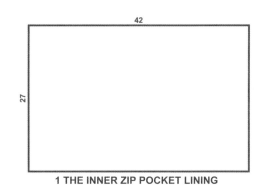

BOTTOM AND SIDES - 1 LEATHER PIECE 1 LINING

Bag measurements:
- Width 37 cm/14.57".
- Height 30 cm/11.81".
- Depth 10.5 cm/4.13".

Pattern for the front and back quadrants:
- Draw a rectangle whose height is equal to the height of the bag (30 cm/11.81") and whose width is equal to the width of the bag (35 cm/13.78").
- Trace the outline as shown in the figure.

Pattern for the facing:
- On a piece of tracing paper, take up the upper part of the pattern of the quadrant, until line A-B for a total height of 7 cm/2.76".

Pattern for the lining with a zip:
- Take up the lower part of the quadrant pattern, until line A-B.
- Draw the position of the zip.

Bottom/side pattern:
- Draw a rectangle whose height is equal to the depth of the purse (7 cm/2.76") and whose length is equal to the length of the external border of the quadrant (84 cm/33.07"). Outline as in the figure.

Pattern for the zip pocket lining:
- 27 x 42 cm (9.06 x 16.54") rectangle.

Pattern for the chap, handle attachment and handle:
- As illustrated.

1 THE INNER ZIP POCKET LINING

1 DOUBLE LEATHER PIECE FOR PLAIN SEAM EDGES

2 PIECES OF LEATHER FOR THE HANDLE ATTACHMENT

4 LEATHER SECTIONS FOR HANDLE KEEPER LOOPS

Trapezoid hobo bag

INSIDE-OUT ASSEMBLY

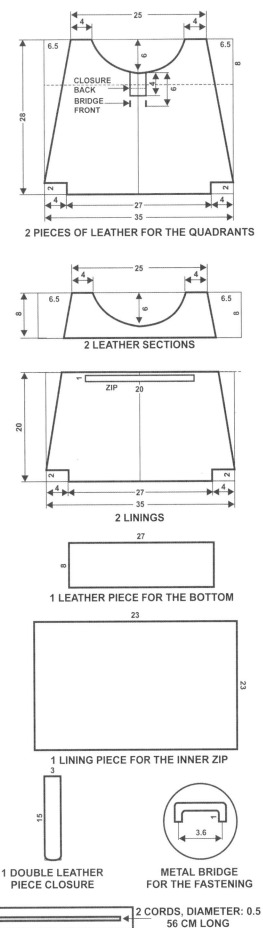

2 PIECES OF LEATHER FOR THE QUADRANTS

2 LEATHER SECTIONS

CLOSURE
BACK
BRIDGE
FRONT

ZIP

2 LININGS

1 LEATHER PIECE FOR THE BOTTOM

1 LINING PIECE FOR THE INNER ZIP

1 DOUBLE LEATHER PIECE CLOSURE

METAL BRIDGE FOR THE FASTENING

Bag measurements:
- Width 26 cm/10.24".
- Height 26 cm/10.24".
- Depth 10 cm/3.94".

Pattern for the front and back quadrants:
- Draw a rectangle whose height is equal to the height of the bag +2 cm/0.79" (28 cm/11.02") and whose width is equal to the width of the bag +8 cm/3.15" for the depth of the side (35 cm/13.78").
- Trace the outline as shown in the figure.

Pattern for the facing:
- On a piece of tracing paper, take up the upper part of the pattern of the quadrant, until line A-B for a total height of 8 cm/3.15".

Pattern for the lining with a zip:
- Take up the lower part of the quadrant pattern, until line A-B.
- Draw the position of the zip.

Bottom pattern:
- Draw a rectangle that's 8 cm/3.15" high and 27 cm/10.63" long.

Pattern for the zip pocket lining:
- 38 x 23 cm (14.96 x 9.06") rectangle.

Pattern for the leather closure and handle:
- As illustrated.

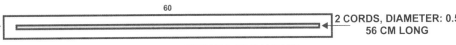

2 STRIPS OF LEATHER FOR THE TUBULAR HANDLES

2 CORDS, DIAMETER: 0.5
56 CM LONG

SMALL SOFT RECTANGULAR BAG

INSIDE-OUT ASSEMBLY

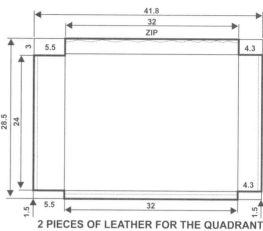

2 PIECES OF LEATHER FOR THE QUADRANT

Bag measurements:
- Width 32 cm/12.60".
- Height 24 cm/9.45".
- Depth 9 cm/3.54".

Pattern for the front and back quadrants:
- Draw a rectangle whose height is equal to the height of the bag +4.5 cm/1.77" (28.5 cm/11.22") and whose width is equal to the width of the bag +9.8 cm/3.86" for the depth of the side (41.8 cm/16.46").
- Draw the outline as shown in the figure to get the sides, bottom and top.

Pattern for the lining with a zip:
- Draw a rectangle that's 33.5 cm/13.19" high and 41.8 cm/16.46" wide.
- Draw the outlines as shown in the figure to get the sides, bottom and top.
- Draw the position of the zip.

Bottom pattern:
- Draw a rectangle that's 9 cm/3.54" high and 32 cm/12.60" long.

Pattern for the zip pocket lining:
- 27 x 37 cm/10.63 x 14.57" rectangle.

Pattern for the leather handle:
- As illustrated.

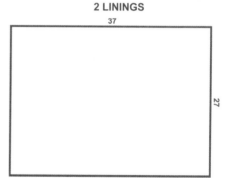

2 LININGS

1 LINING PIECE FOR THE INNER ZIP

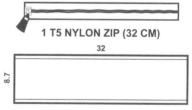

1 T5 NYLON ZIP (32 CM)

1 LEATHER PIECE FOR THE BOTTOM

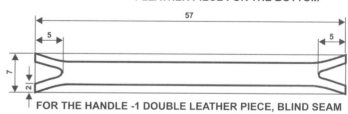

FOR THE HANDLE -1 DOUBLE LEATHER PIECE, BLIND SEAM

SMALL BAG WITH A HANDLE

CUT OUT FROM THE QUADRANTS

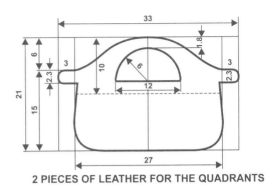

2 PIECES OF LEATHER FOR THE QUADRANTS

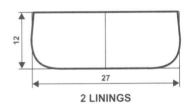

2 LEATHER PIECES FOR THE FACING

2 LININGS

CHAP - 2 DOUBLE
LEATHER PIECES

2 RINGS, DIAMETER: 6

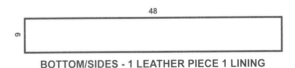

BOTTOM/SIDES - 1 LEATHER PIECE 1 LINING

Bag measurements:
- Width 27 cm/10.63".
- Height 15 cm/5.91".
- Depth 9 cm/3.54".

Pattern for the front and back quadrants:
- Draw a rectangle whose height is equal to the height of the bag +6 cm/2.36" (21 cm/8.27") and whose width is equal to the width of the bag +6 cm/2.36" for the tabs for the rings (33 cm/12.99").
- Trace the outline as shown in the figure.
- Draw the hold for the handle as illustrated.

Pattern for the facing:
- On a piece of tracing paper, take up the upper part of the pattern of the quadrant, until line A-B for a total height of 10 cm/3.94".

Pattern for the lining with a zip:
- Take up the lower part of the quadrant pattern, until line A-B.

Bottom/sides pattern:
- Draw a rectangle that's 9 cm high and with a length equal to the perimeter of the lower part of the quadrant (48 cm/18.90").

Chap pattern:
- As illustrated.

Semi-structured bag 1

PIPING ON THE BOTTOM

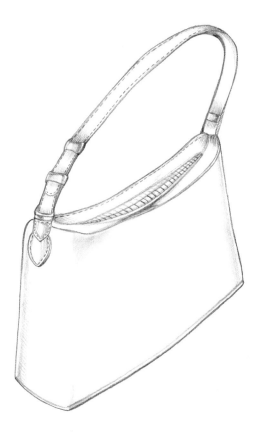

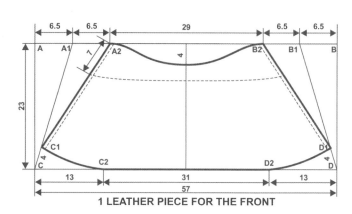

1 LEATHER PIECE FOR THE FRONT

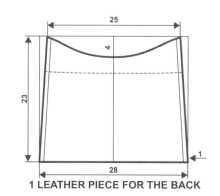

1 LEATHER PIECE FOR THE BACK

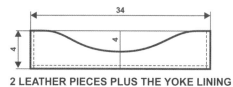

2 LEATHER PIECES PLUS THE YOKE LINING

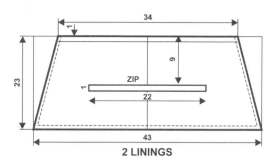

2 LININGS

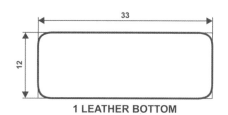

1 LEATHER BOTTOM

Bag measurements:
- Width 33 cm/12.99".
- Height 23 cm/9.06".
- Depth 12 cm/4.72".

Front quadrant pattern:
- Draw a rectangle whose height is equal to the height of the purse (23 cm/9.05") and a width of 57 cm/22.44".
- Curve up by 6.5 cm/2.56" + 6.5 cm/2.56" per side to create the taper, as illustrated.
- Measure 29 cm/11.42" at the top and create a curved outline, dropping down by 4 cm/1.57".
- Create the outline of the lower part, raising the sides by 4 cm, as illustrated.

Back quadrant pattern:
- Draw a rectangle whose height is equal to that of the front quadrant (23 cm/9.05") and with a length of 28 cm/11.02".
- Curve in at the top by 1.5 cm/0.59" cm per side and shape as illustrated.

Yoke lining pattern:
- Draw a rectangle that's 7 cm/2.76" high and 34 cm/13.39" long.
- Shape as in the figure.

Pattern for the lining with a zip:
- Draw a rectangle that's 17 cm/6.69" high and 43 cm/16.93" long.
- Narrow the top by 4.5 cm/1.77" per side and trace.
- Draw the opening for the zip as illustrated.

Bottom pattern:
- Draw a rectangle 12 cm/4.72" high and whose length is equal to the width of the purse (33 cm/12.99").
- Shape as in the figure.

Shoulder strap pattern:
- As illustrated.

SHOULDER STRAP

Young girl's purse

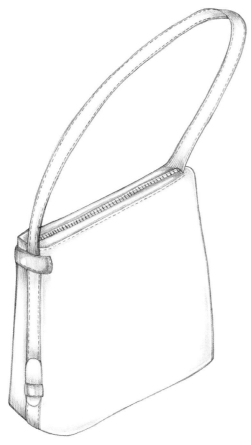

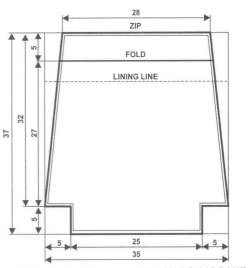

2 PIECES OF LEATHER FOR THE QUADRANTS

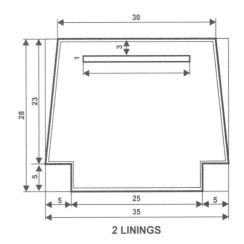

2 LININGS

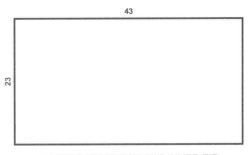

**1 LINING PIECE FOR THE INNER ZIP
23 X 43 CM**

Bag measurements:
- Width 24 cm/9.45".
- Height 27 cm/10.63".
- Depth 9.5 cm/3.74".

Pattern for the front and back quadrants:
- Draw a rectangle whose height is equal to the height of the purse +10 cm/3.94" (37 cm/14.57") and whose width is equal to the width of the purse +11 cm/4.33" for the sides (35 cm/13.78").
- Trace the outline as shown in the figure.

Pattern for the lining with a zip:
- Draw a rectangle 23 cm/9.06" high and whose width is equal to the width of the quadrant (35 cm/13.78").
- Shape as illustrated and draw the opening of the zip in the position illustrated.

Bottom pattern:
- Draw a rectangle whose height is equal to the depth of the purse -5 cm/1.97" (7 cm/2.76") and whose length is equal to the width of the purse (34 cm/13.39").

Pattern for the zip pocket lining:
- 23 x 43 cm (9.06 x 16.93") rectangle.

Handle, snap hook and belt loop and loops.
- As illustrated.

**BELT LOOPS:
1 DOUBLE LEATHER PIECE**

**SNAP HOOK LOOP
1 LEATHER SECTION**

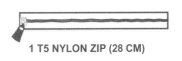

1 T5 NYLON ZIP (28 CM)

1 DOUBLE PIECE OF LEATHER FOR THE HANDLE

SEMI-STRUCTURED BAG 2
WITH PLAIN (BLIND) SEAMS

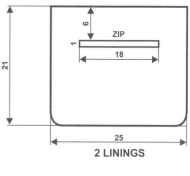

2 PIECES OF LEATHER FOR THE QUADRAN

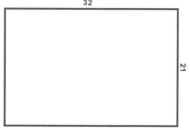

2 LININGS

1 LINING PIECE FOR THE INNER ZIP

1 T5 NYLON ZIP (27 CM)

2 LEATHER SECTIONS

60

1.5

2 LEATHER PIECES TO ASSEMBLE THE QUADRANTS INSIDE-OUT

60

2.5

1 DOUBLE LEATHER PIECE FOR THE PLAIN STITCHED HANDLE

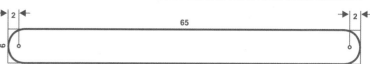

1 LEATHER PIECE - 1 LINING FOR THE HEM/SIDE IN A PLAIN SEAM

Bag measurements:
- Width 25 cm/9.84".
- Height 18 cm/7.09".
- Depth 6 cm/2.36".

Pattern for the front and back quadrants:
- Draw a rectangle whose height is equal to the height of the purse +3 cm/1.18" (21 cm/8.27") and whose width is equal to the width of the purse +2 cm/0.79" for the sides (27 cm/10.63").
- Trace the outline as shown in the figure.

Pattern for the lining with a zip:
- Draw a rectangle 21 cm/8.27" high and whose width is equal to the width of the quadrant (25 cm/9.84").
- Shape as illustrated and draw the opening of the zip in the position illustrated.

Bottom/side pattern:
- Draw a rectangle whose height is equal to the depth of the purse (6 cm/2.36") and a length of 65 cm/25.59".
- Shape as in the figure.

Pattern for the zip pocket lining:
- 21 x 32 cm (8.27 x 12.60") rectangle.

Handle pattern and leather pieces to assemble the quadrants:
- As illustrated.

STRUCTURED PURSE
PLAIN STITCHED, CLOSED WITH A MAGNET

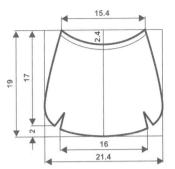

**2 LEATHER PIECES - 2 LININGS
FOR THE QUADRANTS**

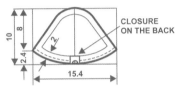

CLOSURE
ON THE BACK

**4 LEATHER SECTIONS
FOR THE PLAIN STITCHED HANDLE**

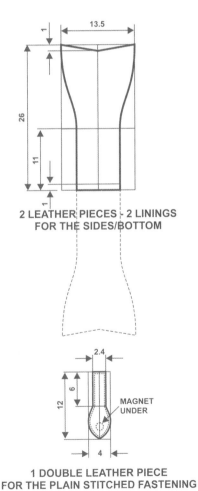

**2 LEATHER PIECES - 2 LININGS
FOR THE SIDES/BOTTOM**

MAGNET
UNDER

**1 DOUBLE LEATHER PIECE
FOR THE PLAIN STITCHED FASTENING**

Bag measurements:
- Width 21.5 cm/8.46";
- Height 19 cm/7.48" (plus the handle);
- Depth 7 cm/2.76".

Pattern for the front and back quadrants:
- Draw a rectangle whose height is equal to the height of the bag (19 cm/7.48") and whose width is equal to the width of the bag (21.5 cm/8.46").
- Trace the outline as shown in the figure.
- Create two small darts on the lower edge to round out the corners.

Pattern for the handles:
- Draw a rectangle whose height is equal to the desired height of the handles (10 cm/3.94") and whose width is equal to the upper part of the purse (15.4 cm/6.06").
- Shape as in the figure.

Pattern 1/2 bottom/side:
- Draw a rectangle whose height is equal to the depth of the purse +6.5 cm/2.56" (13.5 cm/5.31") and a length of 26 cm/10/24".
- Sew the two halves.
- Shape as in the figure.

Pattern for the zip pocket lining:
- As desired.

Chap pattern:
- As illustrated.

SOFT BAG

IN LEATHER OR FABRIC

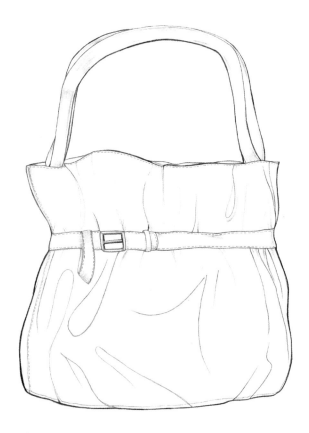

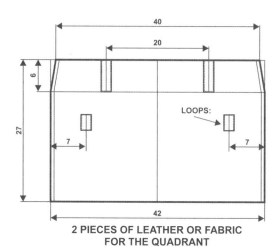

2 PIECES OF LEATHER OR FABRIC FOR THE QUADRANT

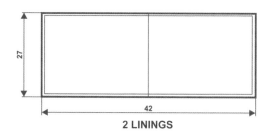

2 LININGS

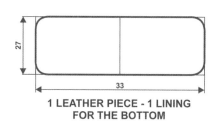

1 LEATHER PIECE - 1 LINING FOR THE BOTTOM

4 PIECES OF LEATHER FOR THE LOOPS

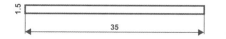

1 DOUBLE PIECE OF LEATHER FOR THE SNAP HOOK LOOP

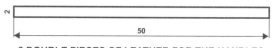

2 DOUBLE PIECES OF LEATHER FOR THE HANDLES

Bag measurements:
- Width 33 cm/12.99".
- Height 21 cm/8.27" (plus the handle).
- Depth 10.5 cm/4.13".

Pattern for the front and back quadrants:
- Draw a rectangle whose height is equal to the height of the purse +6 cm/2.36" (27 cm/10.63") and whose width is equal to the width of the purse +9 cm/3.54" for the sides (42 cm/16.54").
- Trace the outline as shown in the figure.

Lining pattern:
- Draw a rectangle 16 cm/6.30" high and whose width is equal to the width of the quadrant (42 cm/16.54").

Pattern 1/2 bottom:
- Draw a rectangle whose height is equal to the depth of the purse +0.5 cm/0.20" (11 cm/4.33") and a length of 33 cm/12.99".
- Shape as in the figure.

Pattern for the zip pocket lining:
- As desired.

Pattern for the loops, snap hook loop and handles:
- As illustrated.

Satchel bag

with piping

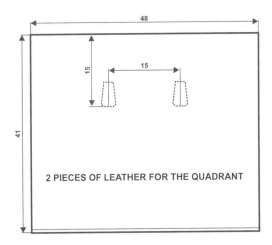

2 PIECES OF LEATHER FOR THE QUADRANT

48

41

15

15

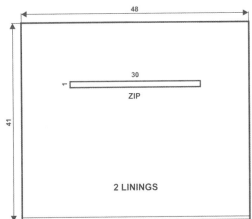

48

41

30

1

ZIP

2 LININGS

Bag measurements:
- Width 48 cm/18.90".
- Height 27 cm/10.63" (plus the handle).
- Depth 23 cm/9.06".

Pattern for the front and back quadrants:
- Draw a rectangle 41 cm/16.14" high and whose width is equal to the width of the bag (48 cm/18.90").

Lining pattern:
- Draw a rectangle 41 cm/16.14" high and whose width is equal to the width of the quadrant (48 cm/18.90").

Side pattern:
- Draw a rectangle whose height is equal to the height of the bag (27 cm/10.63") and whose length is equal to the depth of the purse (23 cm//9.06").
- Shape as in the figure.

Pattern for the zip pocket lining:
- Draw a rectangle that's 33 cm/12.99" high and 40 cm/15.75" wide.

Pattern for the chap, end tabs and handles:
- As illustrated.

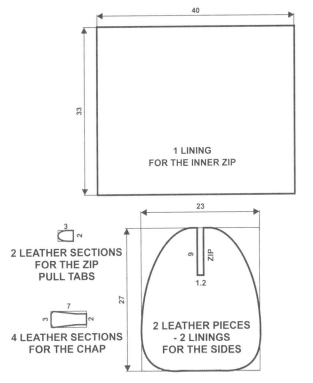

40

33

1 LINING
FOR THE INNER ZIP

3

2

2 LEATHER SECTIONS
FOR THE ZIP
PULL TABS

7

3

2

4 LEATHER SECTIONS
FOR THE CHAP

23

9

ZIP

1.2

27

2 LEATHER PIECES
- 2 LININGS
FOR THE SIDES

60

2 RUBBER PIECES Ø 10 X 55

6

2

2 PIECES OF LEATHER - 2 CORDS FOR THE TUBULAR HANDLES

SEMI-STRUCTURED SHOPPER
WITH PIPING ON THE BOTTOM

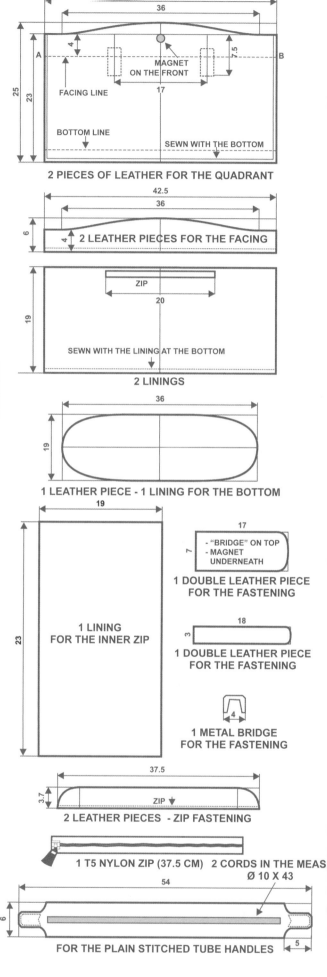

2 PIECES OF LEATHER FOR THE QUADRANT

42.5 / 36 / 25 / 23 / 4 / 7.5 / MAGNET ON THE FRONT / 17 / A / B / FACING LINE / BOTTOM LINE / SEWN WITH THE BOTTOM

2 LEATHER PIECES FOR THE FACING

42.5 / 36 / 6 / 4

2 LININGS

ZIP / 20 / 19 / SEWN WITH THE LINING AT THE BOTTOM

1 LEATHER PIECE - 1 LINING FOR THE BOTTOM

36 / 19

1 LINING FOR THE INNER ZIP

19 / 23

- "BRIDGE" ON TOP
- MAGNET UNDERNEATH

1 DOUBLE LEATHER PIECE FOR THE FASTENING

17 / 7

1 DOUBLE LEATHER PIECE FOR THE FASTENING

18 / 3

1 METAL BRIDGE FOR THE FASTENING

4

2 LEATHER PIECES - ZIP FASTENING

37.5 / 3.7 / ZIP ▼

1 T5 NYLON ZIP (37.5 CM)   2 CORDS IN THE MEAS Ø 10 X 43

FOR THE PLAIN STITCHED TUBE HANDLES

54 / 6 / 5

Bag measurements:
- Width 36 cm/14.17".
- Height 25 cm/9.84" (plus the handles).
- Depth 12 cm/4.72".

Pattern for the front and back quadrants:
- Draw a rectangle whose height is equal to the height of the bag (25 cm/9.84") and whose width is equal to the width of the bag +½ side +0.5 cm/0.20" (42.5 cm/16.73").

Pattern for the facing:
- On a piece of tracing paper, take up the upper part of the pattern of the quadrant, until line A-B for a total height of 6 cm/2.36".

Pattern for the lining with a zip:
- Take up the lower part of the quadrant pattern, until line A-B.
- Draw the position of the zip.

Bottom pattern:
- Draw a rectangle whose height is equal to the depth of the bag (12 cm/4.72") and whose width is equal to the width of the bag (36 cm/14.17").
- Shape as in the figure.

Pattern for the zip pocket lining:
- 23 x 42 cm (9.06 x 16.54") rectangle.

Zip fastening, handles, the upper magnet "bridge", double leather fastening pattern:
- As illustrated.

SHOPPING BAG

WITH PIPING

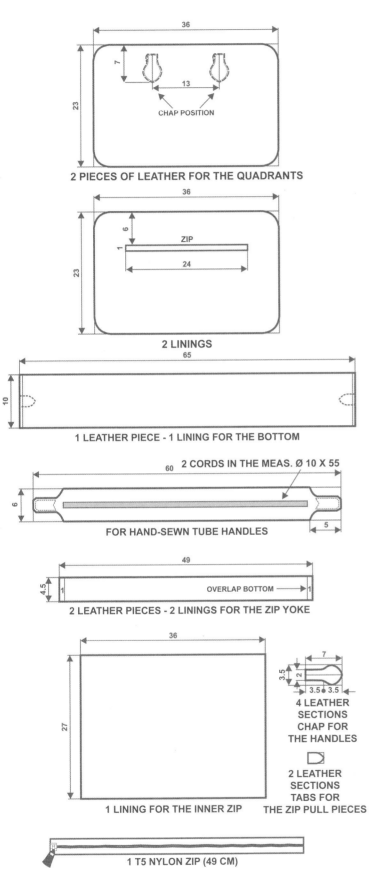

36

7

23

13

CHAP POSITION

2 PIECES OF LEATHER FOR THE QUADRANTS

36

6

23

1

ZIP

24

2 LININGS

65

10

1 LEATHER PIECE - 1 LINING FOR THE BOTTOM

60

2 CORDS IN THE MEAS. Ø 10 X 55

6

5

FOR HAND-SEWN TUBE HANDLES

49

4.5

1 OVERLAP BOTTOM **1**

2 LEATHER PIECES - 2 LININGS FOR THE ZIP YOKE

36

27

1 LINING FOR THE INNER ZIP

7

3.5

2

3.5   3.5

4 LEATHER SECTIONS CHAP FOR THE HANDLES

2 LEATHER SECTIONS TABS FOR THE ZIP PULL PIECES

1 T5 NYLON ZIP (49 CM)

Bag measurements:
- Width 35 cm/13.78".
- Height 22 cm/8.66".
- Depth 9.5 cm/3.74".

Pattern for the front and back quadrants:
- Draw a rectangle whose height is equal to the height of the purse +1 cm/0.39" (23 cm/9.06") and whose width is equal to the width of the purse +1 cm/0.39" (36 cm/14.17").
- Trace the outline as shown in the figure.

Pattern for the lining with a zip:
- The same measurements as the leather quadrant (35 x 22 cm/13.78 x 8.66").
- Draw the position of the zip.

Bottom/side pattern:
- Draw a rectangle whose height is equal to the depth of the purse +0.5 cm/0.20" (10 cm/3.94") and whose length is equal to the width of the purse +30 cm/11.81" (65 cm/25.59").

Zip yoke pattern:
- 49 x 4.5 cm (19.29 x 1.77") rectangle.

Patterns for the chap, zip pull tabs and tube handle:
- As illustrated.

STRUCTURED SHOPPING BAG

OPEN WITH PLAIN (BLIND) SEAMS

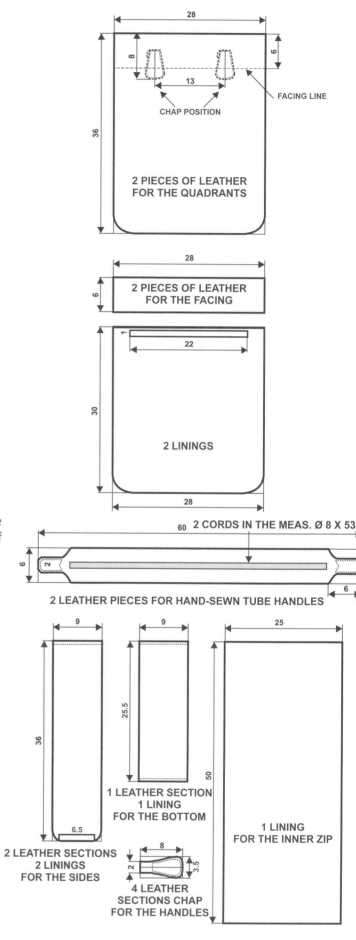

28

8

13

CHAP POSITION

6

FACING LINE

36

**2 PIECES OF LEATHER
FOR THE QUADRANTS**

28

6

**2 PIECES OF LEATHER
FOR THE FACING**

1

22

30

2 LININGS

28

60 **2 CORDS IN THE MEAS. Ø 8 X 53**

6

2

6

2 LEATHER PIECES FOR HAND-SEWN TUBE HANDLES

9

9

25

25.5

36

50

6.5

**1 LEATHER SECTION
1 LINING
FOR THE BOTTOM**

**1 LINING
FOR THE INNER ZIP**

**2 LEATHER SECTIONS
2 LININGS
FOR THE SIDES**

8

2

3.5

**4 LEATHER
SECTIONS CHAP
FOR THE HANDLES**

Bag measurements:
- Width 28 cm/11.02".
- Height 36 cm/14.17".
- Depth 9 cm/3.54".

Pattern for the front and back quadrants:
- Draw a rectangle whose height is equal to the height of the bag (36 cm/14.17") and whose width is equal to the width of the bag (28 cm/11.02").
- Trace the outline as shown in the figure.

Pattern for the facing:
Copy the first 6 cm of the upper part of the quadrant, as illustrated.

Lining pattern:
- Copy the lower 30 cm/11.81" of the quadrant, as illustrated.
- Draw the position of the zip.

Side pattern:
- 9 x 36 cm (3.54 x 14.17") rectangle. Outline at the bottom.

Bottom pattern:
- 9 x 25.5 cm (3.54 x 10.04") rectangle.

Pattern for the inner zip lining:
- 25 x 50 cm (9.84 x 19.69") rectangle.

Chap pattern:
- As illustrated.

ZIP-FASTENED BOWLING BAG

PIPING ALONG THE BOTTOM

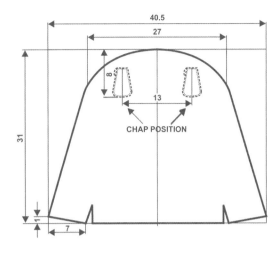

CHAP POSITION

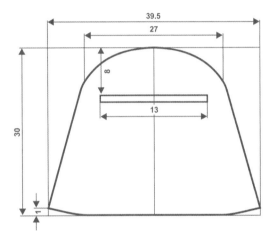

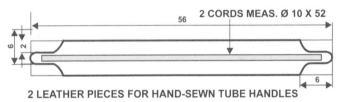

2 CORDS MEAS. Ø 10 X 52

2 LEATHER PIECES FOR HAND-SEWN TUBE HANDLES

Bag measurements:
- Width 30 cm/11.81".
- Height 31 cm/12.20".
- Depth 13 cm/5.12".

Pattern for the front and back quadrants:
- Draw a rectangle whose height is equal to the height of the bag (31 cm/12.20") and whose width is equal to the width of the bag +10.5 cm/4.13" (40.5 cm/15.94").
- Trace the outline as shown in the figure.

Pattern for the lining with a zip:
- Height 30 cm/11.81", width 39.4 cm/15.51".
- Shape and draw the position of the zip.

Bottom/side pattern:
- Draw a rectangle whose height is equal to the depth of the purse (13 cm/5.12") and whose length is equal to the with of the purse (30 cm/11.81").

Pattern for the inner zip lining:
- 23 x 46 cm (9.06 x 18.11") rectangle.

Patterns for the chap, zip pull tabs and tube handle:
- As illustrated.

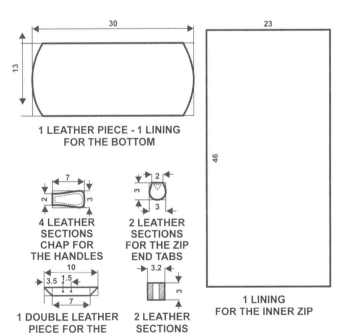

**1 LEATHER PIECE - 1 LINING
FOR THE BOTTOM**

**4 LEATHER
SECTIONS
CHAP FOR
THE HANDLES**

**2 LEATHER
SECTIONS
FOR THE ZIP
END TABS**

**1 DOUBLE LEATHER
PIECE FOR THE
ZIP PULL TAB**

**2 LEATHER
SECTIONS
ZIP TIPS**

**1 LINING
FOR THE INNER ZIP**

FLAT SHOPPER

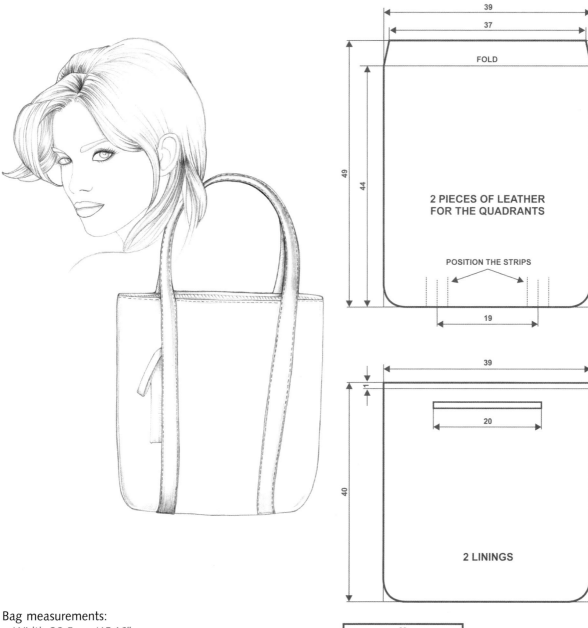

Bag measurements:
- Width 38.5 cm/15.16".
- Height 44 cm/17.32".

Pattern for the front and back quadrants:
- Draw a rectangle whose height is equal to the height of the bag + 10.5 cm/4.13" (49 cm/19.29") and whose width is equal to the width of the purse + 0.5 cm/0.20" (39 cm/15.35").
- Trace the outline as shown in the figure.

Pattern for the lining with a zip:
- 39 x 40 cm (15.35 x 15.75") rectangle.
- Shape and draw the position of the zip.

Pattern for the inner zip lining:
- 23 x 43 cm (9.06 x 16.93") rectangle.

Pattern for the tie, leather for the brand and for the handle:
- As illustrated.

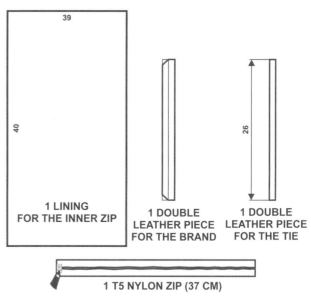

Bucket bag

PIPING ALONG THE BOTTOM

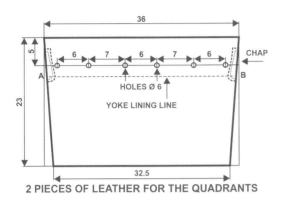

2 PIECES OF LEATHER FOR THE QUADRANTS

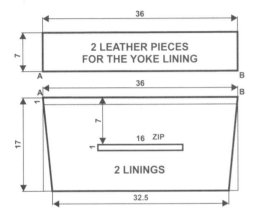

2 LEATHER PIECES FOR THE YOKE LINING

2 LININGS

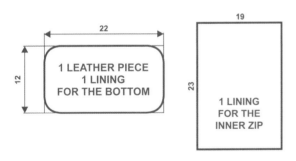

1 LEATHER PIECE
1 LINING
FOR THE BOTTOM

1 LINING
FOR THE
INNER ZIP

2 LEATHER
SECTIONS
CHAP FOR
THE HANDLES

1 LEATHER
SECTION FOR
THE TIE PULL TAB

1 LEATHER
SECTION FOR THE
TIE PULL TAB

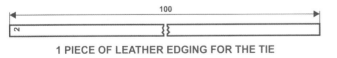

1 PIECE OF LEATHER EDGING FOR THE TIE

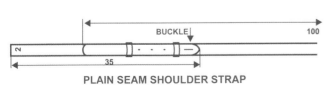

PLAIN SEAM SHOULDER STRAP

Bag measurements:
- Width 22 cm/8.66".
- Height 23 cm/9.06" (plus the handles).
- Depth 12 cm/4.72".

Pattern for the front and back quadrants:
- Draw a rectangle whose height is equal to the height of the bag (25 cm/9.84") and whose width is equal to the width of the bag + the side (36 cm/14.17"). Shape as in the figure.

Pattern for the facing:
- On a piece of tracing paper, take up the upper part of the pattern of the quadrant, until line A-B for a total height of 7 cm/2.76".

Pattern for the lining with a zip:
- Take up the lower part of the quadrant pattern, until line A-B. Draw the position of the zip.

Bottom pattern:
- Draw a rectangle whose height is equal to the depth of the bag (12 cm/4.72") and whose width is equal to the width of the bag (22 cm/8.66").
- Shape as in the figure.

Pattern for the zip pocket lining:
- 19 x 23 cm (14.96 x 9.06") rectangle.

Pattern for the chap, shoulder strap, tie and tie stopper:
- As illustrated.

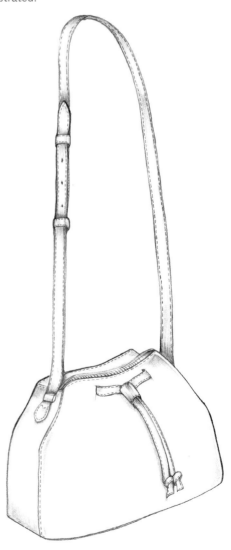

ELEGANT BAG

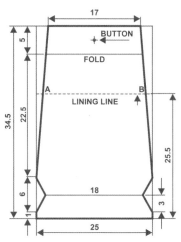

2 PIECES OF FABRIC FOR THE QUADRANTS

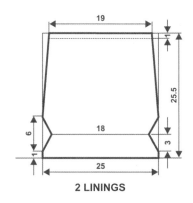

2 LININGS

2 LEATHER PIECES, FOLDED LENGTHWISE FOR THE HANDLES

Bag measurements:
- Width 18 cm/7.09".
- Height 22 cm/8.66".

Pattern for the front and back quadrants:
- Draw a rectangle whose height is equal to the height of the bag +12.5/4.92" (34.5 cm/13.58") and whose width is equal to the width of the purse +7 cm/2.76" (25 cm/9.84"). Shape as in the figure.

Pattern for the inner lining:
- Take up the lower part of the quadrant pattern, until line A-B.
- If desired, draw the position of the zip and the lining of the inner zip pocket.

Pattern for the handle:
- As illustrated.

Shoulder strap: 2 nylon threads, 60 cm/23.62" long, with rhinestone balls.

Variation with handles and a cross-body strap.

PLAIN SEAM BRIEFCASE
CLOSED WITH A TONGUE LOCK

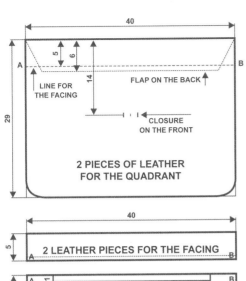

2 PIECES OF LEATHER FOR THE QUADRANT

40

5
6
14

A — LINE FOR THE FACING

FLAP ON THE BACK

B

29

CLOSURE ON THE FRONT

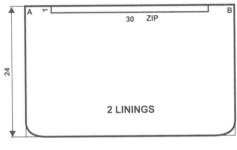

40

5

A — **2 LEATHER PIECES FOR THE FACING** — B

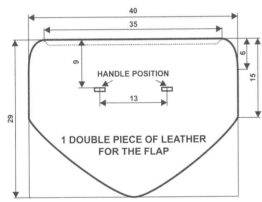

A — 1 — 30 ZIP — B

24

2 LININGS

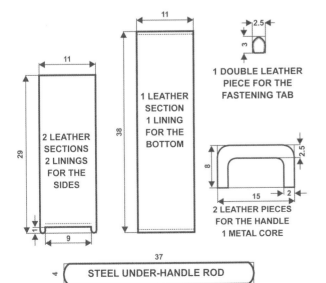

40

35

9

HANDLE POSITION

13

6

15

29

1 DOUBLE PIECE OF LEATHER FOR THE FLAP

11

11

29

2 LEATHER SECTIONS 2 LININGS FOR THE SIDES

9

11

38

1 LEATHER SECTION 1 LINING FOR THE BOTTOM

37

4 — **STEEL UNDER-HANDLE ROD**

2.5
3

1 DOUBLE LEATHER PIECE FOR THE FASTENING TAB

2.5
8

15
2

2 LEATHER PIECES FOR THE HANDLE 1 METAL CORE

Bag measurements:
- Width 40 cm/15.75".
- Height 30 cm/11.81".
- Depth 7 cm/2.76".

Pattern for the front and back quadrants:
- Draw a rectangle whose height is equal to the height of the bag -1 cm/0.40" (29 cm/11.42") and whose width is equal to the width of the bag for the sides (40 cm/15.75").
- Trace the outline as shown in the figure.

Pattern for the facing:
- Take up the first 5 cm/1.97" of the upper part of the quadrant from A-B, as illustrated.

Pattern for the lining with a zip:
- Copy the lower 24 cm/9.45" of the bottom part of the quadrant from A-B, as illustrated. Shape as in the figure.

Pattern for the flap:
- Draw a rectangle that's 29 cm/11.42" high and 40 cm/15.75" wide. Shape and draw the position of the handles as shown.

Bottom pattern:
- Draw a rectangle whose width is equal to the depth of the purse +2 cm/0.79" (11 cm/4.33") and whose height is equal to the height of the quadrant -1 cm/0.39" (38 cm/14.96").

Pattern for the sides:
- Draw a rectangle that's 29 cm/11.42" high and 11 cm/4.33" wide. Shape as in the figure.

Pattern for the zip pocket lining:
- 33 x 50 cm (12.99 x 19.69") rectangle.

Pattern for the handle:
- As illustrated.

BAG WITH BELLOWS POCKETS

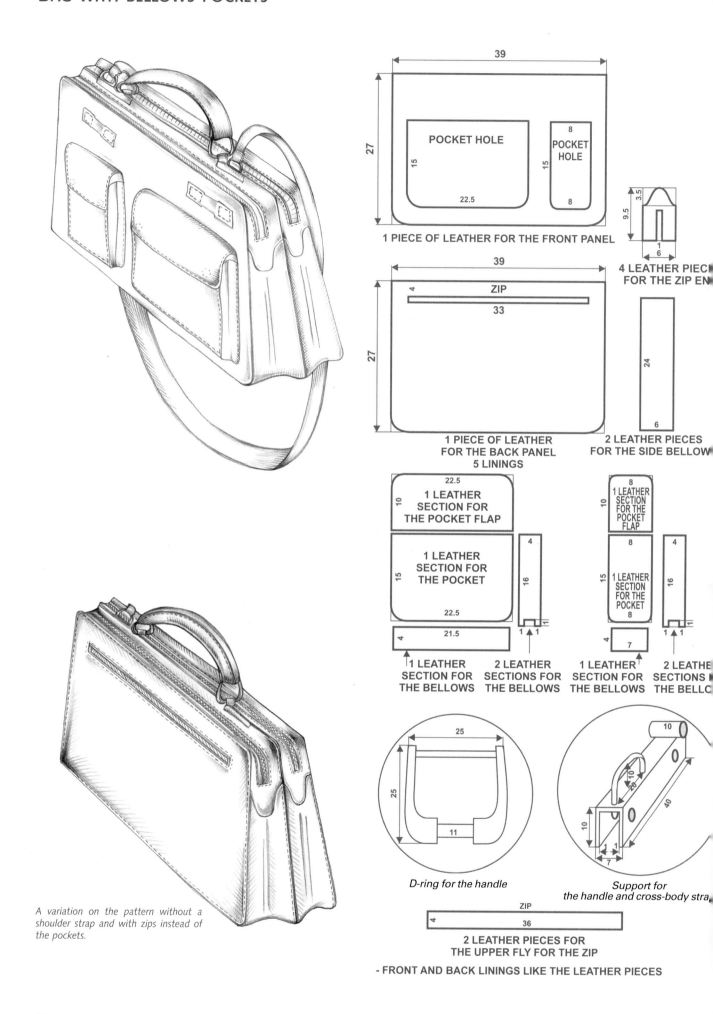

39

27

15

POCKET HOLE

22.5

8

POCKET HOLE

15

8

1 PIECE OF LEATHER FOR THE FRONT PANEL

3.5

9.5

1

6

4 LEATHER PIEC[FOR THE ZIP EN[

39

4

ZIP

33

27

24

6

1 PIECE OF LEATHER FOR THE BACK PANEL 5 LININGS

2 LEATHER PIECES FOR THE SIDE BELLOW[

22.5

10

1 LEATHER SECTION FOR THE POCKET FLAP

15

1 LEATHER SECTION FOR THE POCKET

22.5

4

21.5

1 LEATHER SECTION FOR THE BELLOWS

4

16

1

1 1

2 LEATHER SECTIONS FOR THE BELLOWS

8

10

1 LEATHER SECTION FOR THE POCKET FLAP

8

15

1 LEATHER SECTION FOR THE POCKET

8

4

7

1 LEATHER SECTION FOR THE BELLOWS

4

16

1 1

2 LEATHE[SECTIONS [THE BELLO[

25

25

11

D-ring for the handle

10

10

10

40

10

1 1

7

Support for the handle and cross-body stra[

ZIP

4

36

2 LEATHER PIECES FOR THE UPPER FLY FOR THE ZIP

- FRONT AND BACK LININGS LIKE THE LEATHER PIECES

A variation on the pattern without a shoulder strap and with zips instead of the pockets.

98

Hard shell suitcase

IN TARTAN FABRIC

This type of luggage is made up of various pieces: a hard shell, tartan fabric and applied leather.
- Parts in tartan: the lid, the base, the strip on the lid, the strip on the base.
- Parts in leather: the eight corners, the four applications in the grooves at the side of the strap, the strap, the handle.
- Metal accessories: 2 rings for the handle; 1 buckle for the strap; 8 feet; 2 hinges.
Interior: lining; fabric pocket on the lid; crossed leather pieces to hold clothing in place.

Measurements

This type of suitcase can be made in different sizes:
50, 55, 60, 65, 70, 75, 80 and 85 cm (19.69, 21.65, 23.62, 25.59, 27.56, 29.53, 31.50, 33.46").
Measurements of the suitcase shown here
- Lid: length 60 cm/23.62"; width 40 cm/15.75"; side band height 3 cm/1.18".
- Lower half: length 58 cm/22.83"; width 38 cm/14.96"; height 15 cm/5.91".

Construction

1) Glue the tartan fabric on the cardboard-leather of the lid quadrant, the bottom quadrant and the two bands, being careful not to create creases or bumps.
2) Fold the excess fabric over on the side bands and the bottom.
3) Apply the leather faux corners to the two quadrants, along with the grooving.
4) Prepare, by sewing and reinforcing, the strap and the handle supports, which should be applied to the side of the box, and the inner straps and address tag.
5) Prepare the linings, mark the cover with the reference points where the gathered pocket should go.

Creating the shell on the form

The form can be one or two pieces, depending on if the lid and box line up exactly or dovetail, as in the model illustrated here. It should be of well-cured wood so as the measurements aren't altered due to distortion. In addition, the dimensions of the form should be calculated considering the thickness of the material that the suitcase is made of, especially when dealing with dovetailed pieces. In this latter case, the difference in the measurements between the lid and lower half should be considered to ensure the luggage closes properly.
Implementation
1) On the two forms, apply two bands of card stock in measurements corresponding to those of the two bands of the lid and lower half, affixing them with tacks.
2) Apply the fabric and card stock quadrant to the lid and the lower half of the form, turning the edges over the card stock, ensuring that no bumps form at the corners.
3) Apply the leather faux corners after having created small slits on the edges to make them adhere better.
4) Apply the bands of fabric on the paper stock bands, already affixed to the form, with strong glue.
5) On the back of the lid form, apply the caseback, which should already have the leather strap sewn to it. Then, also on the back of the lower half, glue the part of the base onto which the hinge (the strip of leather that will hold the box and lid together after being taken off the form) will be sewn.
6) When the glued parts are dry, remove the lid and the box from the form.
7) Hand or machine sew the lid and the lower half.
8) Apply the hardware, handle, and feet.
9) Line the inside and apply the braces, keeper straps and outer strap.

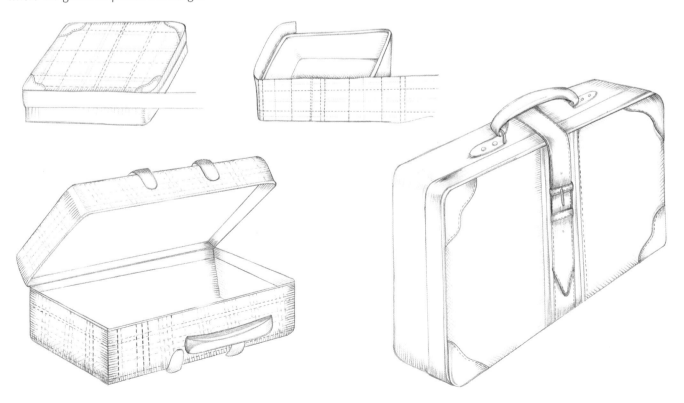

SMALL SUITCASE WITH A WOODEN FRAME

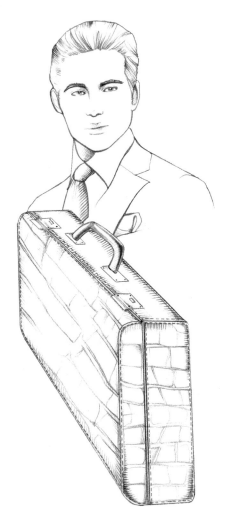

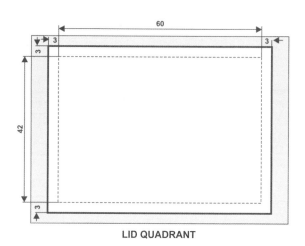

LID QUADRANT

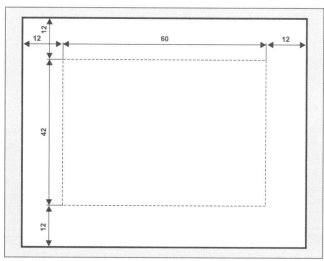

BOX QUADRANT

This small suitcase is constructed on a wood frame (or another type of hard material) with rounded or right angle corners, in English-style aniline leather or any other type of leather. The detailing should be fine, with turned-over edges; the stitching all faux and hand-sewn; the handle is shaped with an inner frame in plastic, which will then be covered in leather. The accessories, in cast brass, are: 2 hinges; 2 rings for the handles; 8 metal feet.

The inside should be in prized fabric such as hemp, with a gathered pocket on a lid that, when open, is held open by the copper arms. It can be embellished by straps to hold clothing in place or with other supports, depending on the intended use of the suitcase.

Measurements of the wood frame of the suitcase:
- Width 60 cm/23.62".
- Height 42 cm/16.54".
- Total depth 15 cm/5.91".
- Lid depth 3 cm/1.18.
- Box depth 12 cm/4.72".

Box and lid quadrant patterns:

The lower quadrant includes the bottom, the height of the front and the back, with the addition of the necessary allowances for the edges that get turned over, which must be wider for the two ends.

The lid quadrant includes the front, the top, the rear part of the lid, which should also have turned-over edges.

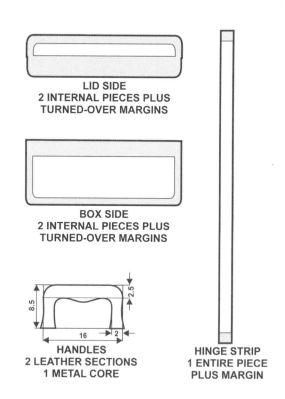

LID SIDE
2 INTERNAL PIECES PLUS
TURNED-OVER MARGINS

BOX SIDE
2 INTERNAL PIECES PLUS
TURNED-OVER MARGINS

HANDLES
2 LEATHER SECTIONS
1 METAL CORE

HINGE STRIP
1 ENTIRE PIECE
PLUS MARGIN

Sides

There are four sides to this suitcase: two for the lower half and two for the lid.

- The two sides of the lower half have a larger flap to be turned over on the ends and regular flaps along the outline.
- The two sides of the lid have regular flaps along the outlines, but they have a double side because half is needed for the flap along the corresponding inner part.
- The strip of leather for the zip on the back is equal in length to the quadrants.

Handle

- Draw as in the figure.

Steps for the suitcase with a wood frame

1) Carefully sand and smooth the wood frame, first using a larger grain sandpaper and then a finer grain one.

Sides

2) Prepare the two leather sides of both the lid and the bottom half, applying lightweight n. 90 cardboard in the same shape as the sides of the wood frame.

3) Create the faux hand-stitching along the entire outer perimeter of the sides.

4) Apply the sides to the frame with glue, ensuring that they adhere securely to the entire surface.

5) Turn over the edges and glue them to the frame, creating small cuts along the curves if necessary.

Quadrants

1) Apply four strips of bonded (or regenerated) leather 3 cm/1.18" in width to the edges, working in the respective lengths, applying just a little bit of glue so they remain puffy.

2) Between the bonded leather and the leather, insert a layer of 0.5 cm/0.20" thick foam rubber that's the same size as the quadrants.

3) Turn over the edges of the quadrants, creating faux stitching on them, just like on the sides.

4) Join the lid with the bottom frame on the respective ends on the back, with a 3 cm/1.18" strip of leather, previously set up with the turned-over lateral ends.

When carrying out this operation, it's important to leave a 6-7 mm/0.24-0.28" space between the two quadrants to ensure ease of movement, since this strip acts as a hinge between the lower half and the lid.

5) Cover the wood frame as follows:

a) Starting from the edge of the cover, glue the bonded leather, apply the foam rubber, and then lay down the leather quadrant of the cover, affixing it to the still uncovered surface. When doing so, ensure that the edges being laid down are perfectly adherent to those of the frame and avoid compressing the part with the foam rubber too much to ensure the end result looks harmonious.

b) Proceed in the same way for the lower half.

c) Turn over the inner edge of the lid: this will act as a guide for the lower half.

Applying accessories

After having carefully checked that the above-described operations have fully and effectively covered the two frames, move on to applying the accessories.

- First apply the locks, for which you will need to ensure the pieces line up correctly, matching up the positions of the female and male pieces so that the suitcase closes perfectly.
- Apply the rings that support the handle, which can be hooked to the handle in advance and then applied to the bottom frame with a hog ring.
- Apply the feet to the bottom.

Interior

- Glue the already-prepared linings to the inside of the lid and lower half.
- Use two screws to affix the two metal hinged arms between the lower half and the lid, used to hold the lid open.
- If desired, apply the cross-shaped straps to hold clothing in place.

LEATHER 24-HOUR BAG
INSIDE-OUT CONSTRUCTION

This item, with inside-out construction in black hand-grained calf leather and with suede lining (or in any other material), is a "24-hour bag" due to its smaller size, designed to take up the least amount of space during short trips.

It is semi-rigid with medium finishings. The handles are applied to the quadrants, affixed with handle anchors that are also in leather. On the front quadrant, the flap that closes the open pocket that covers about three quarters of the same quadrant is closed with a suitcase-style lock.

Measurements and components of the leather 24-hour bag:
- Width 45 cm/17.72";
- Height 35 cm/13.78" (plus the handles);
- Depth 12 cm/4.72".
- The front quadrant is cut in two pieces to create the external pocket.
- There are two side bands: one which is narrower and one which is wider, almost as long as the perimeter of the quadrants.
- The bottom, which is the leather rectangle that is applied to unite the two halves, like a hinge, is less than 5 cm/1.97" in length per side with respect to the length of the suitcase (35 cm/13.78"). This makes it possible for the two zips applied along the side bands to run smoothly around the rounded edges.
- The handles are about 40 cm/15.75" long and are made with tubular construction, that is, with an inner core in rope or a plastic material or in a cylindrical form.
- The pocket-affixing flap, in addition to closing the pocket, acts as a safety element, reinforcing the bag when it's full. It is made of double leather and has a plate clasp at the end.
- There are four leather handle supports (called "chaps") and they are applied to the quadrants in the most suitable position, with the relative metal rings.
- The lining is in suede (or velvet) in a light colour; a gathered pocket is applied inside the lid quadrant; and straps to hold clothing in place are also affixed to the inside.
- The metal accessories generally used on suitcases are: 4 metal rings as handle supports; 4 metal feet; 2 strap buckles, 2 iron frames; 1 flap clasp/lock; 1 external zip.
- Other materials used to create the 24 hour bag are: hemp fabric as a reinforcement; compressed paperboard to make the sides rigid; synthetic fabric or wool paper for the lining; yarn; glue.

Processes
The edges of this bag are cut edges, that is, not turned over, and dyed.

Quadrants
1) Sew the chaps or handle supports, which should be prepared in advance with their rings, on the entire back and on the largest part of the front quadrant.
2) Apply the lower part of the lock on the largest part of the front quadrant.
3) Line the inside of the larger front quadrant.
4) Apply a band of leather about 3 cm/1.18" wide on the raw edge (inked by hand) on the larger front quadrant.
5) Apply the lining to the smaller part of the front quadrant with a plain seam.

6) Join the two pieces of the front quadrant, creating the external pocket, while maintaining the measurements of the inner quadrant.
7) Apply the previously prepared frames (with the trim, i.e. the frames should be covered in leather) to the two quadrants and sew them along the perimeters.

Sides and bottom reinforcement
The side bands are hand dyed on the edges and, along them, the two halves of the zip (open-able at the centre) are glued, lining them with the edges turned over, sewing them along the zip.

The bottom reinforcement strengthens the lower half and the lid. Prepare it by gluing two pieces of compressed paperboard so as to encourage the hinge movement. Turn over the lateral parts and dye the upper and lower parts.

Joining the halves
1) At the ends of the two side strips, affix the bottom reinforcement by sewing it.
2) The thus-prepared side bands should be affixed around the quadrants, being sure to centre them perfectly so that the suitcase is perfectly balanced.
3) At the centre of the band on the lower half, apply the pocket-affixing double leather flap (previously prepared and sewn, with the top part of the clasp already applied).
4) Turn all the sewn parts inside out, being sure not to ruin the leather with scratches or creases.

Finishes
1) With the compressed paperboard, reinforce the strips, gluing them with heavy-duty glue.
2) Apply the feet to the bottom.
3) Glue the edges of the lining strips to the lower half and lid.
4) Apply the two quadrants of the lining, including that for the lid with a gathered pocket, gluing them to the edges without staining them.
5) Apply the straps to hold clothing in place.
6) Apply the tubular handles (previously sewn).
7) Clean all the surfaces.

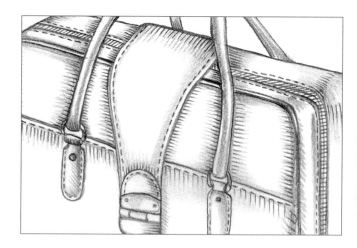

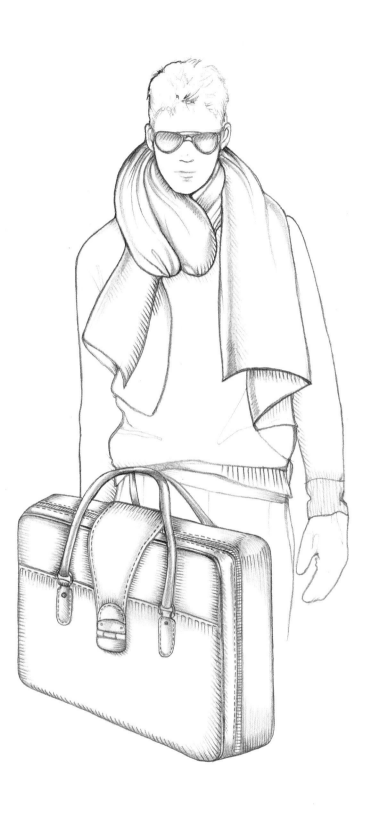

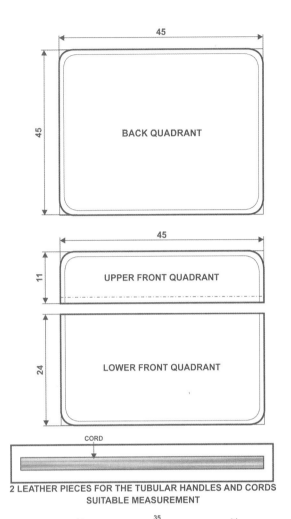

BACK QUADRANT

45
45

UPPER FRONT QUADRANT

45
11

LOWER FRONT QUADRANT

24

CORD

2 LEATHER PIECES FOR THE TUBULAR HANDLES AND CORDS
SUITABLE MEASUREMENT

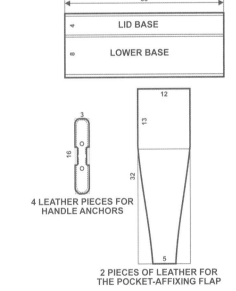

35

LID BASE
4

LOWER BASE
8

12
13
3
16
32
5

**4 LEATHER PIECES FOR
HANDLE ANCHORS**

**2 PIECES OF LEATHER FOR
THE POCKET-AFFIXING FLAP**

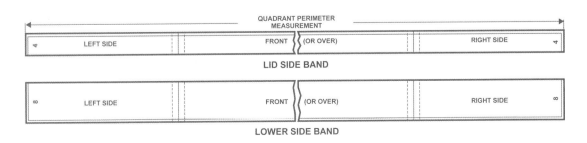

QUADRANT PERIMETER
MEASUREMENT

| 4 | LEFT SIDE | | FRONT | (OR OVER) | | RIGHT SIDE | 4 |

LID SIDE BAND

| 8 | LEFT SIDE | | FRONT | (OR OVER) | | RIGHT SIDE | 8 |

LOWER SIDE BAND

Bag with a motif and gathering

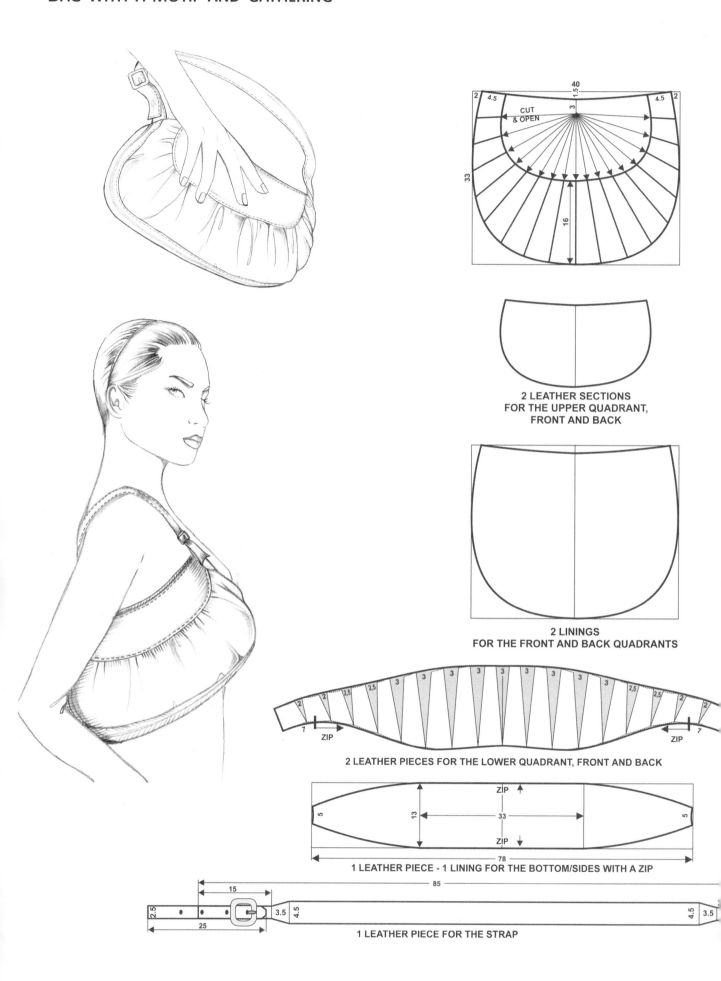

2 LEATHER SECTIONS FOR THE UPPER QUADRANT, FRONT AND BACK

2 LININGS FOR THE FRONT AND BACK QUADRANTS

2 LEATHER PIECES FOR THE LOWER QUADRANT, FRONT AND BACK

1 LEATHER PIECE - 1 LINING FOR THE BOTTOM/SIDES WITH A ZIP

1 LEATHER PIECE FOR THE STRAP

SHOULDER POUCH BAG

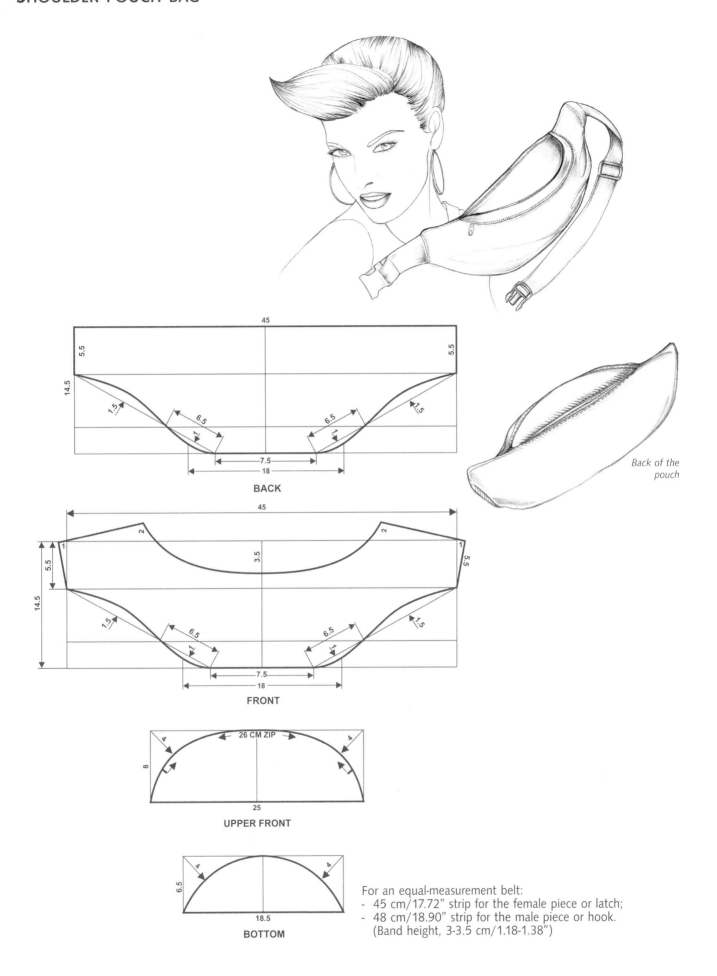

45

5.5

14.5

1.5

6.5

6.5

1.5

1

1

7.5

18

BACK

Back of the pouch

45

2

2

1

1

5.5

5.5

3.5

14.5

1.5

6.5

6.5

1.5

1

1

7.5

18

FRONT

4

26 CM ZIP

4

8

25

UPPER FRONT

4

4

6.5

18.5

BOTTOM

For an equal-measurement belt:
- 45 cm/17.72" strip for the female piece or latch;
- 48 cm/18.90" strip for the male piece or hook.
(Band height, 3-3.5 cm/1.18-1.38")

POUCH BAG BASE

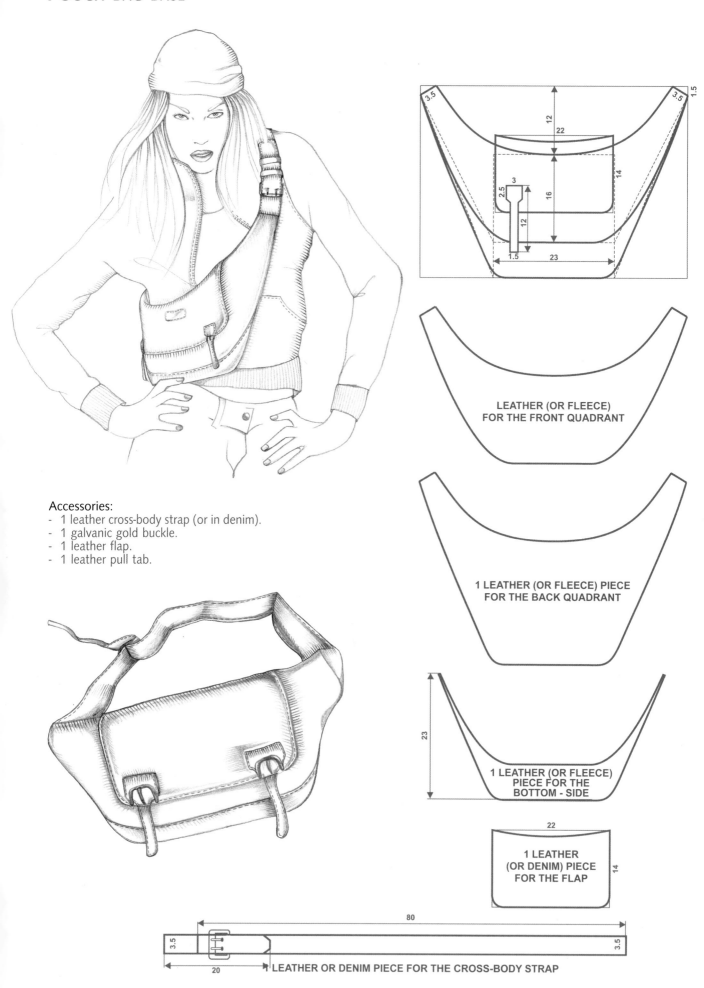

Accessories:
- 1 leather cross-body strap (or in denim).
- 1 galvanic gold buckle.
- 1 leather flap.
- 1 leather pull tab.

3.5   12   22   3.5   1.5   14   3   2.5   16   12   1.5   23

LEATHER (OR FLEECE) FOR THE FRONT QUADRANT

1 LEATHER (OR FLEECE) PIECE FOR THE BACK QUADRANT

23

1 LEATHER (OR FLEECE) PIECE FOR THE BOTTOM - SIDE

22   14

1 LEATHER (OR DENIM) PIECE FOR THE FLAP

80   3.5   3.5   20

LEATHER OR DENIM PIECE FOR THE CROSS-BODY STRAP

RUCKSACK WITH A POCKET

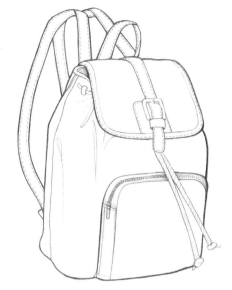

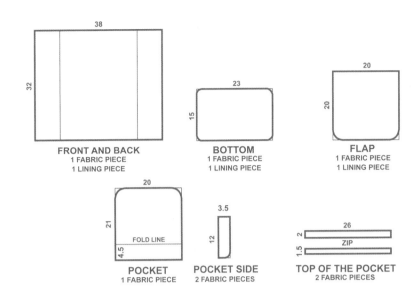

FRONT AND BACK
1 FABRIC PIECE
1 LINING PIECE

38
32

BOTTOM
1 FABRIC PIECE
1 LINING PIECE

23
15

FLAP
1 FABRIC PIECE
1 LINING PIECE

20
20

POCKET
1 FABRIC PIECE

20
21
FOLD LINE
4.5

POCKET SIDE
2 FABRIC PIECES

3.5
12

TOP OF THE POCKET
2 FABRIC PIECES

26
ZIP
2
1.5

Accessories:
- 2 shoulder straps, 3 x 80 cm/1.18 x 31.50".
- 1 handle strap, 40 cm/15.75".
- 1 strap for the flap, 30 cm/11.81".
- 8 eyelets.
- 1 closure cord, 80 cm/31.50".
- 1 zip, 30 cm/11.81".
- Border, 120 cm/47.24".

RUCKSACK WITH TWO POCKETS

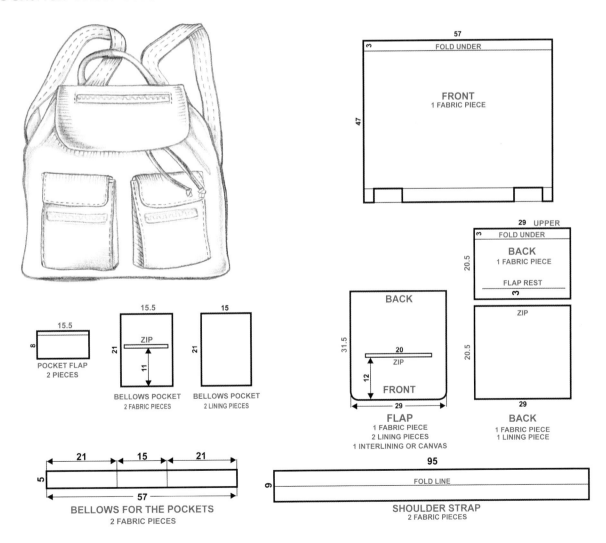

FRONT
1 FABRIC PIECE

57
FOLD UNDER
3
47

29 UPPER
BACK
1 FABRIC PIECE
FOLD UNDER
3
20.5
FLAP REST
3

ZIP
20.5
BACK
1 FABRIC PIECE
1 LINING PIECE
29

POCKET FLAP
2 PIECES

15.5
8

BELLOWS POCKET
2 FABRIC PIECES

15.5
ZIP
21
11

BELLOWS POCKET
2 LINING PIECES

15
21

BACK
ZIP
20
ZIP
31.5
12
FRONT
29

FLAP
1 FABRIC PIECE
2 LINING PIECES
1 INTERLINING OR CANVAS

BELLOWS FOR THE POCKETS
2 FABRIC PIECES

21 15 21
57
5

SHOULDER STRAP
2 FABRIC PIECES

95
FOLD LINE
9

MOUNTAIN RUCKSACK

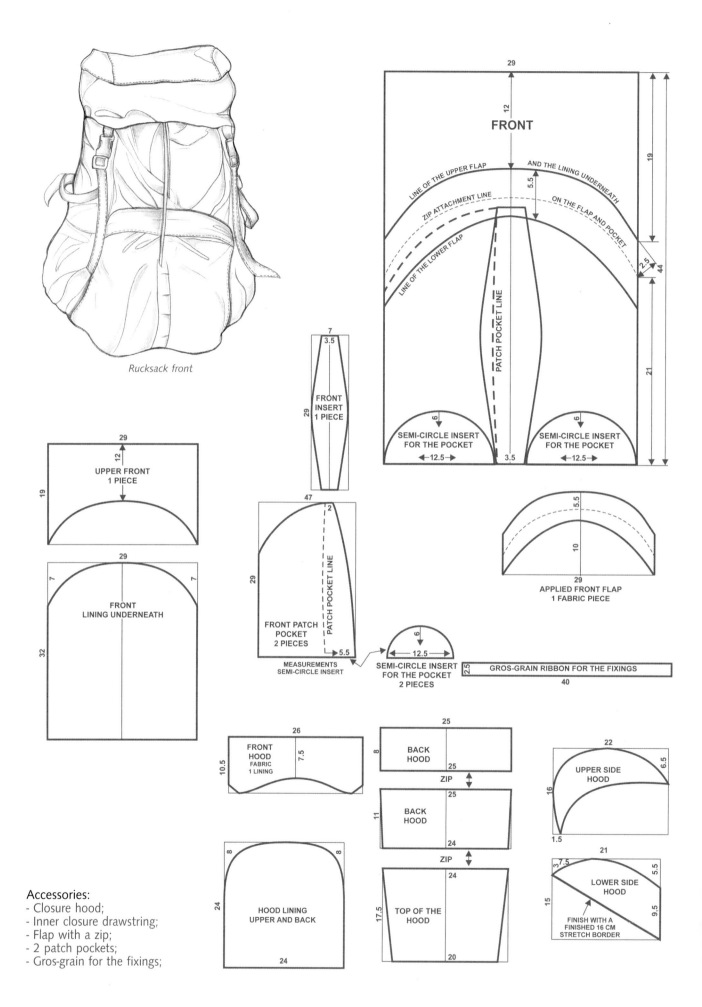

Rucksack front

FRONT

29

12

LINE OF THE UPPER FLAP

AND THE LINING UNDERNEATH

ZIP ATTACHMENT LINE

ON THE FLAP AND POCKET

LINE OF THE LOWER FLAP

5.5

2.5

19

44

21

PATCH POCKET LINE

3.5

SEMI-CIRCLE INSERT
FOR THE POCKET

6

←12.5→

SEMI-CIRCLE INSERT
FOR THE POCKET

6

←12.5→

7
3.5

FRONT
INSERT
1 PIECE

29

UPPER FRONT
1 PIECE

29

12

19

FRONT
LINING UNDERNEATH

29

7   7

32

47
2

FRONT PATCH
POCKET
2 PIECES

29

PATCH POCKET LINE

5.5

MEASUREMENTS
SEMI-CIRCLE INSERT

SEMI-CIRCLE INSERT
FOR THE POCKET
2 PIECES

6

←12.5→

5.5

10

29
APPLIED FRONT FLAP
1 FABRIC PIECE

2.5 GROS-GRAIN RIBBON FOR THE FIXINGS

40

26

FRONT
HOOD
FABRIC
1 LINING

10.5

7.5

25

BACK
HOOD

8

25

ZIP

25

BACK
HOOD

11

24

ZIP

24

TOP OF THE
HOOD

17.5

20

22

UPPER SIDE
HOOD

16

6.5

1.5

21

3 7.5

LOWER SIDE
HOOD

15

5.5

9.5

FINISH WITH A
FINISHED 16 CM
STRETCH BORDER

8   8

HOOD LINING
UPPER AND BACK

24

24

Accessories:
- Closure hood;
- Inner closure drawstring;
- Flap with a zip;
- 2 patch pockets;
- Gros-grain for the fixings;

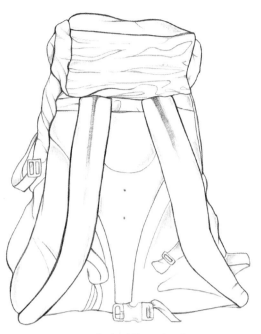

Back of the rucksack

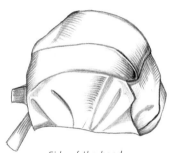

Side of the hood

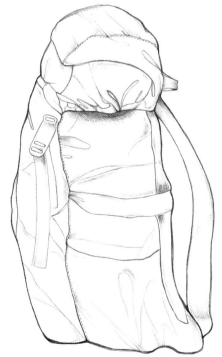

Side of the rucksack

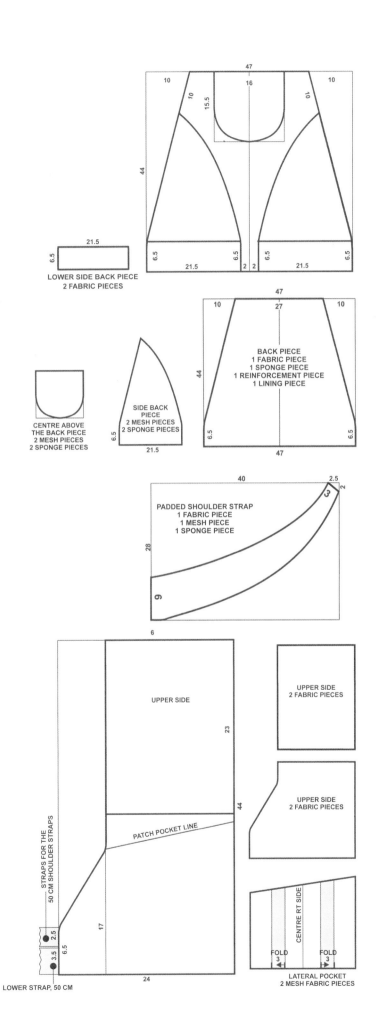

LOWER SIDE BACK PIECE
2 FABRIC PIECES

CENTRE ABOVE
THE BACK PIECE
2 MESH PIECES
2 SPONGE PIECES

SIDE BACK
PIECE
2 MESH PIECES
2 SPONGE PIECES

BACK PIECE
1 FABRIC PIECE
1 SPONGE PIECE
1 REINFORCEMENT PIECE
1 LINING PIECE

PADDED SHOULDER STRAP
1 FABRIC PIECE
1 MESH PIECE
1 SPONGE PIECE

UPPER SIDE

UPPER SIDE
2 FABRIC PIECES

UPPER SIDE
2 FABRIC PIECES

PATCH POCKET LINE

STRAPS FOR THE
50 CM SHOULDER STRAPS

LOWER STRAP, 50 CM

CENTRE RT SIDE

FOLD
3

FOLD
3

LATERAL POCKET
2 MESH FABRIC PIECES

STITCHED SPORTY BAG

MEASUREMENTS: 53 x 22 x 35 CM (20.87 x 8.66 x 13.78")

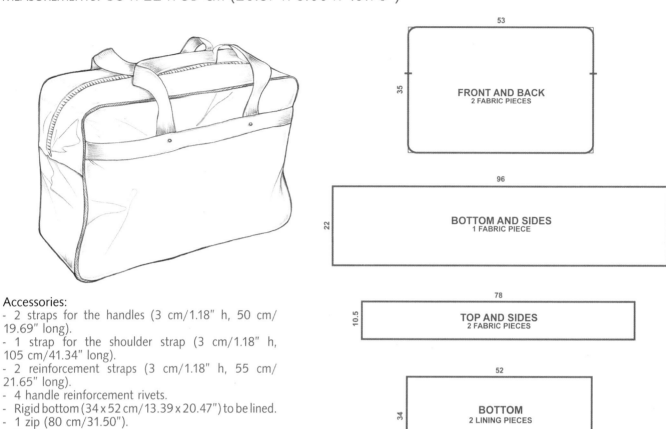

FRONT AND BACK
2 FABRIC PIECES
53
35

BOTTOM AND SIDES
1 FABRIC PIECE
96
22

TOP AND SIDES
2 FABRIC PIECES
78
10.5

BOTTOM
2 LINING PIECES
52
34

Accessories:
- 2 straps for the handles (3 cm/1.18" h, 50 cm/19.69" long).
- 1 strap for the shoulder strap (3 cm/1.18" h, 105 cm/41.34" long).
- 2 reinforcement straps (3 cm/1.18" h, 55 cm/21.65" long).
- 4 handle reinforcement rivets.
- Rigid bottom (34 x 52 cm/13.39 x 20.47") to be lined.
- 1 zip (80 cm/31.50").
- 2 rings.
- 2 snap hooks.

GYM BAG

MEASUREMENTS: 60 x 28.5 x 30 CM (20.87 x 8.66 x 13.78")

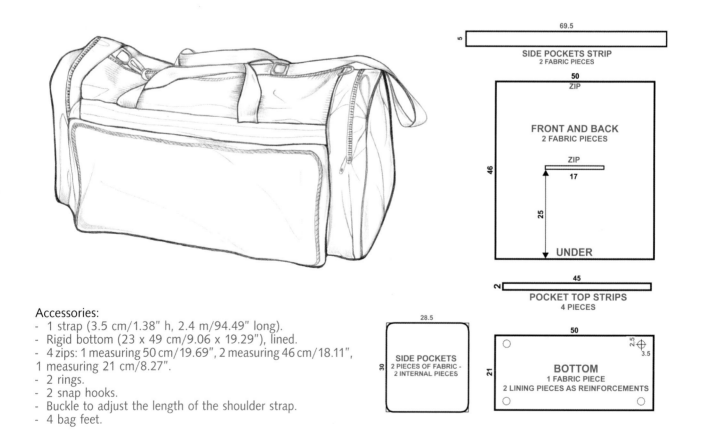

SIDE POCKETS STRIP
2 FABRIC PIECES
69.5
5

FRONT AND BACK
2 FABRIC PIECES
50
ZIP
ZIP
17
25
46
UNDER

POCKET TOP STRIPS
4 PIECES
45
2

SIDE POCKETS
2 PIECES OF FABRIC -
2 INTERNAL PIECES
28.5
30

BOTTOM
1 FABRIC PIECE
2 LINING PIECES AS REINFORCEMENTS
50
21
2.5
3.5

Accessories:
- 1 strap (3.5 cm/1.38" h, 2.4 m/94.49" long).
- Rigid bottom (23 x 49 cm/9.06 x 19.29"), lined.
- 4 zips: 1 measuring 50 cm/19.69", 2 measuring 46 cm/18.11", 1 measuring 21 cm/8.27".
- 2 rings.
- 2 snap hooks.
- Buckle to adjust the length of the shoulder strap.
- 4 bag feet.

Volleyball bag

HEIGHT: 63 CM (24.80") - BASE 42 x 25 CM (16.5 x 9.84")

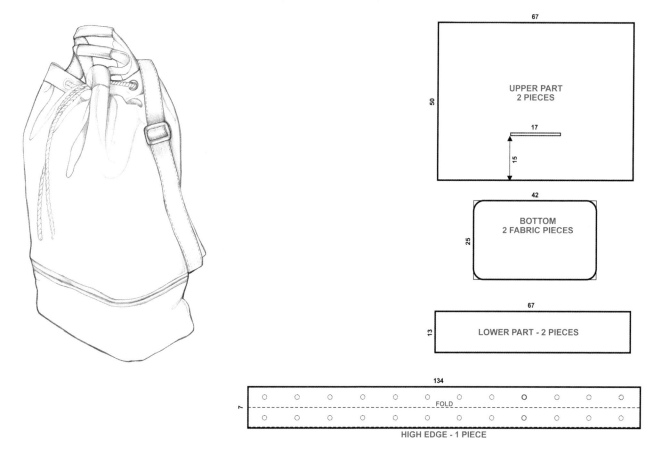

	67
UPPER PART **2 PIECES**	

50

17

15

42
BOTTOM **2 FABRIC PIECES**

25

67
LOWER PART - 2 PIECES

13

134

FOLD

7

HIGH EDGE - 1 PIECE

Round sack

HEIGHT: 58 CM (22.83") - BASE Ø 30 CM (11.81") DIAMETER

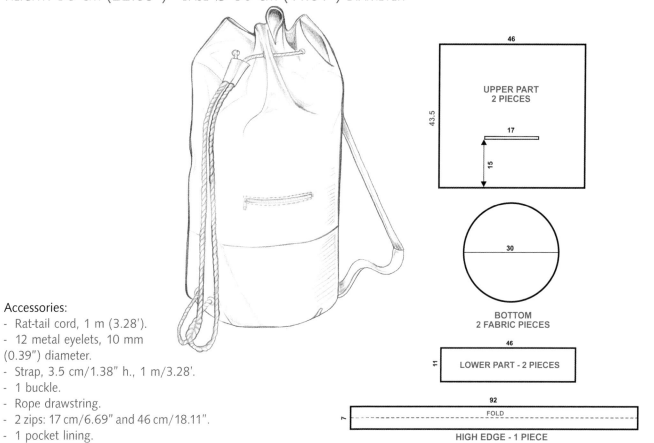

46
UPPER PART **2 PIECES**

43.5

17

15

30

BOTTOM
2 FABRIC PIECES

46
LOWER PART - 2 PIECES

11

92

FOLD

7

HIGH EDGE - 1 PIECE

Accessories:
- Rat-tail cord, 1 m (3.28').
- 12 metal eyelets, 10 mm (0.39") diameter.
- Strap, 3.5 cm/1.38" h., 1 m/3.28'.
- 1 buckle.
- Rope drawstring.
- 2 zips: 17 cm/6.69" and 46 cm/18.11".
- 1 pocket lining.

BELTS

Belts are strips of leather or fabric, synthetic material or metal, worn around the waist to hold trousers, skirts or dresses in place, or used as fashion accessories.

The history of the belt, even a condensed one, could fill the pages of a whole book on its own.

It's an accessory that was used even by our pre-historic ancestors.

- In ancient Egypt, the belt was a component of rich, important clothing. Dancers, almost always otherwise nude, wore belts.

- In ancient Rome, there were various type of belts: from those worn by soldiers to those of matrons and young nobles.

- In Italy in the middle ages, warriors hung their swords from their belts, becoming a knightly, high-class symbol, and was prohibited from women within criminal groups. Often satchels, keys, sewing tools, necklaces, small mirrors and bells were attached to belts.

- In 1200 AD, belts, often called 'zona' (zone) by Latin-speakers in ancient trousseau inventories, were almost always made of silver (at times even gold-plated silver) and were often a gift given from husband to wife as a wedding present.

The 'corrigia', or girdle, which also could be made of silver, was a must-have in men's wardrobes, but it never reached the richness of women's gem-encrusted belts.

- In the 1300s, men used leather straps to draw in their surplice or 'gonnella' (a sort of tunic), and sometimes even the mantle and other outerwear such as fur cloaks, at the waist.

Leather belts could be decorated with silver or gold-plated bands, so much so that they were considered precious objects to be held in strongboxes.

For women, 'scheggiale', gemmed garlands, were feminine belts considered prized pieces of jewellery. Like the versions worn by men, these belts were accompanied by a buckle with a pin or ring clasp and a tip.

Inventories of trousseaus or other documents are full of incredibly detailed descriptions of these belts.

- In the 1400s, women's belts became an almost-necessary item of clothing.

At the start of the century, worn under the bust and then a bit lower, they were similar to ropes or cords (leather girdles decorated with silver pin buckles).

Men's belts, the 'correggia', was still quite important, even if not as large as they were in the 1300s. Those made of Genoan silk was particularly famous and so sought-after that, despite a 1455 ban in England on imported silk, an exception was made for belts from Genoa.

- In the early 1500s, as in the 1400s, belts were quite flashy, worn buckled and quite high on the torso.

Later on, they were worn precisely at the waist and were richer - one such example is the 'paternostro', similar to a rosary. Starting from the mid-1500s, women's belts became quite ornate and intricate. Worn much lower, following the line of a sort of doublet, extended at the ends and handing at the centre, joining to almost become a single unit, down to the hem of the clothing, ending in a large knob, featuring a piece of jewellery or golden ball.

Detail of a "Flagellation" in gold-plated silver, circa 1375. Note the ornate belt in pronounced relief, which possibly are meant to represent gems.

Madonna and Child by Cristoforo Scacco, datable to the late 1400s. The belt is made of a simple ribbon worn under the bust.

- From the 1700s to the late 1800s, women's belts were made of a single ribbon and rarely out of leather as, following the fashions of the empire, they were worn just under the bust line. Once suits appeared, men's style belts began to be worn, supporting the skirt underneath the jacket.

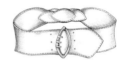

Portrait of Caterina Ferrari, the first wife of R. Trivulzio, the marquis of Vigevano, Italy. Anonymous, circa 1560.

Engraving representing Diana di Poitiers from the late 1500s, showing her wearing a long belt.

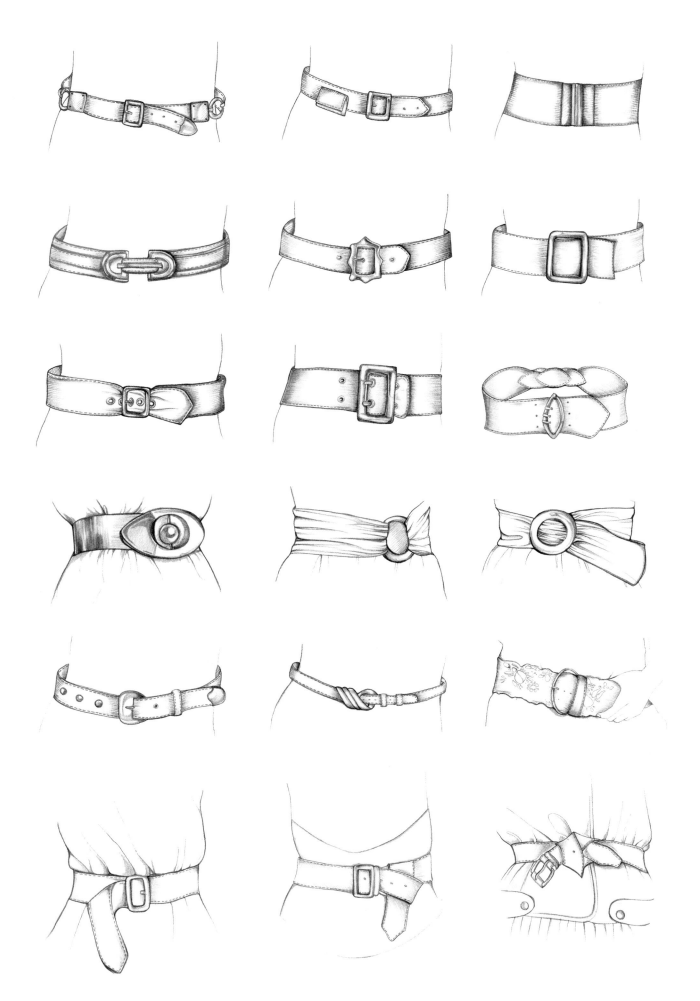

BELT PRODUCTION STEPS

Belts can be divided into three main categories, each of which requires different or complementary production steps:

1) Casual belts: an unlined leather belt with a larger, bolder buckle;
2) Classic men's belts: rounded, lined in a second layer of leather or with faux or bonded leather; Usually 3, 3.5 or 4 cm high (1.18, 1.38 or 1.57") and almost always slightly curved along the surface;
3) Women's belts: generally quite varied, depending on fashion trends. They can come in different heights, from 8 mm to 6 cm (0.31-2.36") and beyond.

Leather

Leather is delivered to the workshop from the tannery, already tanned and dyed, in the thickness and finish desired.
Belt leather can be divided into two categories:

1) Top grain, the prettier hide covering the dermis.
2) Flesh split, the part below the dermis.

The best section of the hide is used for belts:
- the bend (the central/upper part)
- the shoulder and butt.

Production steps for classic belts

The main production phases for classic belts are: 1) Squaring the hides. 2) Cutting the squared edges. 3) Cutting the strips/belts. 4) Skiving. 5) Gluing. 6) Joining. 7) Punching. 8) Trimming and sanding. 9) Stitching. 10) Finishing the edges. Special steps may also be required, depending on the needs and the belt to be made.

Squaring and cutting the squared hides

Depending on the client's requests, the leather is squared in the proper measurements and cut with a leather die or manually.

Cutting into strips

This is the true "cutting" of the belt. Loading the hides into a steel-spacer strap cutter, in the length requested, and according to the orders and the width of the belts, the leather is cut into strips with circular blades mounted after each spacer.

Skiving

Skiving is necessary to create the curved aspect of the belt, removing part of the material along the edges.
This operation is done with a hide splitter, a machine used to bring the leather to the proper thickness. In this case, a special device with single or multiple rollers, shaped specifically for skiving, is used.

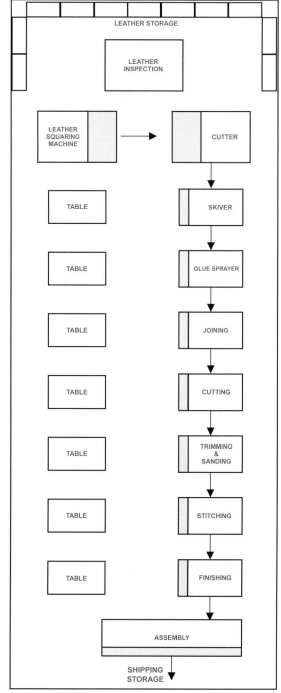

Production steps for classic belts

Oil-hydraulic die cutter with moving carriage

Strap cutter

Leather splitting machine

Skiver

Gluing

In this step, glue (a natural latex is almost always used) us applied to the two strips of leather that compose the belt, completely joining them. Gluing can be done with a nozzle affixed to a special machine made up of a conveyor belt and automatic spray nozzles, or via contact with a gluing machine made of two pressure rollers.

Joining

This step joins the two parts that make up the belt. The machines used are: the joiner, to join the multiple bands, and the joiner-trimmer for single strip belts.

Specially-shaped upper and lower rollers are installed on the machine that, through intense pressure, unites the two parts that make up the belt.

Cutting

A step that is necessary to die-cut the following forms and holes, using a die-cutter and specially-shaped dies:
- The shape of the end of the belt.
- Holes for the notches.
- The hole or slit or attachment for the buckle.

In addition, and at times even via the same operation, while the back of the belts are being die-cut, the client's logo, size, type of leather and other information about the item is applied.

Cutting takes place through a dual-head cutting machine: one for the tip of the belt and the other for the buckle end. The settings are determined according to the type of belt and the shape of the tip. The operation takes place via a press-stroke operation.

Trimming

In this step, multiple belts are separated and cut into single belts. For single belts, the edges are finished, removing all excess materials. Trimming takes place via a trimmer, a machine made of an upper roller where the width spacers for the belt are mounted, along with the cutting blades and a lower roller featuring steel pieces that act as counter-blades.

Stitching

Classic, single belts are stitched along the edges with machines for flat, straight stitches, with 34-38 stitches every 10 cm/3.94" and 20/30 gauge yarn; for casual belts, 15, 10, 8 or 5 gauge thread is used and there will be about 20-30 stitches every 10 cm/3.94".

Finishing the edges

This step is required to round, smooth or ink the edges of the belt. These three steps can be done separately (one after the other) or grouped into a single production line.

In practice, the belt is:
1) Rounded with edge trimmers or filers, passing on shaped rollers that, moving quickly, remove the corners of the belt.
2) Inking/dyeing via two rotating rollers that apply dye to the outer edges of the belt.
3) Drying in a special oven.
4) The belt is then repositioned in another machine with cloth rollers, dyed and dried again in a second oven.
5) Finally it gets to the unloader, which also colours the tip of the belt.

Spray system for water-based glue with an intake grille

Joining

Oven

Trimming

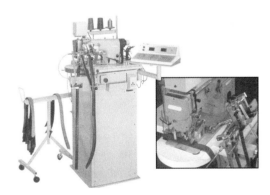

A computer-operated machine for stitching around the edge of belts

6) In higher-quality belts, the last operation is carried out manually, inking the edges with a special tool.

For casual, unlined belts, the step of finishing the edges is done differently. Essentially the edges are rounded with a machine via shaped knives with a range that varies according to the thickness of the leather.

FINISHING TOUCHES

Special procedures

For items or models with special designs, various, specific procedures can be used to characterise the product.
For example:

1) Decorative embroidery at the centre of the belt.
2) Zig-zag rather than straight stitching.
3) Stitching with a stitch marker that, in addition to creating normal stitches, features a shaped foot that cuts and burnishes the leather along the stitching.
4) Knurling, cutting the leather above the seams with rollers that imprint specially-made designs.
5) Embossing, similar to knurling, but made with fixed plates that are as long as the belt.
This ensures even the ends of the belt are finished properly.
6) The application of metal rivets or eyelets through special machines called riveters or eyelet machines.

Loops

The scraps of leather produced from making the belt can be cut into small strips, used to create the loops.
The strips are then joined together in a long chain to speed up the process.

Tail (buckle) end attachments

The leather scraps can also be cut and sliced to create attachments for the buckle, which are then dyed and screwed on to the shaft.

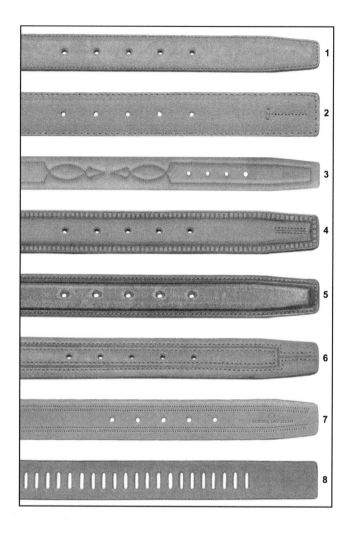

Belt detailing
1) Plain stitching, trapezoid tip; 2) Plain stitching, square tip; 3) Decorative stitching 4) Belt with knurling; 5) Belt with a curved surface; 6) Double belt with recessing; 7) Belt with zig-zag stitching; 8) Belt with cut-outs.

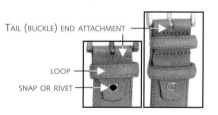

TAIL (BUCKLE) END ATTACHMENT
LOOP
SNAP OR RIVET

Loops and buckle attachment

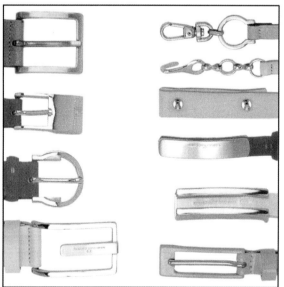

Belt buckles and attachments

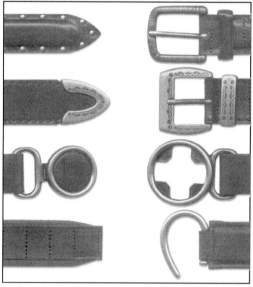

Vintage belts

HATS AND BEANIES

A short history 118
Main types of hats 120
Sports hats and beanies 121
Hat materials 122
Hat measurements 123
Hat terminology 123
Felt hats 124
Manufacturing felt 125
Milliners and their tools 127
Frames and brass wire ridges 128
Esparto bases 129
Felt hats for women 130
Felt hats for men 131
Felt hat production steps 132
Washing the hat 135
Statement hats 136
Sporty hats 137
Straw hats 138
The fundamentals of straw hats 139
Using straw 140

Hat hoods and trimmings 141
Trimming the brim with ribbon 142
Sewn fabric hat 144
Hat with a central panel 145
4 panel hat 146
Bucket hat 147
Beret 148
Cap with a visor 149
Wedge Gatsby 150
Patterned flat cap 151
Schoolboy cap 152
Brimless cap 153
Cuffed micro fleece beanie 153
Baseball cap 154
7 panel baseball cap 155
Baseball cap with a central panel 156
Equestrian helmet 157
Colback with ear flaps 158
Russian fur cap 159
Bandanna 160

A SHORT HISTORY

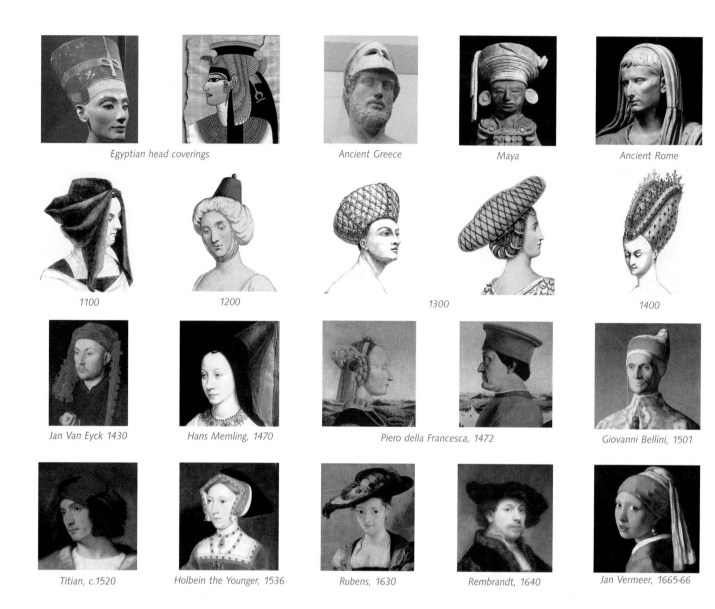

Egyptian head coverings   Ancient Greece   Maya   Ancient Rome

1100   1200   1300   1400

Jan Van Eyck 1430   Hans Memling, 1470   Piero della Francesca, 1472   Giovanni Bellini, 1501

Titian, c.1520   Holbein the Younger, 1536   Rubens, 1630   Rembrandt, 1640   Jan Vermeer, 1665-66

Hats are head coverings for men and women with brims that are wide or narrow, in various materials and shapes. They change according to the dictates of fashion and the use they are intended for (military, religious, sports, etc.)

Their shapes have changed frequently over the centuries, in part because hats have mainly had an ornamental purpose (which is still true today, especially in women's fashion).

Hundreds of centuries before Christ, people used to wear extraordinary objects on their heads: tiaras, large wigs, or imaginative constructions decorated with serpents or sparrow hawks, which symbolised the power of warriors, priests and Pharaohs.

The ancient Greeks wore hats that matched their draped togas: a 5th century BC vase depicts Helen of Troy's kidnapper in long clothing and a large head covering. In other images depicting ceremonies, young men on horseback wear headgear similar to that of American cowboys, thrown back on their shoulders and held on via a chin strap.

In ancient Rome, the hat symbolised personal freedom: the first gift given to freed slaves was a *pileus*, a sort of brimless felt cap. In the imperial period, tiara-shaped headgear from which a shawl cascaded down was common. In this same period, there were different head coverings in different parts of the

world: Egyptian, Spanish and Greek, in addition to Roman hats such as the *cucullus* (a sort of hood attached to a small shawl), and the *galea* (the Roman helmet).

In the Middle Ages, in addition to the woven silver hoods, the most common hat was the cloche, while pilgrims and wayfarers wore bell-shaped hats affixed by an adjustable cord under the chin, or with a raised brim on the back or two sides, decorated with peacock feathers or covered in fur.

In the 1400s, young people in particular wore sugar-loaf hats, posed brazenly over a short shock of hair. In addition, during this time, people often wore two hats, one over the other: the first was a more or less curly stocking or bonnet, worn straight; the second was a toque, shaped like a round pie, that was positioned "at twenty-three".

In the early 1600s, a black, rigid, cylindrical hat appeared in England: the ancestor of the top hat. Then, towards the end of the century, the first tricornes appeared, placed atop men's wigs. In the 1700s, wigs got smaller but, being covered in powder, they made it impossible to wear hats. However, men carried their tricornes under their arm, while women wore a high crest of randomly applied ribbons applied to a wire frame called a *fontage* or *frelange*. Then, women's heads began to swell again and the "Pompadour" hat, tied under the chin, appeared.

1775   1794   1798   1825   1874

1885   1900   1905   1912   1920

1930   1940   1950   1960   1970

1975   1980   1990   2000   2009

During the French Revolution, capricious hats were at their peak: the Incroyables wore brimmed, crescent-shaped bicornes and cylinder-shaped hats in every height and width, while the Merveilleuses, their female counterparts, wore cockades and three-toned ribbons on their heads.

After Napoleon fell from power, cylindrical hats came back into favour for men, while women began wearing turbans and caps in lace again. Subsequently, small hats made of straw, felt or fabric, richly embellished with flowers, fruit and bows, similar to a cap with a brim and ribbons, appeared.

Towards the 1800s, dames adopted small hats with flat or curved brims, which were embellished upwards and which rested directly on the forehead or the nape of the neck. Men wore high, stiff top hats with a tailcoat or suit with a long coat, while for strolling about they wore a bowler hat or, in summer, straw boater hats.

In the early 1900s, it was in vogue for women to have protruding hairstyles, so hats also underwent a transformation to have a wide brim, richly adorned with feathers, flowers, ribbons and bows.

In the 1920s, women wore cloches over their hair, lowered in the front, or turbans with an ornamental feather for social oc-

casions. Men wore soft felt hats with a dip in the crown or sporty caps.

In the 1930s, women wore small decorated hats or close-fitting caps, while men wore soft or stiff felt hats or sporty caps.

In the 1940s, with the 'new look', women adopted short, curly hair styles and elegant hats without brims or with quite wide brims, while men wore soft felt hats, visored caps or even berets.

In the 1950s, women wore wide brimmed hats or small, graceful, ornate hats, while men continued to wear soft felt hats and sporty caps.

In the 1960s, when back-combed hair was stylish, hats weren't worn very often, though young people with bobs wore berets or hats with upturned brims.

In the 1970s, it was fashionable once again for women to wear hats with a veil and a bell shape, while men rarely wore hats, except for casual, sports headgear.

In recent years, women have worn hats mostly for special occasions and celebrations, while men have worn them sporadically, especially to protect against the cold or for sports uses.

MAIN TYPES OF HATS

Bowler

Top hat

Straw hat

Felt

Pillbox

Toque

Pamela

Cowboy

Calot

Fur

Ballon

Russian fur cap

Visor cap

Turban

Cloche

MEN'S HATS

Pitch helmet

Safari

Felt

Panama

Fabric

Hats are an essential accessory for men's wardrobes as well and, even if barely worn at all today (rendered unnecessary by the diffusion of cars that protect from the cold), it will always be a wonderful accessory to complete any man's outfit, giving him elegance and poise.

Men's hats are divided into:

1) Traditional hats, mostly made in felt shaved to various lengths, fabric, rabbit fur, mink, beaver, Astrakhan, etc.

2) Summer hats made of straw.

Hats, depending on their shape, take on different names, even in relation to their use.

- Bowler and top hats for special occasions, accompanied by suitable clothing such as a dinner suit or tailcoat;

- Soft felt hats like the ones made by Windsor or Borsalino, called a homburg, with a deep single dent running down the crown (a gutter crown), with brims that range in size.

- A floppy hat; straw; cowboy hat; colback or Russian fur cap; fabric hats, generally sporty in character, often soft and un-lined, in tweed or loden, etc.

SPORTS HATS AND BEANIES

In canvas
Reversible
Floppy
Winter

Newsboy
Golf
Caps with ear flaps and visors
Hunter's cap

American beret
Yacht cap
Chefs caps
Riding helmet

Beret
Tall beret
Wool beanie
Wool beanie
Visor cap

Sailor's cap
Newsboy
Hood
Aviator
Fabric

Even for women, hats that were once quite popular have lost their charm and, except for a few cases, today they're worn infrequently and with little conviction.

The most common winter outerwear aside from the overcoat or cape is the felt cloche (the most authentic being made by Borsalino in various colours), or the velvet toque for certain occasions. In summer, the most popular hats are panamas in straw or similar materials, without the addition of flowers, fruit or various frills, except perhaps for the presence of silk or synthetic flowers or ribbons in matching colours.

Sporty caps, mostly made of fabrics such as tweed, Loden, cotton, or water-repellent synthetic materials, may be lined or unlined, and with or without a visor of varying lengths.

Skull caps are made in segments or with an upper base and a lateral band, while the flap or visor is sewn to the base of the underlying border.

Types of sports caps and beanies: Beret - Beanie - Floppy hats - Reversible hats - Cloche - Peaked cap - Army caps - Chefs hats, etc.

Hat materials

To make hats, especially those for women, a wide range of fabric types may be used.

To get the best results, the fabric used for millinery must have the right qualities for the type of hat, the season it will be worn in and the use and purpose or occasion it is destined for.

Main materials

Wool felt: a textile of a uniform thickness made by matting and pressing fibres together, taking advantage of wool's properties and ability to be compacted via heat, steam and pressure.

Rabbit felt (lapin or hare): the most commonly used felt for men's hats. To felt rabbit fur, acid compounds, mercury and nitric acid need to be added.

Satin: a fabric made of any fibre, characterised by minimal weaving of the threads, both weft and warp, giving the surface a flat, shiny look on the "right" side and a matt effect on the other.

Velvet: a fabric often made of silk or other fibres such as wool or synthetics. It comes in two types: warp velvet and weft velvet (velveteen). The tufts that are formed by weaving the two layers of the fabric are then cut, creating the pile on the surface.

Silk: fabric created with filaments secreted by silkworms; a noble, costly fibre. Its qualities include durability and flexibility with hygroscopicity, but also a soft handle and warmth, excellent drape and a brilliant surface.

Georgette: a sheer silk or wool fabric with a slightly crinkly surface.

Tulle: a very fine fabric with a wide knit, wide enough to make the material resemble voile. It was often used for veils, made of thin cotton, silk or nylon threads, creating a polygonal bobbinet structure.

Lace: a material that can trace its origins to mesh, dating back to ancient times. The technique requires a high level of skill. There are various types of lace, often named after the town they come from (Chantilly, Brussels, Cluny, Lille, Maltese, etc.).

Veiling: a lightweight widely-knit material or lace used for veils, sometimes found with small applied chenille tufts.

Crinoline (or crin): a type of tulle made with a thick-yarn rayon.

Rubberised mesh: an open-knit mesh, coated with special materials such as rubber, lacquer or resin.

Rayon (viscose): a fabric obtained from viscose rayon, produced from the cellulose of pulp from trees (often poplars, firs or pines), the same used to make paper.

Sisal (straw): a textile fibre created from the leaves of a type of agave, a plant originally from South America but now grown in other parts of the world.

Parasisal (straw): a fibre composed of ultra fine natural straw, finely woven by hand.

Paper: a fibrous celluloid material produced by pressing together pulp, reduced to strips of different sizes, suitable for being woven.

Twisted paper: a type of paper that has been twisted before being woven to make it more durable and to give the weave or braid a rustic look.

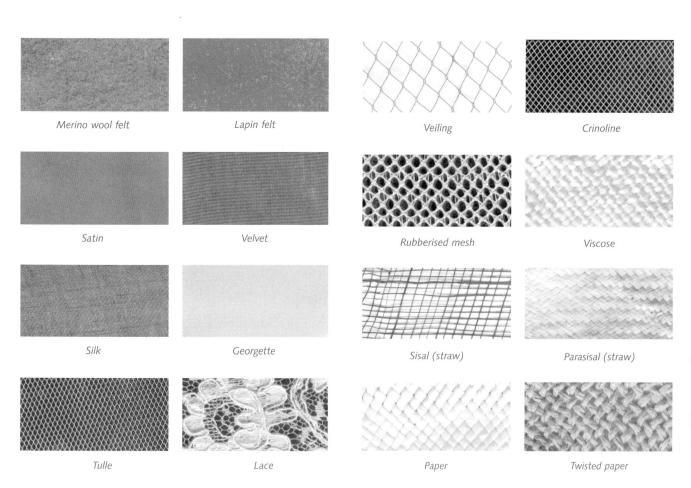

Merino wool felt	*Lapin felt*	*Veiling*	*Crinoline*
Satin	*Velvet*	*Rubberised mesh*	*Viscose*
Silk	*Georgette*	*Sisal (straw)*	*Parasisal (straw)*
Tulle	*Lace*	*Paper*	*Twisted paper*

HAT MEASUREMENTS

The main measurement to take when making a custom hat is the circumference of the head, while the height of the hat varies according to the pattern being used and style.

Head circumference

When taking the measurements, make sure the customer's head is in a normal position, erect and perfectly vertical, with his/her hair down and without bulky accessories.
- Measure from one temple to the other, passing the centimetre tape from the nape of the neck to the forehead, about a centimetre below where the hairline begins.

The measurements used in industrial manufacturing are determined by a table that goes from size 52 to 60 in the EU and 6 1/2 to 8 (going up in 1/8th increments) in the UK, or in measurements of XS -S - M - L - XL for adults, and from size 45 to 56 (EU), or XS - S - M - L - XL, for kids.

The numbered size corresponds to the measurement of the circumference of the head, while the letters may refer to the measurements of two sizes.

Fit

The hat measurement must correspond exactly to that of the head.

The classic hat, when worn on the head, must rest perfectly on the upper part of the forehead and must be lifted off the hair by at least 1 cm (of course, hats with super tall crowns will be even higher off the head). If the hat's measurements are slightly greater than that of the head, which would make it fall down, the hat can be brought to the correct measurement by adding grosgrain ribbon in a suitable thickness to the inside, until obtaining the perfect fit.

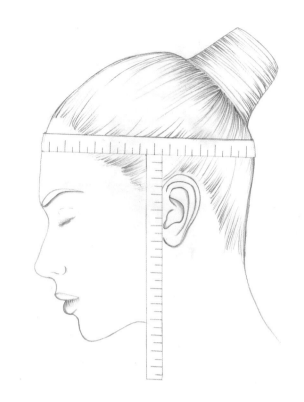

HAT TERMINOLOGY

1. **Crown:** the upper part of a hat or cap. This can be in different shapes (rounded or flat, with just the centre or the centre and sides pushed in, called a crease and dents, respectively), and different heights.

2. **Brim:** the lower ring of the hat which is sewn along the edge of the crown. The brim may vary in size; it may be asymmetrical with the front wider than the back; it may be curved upwards or downwards, or with the front curved down the back up and vice versa.

3. **Hat band:** the ribbon of silk or another material affixed to the lower edge of the crown (the shoulder) to cover the seam or as an embellishment. The hat band can be finished with a flattened bow, which often is placed at the side of the hat, or with other similar accessories suitable to the hat type and purpose.

4. **Lining:** material affixed to the inside of the crown of the hat, in either natural or synthetic fibres.

5. **Sweatband:** the strip of material, often leather or grosgrain, affixed along the inside rim of the hat or cap, coming into direct contact with the head.

6. **Visor:** a short, stiff brim in the shape of a half-crescent placed on the front of a cap. The visor may come in different sizes, lengths and shapes, also according to its purpose and features.

Felt hats

The role of milliner, or hat-maker, is an ancient job that has been reduced due to changes in clothing styles that took place in the second half of the 1900s, starting in Western nations. As a result, felt and straw have almost entirely disappeared, despite once being an essential part of elite wardrobes.

Today, people cover their heads for protective reasons (motorbike helmets, turbans to protect from the sun, beanies for the cold, etc.), technical and sports reasons (horseback riding, baseball, ski helmets, etc.) or symbolic reasons (components of a military uniform, or that for doormen, firemen, guards, clergy, etc.).

The drastic reduction in the use of hats has naturally caused there to be fewer companies that make them and reduced the entire supply chain, causing a few cities that once had a robust hat industry (such as Monza and Alessandria in Italy) to change quite notably, even in terms of the city's layout and feel.

Headgear production is not, as is the case with other garments, geared towards a mass market. Instead, it's a niche of its own, often lumped in with other products, such as: sports items, various accessories or clothing in general. There are very few shops that sell hats exclusively, as they once did in the past. Of course this phenomenon of stagnation, like any historical process, could be susceptible to changes and further developments in the future, both negative or positive, brought about by changes in tastes and fashions.

Felt or fur hat production

For centuries, hat making was an artisanal activity carried out in urban areas, in a sort of cavernous room, where all the pattern design, preparation and finishing steps where carried out, where the name of the craftsman was synonymous with the factory's brand and guaranteed the quality and durability of the hats.

Types of fur used for felt

The felt used for hat is made form animal fibres that have undergone "felting", a process by which the their criss-crossing is intensified mechanically or chemically to create a single piece of felt that is durable, waterproof, versatile and malleable.

It is probable that the first material used for hats was wool, but the best felt for hats has always been made from short animal

fibres, such as otter, beaver or muskrat, which can even be felted by hand; or domesticated or wild hare and rabbit. To felt these types of fur, different types of acids must be added (and mercury was once used as well), in a step that's called secretage or carroting. Suitable blends of animal fibres are chosen according to the type and quality of hats to be produced.

During the felting process, the fibres are pulled parallel to each other (carding), creating a thin web of uniform thickness. Different webs can be combined in order to create the different gauges of felt.

Felt has no warp or weft nor selvedges as it is not a woven material, which simplifies its use in the preparation of hats. For the same reason, it will not fray or wear out. Felt is not stretchy nor does it drape well, but it can be cut and shaped into the desired shape, maintaining that form as long as it isn't placed under extreme tension.

However, given that it is made without the use of thread, which can be twisted, and without being knit, felt is a type of fabric with low textile resistance and, when torn, the fracture zone is jagged and fuzzy.

Felt is quite insulating, keeping warmth in, and it absorbs noise and impact. It is also more waterproof than traditional uncoated fabrics.

Manufacturing felt

Since ancient times, felt has been made in two steps:
1) 'White' processes (so-called for the characteristic white pinafore worn to avoid dirtying the mixture of fur being worked), which includes preparation and mixing of the fibres, bowing, basoning and planking;
2) 'Black' processes, that include dying, shaping the felt, blocking, lining and finishing.

WHITE PROCESSES
Mixing the fibres
In the past, fibres were mixed with a machine called the 'violone' in Italy, a sort of harp whose cords were placed between the fur and plucked, causing the fibres to vibrate and mix together. The mixture was then separated in to the weights required for two or three hats, then passed along to the next operation: carding and the creation of the batt.

Bowing
In the past, this step was done with the 'arçon', arsone or hatter's bow, equipment made of a 2 meter (6.5 ft) beam, with one seven-prong end and the other in the shape of a hook, upon which a nerve cord was placed, stretched with a small axis covered in goatskin. The worker, called an 'arçonneur', vibrated the cord of the instrument (affixed to the ceiling) between the 'fluff' (the fibres) spread out on a work table called a 'canisse', causing them to fall on a dense mesh placed at the side of the table. The vibrations provoke the carding and bonding together of the fluff. The fluff that fell back onto the metal net created a triangular *capade* (French) or batt (English) of fibres that were crossed in every direction, composed of two parts of the amount weighed.
Today, these two steps are united and carried out with a single machine called a carding machine, which makes it possible to create hundreds of hats per day, significantly more than the 125 hats per day made on average by the hand-operated 'arçon'.

Basoning
The four light-weight batts, created by the bowing and carding, are then basoned and shaped into a cone shape by manually uniting, two by two, the triangular batts, felting the overlapping edges to ensure the joints are no longer visible. These are then wrapped around thick paper forms in the shape of a double cone

attached at the base, then cut to create two bells or hoods. They are immediately hardened and matted together, pressing them in every direction on a square made of wicker or iron wire (called a 'claion', 'calcatoio'). At this point, the capades are rolled over a hot table (at times heated with charcoal or steam).

Planking
Planking is an operation that solidifies the capades so that they can be shaped. This step consists of the aggressive, repeated compression of the capades, hardened in tanks that contain boiling water with a sulphuric acid solution. By doing so, the fibres deflate, becoming viscous yet compact, durable and waterproof. After drying, the milliner takes the cone-shaped caps and places them over a special form, shaving them with special clippers. They are then sanded with a sanding machine using very fine sandpaper to get rid of any rough spots on the surface. The milliner then divides them up into those to be dyed and those which will remain their natural colour.

Dying the felt
The felt pieces to be dyed are brought to the dye-house and the colours are established.
In the past, they were immersed repeatedly in copper vats for a few hours, continuously mixing them and drying them out every so often.
Natural colours such as brown, grey, silver and cream are created by each milliner with his own special recipe, which means it is difficult to find two colours that are exactly the same. Black, on the other hand, is much more difficult. Once it was created with special types of wood, walnut with a black exterior, vitriol of Cyprus, etc. Today black is created with synthetic dyes.
Sometimes the felt is planked again to make it even more compact.

Opposite page. Top: *old milliner equipment still in use today.*
Bottom: *Basoning and pressing the felt.*
Above: *dying and shaping.*
At right: *an artisan hat-making laboratory.*

Above: shaping the brim and shaving. Below: lining and packaging.

'Black' processes or shaping

At this point, according to the technical and professional practices still used in Italy, the 'white' or 'wet' processes end here and the 'black' processes or shaping begins. The name derived not only from the prevalent colour, but the fact that the milliners wore a black pinafore.

In the past, shaping (or blocking) consisted of giving the desired shape to the felt. It was always done by hand, working while the felt was hot and moist, with the help of a wood head or block, around which the hat was shaped. A puller downer (a special wood circle) is used to shape the brim of the hat.

After having given the felt the right shape, it was affixed to the block and to the puller downer, pressed while bags of hot sand rested on top, helping it dry.

Lastly, patiently ironing it with a very heavy iron, the rigid parts were corrected, giving the hat its definitive shape and creating the commissioned form.

Once the hat is completed, hat makers proceeded to the internal and external finishing of the piece, applying the sweatband, ribbons, edgings, etc., that were to decorate the finished hat. With the industrialisation of production, all these operations were carried out with the help of increasingly precise machines, starting from studies aimed at estimating the yield of fur obtained from a rabbit, to tests designed to verify the compactness and regularity of the layer of felt and the degree of deformation of the capade, from heat presses with automatic heat controls that replaced sand bags to steamers derived from heavy irons, etc.

Of course, this was all to improve hat quality and production quantities.

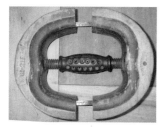

MILLINERS AND THEIR TOOLS

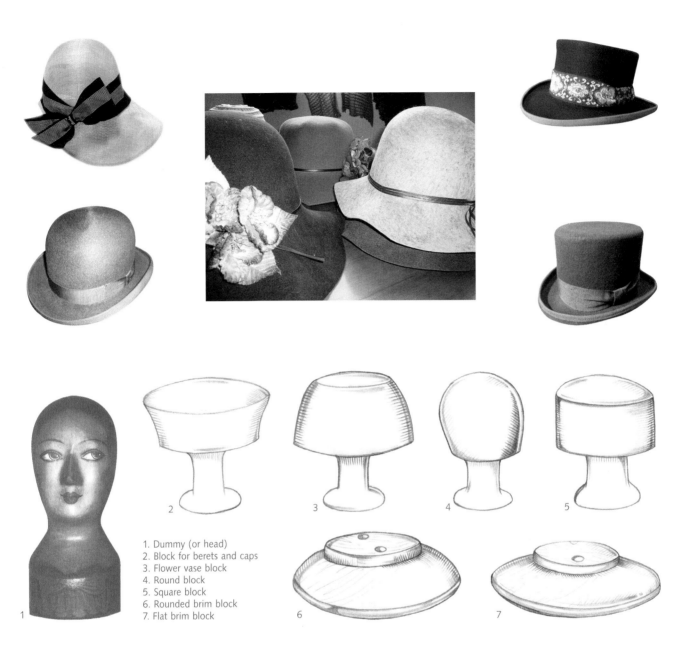

1. Dummy (or head)
2. Block for berets and caps
3. Flower vase block
4. Round block
5. Square block
6. Rounded brim block
7. Flat brim block

Today, the word milliner is used to indicate any man or woman who makes, decorates or sells women's hats, in multiple materials and various models, brim and crown shapes, in felt, natural straw and synthetics. The word derives from "Milaner", meaning someone from Milan. In Italian, the word is "modista", a term that up until the late 1700s (directly related to 'moda', or 'fashion') was used generically to indicate not just a creator of hats, but all the workers and experts of any clothing product sector, in addition to their salesmen: from the haberdasher to those who produced ribbons, lace and buttons.

Only in 1776 in France, where they were called "fashion sellers", with the decline in the popularity of powdered wigs and when seamstresses began to expand their expertise into the realm of head coverings, was a reform passed recognising milliners, mainly women, as a separate trade, giving them the chance to create, dye and apply floral decorations to women's hats.

The tools of a milliner are quite simple:
- Irons and pressing cushions;

- A small "Polish" iron, that milliners heat up and pass over the forms, holding them on the inside with one hand protected by a ball of cotton or a rag, while using the other hand to iron the outer surface.
- Egg iron: an iron in the shape of a ball, called an egg, that is used for rounded and concave surfaces.
- Hat stretcher or conformateur: used to measure the opening of the hat and, eventually, to stretch it and adapt it to the head of the client, when an already-made hat needs adjusting. In this case, the hat, before being put on the hat stretcher, should be dampened on the inside.
- Dolly (female head): a mould of the head used to make hats, composed of a wood base and a head covered in canvas to help the milliner affix the pins (like a dress form for seamstresses). Some heads are in cardboard and even are painted with beautiful women's faces.
- Block: a wood shaping block in different forms, based on their intended use. There are round, square, flower vase and rounded (for berets) blocks. To increase the circumference of the head of the blocks, the milliner uses knit sleeves placed over the wood.

FRAMES AND BRASS WIRE RIDGES

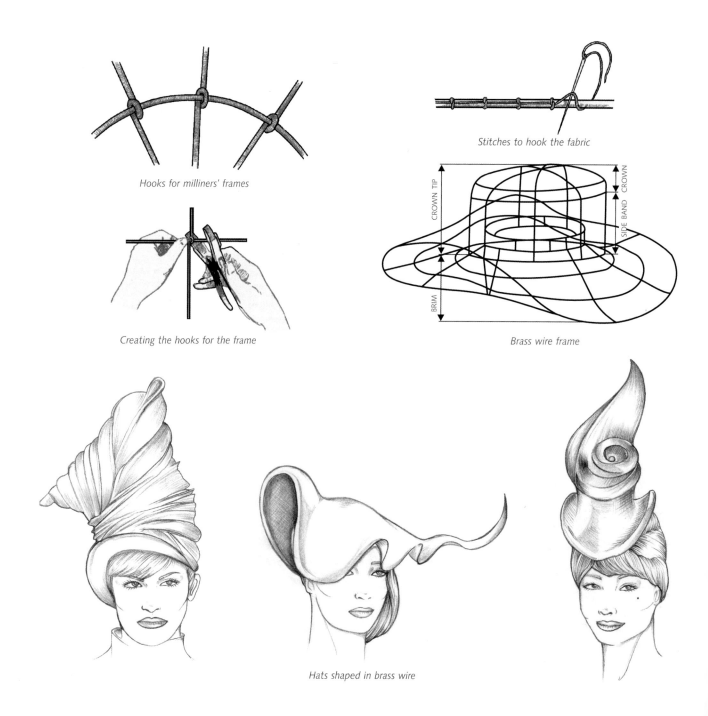

Hooks for milliners' frames

Creating the hooks for the frame

Stitches to hook the fabric

CROWN TIP   CROWN   SIDE BAND   BRIM

Brass wire frame

Hats shaped in brass wire

The frame of a hat is what gives it shape. Frames were created by the milliner with brass wire or with "sparterie" (from 'esparto', a vegetable fibre fabric, lined with starched cotton muslin), creating the desired shape based on personal tastes and the trends of the day.

Brass frames. Brass wire wrapped with silk or cotton yarn was needed to strengthen the esparto shapes and to act as supports over which the fabric of hats was pulled. Those wires were hooked with the help of a thin steel wire, or knotted with the help of strong, shiny yarn.

The brass wires came in 13 different gauges, in varying degrees of pliability. The shapes created with brass wires made it possible to stretch, drape, gather and trim all types of fabric, from tulle to velvet, not just straw and felt. The milliner prepared the brass write frame, a sort of skeleton intended to affix the shapes. This frame included the two parts of the hat: the crown (top and sides) and the brim. With the same frame, changing the arrangement of the fabric and the trimmings, it was possible to create quite different hats. It all depended on the milliner's ability to create and come up with new models.

This system of brass frames, used to hold up the fabric, began to disappear around 1920. Brass remained to support to the esparto to make some models, in addition to being used to reinforce the base of the crown and the external edge of the brim. It remains, however, indispensable for stretching or draping lightweight fabric such as tulle or muslin for fancy hats.

Starting in the late 1930s, hat manufacturers and milliners began to prefer working directly with straw, felt or other materials as sombre, shaped forms where in style, not just those barely decorated with ribbons.

ESPARTO BASES

Ditching frames due to their complexity, milliners began using sparterie or jute to create their desired shapes and models, with less difficulty and more satisfying results.

Sparterie is a type of fabric made of the vegetable fibres deriving from the broad leaves of a grassy plant called esparto. It is lined with starched cotton muslin or with starched stiff or semi-stiff gauze.

Jute is a textile fibre made from the bark of certain trees that grow in Asia and Africa. It can be starched or lined with muslin. Milliner's forms can also be made with synthetic fibres such as laminated paper, when used along with gauze.

Today sparterie is difficult to come by, so milliners and workshops are much more likely to use a stiff starched fabric that, after having been dampened, is shaped on specially prepared wood blocks. When the fabric dries, it takes on a very durable shape and can then be used as a base for the external fabric of the hat.

It's important to remember that:

- Cut on the bias, sparterie can be worked with an iron until the desired shapes and undulations are created.

- When you have a hat with a drastically raised silhouette, it's convenient to put the cotton side of the form in the upper part, to ensure that the subsequently applied fabric is more adherent.

- When it dries, the hardened form is to be removed from the block used to create the shape. It is then possible to introduce and affix the brass wires at the opening for the head and along the edge of the brim.

- Sparterie is more solid when, before letting it dry, it is coated with a layer of wheatpaste (derived from flour or starch).

- Sparterie must be starched before the fabric is stretched or draped.

- It is also possible to shape forms in muslin, executed in dampened pattern paper, made from double or tripe gauze, worked on the bias for rounded crowns and in rough, stiff cotton tulle, which is sprayed with a coat of varnish while it's still wet to make it even stiffer.

Cotton tulle can be found in all the colours of the rainbow and makes it possible to decorate hats using almost any shade of transparent fabric.

- Jute fabric can also be used, lined or unlined with gauze, to create the forms.

Hat fabric

Once the form has been given the desired shape, the fabric garnish can be added, perfectly stretched or well affixed, or even fringed, pleated or draped.

All types of fabric are suitable for this use: silk, jersey, muslin, velvet, synthetics, etc.

Velvet is particularly well-suited to being worked artfully and with imagination. In addition, velvet is able to withstand glue, which is indispensable for attaching it to the sparterie.

The fabric is first cut precisely on the pattern paper, then rested on the supporting structure. It is then glued by passing a brush or muslin cloth over it, being sure that no gathers or folds are created.

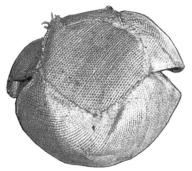

Crown form made of sparterie and muslin

Brim form in starched jute

Crown form in starched gauze which feathers were glued to

Wood hat block

FELT HATS FOR WOMEN

Felt hats for women are worn in winter, but they are manufactured by hat factories or milliners in spring.

The material used to produce these hats may be merino wool, from which medium-quality felted wool capades or hat hoods are created. It may also be felt made of prized or average rabbit or hare fibres, but certainly of better quality than sheep's wool felt. Some of the finest felts are: Flemish, which has longer fibres that look like fur; that from Molise (Italy), with long, silky fibres; and moleskin felt, which looks like velvet.

Felt for women's hats comes in various, yet generally solid, colours though at times they do feature tonal or contrasting motifs.

In hat factories, milliners worked the felt form on the wood block created by the block maker or specialised companies.

The hat block may even be designed and shaped by the milliner him/herself, especially by those who make haute couture or unique hats for exclusive clients.

The hat hood or cone must be prepared the night before, left to rest wrapped in a wet cloth.

It is then placed on the wood block and shaped as desired, according to personal taste or the designer's drawings.

Under the pressure of the milliner's fingers, the felt will behave like a malleable, pliable material.

The crown, after having been pared down, is tightened to the wood block with a thread tied around it.

At this point, the brim is shaped on the block or by hand, gripped and sewn to the shaped crown.

All this work is done with the help of steam from an iron resting on a wet cloth.

Lastly, after having created the desired shape, on the back of the hat, a bit of starch is applied with a brush.

In the past, felt hats were often affixed to brass wires. This system was abandoned and hats became lighter and more flexible. Today, felt is shaped, carved, and worked with draped fabric, sewn and crossed or wrapped with ribbon, braids, etc., according to the trends and the milliner's sense of style.

Felt hat production steps

A felt hat is made by steaming or wetting the felt and then shaping it into the desired hat block. Once dry, it will maintain that shape. Some types of felt are too soft to hold the shape desired but, the application of a bit of starch can solve the problem. Before getting to work, it's important to decide if the hat must be done in just one piece or in two pieces. If it is to be done in just one piece, you'll need to make sure that the felt you have is enough, so as to avoid pulling and stretching it too much, making the hat too thin. For hats made in two pieces, the brim is made first. This is because although the crown or hat body can always be enlarged, the brim cannot.

1. The starting hat body, 100g long-hair lapin.

2. Adding starch, which is quite strong in this case. Left to dry for 12 hours.

3. First manual shaping based on the model and size to be made.

4. Second steaming.

5. Shaping on the brim block, as desired.

6. Properly stretching the hat hood.

7. Make sure it adheres closely to the ring.

8. Third steaming.

The images shown here of working and washing the felt were taken at Cappelleria Melegari in Milan.

132

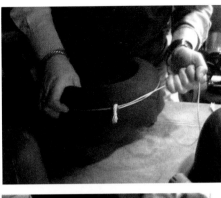

9. Tying a cord to affix the hat form.

10. Fourth steaming.

11. Pulling the hat form tightly and inserting the right block.

12. The milliner presses hard and, if necessary, places it below the press. Left to dry for 24 hours.

13. The hat is removed from the block and smoothed on the lathe.

14. First cut to create the brim.

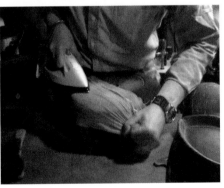

15. First ironing of the brim. Left to dry for 6 hours.

16. With the second cut, the brim is fully defined, as desired.

17. Second, definitive, ironing of the brim.

18. Placing the hat under a bag of hot sand.

19. The crown is shaped as necessary and, only once dry, it's sent to the sewing station.

20. The leather sweatband is sewn on the inside.

21. After having prepared and ironed the hat, a silk ribbon is applied as desired.

22. Adding the lining, sewing it with invisible stitches.

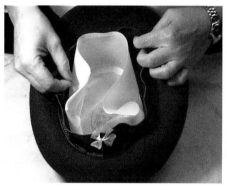

23. Adding the final touches by hand or, if necessary, on the lathe.

24. The hat is ready!

Opposite page:
1. Decorations and linings that will no longer be used are removed from a dirty, rumpled hat.
2. After having washed the hat, it's clean but the shape has been lost.
3. Starch is added to the brim and left to dry for 6 hours.
4. Steam is used to fully wet and heat the crown.
5. The hat form is pulled down over the desired block.
6. A string is used to affix the crown, establishing the exact measurement.
7. The hat is passed over with the lathe to regenerate and smooth the felt. It is then left to rest and dry for 24 hours.
8. The hat is then placed on its brim block (a shaped wooden ring) and the brim is pulled manually with the help of steam.
9. To set the work done by ironing, the hat is placed below a bag full of hot sand.
10. The hat is left under the bag as long as necessary, depending on the type of felt and procedures carried out.
11. The crown and brim are perfectly "shaped", so they are left to dry for 24 hours.
12. A leather sweatband in the appropriate measurements is added to the inside.
13. The outside of the hat is decorated with a silk ribbon in the height and colour desired.
14. The lining is added to the inside.
15. One last steaming of the crown depending on the customer's needs, and a few final touches.

Felt hats from the Museo dell'Arte del Cappello in Ghiffa (VB).
Top left: *Rodolfo Valentino style hat, 1927.*
Cream-coloured felt with a medium brim.
Top right: *Surgeon's hat, 1650.*
Model worn with a long mantel.
At the side: *French Directory style, 1804 Post rider model.*

STATEMENT HATS

Hats made of *sparterie* can easily be shaped into a variety of forms. Large fashion houses may produce up to 80-100 different forms over just one season, in the same model, when its sales are successful. The milliner may make the forms herself, thereby producing the models desired.

STRAW HATS

Straw hats fully came into their own, in terms of fashion, only towards the end of the 18th century.
From that point on, this type of hat has been gaining popularity, especially in women's fashion, so much so that numerous types of hat styles are called 'straw hats'. They're not only made with the stalks of common grasses, but also from a wide range of materials, such as: reeds, bamboo, exotic plants, fuzz from feathers, whalebone, paper and even plastic.

THE FUNDAMENTALS OF STRAW HATS

To create straw hats, you'll need:
1) To prepare the raw materials for their creation: straw, which can be made from the stalks of grasses or other plants, or even from other animal-derived or synthetic materials.
2) The processing, that is the making of the 'fabric'.
3) The finishes, that is: washing and bleaching, dying, starching, shaping, ironing, etc.
4) The decorations, that is: ribbons, faux or real flowers, feathers, haberdashery, etc.

Straw

Straw is produced and sold in three different forms:
1) Braided into skeins.
2) In 'cones' woven into a single piece.
3) Woven into a fabric.
In the past, milliners could make woven straw with very fine single twigs.
Knotting these twigs, they made hats of different shapes, but the resulting product was neither very attractive or successful.

Plaiting

Made in specialised workshops by hand or with special machines, plaiting can be natural or synthetic straw, in different colours and varying gauges.
The plaits are bought by milliners, fold and worked to give them the desired shape. Some hat makers buy semi-finished, already-shaped and woven cone-shaped forms, sewn with almost invisible stitches, from other workshops, then make the straw hat according to their designs.
The straw used for these weaves comes from a large variety of plants. The most common material is straw from grasses that, as was mentioned already, is woven by hand or with a machine, using a variable number of stalks. In fact, the weaves may be done with 4, 7 or 11 pieces, etc., according to the needs and style of the hat. The best types of straw, which have always been used for hat plaiting, are from England. They are quite fine, solid and easy to dye, keeping their brilliance for a long time.
Other commonly-used straws are:
- Belgian straw, which is rather shiny and stiff.
- Swiss straw, which was used not only for plaiting but for small ropes, objects for embellishment, flowers, knots, edging, etc.
- Rice straw, used around the mid 19th century, but immediately replaced by Carpi plaiting, made of a wooden straw deriving from willow trees.
- Tagal, made of processed and braided hemp, which appeared around 1900, a fine, delicate straw with a matt surface.
- Yedda straw, which is flexible and lightweight. It's easy to work and easily takes on delicate colour gradations and is sold in thin or thick, narrow or wide plaiting.
- The tip or fibre of pineapple, used with wide, rustic weaves, with one shiny side and one matt side, was worked after being soaked in moist cloth.
- Plaiting from China (in competition with European straw since the 1870s at very low prices), which can be sewn overlapping by hand or with a machine, making sewn straw hats.

A few phases of straw hat making

USING STRAW

Italian straw
Italian straw is 13-stem wheat straw from Tuscany, which stands out for its unique weave. In fact, due to its braiding method, these weaves can be knotted along a selvedge. So, instead of sewing via overlapping, this type of straw is joined by linking: the knots of the selvedge fit into one another, making it possible to pass the needle from selvedge to the other braid, uniting them. The thread used to assemble the two edges is not visible, making it all seem like one piece with a minimal, lightweight thickness linked along the joint.
Italian straw and hats have long been considered essential in women's wardrobes, both for their light weight and the tasteful finishings they were manufactured with.

Straw hats from the Museo della Paglia e dell'Intreccio in Signa (FI).

Other materials for straw hats
The following materials may be used to make straw hats:
- Wood shavings, taken from suitable types of wood such as willow.
- Raffia, which can be used for original models and ornamentation and compositions.
- Silk braids, at times mixed with chenille or tiny cords.
- Synthetic straws made of gelatine, cellophane and paper.
- Woven natural or synthetic crin. Natural crin is lightweight, shiny and delicate. Its transparency brings out small defects, but it can also be used to make very refined hats. Synthetic crin today is used in different coloured ribbons, especially at hat embellishments.

Working a straw hat on a tool in a craftsman's workshop.

Sewing hats
In the past, the plaits could be sewn over a copper frame or supporting structures made of shaped esparto, cotton or tulle. But these systems, which created rather course forms, were abandoned with the arrival of new executive criteria.
The crown was sewn by hand in a spiral, initially without a hat block, starting from the very top, being sure to create a perfectly flat circle, thus giving it width without ripples or wrinkles, but pressing the straw with the fingers over the needle.
The weave along the brim is done in a small, regular back-weave. For the brims where the edge is wider on one side compared to the other, on the other hand, an edging technique is used.
In this case, one shouldn't make tight weaves. Instead, weave as usual and, when at the point of connecting the new straw to the tightly woven row, stop following the outlines of the already-formed circle to check the circumference and affix the straw.
Affix this last circle by sloping the end of the straw cut on the 'right' side at the closure, which also makes it possible to hide the straw joining points underneath.
The last thing to do is then bridge the gap that is found on the wider rib of the brim, passing through a few ends of the folded straw pieces which will be woven exactly like the rows of straw. This operation is called edging.
Once this operation is finished, and continuing to use the hat block, the milliner passes over the straw with a damp rag to get a better finish. The piece is then dried and removed from the block.

Straw hoods
With time, factories that produce hat hoods or bodies, ready

Panama hat in soft straw with a medium brim and a black ribbon.

Boater hat in stiff straw with a double brim and two-tone ribbon.

to be assembled with brims, started to crop up. They come in a single piece, in a suitable length and in all sorts of straw. The work of weaving is almost always done manually, starting from the very top of the crown.
The quality of the work depends on the regularity of the way each layer is crossed, from the perfection of the weave and the thorough the scrutiny of the raw materials.
Often hats are made with exotic straw, such as Panamas, from Ecuador, resulting in a firm, regular weave with a particular amount of flexibility; Manila bamboo; Javanese rush, Chinese rush, etc.
Over time, straw hoods have gained added value for milliners and creators of elegant fashions because they can be used to highlight a taste for sober, natural forms and their flexibility, as it is possible to use straw hoods like their felt counterparts.

Hat hoods and trimmings

Hoods and capelines to make hats out of one single piece can be created in felt or straw as well as a number of other materials, such as: down, starched and coated cotton with flattened sticks, wicker, Manila hemp, kapok, whalebone, etc.

Today, the most commonly used hat hoods and capelines are produced in different types of fibre, both natural and synthetic.

- Sisal, a machine-woven fibre that is taken from the leaves of a type of agave, a plant originally from South America. It's the best material in terms of the price-quality ratio.

- Buntal, a white, superior-quality fibre, taken from a palm grown in the Philippines. It comes in a tightly-woven fabric which is created by hand within containers full of water to ensure the fibres don't fray. Very fine, this material can easily be dyed in a wide range of colours and tones;

- Viscose is a shiny yet fragile synthetic straw made from cellulose. It is machine-woven and quite inexpensive. A viscose hat body costs up to 5 times less than one in buntal.

Unfinished hat bodies

Straw hoods or cones become unfinished hat bodies when, after having shaped the crown, they are worked and placed on a block while wet and left to dry on the block.

After having been shaped, the hat body is ironed, starched and decorated according to the desired style and taste.

Woven straw fabric

Straw also comes in a woven fabric form, sold by the square metre. Straw fabric produced with natural fibres such as sisal, in addition to being used for trimmings, knots, passementerie, etc., is the ideal raw material for models of hats, toques and turbans that are draped or gathered according to the dictates of fashion. On the other hand, the material produced with synthetic fibres, such as viscose, is broadly used in mass-produced hats and low-cost trimmings.

Trimmings

After they've been shaped and finished, hats made of straw, fabric, felt or any other material are to be dressed with suitable trimmings and decorations, in accordance with the milliner's or designer's choices.

In a hat factory or milliner's shop, that responsibility goes to the decoration expert, following the instructions of the designer or of the trimming department head which proceed this important step. The decoration expert has the delicate job of finding and affixing ribbons, bows, flowers, feathers, etc.

The result of this work phase is that, more than anything else, it expresses the taste, ability and value of the milliner or hat factory.

Flowers and feathers have always been, since ancient times, the preferred trimmings for hats, drastically raising their price point according to the quality and creativity of the ornamentation.

- Flowers, with or without leaves, considered the freshest decoration, are usually applied to summer hats, even if this isn't a hard and fast rule and subject to quick changes in tastes and trends. The most commonly used ones are artificial, made of silk, tulle or veiling, or with leaves or blades of grass applied in bunches or garlands in the desired position. These decorations are produced by specialised companies, using diverse materials such as natural or synthetic fibres, perfectly imitating real flowers and leaves.

- Feathers, on the other hand, are the winter ornament par excellence, being the richest and costliest decoration.

In the past, the use of feathers and plumes to decorate hats has provoked the cruel hunting of birds with prized feathers, causing the risk of extinction for some of them. The bird of paradise is the most striking example of this, but there are also other species such as swans, canaries, geese, Himalayan monals, parrots, peacocks, marabou, pheasants, ostriches, etc.

Today, the highest-prized feathers are made artificially with good results and, conveniently, they have quite low prices.

Other trimmings used for hats are:

- Ribbons, made of silk or synthetic fibres, applied to the crown or as bows.

- Lace, embroidery, trimmings, pearls, veiling, creative compositions, etc.

TRIMMING THE BRIM WITH RIBBON

This edging technique can be used on straw or felt hats and can be both practical and decorative. Before placing the ribbon, it isn't necessary to insert a metal wire along the edge. However, it can be helpful if you are dealing with straw or a particularly wide brim, but it generally isn't needed for felt or when a delicate finish is desired. There are no strict rules that absolutely must be followed.

For the trimming, use a 3, 5 or 9 gauge grosgrain ribbon.

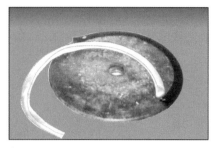

1

2

1-2) Using the 9 gauge grosgrain, wet the ribbon and apply it over the form or over a disc for ribbons. Affix with pins and let dry.

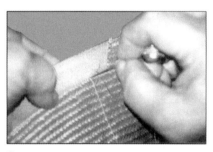

3

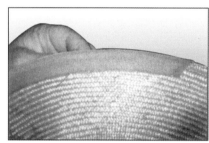

4

3-4) If the straw is thick, turn the edge over and. before adding the ribbon, sew to create a regular hem. Use pins to affix the ribbon and, at the same time, sew the upper and lower edges, going from one side of the straw to the other.

5

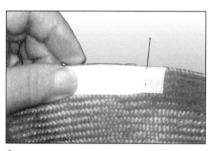

6

5) For simple edging, made by using 3 gauge ribbon, fold the ribbon with your hands, affix with pins and sew as explained above.

6) Rest the ribbon on the edge, right side to right side, and sew along the margin.

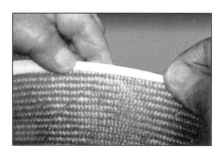

7

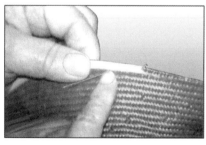

8

7) Flip over.

8-9) Sew just below the strip, taking up the back of the ribbon. The seam should be invisible.

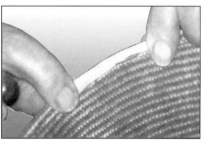

9

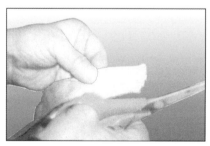

10

10) Cut a piece of ribbon that is three times as wide as the desired finish.

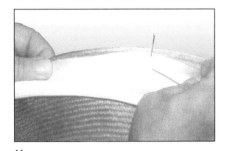

11

12

11) Fold it in the width desired and shape it a bit. Then affix it with pins, right side to right side.

13

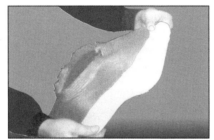

14

12-13) Turn it over and sew through the straw.

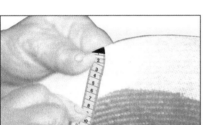

15

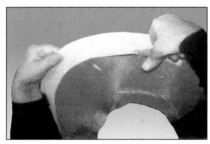

16

14-15-16) Cut a strip of stretch hemp canvas, fold it down the middle lengthwise, and shape it over the brim. Decide on the width and cut it.

17) Turn the strip before the rough part, then slide it off and, next, turn it over from the other part.

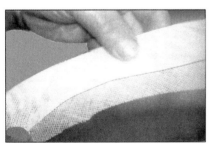

17

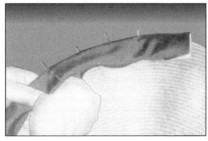

18

18) Cut a strip of fabric in the same width as the canvas piece and pin it to the base. Then pin both the pieces of fabric on the edge so that they perfectly line up.

19-20) Remove the ribbon and sew the two pieces of fabric, on the wrong side, with diagonal stitches. Lightly iron the edging, affix the strip on the edge again with pins and sew each side of the strip separately with diagonal stitches.

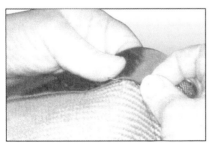

19

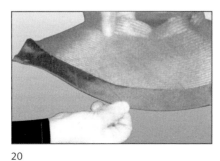

20

Edging with a base

If the fabric is stiff and dense, there probably is no need for a base. However, if the fabric requires a greater thickness, add a strip of adhesive interfacing, ironing it on top of the fabric. This application is ideal for printed fabric. For very thin fabric or for broad edging, hemp canvas can also be used.

Sewn fabric hat

WHOLE UPPER PART

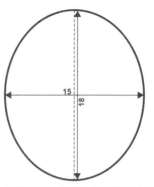

PART ABOVE 1 PIECE OF FABRIC 1 LINING

This type of hat features a crown that is all one piece or divided in two with a central seam. The brim is slightly asymmetrical, being wider in front than in back, even if at times it is the other way around (depending on the design); the sides are also asymmetrical, having the front slightly higher than the back.
To construct the pattern, follow the instructions in the images, based on the measurement of the circumference of the head and the width of the brim desired.

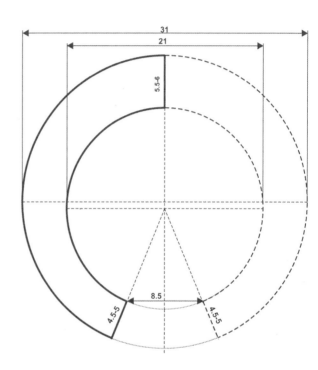

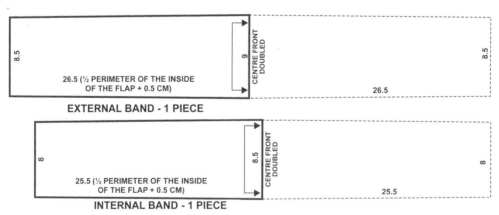

EXTERNAL BAND - 1 PIECE

26.5 (½ PERIMETER OF THE INSIDE OF THE FLAP + 0.5 CM)

INTERNAL BAND - 1 PIECE

25.5 (½ PERIMETER OF THE INSIDE OF THE FLAP + 0.5 CM)

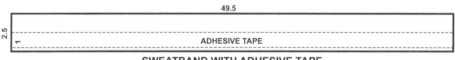

SWEATBAND WITH ADHESIVE TAPE

ADHESIVE TAPE

Hat with a central panel

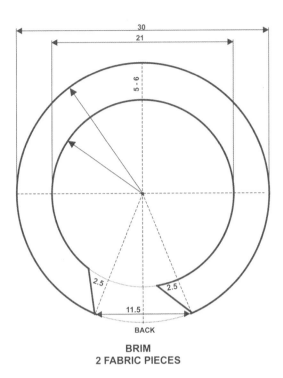

BRIM
2 FABRIC PIECES

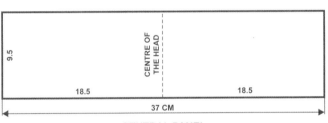

CENTRAL PANEL
1 FABRIC PIECE
1 LINING PIECE

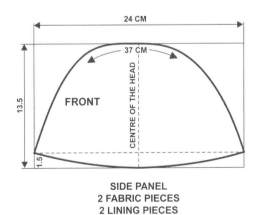

SIDE PANEL
2 FABRIC PIECES
2 LINING PIECES

This pattern features a crown composed of one central panel and two side panels.

The length of the central panel should coincide with the upper cut of the side panels.

The brim can be slightly asymmetrical, that is: larger in the front with respect to the back (even if at times it is the other way round, depending on the design). The side may also be asymmetrical, with the front being slightly higher than the back.

To construct the pattern, follow the instructions in the images, based on the measurement of the circumference of the head and the width of the brim desired.

4 PANEL HAT

PANEL FOR THE CROWN
4 PIECES

17
1.8
1.8
1.8
1.8
39
17
1.8
1.8
CENTRE BACK
1.8
SIDE BAND
1.8
17
39

BRIM
2 pieces

30
21
5 - 5.5
2.5
2.5
11.5
BACK

LINING - CROWN - PIECE

15.5
11.5

LINING - SIDE - 2 PIECES

4
0.5
0.5
4
SIDE BAND
SIDE BAND
CENTRE FRONT AND BACK
11.5
0.5
0.5
29

EXTERNAL BAND

58
2.8

Bucket hat

IN STIFF POLYESTER

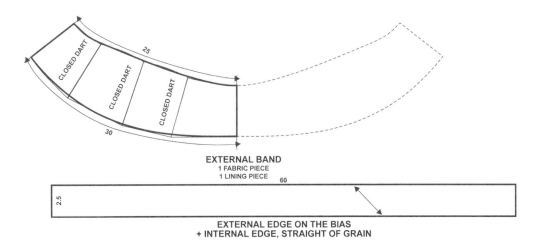

EXTERNAL BAND
1 FABRIC PIECE
1 LINING PIECE

60

2.5

EXTERNAL EDGE ON THE BIAS
+ INTERNAL EDGE, STRAIGHT OF GRAIN

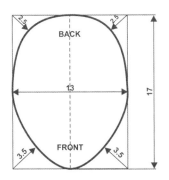

2.5 2.5

BACK

13

17

3.5 FRONT 3.5

PART ABOVE 1 PIECE OF FABRIC 1 LINING

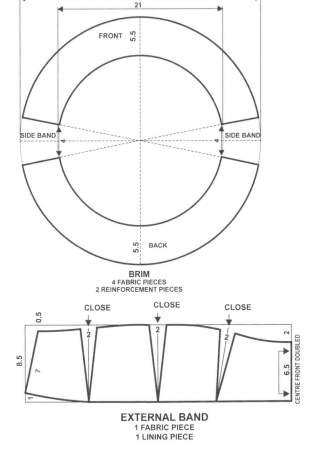

32
21

FRONT 5.5

SIDE BAND SIDE BAND

5.5 BACK

BRIM
4 FABRIC PIECES
2 REINFORCEMENT PIECES

0.5

CLOSE CLOSE CLOSE

2 2 2

8.5

7

1

6.5

2

CENTRE FRONT DOUBLED

EXTERNAL BAND
1 FABRIC PIECE
1 LINING PIECE

This type of hat has an inner covering along the top of the crown and a regular brim (having the front like the back), even if at times it can be asymmetrical.

To construct the pattern, follow the instructions in the images, based on the measurement of the circumference of the head and the width of the brim desired.

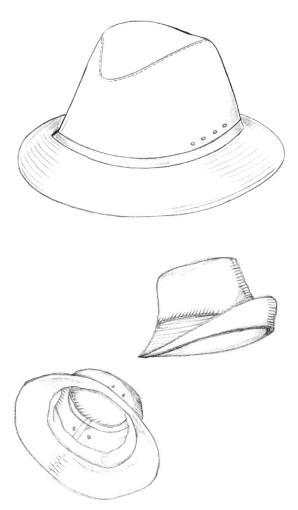

147

BERET

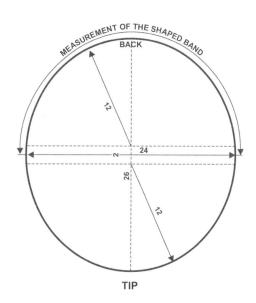

TIP

Introduction

The beret is a head covering typically worn by men, though today it is worn by women as well. It is snug along the head and can have a visor or not. In the past, the beret was used exclusively by workers (*casquette* in France) and by farmers (bonnets), while the bourgeoisie wore a bowler and important members of society wore a *Gibus*.

Berets were made of wool, cotton or waterproof types of fabrics. They are composed of:

- The tip, which is the upper part of the crown, made of just one piece or in panels.
- A shaped side, made of two curved pieces sewn on the sides.
- A lower band in the same fabric.
- An inner reinforcement of the lower leather band.
- An inner sweatband in grosgrain.
- Lining.

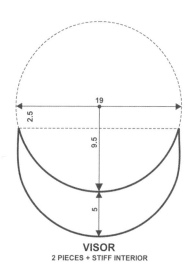

VISOR
2 PIECES + STIFF INTERIOR

Construction

- Size 60 (EU) - 7 3/8 (UK).
- Draw the elliptical tip, with a length of 26 cm and a width of 24 cm, as shown in the figure (10.24 x 9.45").
- Draw half the side, shaped to accommodate the length of the upper part, equal to half the circumference of the tip (38 cm/14.96") and the lower part which is 4 cm/1.57" shorter. The height is 6-6.5/2.36-2.56" on the centre front and back, and 5-5.5 cm/1.97-2.16" at the sides.
- Draw the lower edge, creating a rectangle whose length is equal to the circumference of the head +4 cm/1.57" (64 cm/25.20") and whose height is 3 cm/1.18".
- Draw the visor by creating a circle with a radius equal to that of the circumference of the head (e.g. head cir. 60 cm ÷ 3.4 + 0.5 cm = 19.61/7.72") At 5-5.5 cm/1.97-2.16", draw the outside arc as illustrated.
- Draw the patterns of the inner lining with the same shapes used for the tip and side.

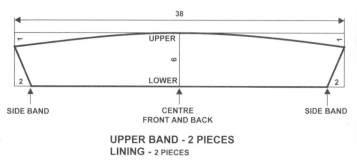

UPPER BAND - 2 PIECES
LINING - 2 PIECES

LOWER STRIP 2 PIECES
+ STIFF INTERIOR - 60.5 CM **+ GROSGRAIN** - 60.5 CM

CAP WITH A VISOR

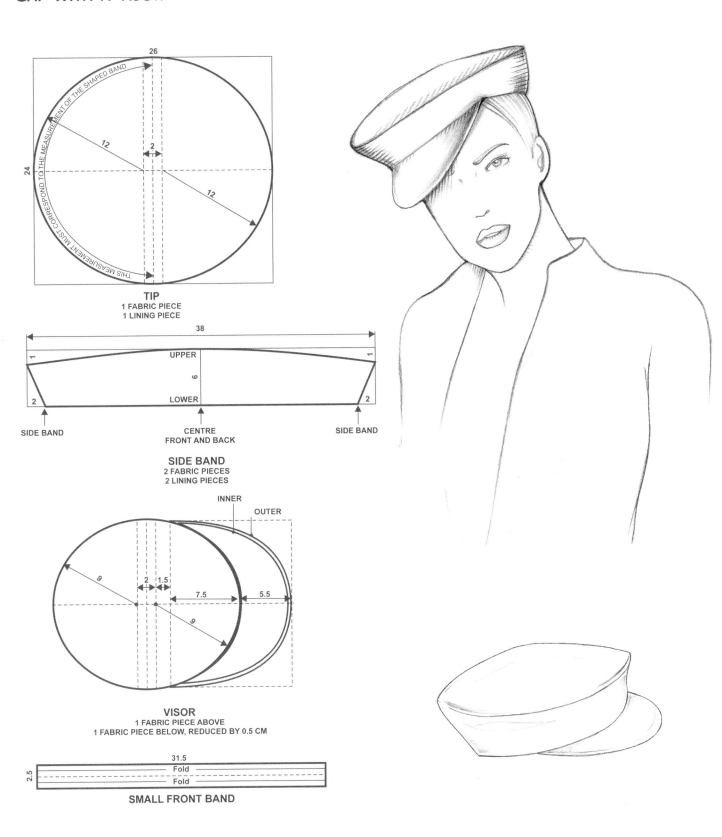

26

THIS MEASUREMENT MUST CORRESPOND TO THE MEASUREMENT OF THE SHAPED BAND

24

12

2

12

TIP
1 FABRIC PIECE
1 LINING PIECE

38

1

1

UPPER

6

2

LOWER

2

SIDE BAND

CENTRE
FRONT AND BACK

SIDE BAND

SIDE BAND
2 FABRIC PIECES
2 LINING PIECES

INNER

OUTER

9

2   1.5

7.5

5.5

9

VISOR
1 FABRIC PIECE ABOVE
1 FABRIC PIECE BELOW, REDUCED BY 0.5 CM

31.5

2.5

Fold

Fold

SMALL FRONT BAND

64

3

LOWER BAND 2 PIECES
+ STIFF INTERIOR - 60.5 CM + GROSGRAIN - 60.5 CM

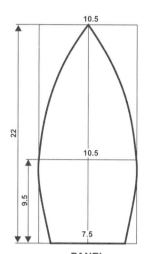

PANEL
9 FABRIC PIECES
9 LINING PIECES

10.5

22

10.5

9.5

7.5

This cap is made in soft fabric (velvet, coated cotton, nappa leather, faux leather, etc.) and can be made as 'one size fits all', as there is an elastic insert at the back, adapting it perfectly to all head sizes.

Draw the pattern, following the indications in the figures.
The seam margins are not included in the patterns, which should be added directly to the fabric or on the final cardboard pattern for mass production.

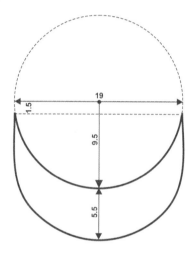

19

1.5

9.5

5.5

VISOR
2 PIECES + STIFF INTERIOR

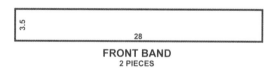

3.5

28

FRONT BAND
2 PIECES

3.5

FOLD

3.5

38

BACK BAND WITH ELASTIC
1 PIECE

ELASTIC - 27 CM/10.63", h. 3.5 CM/1.38"

GROSGRAIN - 62 CM/24.41", h. 2.5 CM/0.98"

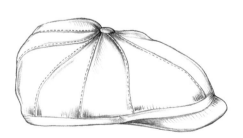

Patterned flat cap

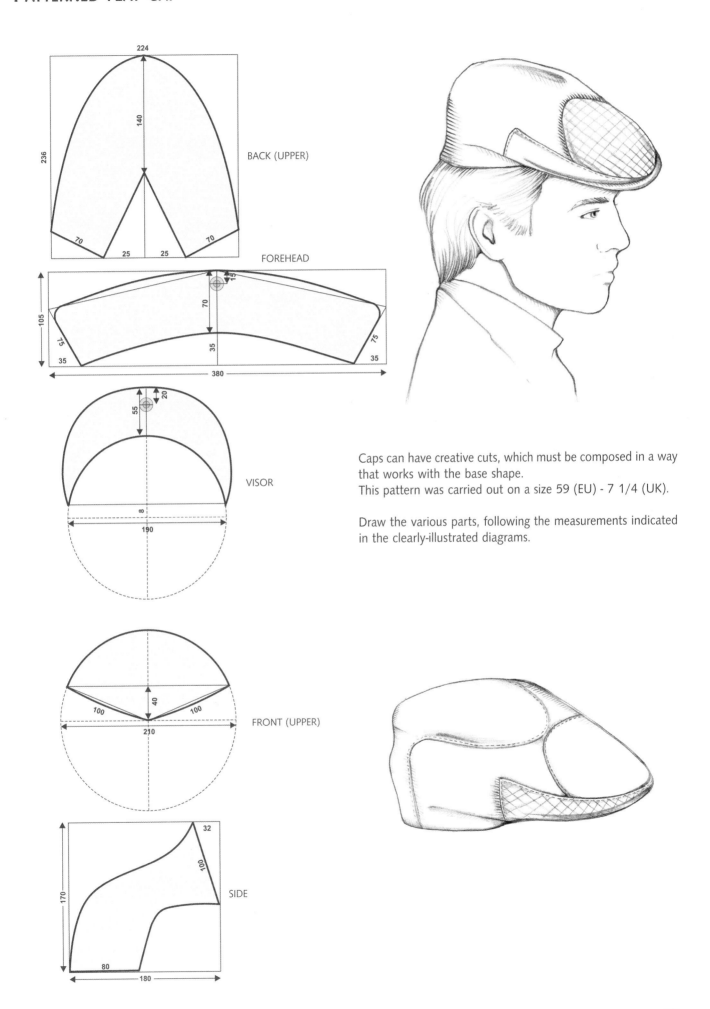

224

140

236

BACK (UPPER)

70   70

25   25

FOREHEAD

105

15

70

75

75

35

35

35

380

20

55

8

VISOR

190

Caps can have creative cuts, which must be composed in a way
that works with the base shape.
This pattern was carried out on a size 59 (EU) - 7 1/4 (UK).

Draw the various parts, following the measurements indicated
in the clearly-illustrated diagrams.

40

100   100

FRONT (UPPER)

210

32

100

170

SIDE

80

180

Schoolboy cap

SIX PANELS, ONE SIZE FITS ALL (60 EU - 7 3/8 UK), WITH AN ADJUSTABLE STRAP

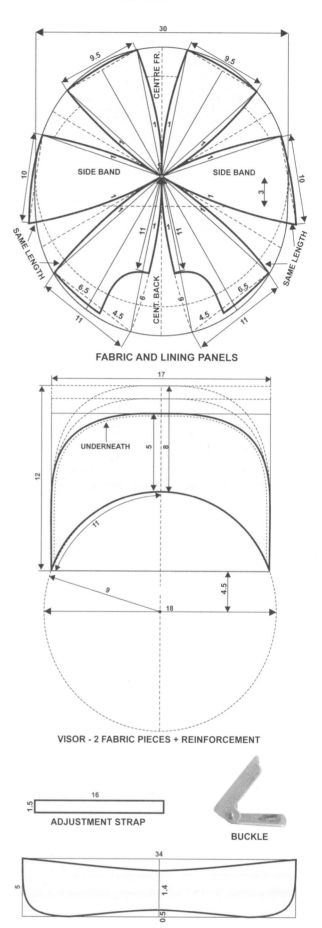

FABRIC AND LINING PANELS

VISOR - 2 FABRIC PIECES + REINFORCEMENT

ADJUSTMENT STRAP

BUCKLE

EAR FLAP: 1 PIECE OF FABRIC AND 1 PIECE OF LINING OR FELT

Size: One size fits all (head circumference 60 cm/23.62")

Crown panels

- Draw two circles with a 15 cm/5.91" radius whose centres are 3 cm/1.81" apart and connect them with an elliptical form.
- Divide the elliptical circle in six equal parts.
- Draw the panels with different measurements, as in the figure.
- Create the opening on the back for the adjustment strap.

Visor (or brim)

- Draw a circle with a 9 cm/3.54" radius.
- At 4.5 cm/1.77" from the centre, draw a rectangle that is 9-13 cm/3.54-5.12" high (or as desired, based on the desired length) and with a length equal to the diameter of the circle that creates the tip circumference minus 7-8 mm/0.28-0.31".
- Shape the visor as in the figure.
- The upper part of the visor should be about 4-5 cm/1.57-1.97" larger to encompass the lower seam.

Brimless cap

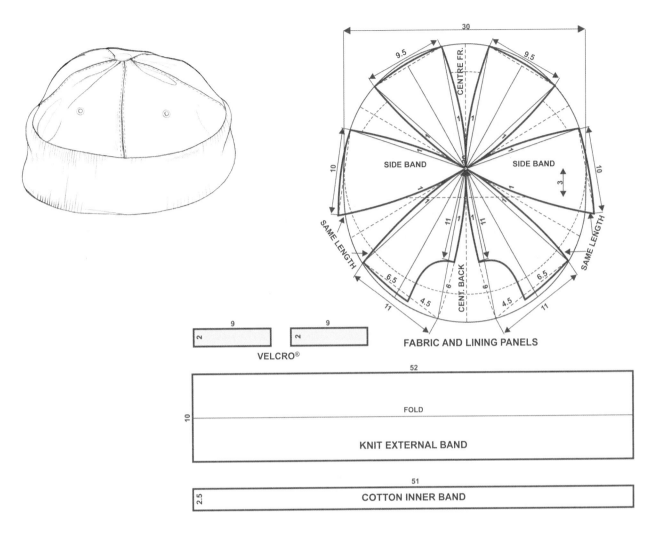

30

9.5   CENTRE FR.   9.5

1 1

SIDE BAND   SIDE BAND

10   3   10

SAME LENGTH   SAME LENGTH

1   1

11 1 1 11

6.5   6   6   6.5

CENT. BACK

11   4.5   4.5   11

FABRIC AND LINING PANELS

9   9

2   2

VELCRO®

52

FOLD

10

KNIT EXTERNAL BAND

51

2.5   COTTON INNER BAND

Cuffed micro fleece beanie

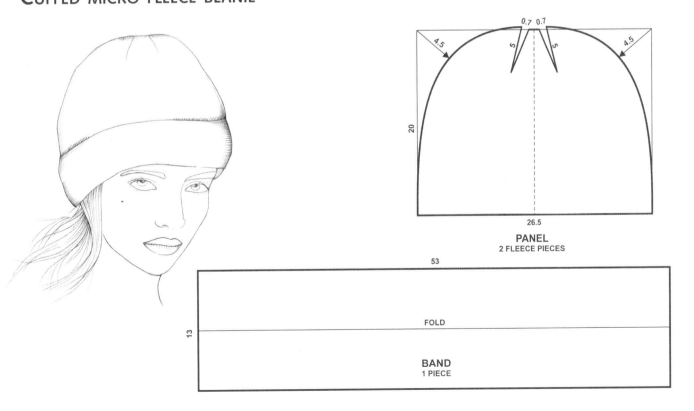

0.7 0.7

4.5   5   5   4.5

20

26.5

PANEL
2 FLEECE PIECES

53

FOLD

13

BAND
1 PIECE

BASEBALL CAP

5 PANELS

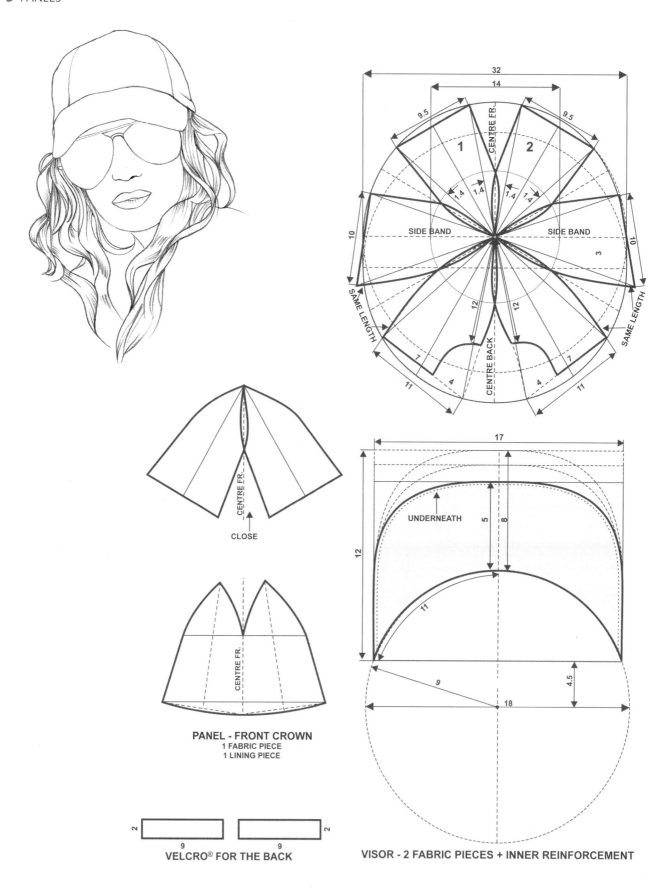

CLOSE

CENTRE FR.

32

14

9.5

9.5

CENTRE FR.

1

2

1.4 **1.4** **1.4** **1.4**

SIDE BAND

SIDE BAND

10

3

10

SAME LENGTH

SAME LENGTH

12

12

CENTRE BACK

7

7

11

4

4

11

17

UNDERNEATH

5

8

12

11

9

18

4.5

PANEL - FRONT CROWN
1 FABRIC PIECE
1 LINING PIECE

CENTRE FR.

2

9

2

9

VELCRO® FOR THE BACK

VISOR - 2 FABRIC PIECES + INNER REINFORCEMENT

To create this type of cap, the front panel needs to be doubled,
sewing the upper part of the centre front.

7 PANEL BASEBALL CAP

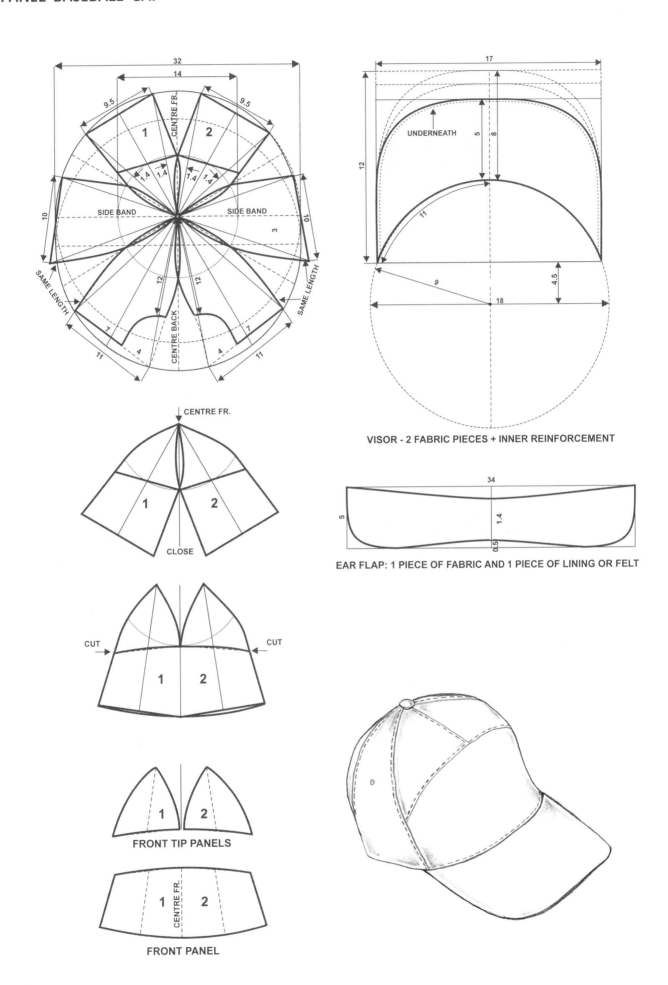

32

14

9.5 CENTRE FR. 9.5

1   2

1.4 1.4 1.4 1.4

SIDE BAND   SIDE BAND

10   10

3

SAME LENGTH   12   12   SAME LENGTH

7   7

11   4   CENTRE BACK   4   11

17

12   UNDERNEATH   5   8

11

9   18   4.5

VISOR - 2 FABRIC PIECES + INNER REINFORCEMENT

CENTRE FR.

1   2

CLOSE

CUT   1   2   CUT

34

5   1.4   0.5

EAR FLAP: 1 PIECE OF FABRIC AND 1 PIECE OF LINING OR FELT

1   2

FRONT TIP PANELS

CENTRE FR.

1   2

FRONT PANEL

BASEBALL CAP WITH A CENTRAL PANEL

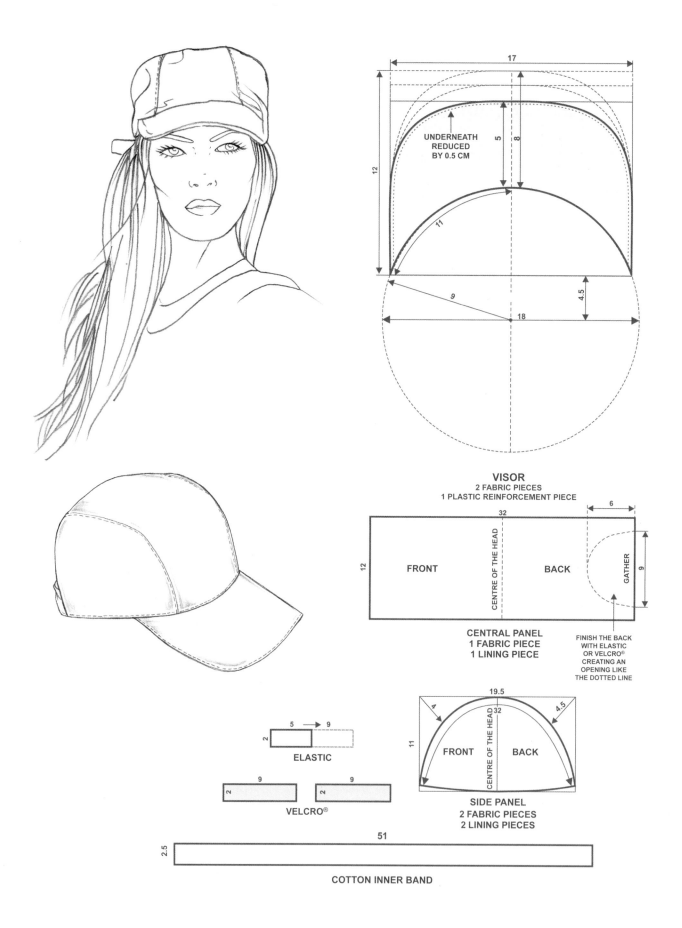

17

UNDERNEATH
REDUCED
BY 0.5 CM

12

5

8

11

9

4.5

18

VISOR
2 FABRIC PIECES
1 PLASTIC REINFORCEMENT PIECE

32

12

FRONT

CENTRE OF THE HEAD

BACK

6

GATHER

9

CENTRAL PANEL
1 FABRIC PIECE
1 LINING PIECE

FINISH THE BACK
WITH ELASTIC
OR VELCRO®
CREATING AN
OPENING LIKE
THE DOTTED LINE

5 → 9

2

ELASTIC

9

9

2

2

VELCRO®

19.5

4

32

4.5

11

FRONT

CENTRE OF THE HEAD

BACK

SIDE PANEL
2 FABRIC PIECES
2 LINING PIECES

51

2.5

COTTON INNER BAND

EQUESTRIAN HELMET

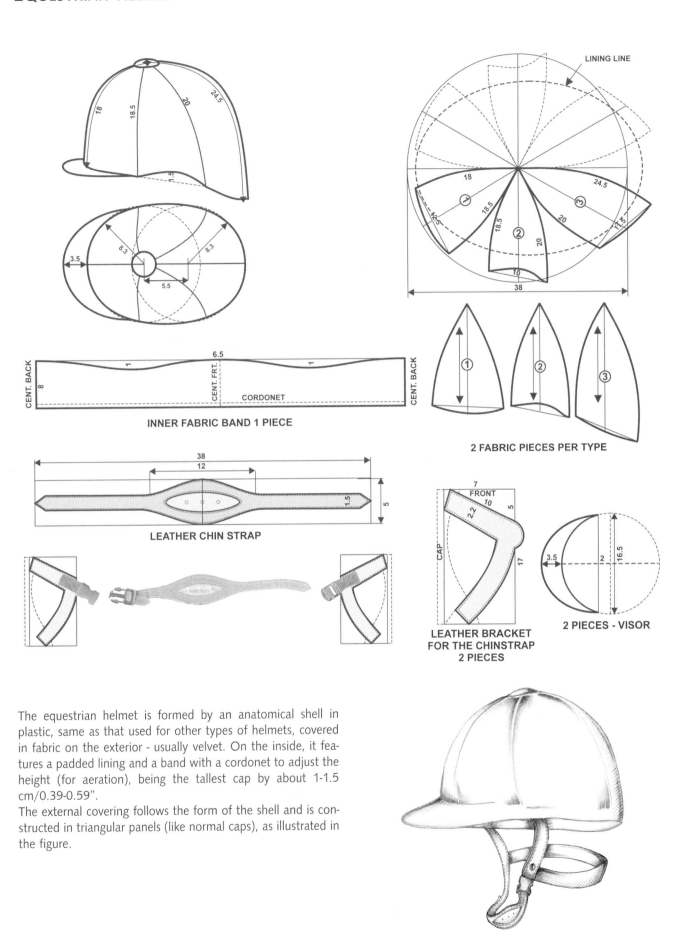

INNER FABRIC BAND 1 PIECE

2 FABRIC PIECES PER TYPE

LEATHER CHIN STRAP

LEATHER BRACKET
FOR THE CHINSTRAP
2 PIECES

2 PIECES - VISOR

LINING LINE

CORDONET

CENT. BACK

CENT. FRT.

CENT. BACK

FRONT

CAP

The equestrian helmet is formed by an anatomical shell in plastic, same as that used for other types of helmets, covered in fabric on the exterior - usually velvet. On the inside, it features a padded lining and a band with a cordonet to adjust the height (for aeration), being the tallest cap by about 1-1.5 cm/0.39-0.59".

The external covering follows the form of the shell and is constructed in triangular panels (like normal caps), as illustrated in the figure.

COLBACK WITH EAR FLAPS
SIZE 59 (EU) - 7 1/4 (UK)

The colback is a natural or synthetic fur cap. Originally it was a military head covering worn by Russian, Turkish (Kolpak) and Armenian soldiers, adopted by the armies of various European regions as well: French, English, Italian (used by cavalrymen). In a more or less elongated cylinder (that used by English imperial guards is quite long), it was often used in men's and women's winter fashions, with various stylistic solutions. This model is quite simple: cylindrical in shape, it has a strip of fur cuffed up and around it and wool earflaps hidden on the inside. To create this pattern, follow the instructions illustrated in the figures.

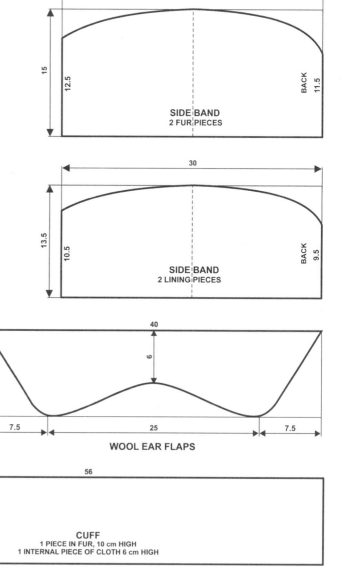

158

RUSSIAN FUR CAP

WITH EAR FLAPS AND A VISOR - SIZE 60 (EU) - 7 3/8 (UK)

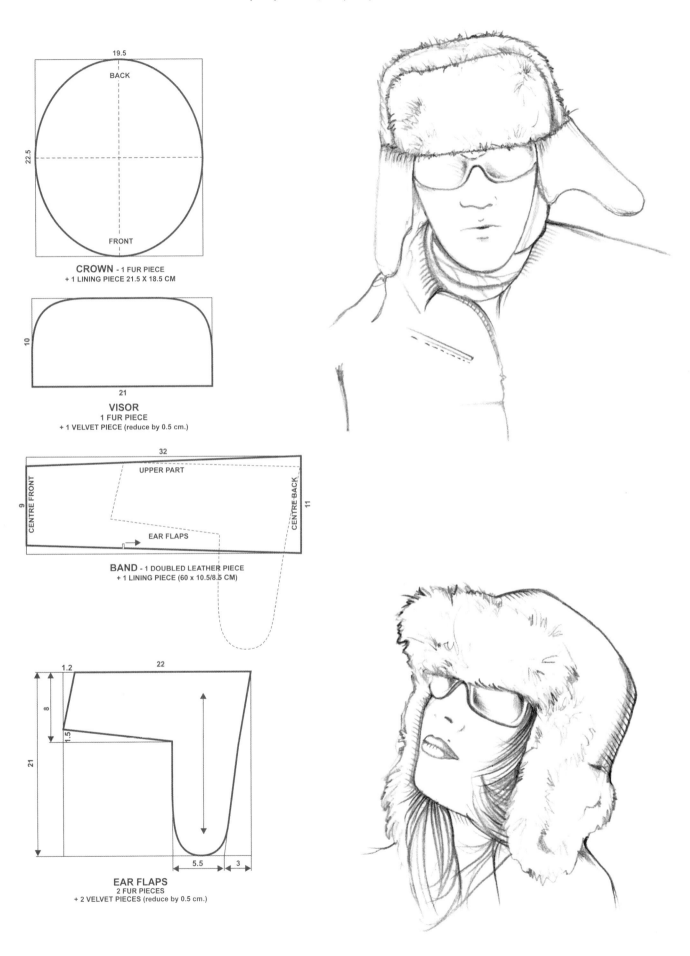

19.5

BACK

22.5

FRONT

CROWN - 1 FUR PIECE
+ 1 LINING PIECE 21.5 X 18.5 CM

10

21

VISOR
1 FUR PIECE
+ 1 VELVET PIECE (reduce by 0.5 cm.)

32

UPPER PART

CENTRE FRONT

9

CENTRE BACK

11

EAR FLAPS

BAND - 1 DOUBLED LEATHER PIECE
+ 1 LINING PIECE (60 x 10.5/8.5 CM)

1.2

22

8

1.5

21

5.5

3

EAR FLAPS
2 FUR PIECES
+ 2 VELVET PIECES (reduce by 0.5 cm.)

159

Bandanna 1

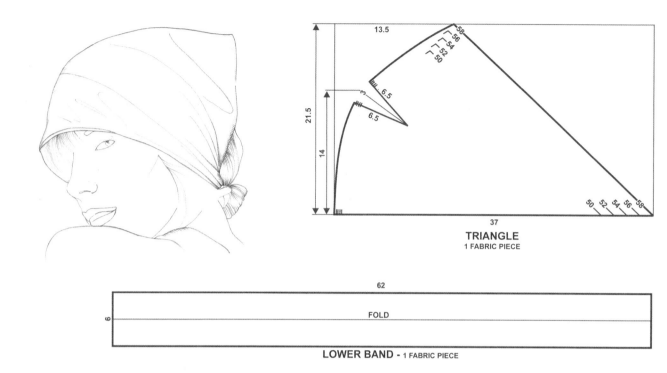

TRIANGLE
1 FABRIC PIECE

13.5
21.5
14
6.5
3
6.5
58
56
54
52
50
50 52 54 56 58
37

62
FOLD
6

LOWER BAND - 1 FABRIC PIECE

Bandanna 2

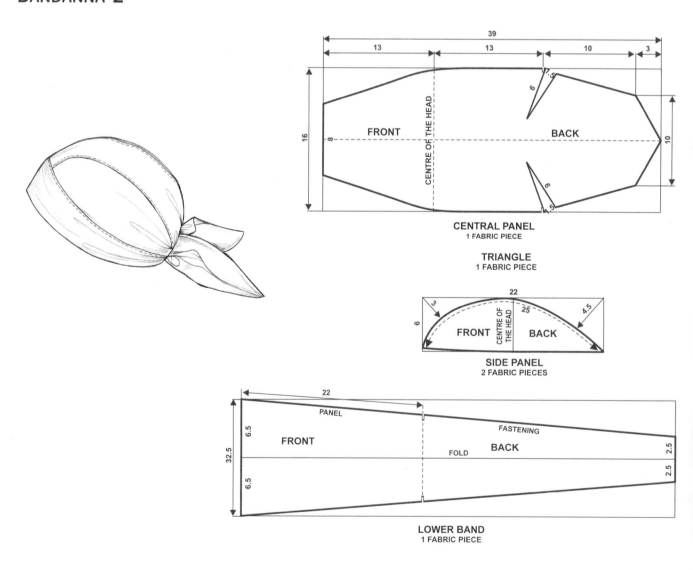

39
13
13
10
3
16
8
FRONT
CENTRE OF THE HEAD
BACK
6
6
1.5
4.5
10

CENTRAL PANEL
1 FABRIC PIECE

TRIANGLE
1 FABRIC PIECE

22
3
25
4.5
6
FRONT
CENTRE OF THE HEAD
BACK

SIDE PANEL
2 FABRIC PIECES

22
PANEL
FASTENING
32.5
6.5
6.5
FRONT
FOLD
BACK
2.5
2.5

LOWER BAND
1 FABRIC PIECE

GLOVES

History. 162
1929 - 2009. 164
Lines and types 166
Glove terminology 167
Tools 168
Anatomy of the hand 169
Measuring the hand 170
Form-fitting glove base (women). 171
Form-fitting glove base (men) 172
Glove seams. 175
Ski gloves. 176
Artisan working phases. 178

Mitten, 16th century *16th century* *Lace, 16th century* *With inserts, 16th century.* *Steel protective glove* *17th century*

Long women's gloves, mid 18th cen. *French Directory* *1830* *19th century* *19th century (Sarah Bernhardt)*

Gloves are coverings for the hand, made to adhere to it and thus created in the same shape.

Already in use by the *Egyptians* and in a few parts of *Asia*, having arrived to *Greece* and *Rome*, they were at first rarely worn as ornamentation. Then, increasingly, gloves became a symbolic tool loaded with meaning in ceremonies, especially following their spread after Barbarian invasions.

In the *Middle Ages*, gloves were part of the feudal investiture rite, a sign of trust in the woman they were given to, or a sign of challenge or contempt if thrown or slammed.

In the *9th century*, the first women's gloves appeared in silk and wool, closed at the wrist with three small buttons, or with a roomy cuff, often lined in fur. Leather versions were worn to ride horses, while only one was needed for falconry.

Frederick II, the King of Sicily, wore gloves similar to those seen in ancient Greece, decorated with golden foil embroidery, precious stones and pearls. Gloves for dignitaries were in finely-embroidered white leather.

In the *1200s*, Italy was famous for especially embellished gloves. Leather was sometimes tanned with fragrant essences but, at at other times (it was suspected), with poison intended to quickly settle a score.

By the *1300s*, gloves were commonly worn. Sumptuous leather gloves, woven with gold threads, dot the first century of the Renaissance, often also including precious applied gems. The novelty of colour (scarlet, violet, green) distinguished ecclesiastical hierarchies: the Pope wore white gloves with pearls.

There were also cloth gloves, called *ciroteca*, or *muffole* (mittens). In the *1500s*, instead of applying gemstones to the gloves, cuts were created to let cabochon rings worn on the fingers show through. Women's gloves, almost entirely in gold thread, became so rich and costly that sumptuary laws were created for them: it was illegal to own more than 32 pairs.

In the *1600s*, there were many different varieties in satin, velvet and cloth, enriched by lace, fringe and embroidery.

In the *1700s*, people began focusing on their utility without losing any of their elegance. Those lined in down were very common but, in general, gloves were almost always carried in the hand. "Iced" (that is, shiny, in glacé leather), these gloves cost twice as much as those in kidskin; if they were then in beaver skin, the glove maker himself was the only one who knew how to wash them without damaging them.

Women possessed an extraordinary number of them, all quite varied, even as many as 72 pairs. Gloves became shorter or longer depending on the length of the sleeve.

At the time of the *French Directory*, fashion dictated that they be tight and long to cover the arms left exposed by evening gowns. Men wore just one, in only one colour: white.

162

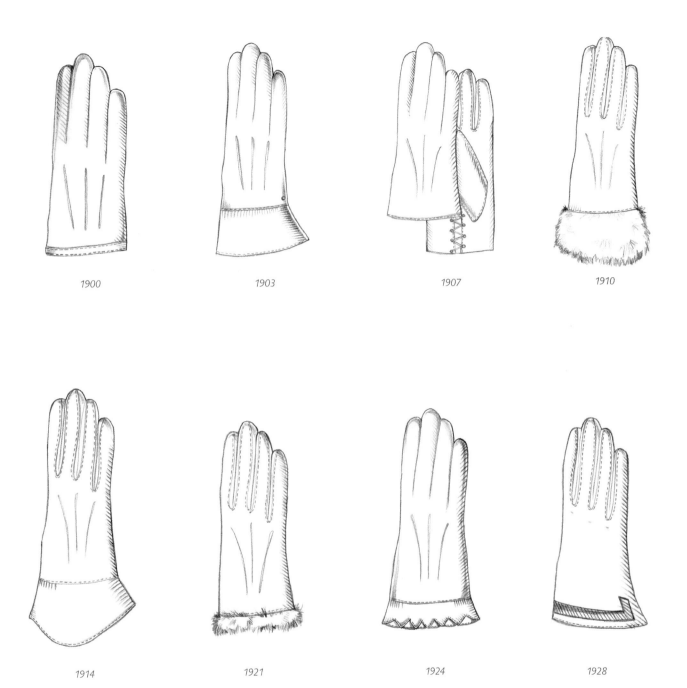

1900

1903

1907

1910

1914

1921

1924

1928

In the first three decades of the 1800s, with the return of elite clothing, even gloves became part of refined style, choosing, according to the outfit, colours tending towards neon: bergamot peel, Boreal blue and fleshy pink. Subtle pin tucking, silver embroidery and woven tulle inserts indicated the gloves were from Naples, the largest producer of this elegant accessory at the time for both Europe and the USA.

It was during this era that fingerless gloves were in fashion, almost always in mesh. Around the mid 1800s, elegant women never left the house without gloves, generally short and closed with two small buttons, or, at times, exceptionally long, decorated at the top by small flower garlands, lace or ermine. Gloves were also worn at home, generally fingerless and in wool, and, rarely, in velvet. For men, the alternative to those in lisle (mercerised cotton) were yellow leather gloves (which became synonymous with the gentlemanly, unsuspicious thief) during the day,

white for the evening. At the end of the 1800s, no longer the essentially elegant accessory or for protection against the cold, gloves took on the role of defending the hand from contact with surfaces. They were a sign of distinction and distance, while the numerous 'good taste' manuals took it upon themselves to draft rules for presenting a bare hand. After the revolution in fashion that took place in the 1920s, which saw the return of long gloves left to fall and ripple softly on the forearm, gloves closely followed evolving tastes. They became more complex with musketeer-like cuffs and colourful inserts; they were made in crocodile and boar; they had straw palms, leather on the back; they met the needs of the hand upon the steering wheel; they disappeared from used except in winter; they reappeared in mesh or silk for summer; and they triumphed in wool among the youth. Forgotten for years, they return every so often to highlight a casual or military-inspired look.

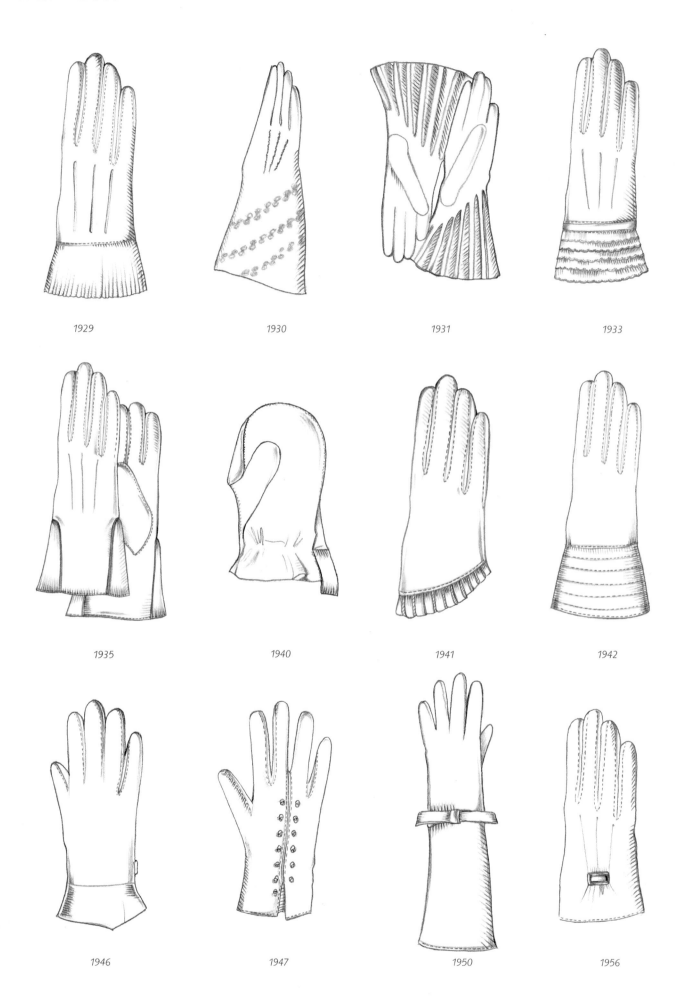

1929

1930

1931

1933

1935

1940

1941

1942

1946

1947

1950

1956

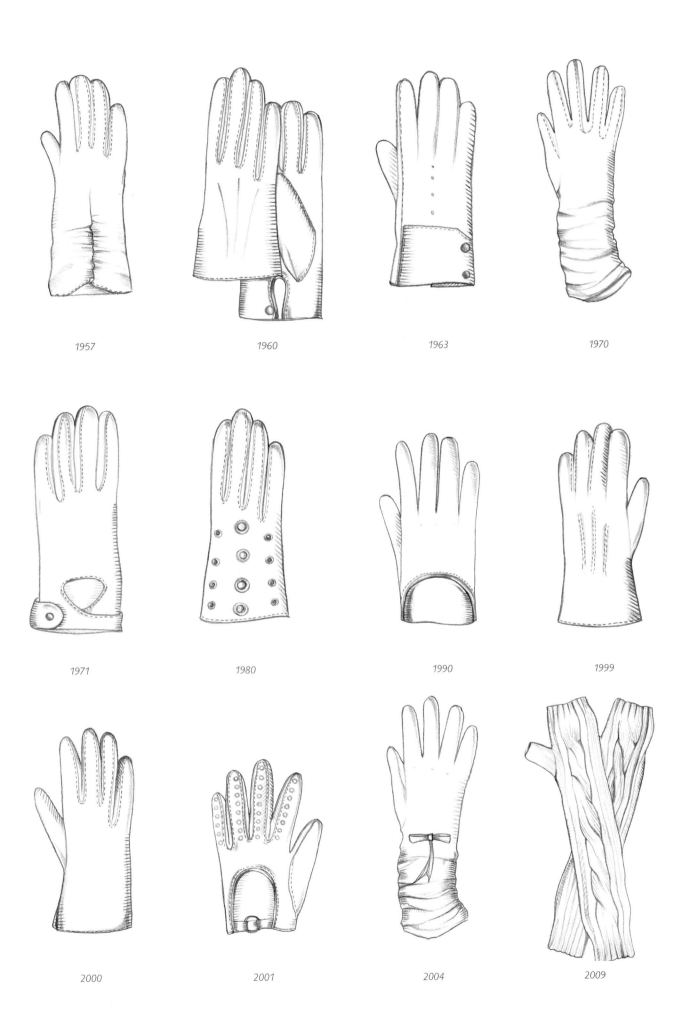

1957

1960

1963

1970

1971

1980

1990

1999

2000

2001

2004

2009

LINES AND TYPES

Women's day gloves

Men's day gloves

Women's evening gloves

Golf gloves

Ski gloves

Snow mitts

Goalie gloves

Weightlifting gloves

Cycling gloves

Boxing gloves

Full contact kickbox-ing gloves

Boxing bag gloves

Kumité gloves

Baseball glove

Unlike the lines of other garments, gloves have changed little in recent years.

Gloves can be: for day, evening or formal ceremonies; for sports or work.

Day, evening and formal gloves

Classic gloves to be worn during the day are usually in kidskin or lambskin. They can be unlined, lined or padded.

After an initial selection, the hides then go through a second selection round according to three main types:

1) Shiny gloves: when the epidermis of the animal (the external or 'grain' side) corresponds to the 'right side' or exterior of the glove.

2) Suede gloves: when the flesh side corresponds to the exterior of the glove. They are velvety to the touch.

3) Split leather glove. when the grain and flesh side are cut thinly until the core of the leather; the face, initially grain, corresponds to the 'right side' of the glove and has a velvety appearance. Soft gloves, in mixed sueded and shiny leather, will generally thus be in suede.

These three main types of leather will be necessary to carry out the four most important types of gloves:

1) Saxon gloves, in which the extension of the glove to its edge doesn't require any openings or vents.

2) "Crispine" gloves whose extension towards the forearm is reinforced, making them stiffer. This extension is why different materials, such as silk, leather, etc. have been sought out and used.

3) Gloves with cuffs or rolls: a type of Crispine glove where the softer extension on the end is folded over the hand.

4) Long (evening) gloves, that often end with a small opening that may extend up the entire arm and which may be closed with buttons, snaps, clasps, clips, hooks or vegetable ivory (corozo).

Sports gloves

These gloves come in different shapes and sizes, depending on the athletic activity they are destined for.

Work gloves

These gloves are made of materials able to protect the hand from chemicals, heat, freezing temperatures, etc.

Glove terminology

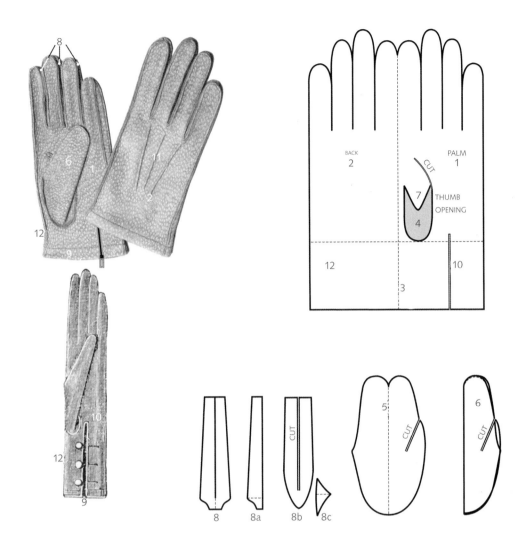

1) The palm.

2) The back.
The ends of the fingers are to be extended; this variant serves to encircle the thickness of the fingers.

3) Glove pattern with two joined parts (called the "trank"), composed of eight fingers, two of which are the same.
The back of the glove pattern should be slightly bigger in terms of its measurements than the palm to fit the hand properly.

4) Thumb hole, executed on the palm side.

5) Pattern for the thumb.

6) Folded thumb.

7) In the thumb hole, a round insert can be added that, connected to the thumb, will act as a bellows, connected directly to the glove or detached, that will offer greater mobility to the hand.

8) Fourchettes. The fingers, which are part of the back and the palm, are united with three doubled or six individual strips of leather per glove, called *fourchettes*, to compensate for the thickness of the fingers.

8a) Half fourchette. A pair of gloves requires 12 half fourchettes; 6 per glove.

8b) Fourchette with a bellows. This type of fourchette makes it easier to move the finger, but it is much more tedious to sew.

8c) Quirk for the bellows.

9) The upper part of the glove will be edged with a strip of soft leather, creating the hem.

10) A small strip to be sewn along the opening called the *button slit* to improve the fit.

11) "Points" to improve the shape. The glove can feature one or three "points" (pintucks or seams), carried out on the back by hand or with a dual-needle sewing machine.

12) The cuff of the glove body.

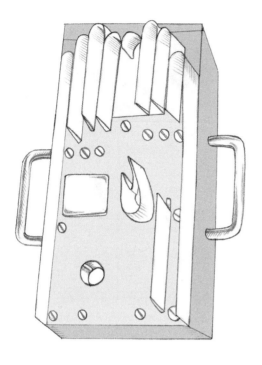

Glove body die punch

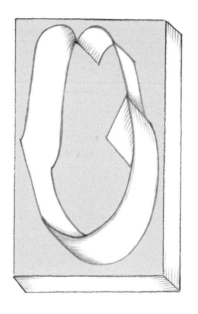

Thumb die punch

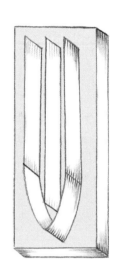

Fourchette die punch

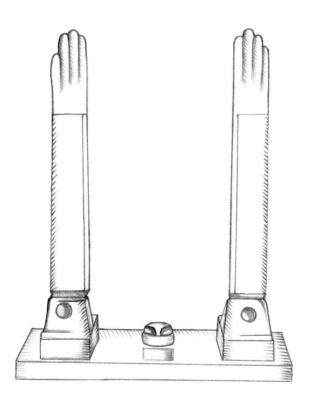

Tool to straighten and iron finished gloves

Glove turner

Anatomy of the hand

Bones

The skeleton of the hand supports a complex system of muscles and tendons. It is made up of 27 bones, divided into three groups: *the carpus, metacarpus, and phalanxes (fingers).*

The carpus corresponds to the wrist and is made up of 8 small bones arranged in two rows: the *scaphoid*, the *lunate*, the *tirquetrum* and the *pisiform* make up the first row, and the *trapezium, trapezoid, capitate* and *hamate* make up the second. The carpus is articulated on one side by the distal extremity of the forearm bone and, on the other, by the bones of the metacarpus, composed in turn of 5 long bones, called metacarpals. Each metacarpal bone is followed by the bones of the corresponding finger, which itself is made up of three elongated *phalanges* (first, second and third *phalanges*, or *phalanxes*, except the thumb, which only has two) that get progressively shorter towards the fingertips. The different bones of the hand are connected to quite complex *capillary*, *ligamentary* and *tendon* systems which grant the hand a wide variety of movements. The two essential fulcrums of hand movements are: *radio-carpal articulation*, which makes it possible to bend, extend, abduct, adduct or, following the movement of the forearm, bring the hand *prone* (ie, brining the palm upwards) or *supine* (with the palm facing down); the metacarpophalangeal joints make it possible to flex, extend and adduct or abduct the fingers. Plus, their opposition (especially when it comes to the thumb), allows the greatest possibility of movement.

Muscles

Above the skeleton of the hand is an extremely complex muscle and tendon system. There are 19 hand muscles, grouped into 3 zones: a lateral region for the thumb, called the *thenar eminence*; a medial region for the little finder, the *hypothenar eminence* and an intermediary zone.

These muscles are joined by tendons that reach the carpal bones and the fingers from the forearm. The first muscles are also called the intrinsic muscles of the hand; the second ones are called the extrinsic muscles of the hand. The latter are the long muscles that originate from the forearm and the humerous; they are the: flexor digitorum profundus tendon, the flexor pollicis longus tendon, the extensor digitorum, the ext. indicis tendon, the extensor digiti minimi, the extensor pollicis longus, and the abductor pollicis longus.

The intrinsic musculature is created by small muscles located, on humans, on the palm. They are: the interossei (3 volarly and 4 dorsally), *four lubrical* muscles, the thenar eminence muscles (adductor, short flexor, short abductor and the opponens pollicis); the hypothenar eminence muscles are the palmaris brevis, the abductor and the flexor of the digiti minimi, as well as the opponens digiti minimi). In particular, the lumbrical muscles determine the ability to flex the first phalanx and the extension of the other two; the interossei muscles flex the first phalanx and extend the other two, drawing the fingers either closer together or further apart.

Above and between the muscle groups, there are bands or *aponeuroses*, which are divided into: palmar and extensor hoods (on the back of the hand). The palmar aponeurosis (palmar fascia) include: the superficial fascia, placed just below the skin, and the deep fascia, placed below the flexor tendons. In

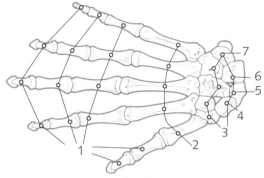

Hand skeleton, posterior view (back)
1. Phalanges; 2. Metacarpals; 3. Carpals; 4. Pisiform;
5. Tirquetrum; 6. Lunate; 7. Scaphoid.

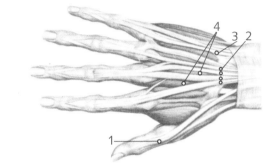

Muscles and tendons, posterior view (back)
1. Extensor pollicis longus tendon; 2. Dorsal interossei muscles; 3. Extensor digiti minimi tendon; 4. Extensor digitorum.

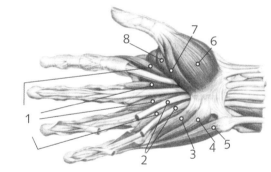

Muscles and tendons, anterior view (palm)
1. Lumbrical muscles; 2. Tendons; 3. Digiti minimi brevis flexor;
4. Opponens digiti minimi; 5. Short abductor of the digiti minimi;
6. Abductor pollicis brevis; 7. Flexor pollicis brevis.

the dorsal region, we also have a superficial dorsal fascia, placed just below the skin, and a deep dorsal fascia, placed in the interosseous spaces. In addition, there are tendons found in special tendon sheaths.

The hand is served by radial and ulnar arteries that are connected by anastomosis, forming a double arch in the palm, from which branches head out directly into the distal parts. Sensory and motor innervation depends on the median and ulnar nerves; the extrinsic muscles are innerved also by the radial nerve. All these nerves are branches of the brachial plexus.

MEASURING THE HAND

The hand is as long as the face, from the chin to the hairline. A person should be 8.5 of their hands "tall". So, if someone is 170 cm/66.23" tall, the calculation would be: 170 cm ÷ 8.5 = approx 20 cm/7.87".
The circumference of the hand should be barely less than its length up to the base of the thumb.

Measurements

HAND LENGTH - This measurement is taken lengthwise, from the base of the thumb, or just before the fold of the wrist, to the very end of the longest finger.

HAND CIRCUMFERENCE - This measurement (the very hand of the glove itself) is taken by passing a centimetre measuring tape around a closed fist to ensure the hand muscles are engaged.

TOTAL GLOVE LENGTH - The comprehensive measurement of the hand length plus the desired extension.

WRIST OR ARM CIRCUMFERENCE - Taken from the position where the edge of the glove happens to be, based on the total length of the glove.

Glove extension

The unit of measurement of the glove extension will be the "button", equivalent to the length of a thumb (25.4 mm/1"). The width of the opening of the glove (the hem), will be proportionate along its length: the longer the glove is, the wider the opening will be, correlated to the diameter of the arm where the hem will ultimately rest.

Gloves are almost always completed in a single piece: hand and extension together.

However, extremely long gloves - those with 18, 20, 24, 30, 32 or 36 buttons - are designed and sewn to dovetail into two parts.

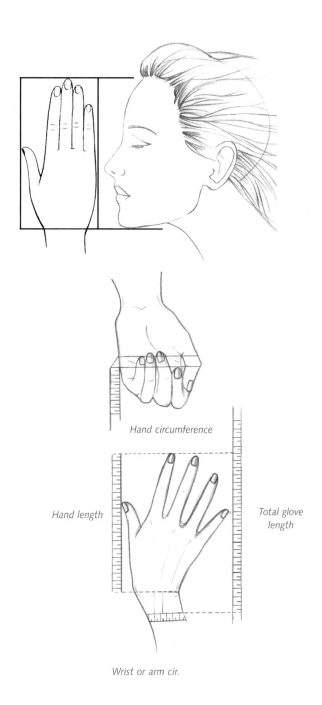

Hand circumference

Hand length

Total glove length

Wrist or arm cir.

WOMEN'S SIZE TABLE								
Size or Measure		S		M		L		XL
		6	6 ½	7	7 ½	8	8 ½	9
Imperial measure In inches	HAND CIR.	6	6 ½	7	7 ½	8	8 ½	9
	HAND LENGTH	5 ¾	6 ¼	6 ¾	7 ¼	7 ¾	8	8 ¼
Metric measure In millimetres	HAND CIR.	152	165	178	191	204	217	230
	HAND LENGTH	145	157	170	185	197	210	222

MEN'S SIZE TABLE								
Size or Measure		S		M		L		XL
		7	7 ½	8	8 ½	9	9 ½	10
Imperial measure In inches	HAND CIR	7	7 ½	8	8 ½	9	9 ½	10
	HAND LENGTH	6 ¾	7 ¼	7 ¾	8 ¼	8 ¾	9 ¼	9 ¾
Metric measure In millimetres	HAND CIR	178	191	204	217	230	243	256
	HAND LENGTH	170	185	190,5	210	222	235	247

Sizes (or measurements)

The measurements or size of the glove, taken in inches, will depend on the size of the hand, taken with the measuring tape so as to have:
- A hand that is 7 inches wide will fit a size M or 7.
- A 7½ inch wide hand will fit a size M or 7½, etc.

Glove eases

Gloves can have the following eases:
- Tight and unlined: with an ease from -10 mm to -25 mm (-0.39 to -0.98"), based on the stretch of the leather or fabric.
- Tight and lined: with an ease of 0.5 mm to 15 mm (0.02 to 0.59").
- Fitted: with an ease of 0.5 mm to 15 mm (0.02 to 0.59").
- Padded: with an ease of 10 mm to 30 mm (0.39 to 1.18").

FORM-FITTING GLOVE BASE (WOMEN)

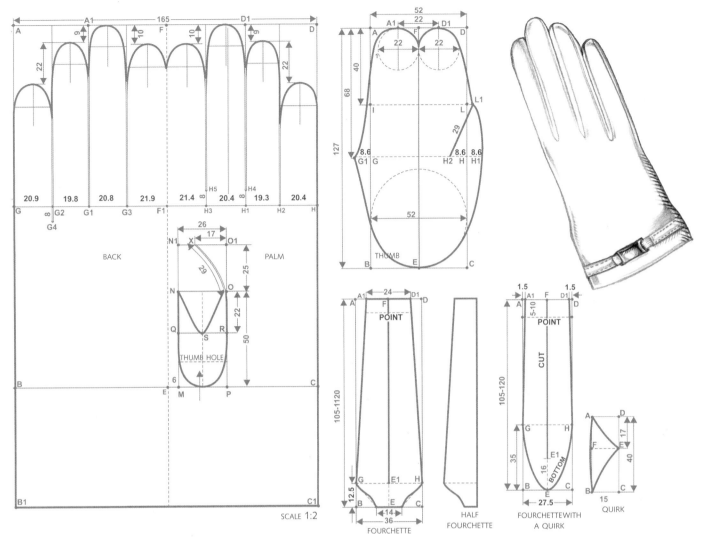

SCALE 1:2

Measurements (Size 7½ or M):
Hand circumference 191 mm/7.52"; hand length 185 mm/7.28";
Circumference ease 25 mm/0.98".

Glove
- Draw rectangle A-B-C-D, with:
- A-B equal to the length of the hand (180-195 mm/7.09-7.68")
- B-C equal to the circumference of the hand minus 2-2.5 cm/0.79-0.98") or the ease (e.g.: 190 - 25 = 165 mm/6.50")
- B-E half of B-C + 1 mm/0.04" (83.5 mm/3.29"). Draw E-F
- B-B1 and C-C1 desired wrist length (e.g. 67 mm/2.64")
- Draw B1-C1
- A-G half of A-B (92.5 mm/3.64"). Draw G-H
- G-F1 like B-E
- G-G1 half of G-F1-1 mm/0.04" (e.g.: 83.5 ÷ 2.= 41.75 - 1 = 40.75/1.60")
- G-G2 half of G-G1 + 0.5 mm/0.02" (20.9 mm/0.82")
- F1-G3 half of F1-G1 + 0.5 mm/0.02" (21.9 mm/0.86")
- H-H1 half of H-F1 - 1 mm/0.04" (e.g. 81.5 mm ÷ 2 = 40.75 - 1 = 39.75 mm/1.56")
- H1-H2 half of H-H1 + 0.5 mm/0.02" (20.4 mm/0.80")
- F1-H3 half of F1-H1 + 0.5 mm/0.02" (21.4 mm/0.84")
- G2-G4 8 mm/0.31". H1-H4 and H3-H5 8 mm/0.31".

Thumb hole
- E-M 6 mm/0.24"
- Draw a rectangle M-N-O-P, where:
- N-M = 50 mm/1.97" and M-P = 26 mm/1.02"
- N-Q and O-R = 22 mm/0.87". Draw O-S-N

- N-N1 and O-O1 25 mm/0.98".
- O1-X 17 mm/0.67"
- Draw the curved line O-X
- Connect the bottom with a curve, as in the figure.

Thumb
- Draw rectangle A-B-C-D, with:
- A-B = 127 mm/5". - B-C = 52 mm/2.05"
- A-G and D-H = 68 mm/2.68". Draw G-H
- G-G1, H-H1 and H-H2 = 8.6 mm/0.34"
- A-I and D-L = 40 mm/1.57". Draw I-L
- L-L1 3 mm/0.12". - Draw L1-H2
- Shape the outline as shown in the figure.

Fourchette
- Draw rectangle A-B-C-D, with:
- A-B equal to the length of the longest finger of the glove + 10-20 mm/0.39-0.79" (e.g.: 95 + 10 = 105 mm/4.13") (when sewing, the excess part will be trimmed)
- B-C = 36 mm/1.42"
- B-E and A-F half of B-C. - Draw E-F
- A-A1 and D-D1 6 mm/0.24".
- E-E1 12-14 mm/0.47-0.55". - B-G = 12.5 mm/0.49"
- Draw the outlines as in the figure.

Fourchette with a quirk
This type of fourchette makes it easier to move the finger, even if it is much more difficult to sew.
- Draw both the pattern of the fourchette and the quirk, as shown in the figure.

171

Form-fitting glove base (men)

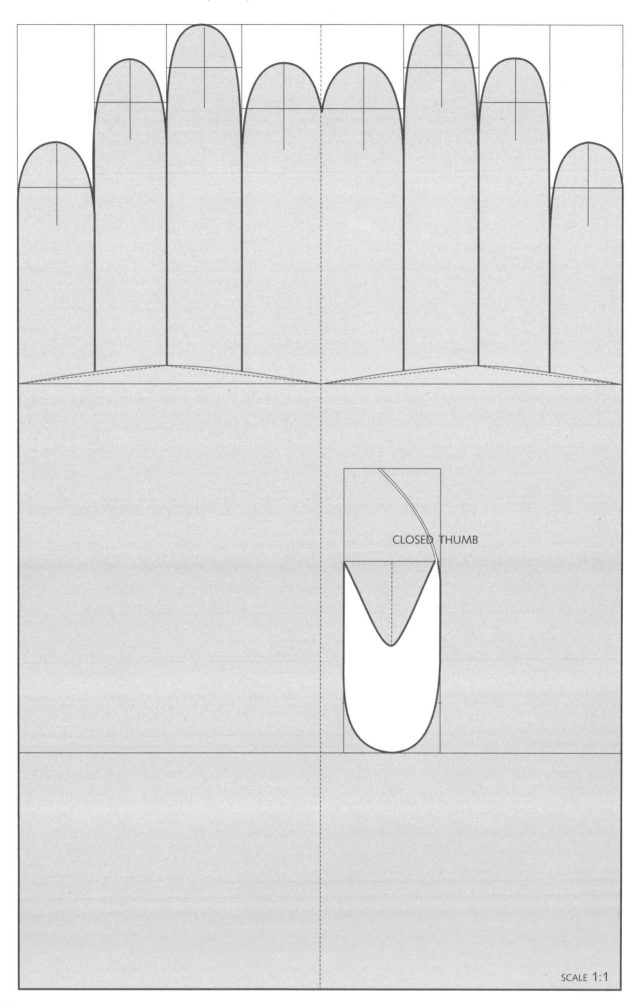

CLOSED THUMB

SCALE 1:1

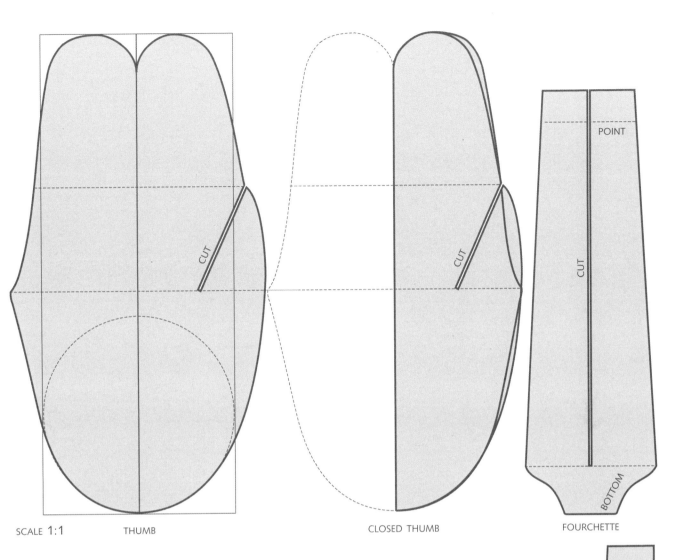

SCALE 1:1   THUMB   CLOSED THUMB   FOURCHETTE

Tight gloves

Tight gloves should be like a second skin when they're worn. For this reason, patternmaking solves three problems:

- The first problem is the need for the leather to adhere to the skin of the hand.
- The second is the principle of instability of the hand, supported by the glove.
- The third is the shape of the hand, composed of five joined yet various fingers, placed curiously atop a small mass.

To create the form of the hand, you'll need a good pattern to create an ideal *form-holder* but, before this, you'll need to consider the quality of a suitable material, so that this holder acts as a second skin to the hand.

Leather thus may meet these demands if it is both *durable* and *fine*.

Thus it will be very important to choose leather with the right qualities: the person in charge of buying the materials must pay close attention to the evaluation and choice of the material.

The highest quality leather on the market is kidskin or lambskin of less than six months. In fact, the skin of animals that have already grazed will lack elasticity, while the the hides of fat animals will create leather of an inferior quality, while the hides of female animals *will be the most prized* for their fineness, durability and tight grain.

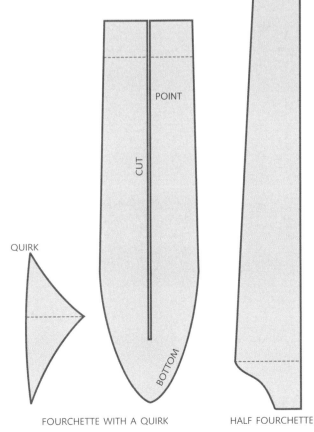

QUIRK

FOURCHETTE WITH A QUIRK   HALF FOURCHETTE

173

FORM-FITTING GLOVE BASE (MEN)

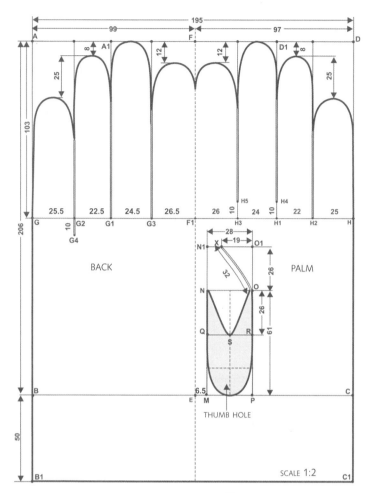

BACK

PALM

THUMB HOLE

SCALE 1:2

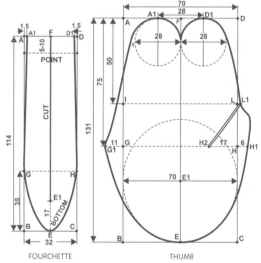

FOURCHETTE

THUMB

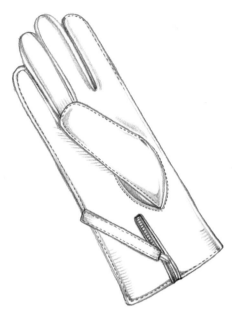

- A-G half of A-B (103 mm/4.06"). Draw G-H
- G-F1 like B-E
- G-G1 half of G-F1 - 1.5 mm/0.06" (e.g.: 99 ÷ 2 = 49.5 - 1.5 = 48 mm/1.89")
- G-G2 half of G-G1 + 1.5 mm/0.06" (25.5 mm/1.00")
- F1-G3 half of F1-G1 + 1 mm/0.04" (26.5 mm/1.04")
- H-H1 half of H-F1 - 1 mm/0.04" (e.g.: 97 mm ÷ 2 = 48.5 - 1.5 = 47 mm/1.85")
- H-H2 half of H-H1 + 1.5 mm/0.06" (25.5 mm/1.00")
- F1-H3 half of F1-H1 + 1 mm/0.04" (25 mm/.98"")
- G2-G4 10 mm; H1-H4 and H3-H5 10 mm/0.39"

Thumb hole

- E-M 6.5 mm/0.26"
- Draw a rectangle M-N-O-P, where:
- N-M = 60-61 mm/2.36-2.40" and M-P = 28 mm/1.10"
- N-Q and O-R = 26 mm/1.02" Draw O-S-N
- N-N1 and O-O1 26 mm/1.02"
- O1-X 19 mm/0.75". Draw the curved line O-X
- Connect the bottom with a curve, as in the figure.

Thumb

- Draw rectangle A-B-C-D, with:
- A-B = 131 mm/5.16"
- B-C = 70 mm/2.76"
- A-G and D-H = 75 mm/2.95". Draw G-H
- G-G1 11 mm/0.43"; H-H1 6 mm/0.24; and H-H2 17 mm/0.67"
- A-I and D-L = 50 mm/1.97". Draw I-L
- L-L1 2 mm/0.08". -Draw L1-H2
- Shape the outline as shown in the figure.

Fourchette

- Draw rectangle A-B-C-D, with:
- A-B equal to the length of the longest finger of the glove + 5-10 mm/0.20-0.39" (e.g.: 94 + 10 = 104 mm/4.09") (when sewing, the excess part will be trimmed)
- B-C 32 mm/1.26"
- B-E and A-F half of B-C. Draw E-F
- A-A1 and D-D1 1.5 mm/0.06"
- E-E1 17 mm/0.67"
- Draw the outlines as in the figure.

Measurements (Size 8½ or M): Hand circumference 217 mm/8.54"; hand length 210 mm/8.27"; Circumference ease 20-25 mm/0.79-0.98".

Glove base

- Draw rectangle A-B-C-D, with:
- A-B equal to the length of the hand (206 mm/8.11")
- B-C equal to the circumference of the hand minus 20-25 mm/0.79-0.98") for the ease (e.g.: 217 - 22 = 195 mm/7.68")
- B-E half of B-C + 1.5 mm/0.06" (99 mm/3.90"). Draw E-F
- B-B1 and C-C1 desired wrist length (e.g. 50 mm/1.97")
- Draw B1-C1

GLOVE SEAMS

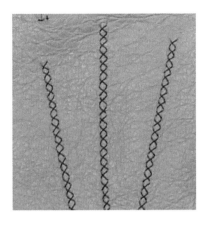

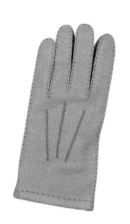

Gloves can be sewn by hand and with a machine.

Hand stitching

Hand stitching is done with a *running stitch* from the 'right' side of the material for soft leather day gloves. The stitches should be regular and relatively close together. This type of stitching is quite prized and decorative but, as is easy to imagine, also quite costly.

Machine sewing

There are four main machine stitches used for gloves:

1) *Bonis:* a type of round stitch, whipstitch or stitch in an external spiral along all the edges, made with just one thread. This stitch is made with a rather old sewing machine.

2) *Double thread:* this stitch may be straight or similar to a *Bonis* stitch, but it is done with two threads instead of one.

3) *Pique:* a straight seam done on the right side of the glove body and on the inside of the fourchettes, requiring the appropriate skill level.

4) *Saddle stitch:* a seam often used in saddlery, created on the right side of the material by joining the two pieces of leather of the glove and the fourchettes or sides.

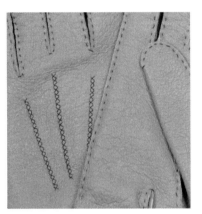

'RIGHT' SIDE

HAND STITCHING

To make sewing easier, small holes can be created with a sewing machine without thread.

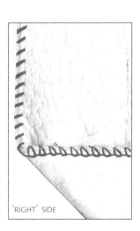

'RIGHT' SIDE

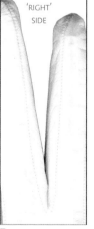

'RIGHT' SIDE

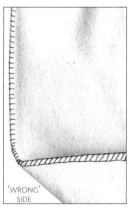

'WRONG' SIDE

TWO-THREAD STITCHING

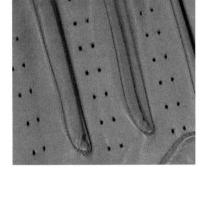

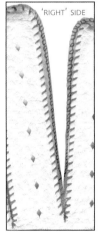

'RIGHT' SIDE

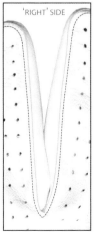

'RIGHT' SIDE

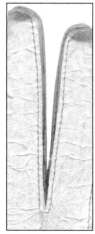

'RIGHT' SIDE

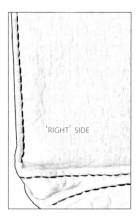

'RIGHT' SIDE

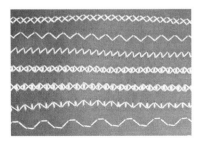

"BONIS" STITCHING   PIQUE STITCH   SADDLE STITCH

Ski gloves

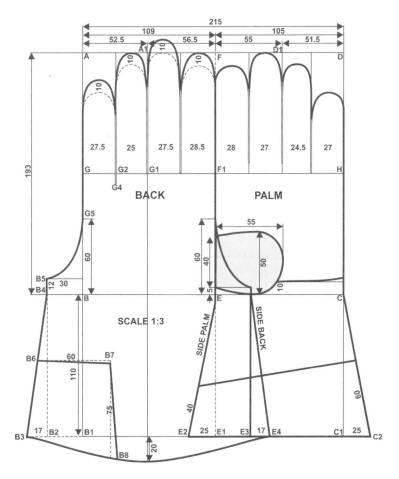

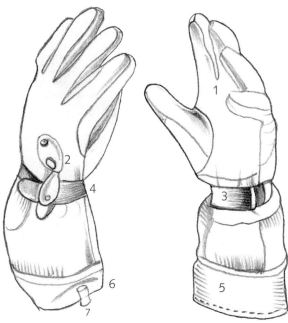

1) No-slip material; 2) Hot air vent;
3) Elastic gathering; 4) Velcro® strap; 5) Extension;
6) Internal drawstring; 7) Drawstring tab.

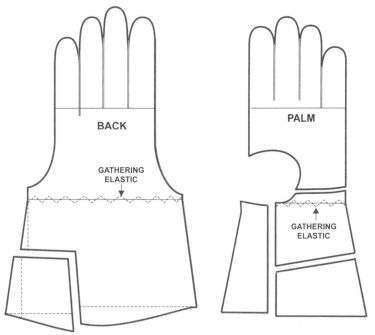

Ski gloves should:

- Have a suitable ease added to the circumference (+22-26 mm/0.87-1.02"), for the padding and to easily surround the hand.
- Have an anatomical shape, with a slightly curved palm, to make it easier to grab the ski poles.

The back of the fingers should be about 8-10 mm/0.31-0.39" longer than the palm side and the inserts at the sides should also be curved.

- The bottom should be enlarged in order to cover outdoor/cold weather clothing, in addition to an extension with a drawstring fastening.
- The palm and the inner part of the thumb should be in a no-slip material (rubber or a knurled synthetic material).
- The bottom of the back should be a bit longer than the palm.

- Draw rectangle A-B-C-D, with:
- A-B equal to the length of the hand +8-10 mm/ 0.31-0.39" (193-195 mm/7.60-7.68").
- B-C equal to the hand circumference + 22-26 mm/0.87-1.02 (215 mm/8.46").
- B-E half of B-C + 4 mm/0.16".
- A-G half of A-B.
- Shape the fingers as in the figure.
- Extend and widen the bottom, as in the figure.
- Draw the thumb hole.
- Draw the cuts as desired.

Shaped thumb
- Draw a rectangle with:
- A-B = 127 mm/5".
- B-C = 52 mm/2.05".
- B-B1 and G-G1 9 mm/0.35".
- D-D1 27 mm/1.06".
- G2-B3 26 mm/1.02".
- D-F1 35 mm/1.38".
- Shape the outline as shown in the figure.
- Take up the parts composing the top and bottom of the thumb on another sheet of paper.

Sides of the index and little finger
- Draw a rectangle that is 155 mm/6.10" high for the index finger and 145 mm/5.71" for the little finger.
- Draw E-F halfway between A-B.
- Cut and open by 11 mm/0.43".
- Shape the outline as shown in the figure.

Shaped fourchettes
- Draw a rectangle whose length is equal to the inner measure of the two fingers and whose width is equal to the sides (28 mm/1.10").
- Cut at the centre of the finger and open by 15 mm/0.59".
- Shape as in the figure.

Glove extension
The extension of the glove is to be done with doubled material, with the upper part in the same measurement of the glove it is to be sewn to. A drawstring is to be inserted as a fastening.

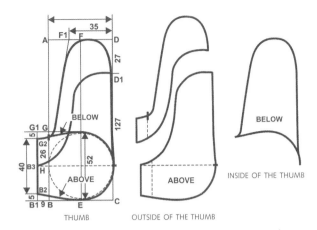

THUMB   OUTSIDE OF THE THUMB   INSIDE OF THE THUMB

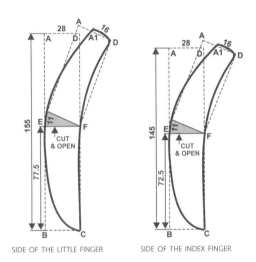

SIDE OF THE LITTLE FINGER   SIDE OF THE INDEX FINGER

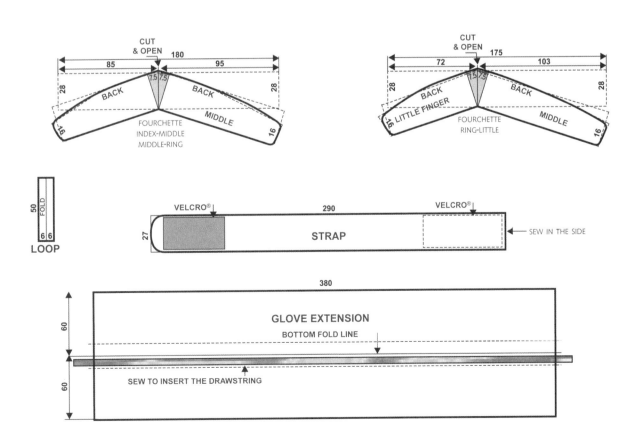

FOURCHETTE INDEX-MIDDLE MIDDLE-RING

FOURCHETTE RING-LITTLE

LOOP

VELCRO®   290   VELCRO®   STRAP   SEW IN THE SIDE

380

GLOVE EXTENSION
BOTTOM FOLD LINE

SEW TO INSERT THE DRAWSTRING

ARTISAN WORKING PHASES

A few steps in the driving glove production process

Leather gloves are often made by craftsmen in small workshops with decades-old machines and tools and techniques handed down from father to son. There are very few businesses operating in this field, generally not in Italy.

Below are a some artisanal working processes for gloves:
1) Selection and sorting of the hides.
2) Wetting the hides.
3) Cutting into strips.
4) Cutting into rectangles and ironing.
5) Checking the colour.
6) Die-cutting the pieces.
7) Open-glove processes and stitching.
8) Final assembly and trimming.
9) Lining.
10) Ironing.
11) Finishing, decorating and packing.

Selecting hides

Once tanned, hides are to be dyed. However, this step requires selection.

Experts who examine the hides visually and by touch find the smallest defects of the leather, which dying tends to bring out. This selection is done according to four colours:
1) Light-colour leather, which must be defect-free.
2) Grey leather, which also must be defect-free.
3) Dark leather, which may have a few defects.
4) Black, which can have a few more.

However, the wet white of grain leather is delicate and cannot be dyed.

This first selection will then be followed by a second round of selection according to the thickness of the leather and its resistance to stitching:
- Thin hides will be used to make evening gloves with whipstitching.

- Thicker, stronger hides will be used to make day or city gloves with topstitching.
- Extra thick and strong hides will be used to make sports or men's gloves, with hand stitching.

The selection expert will then evaluate the number to cut according to the sizes and defects of the hides.

Thinning

Before being wet, the leather will be thinned and printed or embossed, pulled, straightened and pressed on a sheet of marble. Hides are of varying thickness along the back and sides of the animal, and these steps help create a uniform thickness and correct or smooth any variations in the surface of the leather.

Wetting the hides

Before being cut and assembled, leather for gloves must be stabilised.
- The layers of leather are rolled in a wet cloth and left for a certain amount of time to soften.
- The wet pieces of leather are then extracted and pulled by hand in the proper direction and with the right amount of pressure. This operation, which requires a good amount of experience, is very important as, once pulled, the wet leather is stabilised or at least will accept very few modifications.

Cutting into strips

In this step, rectangles of leather are cut into the appropriate size, depending on the measurements of the two sides of the hand, the thumb, the fourchettes and the sides, slightly larger than those of the pre-established sizes.

The clicker (the person who cuts the leather) must consider the direction of the leather and its defects, which s/he will make line up with the seamlines, the thumb hole and the interstices of the fingers.

Cutting into rectangles and ironing

The strips of leather that have been prepared will no longer change in width, however, the length is still to be calibrated according to the desired measurement, pulling them lengthwise by hand, thereby readying the leather for the die cutting process.

Checking the colour for blemishes

Each pair of gloves is prepared for final die cutting. This operation is done very carefully:

1) A final check of the dye/colour, which should be the same for each piece.

2) A final check for any blemishes that may have been missed before.

3) Matching of the parts of the glove, putting them together *mirrored*, that is, right side to right side.

4) Numbering the parts in a sequence, placing the number on the inside of the glove to ensure the pieces and pairs aren't mixed up.

Die-cutting the pieces

The packets of the glove pieces are brought to the hydraulic die cutter where, after having opened them, they are cut by a sort of punch.

The moulds or punches, each one being a different size, are positioned on the hides prepared previously and arranged on the table of the die cutter which, having been given a signal or a push, cuts all the parts of the leather underneath.

After die cutting, the gloves are trimmed and shaped according to the pattern by a worker, using special elongated scissors.

Open glove working process

Before closing the glove with the external stitching, all the steps that can be done on the open glove should be completed. They are: *pintucking, decorative motifs, gatherings,* etc.

1) The creation of piping or stitching on the back of the glove, if any. The pintucking or stitching is usually a set of 3 radiant lines, or just one down the centre of the back. The stitching can be done by hand or with a machine. Hand stitching requires making a faux seam with a two-needle machine without thread to create guide marks.

Machine sewing is done with a special foot which creates the pintucking by lifting the leather at the centre of the seam, creating an embossed effect. The ends of the two threads of each seam are pulled inside the glove and knotted.

2) The creation of applied motifs or embroidery on the back if any.

3) The creation of elasticated gatherings on the back or palm of the glove, or sewing an elasticated piece on the inside, if any.

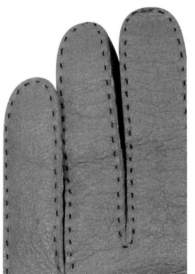

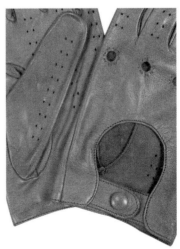

Hem

The hem can be made by turning the leather over on the bottom or with the application of a small strip of leather directly on the edge.

Turned hems are first glued with a small amount of glue and then sewn and trimmed.

Vent and fastening

Gloves can be made with a single vent along the hem, or with a button, zip, snap, buckle, Velcro® or other type of fastening. Vents are to be finished with a small hem or leather edging.

Printing the size

The size number is printed on the inside of the glove with a special stamp dipped in permanent ink.

Final inspection and pairing

At this point, a worker checks to make sure that all the pieces are in the same colour and size. The package is then gathered together and sent on to the assembly room.

Assembly

Once the decorations and trimmings have been added, the glove is assembled.

After having sewn together all the pieces of the thumb, it is sewn to the glove itself. The six fourchettes are sewn to the face of the glove, as are the side pieces. The stitches to use are chosen according to the type of glove and the type of leather: *Hand*, *Bonis*, *two thread*, *pique* or *saddle stitching*.

Lining

The following procedure is used to add the lining:

- Turn the sewn glove inside out with the special tool made for this purpose.

- Tack the lining (already completed in a knit fabric or other material, already sewn) on all five points of the fingers, with a single stitch, without touching the outer leather.

- Turn the lining inside out on the inside of the glove and affix it with an understitch in the inner hem, about 2-5 mm from the edge, so that it isn't visible from the outside.

- Turn the glove inside out again, bringing it right side out, using the tool.

Ironing and straightening

Once the glove is done, due to the multiple manipulations that it has gone through, it will remain a bit more deformed and therefore need to be reshaped.

To do so, the glove will then be slipped on to a special metal form, called a *hot hand*, which is heated electronically to 60-70°C/140-158°F, leaving it there for a few seconds: the time necessary to straighten and iron it, giving it the perfect shape.

Finishes

Once ironed, the leather glove can be *smoothed* with a moving felt wheel, to restore the original shine of the leather. Then the two halves are immediately paired, uniting the two gloves that are identical in colour and size, right and left, with a hand stitch. Then the producer's tag is attached, with all the information necessary to identify the size, colour, model, etc. It is then packaged and sent to the warehouse to be shipped to the customer.

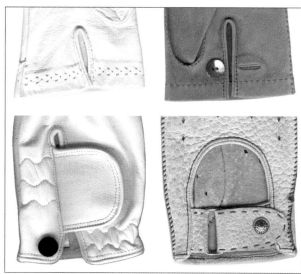

Glove fastenings

Turning the glove inside out

NECK TIES

A short history of neck ties. 182
Main types of neck ties 184
Bow ties. 187
Ascots 187
Cutting and assembly. 188
Parts of the tie. 189
Fabrics, prints, motifs and colours. 190
Neck tie knots 194
Handkerchiefs. 196

A SHORT HISTORY OF NECK TIES

Ties, like other garments, have their own unique history.

- In antiquity, the soldiers of many armies used to wear a piece of fabric knotted around their necks to protect themselves from the cold or for hygienic reasons. Just one of many other examples, the life-size terracotta statues from China (dating to the 3rd century BC) stand out, wearing a handkerchief around their neck. The Roman legions represented on the Column of Trajan appear with a *focale*, a strip of fabric knotted around the neck with multiple functions.

- Around the early 1600s, this accessory, consisting of a strip of fabric knotted around the neck, acting as a decorative and distinguishing element, was worn by a body of Croatian soldiers, mercenaries serving Louis XIII in the Thirty Years War that devastated Europe. French authorities adopted the habit of tying this handkerchief around their neck, finding it to be must more comfortable than the irritating ruff collar, thus spreading it to the aristocracy of the time, which transformed it into a large knot of muslin or lace.

The Italian word for "Croations", *Croati*, seems to be the origin of the present-day term *cravat*.

From then up to today, neck ties and cravats have maintained their same function as pure decoration in classic men's clothing.

- In 1715 a new type of neckwear appeared in England called the *stock*; a strip of batiste or muslin wrapped around the neck without letting the two ends fall on the front, or enhanced by a knot on the front called a *Solitaire*.

- In 1770 many young aristocratic Englishmen called *macaronis* dressed in quite an eccentric style, wearing, among other things, large, knotted white cravats that fell onto the chest.

In France immediately after, during the time of the Directory, the *Incroyables* (young, eccentric, transgressive Parisians) followed the example of the English maraconis, wrapping enormous cravats around their neck and chin, right up to the mouth, resembling shawls in gaudy, flashy colours.

- In the Romantic era (1815-1850), the most important characteristic for men's clothing was the cravat. Knowing how to tie it was considered an art.

In 1828, a Mr. H. Le Blanc published a book titled *The Art of Tying the Cravat*, in which, among other things, he taught readers thirty-two ways to tie a cravat, complete with illustrations.

- In 1838, Maison Charvet was founded, the famous creator of highly prized shirts and cravats.

Today, the fashion house is still a temple to silk fabric neck ties, with the widest assortment in the world.

- In 1880, the *ascot* was in vogue among the upper middle class and the aristocracy, a typical tie with large ends crossed over the chest, still in use today, also called a *hanker-tie*.

Interesting, the name of this accessory was launched much earlier, in 1771 to mark the inauguration of the Ascot horse races, where it was obligatory to wear this type of cravat in the presence of the king.

Terracotta figure, China,
3rd cen. BC

Roman soldiers with the
"focale"

Cravat as worn by the English
macaronis 1770 - 1790

Cravat as worn by the French
Incroyables 1780 - 1790

Aristocratic neckwear from the 1700s

Different ways to wear a cravat in the Romantic era

Ascots

Bow ties

Pussy cat bow or Lavallière

Bandanna

Bolo tie

"Bold look"

Bootlace

- In 1860, the long tie or *four-in-hand* (called *régate* in France) appeared. This neck tie, which was narrow with a small knot and long ends that fell down the torso, is the ancestor to the present-day tie.

- In 1905, *bow ties* were in fashion, following the resounding success of Puccini's Madame Butterfly at La Scala in Milan, giving it the name *papillon* in French. Its form resembles just that - a butterfly - even if it should be stressed that it was worn well before the predominant long tie, but was simply called a*cravat*).

These types of ties were all the rage in the 1920s, 1930s and 1940s, but today, except for formal occasions (black tie or white tie) or important ceremonies, they are rarely worn.

- In the 19th century, the neckwear preferred by liberal intellectuals and artists was the *Lavallière*. This large, floppy bow tie, similar to today's pussycat bow, was worn knotted around the collar. It gets its name from the Duchess of La Vallière, the favourite mistress of Louis XIV, who imitated the king by wearing a strip of prized fabric around her neck, becoming one of the first women to wear a tie.

- At the end of the 18th century in America, James Belcher, a famous boxer, made it fashionable to wear a *bandanna* or kerchief. Also called kerchiefs, they are are silk, cotton or linen squares of fabric, often in bright colours, which is wrapped around the neck with the ends knotted to hold them in place.

- In 1925, the American tie maker Jesse Langsdorf patented a type of long neck tie that was less likely to become rumpled and with a structure that was stabler. This is the neck tie used today, made in three segments of fabric cut on the bias.

- In 1935, the future duke of Windsor started the fashion of the wide knot, which then took his name. It is still quite popular today.

- In the 1940s, a quite whimsical type of tie gained popularity in the United States, featuring images of Hawaiian beaches, pin-ups, skylines, etc., called a *bold look*.

- In the 1950s, among the various appearances of long ties proposed by tie makers, the *bola or bolo tie*, a Western-style of string invented by a cowboy from Arizona, worn around the neck, fastened by a buckle, was in vogue.

- In the id 1950a, English rockers called Teddy Boys popularised the *bootlace tie*, deriving from the bolo.

- In the 1960s, in order to stand out, youths wore *twists* (a name borrowed from the famous dance style), a type of tie with crossed ends, affixed by a seam under a button.

- In 1968, ties became very wide with a large knot, called *kipper ties*.

- In the 1970s in Germany, a machine called a *liba*was built, able to sew nearly 2,000 ties per day, revolutionising tie production.

- In the 1970s, neck ties in knit wool or silk were in vogue.

At the end of the 1980s, the American designer Nicole Miller introduced the first *conversational*ties, with about ten million of them produce per year today.

In Italy, tie production is quite sophisticated and high-quality, with the biggest names of high fashion involved, from Ferragamo to Ermenegildo Zegna, Gucci and many others.

Main types of neck ties

Currently, three types of neck ties are worn for various occasions:
The *ascot*; the *neck tie* or *long tie*; and the *bow tie*.

The ascot

The ascot has wide ends that fall onto the chest, either crossed or parallel and affixed with a pin.

It is worn on elite occasions (usually associated with horse racing) and important weddings, pairing it with formal suits, but rarely tailcoats.

In vogue mainly with the upper middle class starting from 1850 onwards for all social events, the ascot had to respect precise dimensions: 127 cm/50" in length, 2.2 cm/0.87" for the height of the collar, and 7.6 cm/2.99" for the width of the ends.

These measurements are no longer a requirement today, even if the ascot is considered an elegant accessory, almost always sold with the knot already tied.

Neck tie (or long tie)

Today's neck tie is the result of the genius invention of a tie maker from New York, Jesse Langsdorf, who in 1924 had the idea (which he later patented), to cut the tie fabric diagonally (on the bias) and to sew the three fabric segments together, giving them greater stretch and, in particular, the ability to spring back to the initial shape after the knot has been untied. In the past, when the long tie triumphed in the 1920s, along with the soft collar, it was still rather impractical. Being made up of a simple strip of silk or cotton, when the knot was loosened (with difficulty), it was reduced to a crumpled rag, at times even ripping and having to be replaced often.

After Langsdorf's invention, long ties did not undergo any meaningful or important changes, except for a few small variations due to passing fads, such as: the squaring off of the narrow end in the 1950s, or that of the wide end in the 1960s-70s. Every other attempt has always been unsuccessful.

In terms of the dimensions and the form of this type of neckwear, the most balanced ties are 35 cm/13.78" long, 8-9 cm/3.15-3.54" at their widest point near the bottom, and 3-4 cm/1.18-1.57" in their narrowest point.

Foulard Cravats

This type of cravat comes in printed silk, it features a pre-tied knot with a neckband in matching fabric, an elastic, adjustable clasp or none at all (to be tied by hand), used mainly in the early 1900s and in the 1960s-70s.

Neck ties with undulating edges or reversible neck ties

In order to satisfy sophisticated clients with a bit of flair, some tailors and tie makers add cravats with undulating edges or reversible versions, which require special patterns and assembly techniques.

Ascot with a pre-tied knot   *Ascot to be knotted*

Neck tie or long tie

Skinny to be knotted   *Broad to be knotted*

Foulard cravat with a pre-tied knot

Undulated edges

Bow ties

Today, this type of tie is worn infrequently. Except for in a few important formal occasions where it is required, i.e. a *Black Tie* or *White Tie* event, you won't see many bow ties while walking around or as part of office wear.

Instead, the bow tie is considered a special way to distinguish oneself as the wearer is immediately classified as a free spirit, an anti-conformist intellectual or an inspired creative type.

However, it is also considered suitable for those who have a job which requires them to lean over often, such as wait staff or doctors.

The bow tie is much older than the neck tie. It dominated fashion from the end of the 19th century to the start of the 20th (up to around 1940), taking on different forms. Almost every portrait of a famous man at the time immortalises him with the most varied of bow ties: large with rectangular knots, wide with asymmetrical knots, narrow with herringbone patterns, etc.

Wearing a bow tie back then didn't have any particular meaning, nor did it imply participation in a special event.

185

NECK TIE PATTERNS

Measurements and composition of long ties

Today's neck ties are more or less the same as the original 'long tie' versions created in 1924 by Jesse Langsdorf: 140 cm/55.12" in length (for those of an average height, the tie should fall to the belt) and 7-8 cm/2.76-3.15" in breadth.

Over the years, a few tie makers have tried to change these measurements, proposing different lengths, widths and shapes such as *Slim Jim ties*, which were 5-7 cm/ 1.97-2.76" wide with a square end, launched in the 1950s by the English Teddy Boys and the birth of rock and roll culture.

Or the *kipper tie* trend, with widths about 12 cm/4.72", started by the British hippy Michael Fish. This fashion was in vogue from the early Sixties, with the arrival of the hippy movement.

Classic neck ties and cravats are made up of three elements:

1) The outer fabric or shell, which is cut into two or three pieces.

2) The tipping or lining, generally made of two pieces sewn to the two ends of the cravat or, at times, along the entire model.

3) The *interlining*, which is the fabric cut in the shape of the tie and placed within its shell to add support and structure.

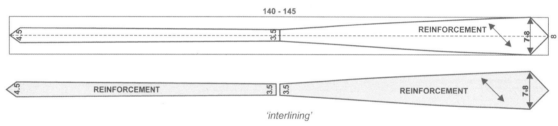

'interlining'

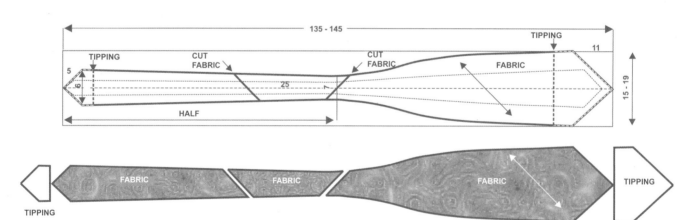

Interfacing

- Draw a rectangle whose base is the length of the desired tie (140-145 cm/55.12-57.09") and whose height is the maximum desired width of the finished product (8 cm/3.15").

Create the outline with the classic shape and dimensions of a neck tie: 140-145 cm/5.12-57.09" in length, 7-8 cm/2.76-3.15" in breadth in the widest part; 4-4.5 cm/1.57-1.77" wide on the opposite end; and 3-4 cm/1.18-1.57" at its narrowest.

Create a cut along the centre.

Base tie in fabric

- Draw a rectangle whose base is equal to the length of the tie and whose height is equal to double the maximum width. Draw the outline, shaping the reinforcement pieces and leaving a margin for the overlap. Create two cuts: one at the centre and one at about 25 cm/9.84", for a better use of the fabric and greater flexibility.

- Lining: the lining can be whole, using the same pattern as the fabric, or it can be just at the two ends (called tipping in that case), obtaining the models always by using the selvedge of the fabric.

Bow ties

TO BE KNOTTED

Bow tie construction

- Draw rectangle A-B-C-D whose base is equal to the desired width (6-7 cm/2.36-2.76") and whose length is equal to ½ of the neck circumference + bow length + ½ bow length + 10 cm/3.94" for the knot.
  (e.g. 42 cm ÷ 2 = 21 + 11 + 6.5 + 10 = 48.5 cm/19.09").
- A-E equal to the length of the bow (e.g. 12-13 cm/4.72-5.12")
- E-G ½ of A-E (e.g.: 13 ÷ 2 = 6.5 cm/2.56").
- Shape the outline as shown in the figure.

NB: Bow ties are assembled with the same fabric,
doubled and sewn inside-out, then flipped to the right side of the fabric.

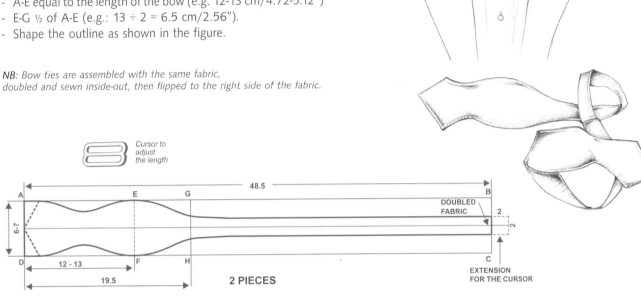

Ascots

TO BE KNOTTED

Ascots are characterised by the ends, which are crossed on the chest or left to drape, parallel, held in place by a pin with two pearls.
Today, ascots are worn at important weddings (for the groom's outfit), or for social ceremonies or events, often connected to horse racing. At times they are worn with tailcoats.
Both bow ties and ascots often feature a pre-tied knot and a collar adjusted by a cursor.

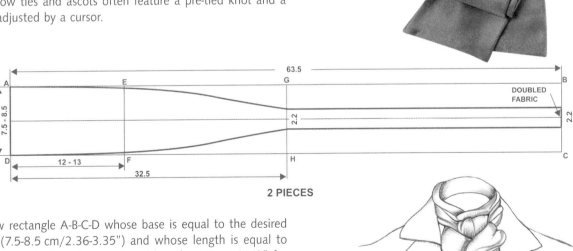

- Draw rectangle A-B-C-D whose base is equal to the desired width (7.5-8.5 cm/2.36-3.35") and whose length is equal to ½ of the neck circumference + end length 10.5 cm/4.13" for the knot (e.g.: 42÷2 = 21 + 32 + 10.5 = 63.5 cm/25.00").
- A-G equal to ½ length + 1 cm/0.39".
  (e.g. 63.5 cm ÷ 2 = 31.75 + 1 = 32.75 mm/12.89").
- A-E 13 cm/5.12".
- Shape the outline as shown in the figure.

CUTTING AND ASSEMBLY

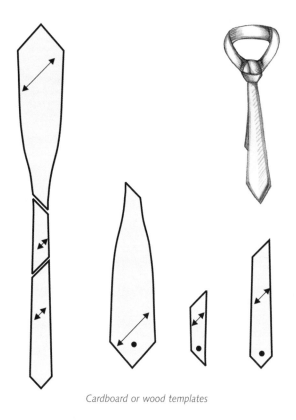

Cardboard or wood templates

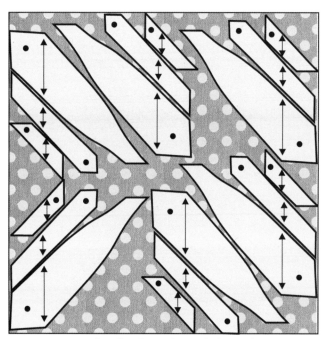

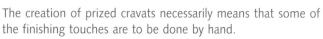

Nesting of cardboard or marking with the templates

Marking, cutting and sewing the cravat

The creation of prized cravats necessarily means that some of the finishing touches are to be done by hand.

There are three ways to make ties:

1) Industrially, entirely with machines.
2) Semi-artisanal, with machines, finished by hand.
3) Artisanal, made completely by hand.

Artisanal or handmade construction requires more time, but the results that are obtained are surely of higher quality and value for each tie.

Semi-artisanal construction produces a higher-quality product in that each tie passes through the hands of the craftsmen for the finishing touches.

Working phases

The steps in making a tie are:

1) Cutting the fabric, which is done perfectly on the bias, meaning the pattern or template must be positioned at a 45° angle across the fabric. In general, 4 to 6 ties are made from every metre of fabric, depending on the design type and how binding the pattern is.

PARTS OF THE TIE

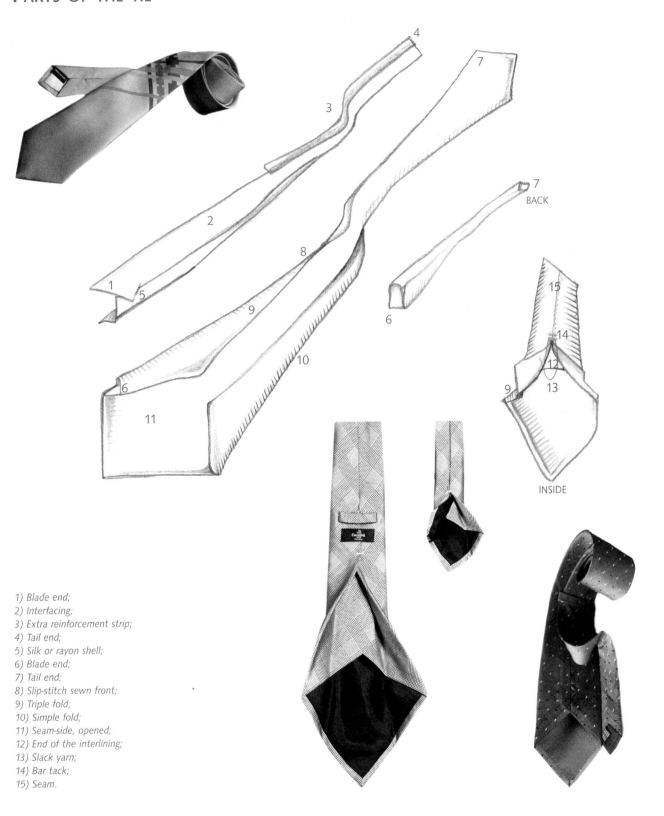

1) Blade end;
2) Interfacing;
3) Extra reinforcement strip;
4) Tail end;
5) Silk or rayon shell;
6) Blade end;
7) Tail end;
8) Slip-stitch sewn front;
9) Triple fold;
10) Simple fold;
11) Seam-side, opened;
12) End of the interlining;
13) Slack yarn;
14) Bar tack;
15) Seam.

2) The sewing of the external shell fabric together with the segments that make up the tie with a sewing machine.
3) The ironing of the fold lines/seams, which are flattened with an iron at a temperature suitable for the fabric.
4) Cutting the lining and machine sewing it to the tips of the fabric tie.
5) Cutting the *interfacing*.
6) Inserting the interfacing.
7) Closing the external fabric shell with a longitudinal seam, inside out, with a long line, also affixing the interfacing.

For fine cravats, this seam is done by hand masterfully, leaving the so-called *slack yarn* which is the end of the thread used for this seam.
8) Turn the tie right out with the special stick, placing the two ends of the interfacing within the two linings sewn on each end of the tie;
9) Sew the loop and the label;
10) Final ironing.

FABRICS AND PRINTS

The main materials used to make ties are: silk, cotton, wool, leather and synthetic fibres.

Silk

Silk is the material which gives ties the most elegance and a smooth, soft *handle or hand*, that is, the tactile impression that results from touching a given fabric.

The properties that sets it apart are: its shine, durability, elasticity, the ease of dying and, in particular, its handle. Silk is the queen of all cravats, even if today synthetics are more common than silk in industrialised manufacturing.

There are many different ways to process and weave silk for ties. The main *families* are: *silk jacquard* or *yarn-dyed* fabric, in which the patterns are woven into the fabric with different colour thread; *printed* or *piece-dyed*, in which each colour is individually printed on to the piece of raw or already-processed silk. Yarn-dyed silk with *woven patterns* is considered the top of the line in terms of cravat materials as it makes it possible to create fine motifs and allows for an unrivalled wealth of textures.

Canvas weaving is used to create reps, ottoman, crepe and faille. Twill, which has diagonal ribbing, is mainly used on printed cravats. Satin weaving generates satin fabric, which is shinier, softer and smoother than other types of silk weaves.

These weaves are often combined, creating refined, original neck ties with paisley motifs, checks, polka-dots, etc.

Cotton

This natural fibre (cotton muslin and batiste) was the most commonly used material to make the very first cravats in the time of Louis XVI.

Today cotton is rarely used for neck ties at it is unattractive and lacks the soft *handle* of silk, even if it may seem alluring due to the colours which cotton accepts and holds quite easily.

Cotton is used mostly for the creation of cravats for children which are often dirtied, as it is a material that's easy to wash and maintain.

Wool

Knit wool cravats were in fashion in the 1960s and 1970s, though always less so than their silk counterparts.

Today, highly prized wool is used such as Scottish wool and cashmere, with tartan, Paisley or tweed motifs.

Wool is often combined with silk, creating a product with an exceptional *hand*, especially when combining cashmere and silk. Wool can also be blended with polyester or cotton, which is quite suitable for the *interfacing* of the tie, the internal support of the cravat.

Leather

Leather ties first appeared in the 1940s in the United States with the *Bolo*. They then made a comeback in the 1970s. In Europe, leather ties had a shining moment in fashion in the 1950s and the 1980s, especially among youths, who wore narrow ties in different colours with a square tip, or even those in suede with a diamond tip.

At left, pure wool; at right, silk and linen. Both by Segni e Disegni.

Patterns and colours

From the birth of the long tie in 1924, this accessory has seen an immense variety of patterns, designs, textures, colours and nuances.

The study and creation of fabric patterns is done while considering the execution of the tie. This may have an influence on the way the material is woven or knit and on the print and construction, giving the cravat its own particular style.

Among the countless motifs that ties are given, the most common ones are: *stripes*, *regimental*, *polka dot*, *paisley*, *animal prints*, *floral*, *sporty*, and *whimsical*. In addition, there are different ways of creating and arranging the motifs on the tie: *all over*, *large designs*, and those that are carefully *placed*.

Stripes

As far as ties are concerned, stripes have played an important role since the beginning. Their almost perennial success is due, in particular, to the fact that they aren't a purely ornamental motif. Instead, they derive from a cost-effective technique which is easy to swap out in terms of the colours of the threads on the loom. In England, stripes indicated different regiments of the army, giving rise to the famous neck ties worn by soldiers, called *Regimental ties*. These ties feature colourful diagonal stripes, coordinated to the colours of the single uniforms of the various regiments. This type of cravat is still quite popular today.

Royal Irish Poplin ties, on the other hand, are striped neck ties in poplin fabric (a fabric with a silk warp and a wool weft, with a very fine *handle*) from *Atkinsons Irish Poplin* of Belfast, a British tie maker established in 1920.

In addition to regimental ties, there are other types of striped ties that fall into this category:

- *Club* and *old school* ties, which are stripes deriving from British colleges or schools.
- *Placement stripe* ties, with the single stripe placed below the knot.
- *Horizontal or vertical* stripes were in fashion in the 1950s.
- *Mogador* stripe ties, which is a fabric made of silk and cotton with a fine, tight weave, similar to that of Moroccan barracan fabric, suitable for spring/summer ties.
- *Ribbon stripe* ties with diagonal or straight stripes of varying widths, set apart by a background colour.
- *Herringbone stripe* ties, in addition to many other types of stripes which have appeared over the years, some in use today and some having completely disappeared.

Paisley

Paisley, whose name derives from the Scottish city outside Glasgow where many of these textiles came be produced. The tear drop shaped motif is either printed or woven into the fabric.

This pattern dates back to Babylonian times, approximately 2000 years BC, when a date palm sapling, a symbol of fertility, was added to cloth. In the 17th century, in northern India's Kashmir region, shawls in fine wool were made with this symbol, along with other types of plants. Near the mid-17th century, the East India Company began importing these shawls from Kashmir to England, where many types of Paisley fabrics were then created. The *curved tear drop* in cashmere, with all the beauty of its nuances and shades, is generally made today in an all-over print stamped on the fabric. Woven paisley patterns are generally rare and much more simplified in form as they are more complicated to produce.

All-over prints

The term 'all over', in tie terminology, means the repetition of a motif across the entire surface of the tie.

There are infinite types of all-over prints, from tiny checks to polka dots, small animals to objects, trees to flowers, mini tennis rackets to musical instruments, etc.

The objects and designs can vary in size from one tie to the next, combined with other motifs or even stand-alone or unevenly spaced depictions.

The absence of a precise, obligatory orientation of the designs makes all-over prints quite economical to produce, making it possible to cut the fabric in any direction.

Polka dots

Polka dots were one of the first designs added to ties, along with small geometric shapes.

Around 1920, Thomas Lipton consecrated these small patterns with an inseparable blue and white polka dot bow tie of his own design.

The most classic polka dot size for Lipton's ties was comparable to a piece of confetti, but by 1930, Charvet offered elegant polka dots as large as a coin.

Polka dots also can have a medium size, and they are often arranged in a *quincunx or quinconce*, that is, at the points of a perfect rhombus.

Affirmed in its main forms, the primary elements of the tie were the colour and the pattern, either woven or printed.

In addition to their style and type, such motifs are also defined by their placement and the quality of their execution.

The arrangement of the motif, in addition to often bringing a certain style to the cravat, may also determine the way the fabric is woven, printed or assembled.

The motifs used over the years are quite varied: *large flowers, leaves, plants* and *animals*; small *geometric motifs* or other repeated subjects (all over); designs regarding *sport; monograms* and *brands; extravagant* and *whimsical* designs; advertising and promotional images and lettering; and even works of art by famous artists are reproduced on ties.

At first, tie colours were classic and sober, but in the 1950s-60s they began to take on lighter, more delicate tones, from pastels to intense hues. In the 1970s-80s more natural colours were favoured, echoing stone or earth tones, paired with browns, greens and greys, offered by important stylists that had begun to present their collections.

In recent years, tie colours have been flashier, with a chromatic composition made with cutting-edge computerised systems. Tie *motifs* vary greatly and are chosen and coordinated according to the type, colour and pattern of the shirt or jacket the tie is to be worn with.

The flowers and the small leaves of ties are a classic genre that appeared around 1980-1990, available as all-over prints repeated across the entire surface.

Large, more realistic flowers appeared on American neck ties in the 1940s, popularised in Europe among the young middle class during the period dominated by the hippy movement.

After a period where they were out of vogue, starting in 1995 ties with large flowers sporadically have reappeared on the fashion scene.

Geometric patterns are also a classic neck tie motif, especially those woven into an all-over design, seen starting from the late 1800s, and *Macclesfield* neck ties (all-over patterns with small motifs), worn in Europe starting in 1920.

Creative and artistic motifs

Creativity in terms of tie patterns has no limits. Monograms and brands range from small embroidered letters to large characters printed and incorporated in the entire printed motif, to full signatures.

In sports, the themes that are most often seen on ties are those relating to fishing, hunting, polo, golf and horseback riding, with related details of the objects and tools relating to them, often small-scale, woven, all-over prints.

Peculiar, funny or promotional designs on ties are mainly worn by Americans. Subjects of every type can end up on a tie and satisfy all those who who wish to make an impression as funny people with a strong sense of humour, from classic horseback cowboys to macabre or lively scenes, from pistols to bank notes. Art also has a close relationship with cravats. A few painters, such as Salvador Dali, Picasso and Jean Cocteau, all created ties, signing them directly, just like a painting. Starting in the 1940s, many European and American designers created ties with large geometric motifs inspired by Art Deco and Abstract Expressionism, or even by Japanese, Gothic or Italian Renaissance art.

Others have used the detail of a painting to completely cover the tie, or they've shrunken the full image to the size of the tie.

NECK TIE KNOTS

The knot of a neck tie has always been a decisive factor in men's elegance.

In the past, the art of tying a tie was given fundamental importance, so much so that entire books were written about the subject. Vain perfectionists such as Lord Brummel took hours to get just the right knot, using up dozens of ties as they were made of un-starched fabric.

Today, no one has the time to spend tying a strange or special knot. The knots that are used are mainly those for long neck ties, especially the *simple knot* or the *four-in-hand* and the *Windsor* or a *cross knot*.

Very few people tie their own *bow ties*. Almost all of those sold today have a pre-tied or sewn knot, equipped with a collar with a fastening and adjustment system via a buckle, a slot sewn on the inside of the collar that a small hook is attached to, or with two Velcro® strips.

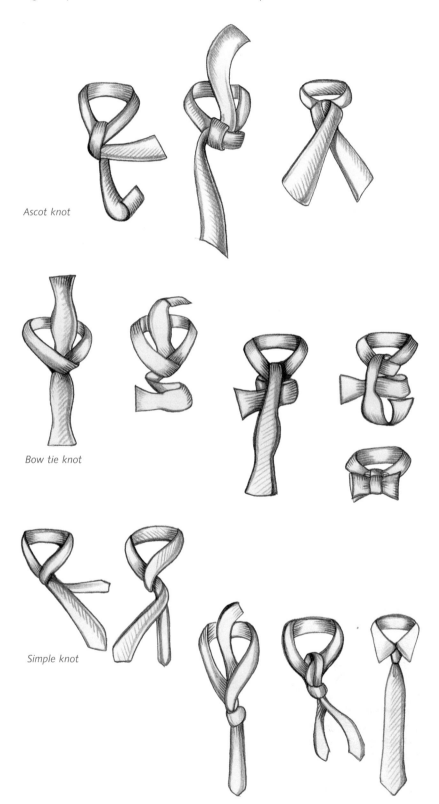

Ascot knot

Bow tie knot

Simple knot

ASCOT KNOT

The ascot knot is one of the simplest to tie. It should be mentioned that the ascot is found in shops almost always pre-tied, being of a very limited use.

To create this knot, follow the instructions illustrated in the figures.

BOW TIE KNOT

An un-tied *bow tie* looks like a band of ribbon, with squared or slightly rounded ends (battoir) or with pointed ends (butterfly).

1) Pass the bow tie around the neck, cross sides 1 (right) and 2 (left), then pass end 1 under end 2.

2) Pull the two ends and fold end 2 in the opposite direction, while holding end 1 taut.

3) Bring end 1 over 2, vertically.

4) Take end 1, wrap it completely around end 2 and insert it in the opening that has been created at the start of the neck.

5) Pull to finish the step and adjust both the ends.

SIMPLE KNOT (FOUR-IN-HAND)

The knot for long neck ties, the *simple knot*, is the one most often used today and, if done properly (not too wide nor too big, tight at the right point so as to create the vertical mark called a *couillèr* in French or a *dimple* in English), it is also one of the best

1) Wrap the tie around the neck, cross the ends, passing the wider one under the narrower one.

2) Wrap the wider piece around the narrow piece.

3) Pass the wide end along the inside of the neck.

4) Slip the wide end into the space created.

5) Pull and adjust the knot and the length of the front of the tie, which should reach the belt.

WINDSOR KNOT

This knot, started by King Edward VIII in 1933 and then adopted by the Duke of Windsor, is quite large in volume, useful for filling the empty space at the collar, especially with collars that feature wide points. It has a triangular shape and, after its execution, the wider end should drop down below the narrower end by about 35 cm/13.78".

To create this knot, carefully follow the steps illustrated in the figures.

CROSS KNOT

This knot is rarely used, though it may be useful simply to add a bit of variety and to fill the space of wide-set collar points.

To complete it, follow the steps shown in the figure.

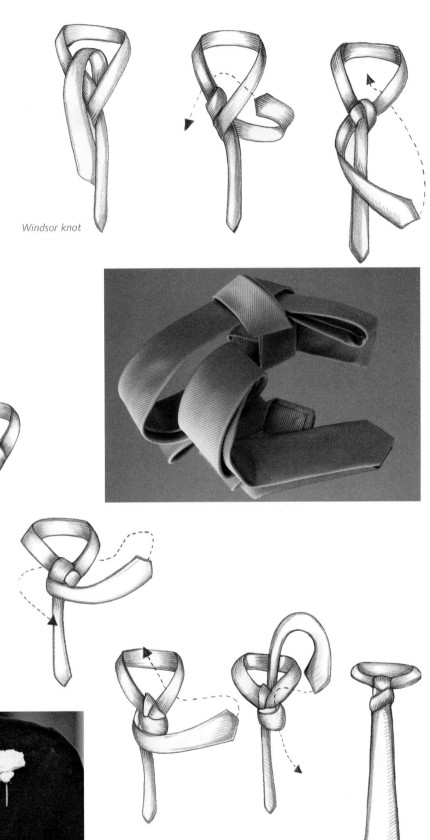

Windsor knot

Cross knot

195

HANDKERCHIEFS

The handkerchief is a square piece of linen, cotton, silk or synthetic fabric in varying sizes according to its destined use: hygiene if it's to be used to clear one's nose or dab sweat, as an embellishment worn in shirt and jacket pockets; a head covering, wrapped at the wrist or neckline.

It is an ancient accessory. It is seen in the portrait of a Chinese emperor who lived about 1,000 years before Christ while, later on, the Romans of the Late Roman Empire always had a *sudarium* with them, inserted in their belt and used for different purposes. In the past, handkerchiefs were an elegant, refined element and often as many as 12 dozen of them were found in wedding chests. Particularly rich handkerchiefs featured embroidered leaves, flowers and figures, extending along the entire surface of the sheer batiste fabric, while crests and symbols were presented at the corners.

In the early 1600s, it was considered quite elegant to carry a handkerchief in one's hand, or to have it sticking out of the end of the sleeve, including in men's fashion about the time snuff appeared.

In 1848 in Italy, people wore patriotic kerchiefs in the colours of the Italian flag. Most men began to place a pocket square in their jacket in addition to the kerchief carried in the pocket.

Pocket squares

Pocket squares are an indispensable accessory for elegantly-dressed men. In the past, the pocket square was only in white, folded at right angles and stuffed into the chest pocket so that only one triangular corner was visible. Today this accessory, though still every bit as elegant, is rarely worn, mostly by older generations.

The most commonly worn pocket squares are in pure silk or cotton, sprouting up from the pocket, never in the same colour as the tie, nor in similar tones, but always in a colour different than the rest of the outfit.

Head scarves or foulards

Going back to the ancient days, this type of kerchief was worn by commoners.

Foulards can be worn on the head or around the neck, but in the past those worn around the neck in Italy were a special item called a *fisciù*, used to cover a neckline that was perhaps too deep. In the 1800s it was called a *modestina*, deriving from the word for "modest". Men of days past also wore a kerchief around the neck to soak up sweat, like American *cowboys* and the "gauchos" of the Pampa still do today.

HANDKERCHIEF MEASUREMENTS

Handkerchief measurements can vary from one manufacturer to another. However, as a general rule, they are all more or less the same, with foulards being an exception as they come in different sizes.

- 40 x 40 cm/15.75 x 15.75" women's handkerchiefs.
- 45 x 45 cm/17.72 x 17.72" and 50 x 50 cm/19.69 x 19.69" men's handkerchiefs.
- 33 x 33 cm/12.99 x 12.99" pocket squares.
- 90 x 90 cm/35.43 x 35.43" foulards.

UMBRELLAS AND WALKING STICKS

The history of umbrellas 198
Main types of umbrellas 199
Umbrella terminology 200
Sections for umbrellas 202
Walking sticks 203
Types of walking sticks 204
Special walking sticks 205
Artisan working phases and materials 206
Crookneck walking sticks 207
Walking stick from two pieces of wood 208
Buffalo horn handle 209
Finishing horn handles 210

THE HISTORY OF UMBRELLAS

In antiquity, the umbrella was a symbol of the power of a divinity and great priests, as shown by the representations of a few Indian divinities such as Vishnu and Buddha carrying this object above their head.

In China, the parasol was in use 1,000 years before Christ; in ancient Greece, it was present in mythology; Etruscan images portray the umbrella above the heads of priests; in ancient Rome, Roman matrons widely carried a parasol, made of precious silk and at times embellished by gems and stones of all types; in the Middle Ages, it was used exclusively in religious ceremonies and by the powerful.

In the Renaissance, the umbrella became an indispensable accessory for ladies of the court and for nobility, triumphantly coming into use by women in the 1600s, with a lighter structure and artistically carved handles.

In the Neoclassical era, after the end of Napoleon's rule in particular, small umbrellas became a common accessory in women's fashion, resulting in charming or whimsical variations and gimmicks: umbrellas with drapery; overturned umbrellas; pagoda-shaped umbrellas; Japanese-style parasols; umbrellas with a foldable or detachable handle.

The rods were made of Indian rush or strips of Indian shot. The fabric went from raw batiste, which was far from waterproof, to nankeen taffeta or Carolina canvas, lined in pink, or in white muslin with a taffeta lining.

1801

1896

1901

Images from "Memoir of a Geisha"

The umbrellas of this time were smaller than the hats of the day, and the colours and forms of their handles had rather bizarre characteristics: handles in the shape of snakes, lion's heads or vultures, made of Chinese laurel oak, rosewood, rosewood with a small polished gold orb, or fluted bamboo with the owner's initials etched into a gold plate, etc.

In 1835, umbrellas that featured an ingenious spring-based system that allowed them to fold in half began to appear, called brisés.

In 1851, Englishman Samuel Fox was the first to replace the whalebones used to construct the skeleton of the umbrella with steel rods.

Men's umbrellas were quite practical, able to protect the entire family, generally of eight panels of red, light blue, or black silk, with a hooked horn handle, carried under the arm with the brass tip facing backwards.

1910

1911

1912

Main types of umbrellas

Despite its use as protection from water, the umbrella continued to play an important role in fashion until after WWII, with multiple original and creative forms: from practical foldable models to thin, long models; from those in elegant printed fabric to *summer* versions in lightweight cotton with a floral print and others in curved clear plastic and those with a short rod to be worn with a shoulder strap. Even the handles, imitating those of walking sticks, took on strange and even refined shapes for both men's and women's versions.

Today, despite the use of cars, umbrellas are still in use, even if they no longer have the same characteristics as a *fashion accessory* in the true sense of the word, like they did in the past. They also are now used exclusively for one purpose, protection from the rain. Perhaps the English (though not all of them) still use umbrellas as a walking cane even when it isn't raining, with the fabric rolled up and affixed.

The differences between modern umbrella models mostly has to do with the technical aspect and the fabric used.

Main types of umbrellas:

1) *Classic umbrella:* with a handle//shaft/points in wood, or with a metal shaft and a plastic or wood handle; nylon or another water-repellent fabric cover; manually opened, with a radius from 59 to 63 cm/23.28-24.80".

2) *Automatic umbrellas:* equipped with a spring opening mechanism; steel shaft; plastic or wood handle; nylon cover; 59-63 cm/23.28-24.80" radius.

3) *Anti-lightening umbrellas:* featuring a Bakelite shaft and straight handle in a rubbery material; 59-63 cm/23.28-24.80" radius.

4) *Golf umbrellas:* featuring an enlarged radius of 75 cm/29.53", the handle is generally straight with a metal shaft.

5) *Mini umbrellas:* smaller in size, with a radius of only 50-54 cm/19.69-21.26"; the metal shaft is retractable; it can come with a button for automatic opening and closure. When closed it's generally about 18-28 cm/7.09-11.02" long. It comes with a nylon bag with a handle or carabiner to contain it and carry it.

6) *Drip-catcher umbrellas:* an accessory applied to the outer tip of the umbrella (usually automatic with a normal radius of 58-63 cm/22.83-24.80"), consisting of a telescopic container that, when the umbrella is closed, covers it entirely so it doesn't drip.

UMBRELLA TERMINOLOGY

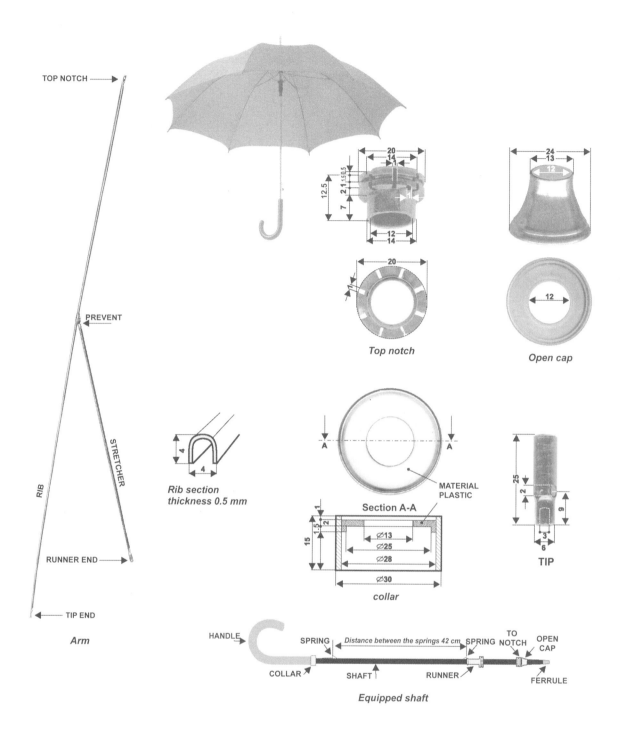

Arm

Top notch

Open cap

Rib section thickness 0.5 mm

Section A-A

MATERIAL PLASTIC

collar

TIP

Equipped shaft

- *Canopy:* the outer fabric part of an umbrella, usually made of nylon but at times waterproof or rubberised cotton. The height of fabric for umbrellas with a radius of 59-65 cm/23.23-25.59" is 60 cm/23.62"; the height for umbrellas with a radius of 75 cm/29.53" is 70-80 cm/27.56-31.50" according to the design.
- *Shaft:* the central axis of the umbrella upon which the handle and all other parts are affixed. It can be in wood or metal (iron or aluminium). Wood shafts generally have a 14-20 mm/0.55-0.79" diameter; metal shafts range from 10 to 12 mm/0.39-0.47" in diameter (used mainly for automatic umbrellas).
- *Handle:* the end of the umbrella that is gripped by the hand. It can be in different forms and sizes: curved, straight, a knob or shaped like an animal's head or famous person's head, etc.
- *Frame* (iron rods): the group made of the stretchers and the ribs.

- *Top notch:* the metal or plastic ring affixed to the part of the *shaft* where the ribs that support the fabric canopy are attached.
- *Rib:* the rod that attaches to the *top notch* and that supports the fabric that covers the umbrella. The canopy is attached to the rib with a stitch.
- *Runner:* the part that runs along the shaft, where the *stretchers* are attached. It's diameter is greater than that of the shaft, with a height of about 4 cm/1.57". It can be made of metal or plastic.
- *Stretcher:* the rod that is hinged and attached to the runner and the rib to act as a support and reinforcement to the fabric.
- *Frame:* the 8 ribs, stretchers, top notch and runner as a group, already assembled.
- *Tips:* small metal or plastic caps affixed to the fabric canopy and placed on the outer end of each rib.

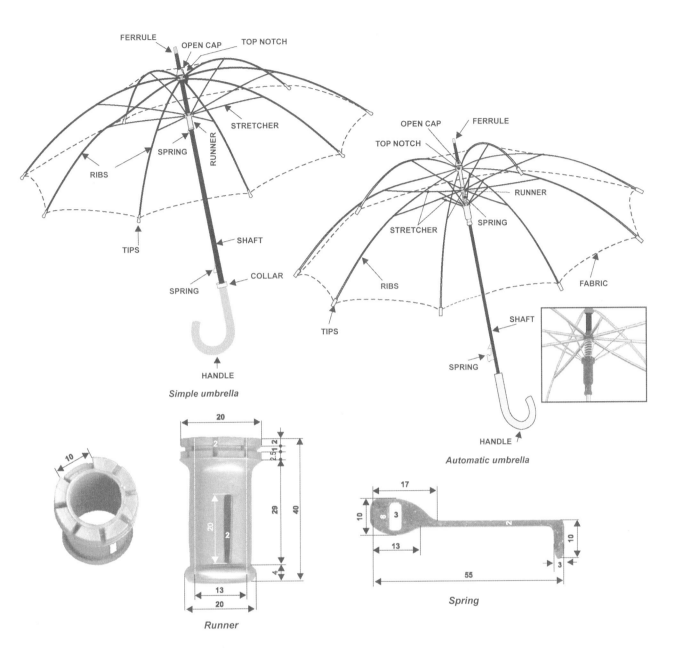

Simple umbrella

Automatic umbrella

Runner

Spring

- *Open cap:* a ring-shaped cap that is placed on the shaft above the canopy, used to finish and cover the fabric and ensure water doesn't get in. After being positioned, the open cap is affixed with a small nail or other side stopper.
- *Ferrule:* a metal or plastic topper placed at the very upper end of a wood shaft.
- *Fit-up:* the finish on the top end that groups the open cap and the ferrule, to cover the canopy.
- *Springs:* the two pieces inserted on the shaft that keep the umbrella open (near the top, called a top spring), or closed (called a button spring).
The distance between the two springs is in relation to the length of the *stretcher* and the shaft (e.g..: for a 61 cm Italian umbrella, the distance is 42 cm/1.65″.

- *Collar:* the ring placed above the handle, which is used to stop the tips attached to the canopy at the end of the ribs.
- *Strap:* a ribbon of fabric with a hook or Velcro® sewn to the canopy to affix it when closed.

Assembly
1) Assemble the frame, connecting the *stretchers and ribs* with the runner and the top notch with iron wire.
2) Affix the top notch to the shaft with a small nail.
3) Affix the fabric canvas (already sewn) to the frame: with a stitch on the ribs, inserting the tips onto their ends.
4) Iron the canvas with a jet of steam.
5) Affix the open cap on the top, with a nail or with glue or a ring.
6) Insert the handle, affixing it with a bit of glue.

Sections for umbrellas

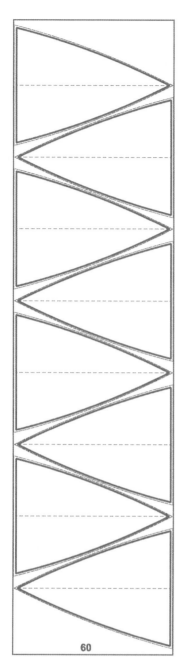

60

Section layout

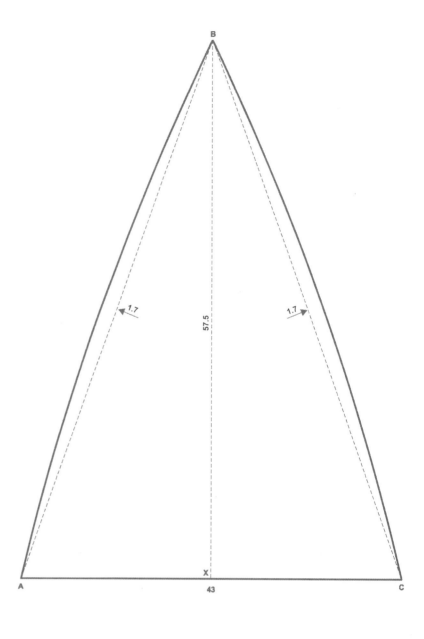

B

57.5

1.7   1.7

A   43   C

X

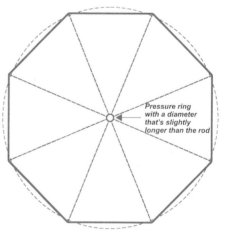

*Pressure ring
with a diameter
that's slightly
longer than the rod*

8 panel umbrella

(Construction for an umbrella with a coverage radius of 61 cm/2.40")
- Draw triangle A-B-C, with the base of A-C as 43 cm/1.69" and the height B-X as 57.5 cm/2.26".
- Curve sides A-B and C-B with an arc as shown in the figure, keeping them pulled away from the centre by 1.7 cm/0.07".

WALKING STICKS

1796 - Incroyables

1912

Around the 1760s, walking sticks with a twisted or curved handle became a natural complement for English clothing, typical of the Neoclassical period.

In the early 1800s, an ingenious model of cane was made in Italy, as the *Corriere delle Dame* wrote at the time, "it closes like a telescope and can be carried in one's pocket", with various forms and finishes: straight, with a derby handle, a smooth gold knob, with a cord loop or chain to hold it to the wrist, etc. In this period, walking sticks, also called canes, were quite in fashion, made of highly-prized wood. They often came with many inventions, like that of hiding just about anything one needs to smoke tobacco in the knob, or hiding a small dress sword within it (called a swordstick).

Youths preferred thinner walking sticks called "gannette" in Italy, made to be continuously rotated between the fingers as one walked.

After 1890, still an indispensable fashion accessory, the walking stick generally had a crookneck handle with a vein of gold at the point of attachment with the handle, along with those with an ivory top or motifs carved in Art Nouveau style.

Walking sticks are generally a men's accessory. Today, they are almost exclusively used by those who need them to walk.

In the past, robust walking sticks were carried for safety and even as a defensive weapon, often also by women.

Around the mid 1500s, walking sticks began to turn into a quite common accessory, especially for affected decoration.

In this period, they also took on a social function, so much so that the authorities of the era gave worthy persons a cane of honour, a sort of award or personal merit.

In the 1600s, the habit of carrying a long walking stick with a knob at the top became quite popular, marking one's step by hitting it on the cobblestones, military style.

In the 1700s, the cane was at the height of its splendour. In fact, it was a very common to go out dressed elegantly, with a rich, long, thin walking stick topped with a golden knob, semi-precious stone or ivory.

Northern European walking stick, 1700-1730

TYPES OF WALKING STICKS

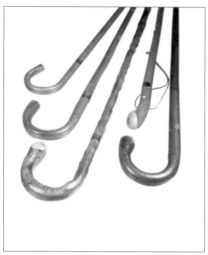

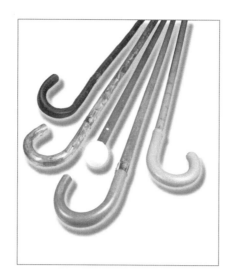

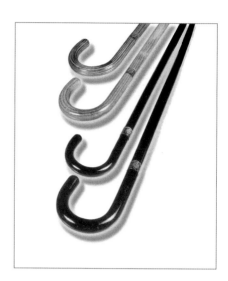

NATURAL WOOD

Type "A" (90 cm/3.54")
- 1 Crookneck in ash with a Savoy band
- 2 Crookneck in chestnut with a Savoy band
- 3 Crookneck in Congo wood with a Savoy band
- 4 Straight shillelagh in chestnut with a Savoy band
- 5 Crookneck in hazelnut with a Savoy band

Type "B" (90 cm/3.54")
- 1 Crookneck in striped durmast oak with a Savoy band
- 2 Crookneck in durmast oak with a Savoy band
- 3 Crookneck in black acacia with a Savoy band
- 4 Crookneck in black acacia with a Savoy band
- 5 Crookneck in brown acacia with a Savoy band

Type "C" (90 cm/3.54")
- 1 Crookneck in marasca cherry with a Savoy band
- 2 Crookneck in Scotch broom with a Savoy band
- 3 Crookneck in natural malacca with a Savoy band
- 4 Crookneck handle in light boar, natural malacca shaft

Type "M" (90 cm/3.54")
- 1 Dachshund head, brown wood shaft
- 2 Mastiff head, brown wood shaft
- 3 Dog's head in horn, wood shaft
- 4 Brown dog's head, wood shaft
- 5 Cocker spaniel head, black wood shaft
- 6 Pointer head, brown wood shaft

ANIMALS - Type "I" (90 cm/3.54")
- 1 Woodpecker head, brown wood shaft
- 2 Eagle head, brown wood shaft
- 3 Toucan head, brown wood shaft
- 4 Falcon head, brown wood shaft
- 5 Pheasant head, brown wood shaft
- 6 Parrot head, black wood shaft

CHARACTERS - Type "N" (90 cm/3.54")
- 1 Dante Alighieri, black wood shaft
- 2 Schiller, black wood shaft
- 3 Napoleone Bonaparte, black wood shaft
- 4 Goethe, black wood shaft
- 5 Mussolini, black wood shaft
- 6 Francesco Giuseppe, black wood shaft

SPECIAL WALKING STICKS

Cane with a hidden compartment, 1890

*"Telescopic" cane,
late 1800s*

"Sewing" cane

"Sommelier" cane

"Watch" cane

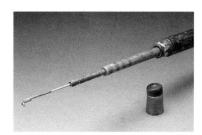

"Fishing rod" cane

"Lipstick" cane

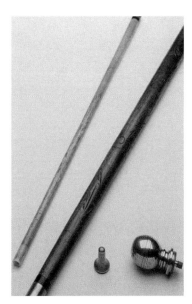

"Cue stick" cane

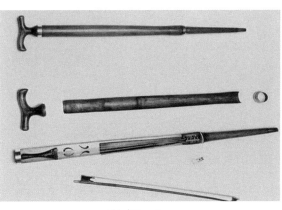

"Violin" cane

"Emergency professional" cane

Walking stick in just one piece

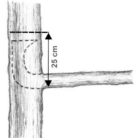

Choosing the branch

Rough cutting the branch

Trunk with the part of the root ready to be worked

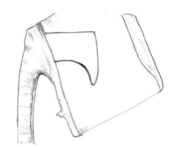

Drawing the outline of the walking stick

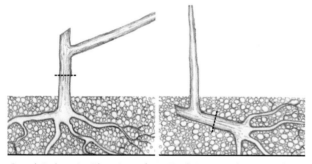

Branch to be cut with a piece of the main trunk

Trunk to cut with a piece of the root

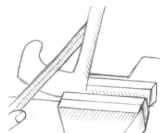

Cutting with the jigsaw and finishing

Materials

The quality of a walking stick depends on many factors: good manufacturing techniques, proper design and the artistic element of the handle or knob, but, most importantly. by the quality of the material it is made from.

The most commonly used material for canes is wood, even if handles are often in prized materials such as horn or ivory.

The main types of wood used for walking sticks are: *chestnut*; *ash*, *birch*, *hawthorn*, *hazelnut*, *holly*, *honeysuckle*, *mountain ash*, *sycamore*, *willow*. Some of these trees not only offer flavourful fruit and prized wood, but their branches are also integral to the creation of prized walking sticks. Carefully chosen and worked, they turn into walking or hiking sticks. These types of wood were once used for artisanal manufacturing, quite common in the past. Today, in Europe, there are a few companies working at full capacity. One of them is the Fabrique de cannes B. Boursier in Entre deux Guiers, a small town in Isère. A family company founded in 1898, they've produced walking sticks for six generations. Six employees produce 60,000 pieces per year in different varieties: with a crook neck, or straight and with a leather loop, simple or a top sculpted into the shape of a

Eurasian eagle-owl, symbol of the Parc régional de la Chartreuse. Boursier was the first to be awarded the *park's brand* in 1999. It is difficult to imagine that a chestnut walking stick could require 32 phases for its creation, often still made with old machinery.

Choosing the wood

Different types of wood grow in various climates, thus giving them different qualities and flexibility. Selection is then based on the use the walking stick is intended for, as are the processes used, tied to the shape and length of the chosen branch.

New growths of trees (shoots) and other plants along the banks of rivers are the best types of branches to use for walking sticks, as they are often already in the desired shape.

Walking sticks in just one piece

After having chosen the desired branch, cut the main trunk including the branch, in a length of about 25 cm/9.84".

- Rough cut and mark the outline of the handle or the knob as desired, preferably con a cardboard pattern.

- Cut out the shape with a jigsaw, working it with a rasp. Finish with sandpaper in various gauges.

CROOKNECK WALKING STICKS

This type of walking stick is a humble, affordable and functional one. It can be found in numerous health-care stores and among items for the mountains, but it must be made with utmost attention in order to avoid folds or breakages.

The wood generally used for mass production of this model is ash or sweet chestnut. If ash is being used, the bark is usually left on, while those made of sweet chestnut are free of bark and dyed.

Creating the handle

To create the rounded handle, two tools are required:

1) A heating accessory, to warm the part of the stalk that is to be curved (usually the last 38 cm/1.50").

2) A piece or form around which the handle is shaped and which will keep it in the right shape until its definitively set.

Prepare the tool to curve the handle:

A) Cut a sheet of hard wood measuring 25 x 10 x 2 cm/9.84 x 3.94 x 0.79".

B) Lathe a hard wood wheel with an indented canal along the outside edge, 9 cm/3.54" in diameter and 3 cm/1.18" in thickness.

C) Prepare a metal cylinder that is 10 mm/0.39" in diameter and 5-6 cm/1.97-2.36" high, screwed to the flat plane (it can be created from an already threaded bolt, with a smooth part above and the head to be cut off).

D) Get a bolt to affix the curved wheel.

Assemble the pieces as illustrated.

Heating the walking stick

Different systems can be used to heat the walking stick:

1) A hot basin of wet sand (the ancient, traditional method), though it is inconvenient to build and move or put away.

2) A hot air generator, though with this system the air won't be quite hot enough and it will be poorly distributed.

3) With a water boiler placed on an electric burner or a gas flame, the most suitable method for both straightening the shaft and curving the handle.

Creating the walking stick

To create this type of walking stick, start with a straight trunk, about 120 cm/4.72" long and with a diameter of about 2.5 cm/0.10" proceeding as follows:

1) Create a notch at about 12 mm/0.47" from the end of the handle and wrap a robust cord around it, about 38 cm/14.96 long, so that the ends of the cord are equal in length. The two ends of the cord will then be used to hold the curved handle in place.

2) Steam the handle for about an hour, covering it with a canvas sack or something similar, so as to maintain the heat around the part to be curved. It isn't possible to say precisely how much time the cane needs to be steamed, because there are lots of variables and only practice makes perfect. If the cane doesn't bend on your first try, don't force it as it will break. Steam it some more and try again later.

3) Quickly place the heated end between the *stopper* and the wheel, keeping it snug. Move the handle clockwise around the wheel.

4) Snugly tie the cord around the trunk in a point that's lined up with the notch, perhaps with the help of another person. Bending the handle in this way can cause splintering on the crown of the handle, which will then be removed with a very sharp knife, working with the grain, then sanded delicately with sandpaper of various gauges.

Curved walking stick.

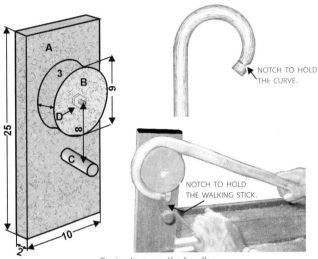

NOTCH TO HOLD THE CURVE.

NOTCH TO HOLD THE WALKING STICK.

Device to curve the handle.

Keep the curved part of the cane around the wheel with a string held in place by the notch.

Remove the wheel with the cane attached and let it set for a night.

THE "TURN UP" SHAPE.

5) Remove the wheel with the entire cane from the device and let the unit rest so that the handle cools and the curvature sets.

6) After about 20-24 hours, remove the cord. This will cause the curvature to open slightly. Remove the wheel and, to ensure that the handle is fully set, dry it with a hair dryer with hot air for about 2-3 minutes.

7) Finish the handle by cutting the bump away and rounding out the end with sandpaper, or thin it with a knife to give it a *turn up*, often seen on shepherds' crooks.

WALKING STICK FROM TWO PIECES OF WOOD

Two-piece walking sticks have the advantage of not having to be tied to or limited by the shape, colour and size of the raw natural material, as often happens with walking sticks made of one piece of wood. For the handle, you can use any type of wood and its design can be simple or complex, as desired.

The main problem is, of course, how to attach the handle to the shaft. This isn't particularly difficult but, no matter how the handle is fit into the wood block, the direction of the grain will inevitably create weak points. A way to reduce, if not entirely eliminate, this problem is to carve out the handle from a piece of wood that is already curved naturally, close to the form you wish to obtain. As such, the grain follows the line of the handle, reinforcing it, instead of running transversally. Although you may be lucky enough to come across a piece of wood suitable enough to produce the handle of a shepherd's crook, it's much more likely that you'll find smaller pieces of wood that you can create the handle of a market walking stick. This makes it possible to produce handles that are less attractive than those made of carefully selected blocks of wood, though they are surely much more durable.

Shaping the handle

For the two-piece walking stick shown here, the handle can be made of one piece of sycamore. This smooth, durable wood features a narrow grain and light colour, and is easy to work. This requires a block measuring 15 x 15 x 3 cm/5.91 x 5.91 x 1.18". These pieces can easily be made from wide planks bought at carpentry shops or sawmills.

The outline of the handle is shown in the figure. Transferring it to Plexiglas or another transparent, durable material, and resting it on the wood block, you will note the direction of the grain and thereby establish the most suitable position. When creating this type of handle, it's best if the grain is in a diagonal direction. With a diagonal grain, the risk of weak points is reduced. Once you've found the correct position, use a pencil to draw a line around the outline, then cut the form with a saw. Then select a stalk or trunk suitable to be united with the handle (or, for a sycamore handle, you can choose a dark hazelnut shaft or one with a pronounced grain). After having chosen and decided upon the diameter to which the handle needs to be shaved, you'll need to use a rasp or file to round the edges until the neck of the handle is 3 mm/0.12" greater in diameter than that of the upper part of the shaft.

Adapting the handle to the shaft

Different methods can be used to unite the two parts of wood. It is, however, best to create a wooden peg in the shaft that fits perfectly with a cavity carved out of the inside of the handle, then affix the two pieces with glue. It is very important for the peg to fit perfectly with the cavity so that the handle, once assembled, is aligned perfectly with the shaft and the joint created is precise and neat. This part of the process requires plenty of patience. A poorly-done joint can ruin an otherwise perfect walking stick.

To create the peg, create a mark on the shaft measuring 3 cm/1.18" below the upper edge and carefully wrap a piece of protective adhesive tape below the mark. The upper edge of the tape is the point at which you should cut. With a saw, make a 6 mm/0.24" deep cut following the line of the tape. Then, with

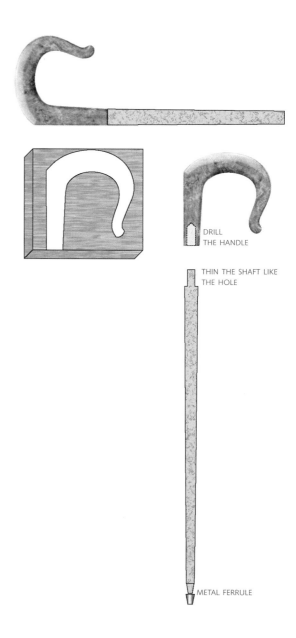

DRILL THE HANDLE

THIN THE SHAFT LIKE THE HOLE

METAL FERRULE

a sharp knife, whittle the wood to create the peg and finish it with a file to create a diameter of 13 mm/0.51".

Then, in the middle of the handle, use a drill to create a 13 mm/0.51" diameter hole. Then, perhaps with the help of a spacer so you don't go through the other side, drill to the depth of 32 mm/1.26". Smooth the opening of the hole and try inserting the shaft. When you're sure it enters perfectly, spread a good amount of resin glue over the surface, ensuring the peg enters easily, without the risk of creating cracks in the handle.

After the glue has dried, finish the handle, filing it around the joint, bringing it to the same diameter as the shaft. Sand the handle carefully in the same direction as the grain until the two surfaces are perfectly flush.

Buffalo horn handle

The easiest shape of a horn walking stick to make is the variety similar to the wood one described before.

Reducing the size of the horn

To start, you'll need to reduce the transversal section of the buffalo horn at the point in which it will become the neck of the handle. This makes it easier to curve the material and less likely that folds will be created on the inner part.

Starting from the assumption that you will have to work with a horn that is at least 35 cm/13.79" long, you can expect its oval base will be 5 cm/1.97" in diameter at its widest point and 2.5 cm/0.98" at the narrowest point. That which must be reduced is the widest part, to the same dimensions of the smaller one so that the cross-section is more or less square. Using a coloured pencil, roughly draw this outline on the horn and then cut the shape with a band saw or a mechanical jigsaw. In this phase, you'll need to pay close attention to not remove too much material, so as not to compromise the final dimensions.

Once done cutting, use a rasp or file to round the squared edges.

Heating and bending

The next step is that of boiling the horn for about 30 minutes, so that it will become softer, helping speed up the bending process with a hot air gun. Use a pair of pliers to remove it from the pot and check that it can be handled without issue before putting it in the bending device.

If using a shaft jig like that shown in the figure, affix the part of the neck between the adjustable grips and the mould and tighten so that the surface of the horn is entirely touching the shaft jig. Don't pull the grip too tight, so as not to ruin the horn or the mould.

Before heating the horn, sprinkle lubricating oil over it to reduce the risk of splintering. Apply the hot air gun for about 5 minutes along the section of the horn that is to be curved around the mould (to become the crown of the handle).

Use a G-clamp to force the horn around the mould. Tighten it until the horn is snug against the surface of the mould, across the entire length of the crown (see the figure).

You can also use roughly concave and convex wood blocks and wedges to help in this process.

Continue, heating the part of the horn that is still free (that is, the tip), using another G-clamp and a block of wood to line up this last part as well. However, do not tighten the clamp so much that the tip touches the concave part of the mould.

To make the cane, that which you should obtain in this phase is a shape similar to that shown in the figure.

After having positioned all the clamps, check that the horn hasn't shifted from the rear surface of the shaft jig. If that has happened, you'll need to apply one or two more clamps to line everything up. Leave the horn in the jig overnight.

Walking stick with a horn handle

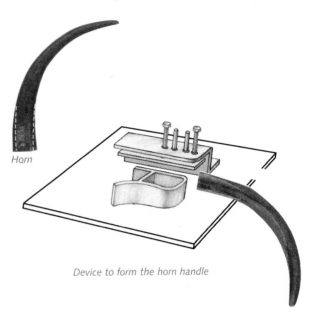

Horn

Device to form the horn handle

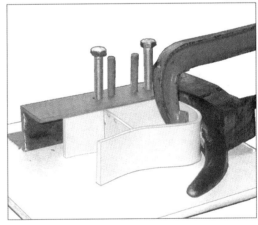

First bending of the horn

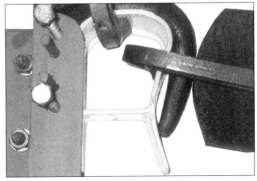

Second bending of the horn

FINISHING HORN HANDLES

Now you'll need to curve the tip of the handle inward. To do this, you'll need to heat the part close to the tip (that is, the last 10 cm/3.94" or so) and tighten it with a clamp. Tighten the handle, heat the tip, and delicately tighten the clamp until the end is curved inwards, reaching about 5 cm/1.97" from the neck. Leave it in the clamp until it is fully set.

Final shaping

The overall length of the handle, from the point in which it is united to the shaft to the tip, should be around 30 cm/11.81". The last thing left to do is to shape the final form of the handle and finish it using a series of rasps and sandpapers. The effect to try to create is that of a round handle that thins towards the tip into a point.

Before starting, remember that this material is an easily-worked material, and it's much easier to create undesired marks than remove them.

As much as possible, file and sand along the front of the length instead of around the circumference of the handle, and do not remove too much material from the same place all at once. At this point, be sure to pause and carefully look at the piece, then proceed.

Pay careful attention to the tip, which must be slightly flattened, thereby making the external surface semi-circular.

Affixing the handle to the shaft

Affix the handle using self-tapping screws, set both on the handle and on the shaft with a depth of about 5 cm/1.97" per side, as shown in the figure.

You can add a *spacer* to this type of handle, which will be positioned between the handle and the shaft, embellishing the joint. The spacer may be made of different materials, including: hard wood, such as ebony; horn or deer antlers; metal, such as brass; synthetic materials, such as nylon or Teflon®; ram or sheep horn to lighten a dark handle, or water buffalo horn when the handle is light in colour.

The spacer should be no more than 19 mm/0.75" thick.

The upper and lower surfaces of the spacer should be completely flat, smooth and flush so that, once inserted between the handle and the shaft, it's perfectly joined with both. The simplest way to create perfectly flat surfaces is to rub the spacer on a piece of fine sandpaper resting on a flat surface: this reduces the risk of ruining and rounding the edges of the spacer. After having sanded the surfaces, remove the majority of the material to be discarded from the circumference of the spacer with a rasp. Centre and pierce the spacer and thread it onto the shaft.

Using sand paper, rub the spacer until its circumference is exactly equal to that of the handle.

Finish the walking stick by placing a cap on the end and applying paint, oil or enamel.

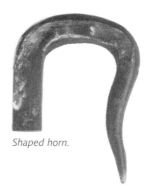

Shaped horn.

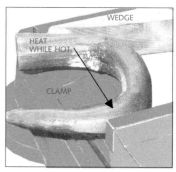

Delicately close in on the heated horn with the clamp.

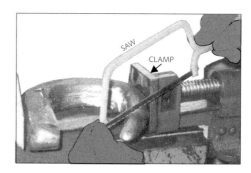

Cut to the desired length and round.

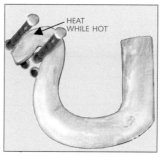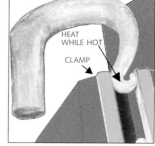

Or create the desired shape.

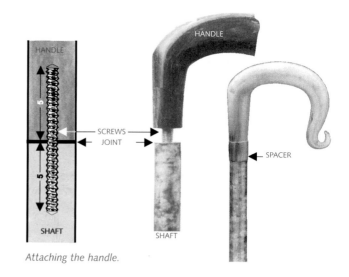

Attaching the handle.

BUTTONS

A short history 212
Paper, doum and snap buttons 214
Button sizes and working processes 215
Button working processes 216
Button measurements 217

A SHORT HISTORY

Buttons are small discs of various materials that, when inserted into an eyelet, serve to join or unite two parts of clothing. They can be flat, convex or even covered in fabric. Buttons can be both decorative and functional, or simply used as decoration or as a button-jewel.

Buttons can be made of natural materials (wood, bone, horn, mother of pearl, metal or vegetable ivory (corozo) or synthetics (polyester, polyamide, acrylic and casein). In addition, plastic and metal can be combined, like when a metal circle acts as a setting or crown for a button, and plastic may be covered in the same fabric as the garment.

Natural materials create buttons of different colours, shapes, sizes and outlines, though they generally have a higher price point, while man-made materials are more uniform and cost less. The material that is eventually chosen depends in large part on the type of garment and the market, however the main necessity in terms of the creation of the garment is that, in any case, the buttons can be machine-sewn.

Buttons as we know them came into use only in the 17th century in France. Before that, clothing was sewn and un-sewn with running stitches each time it was worn, with the understandable discomfort that this implied.

After that date, especially among nobility and the wealthy, buttons became another way to show wealth and luxury, with jewel-like buttons in gold and precious stones.

During the time of Louis IX, *boutoniers* were recorded in the "Book of Trades" compiled by the Provost of Paris, Etienne Boileau, alongside the manufacturers.

Chapter LXXII of this historic document reveals the main requirements suitable for the job of buttoner, who must be first and foremost a person of good moral standing, skilled, wise and loyal.

Despite its practical function, button making remained mainly in the hands of jewellers.

In the 18th and 19th centuries, when their use was by now in full swing, industrially-made buttons appeared in England and France.

The evolution of buttons produced on an industrial scale was systematic and considerable.

Buttons are dividable into a few categories:
- *Buttons for eyelets or buttonholes - Post snap fasteners Prong snap fasteners*.

They can be made of different materials, the most common of which are:
1) Metal; 2) Ceramics; 3) Mother of pearl; 4) Fabric; 5) Glass; 6) Paper; 7) Doum palm (a type of "vegetable ivory").

Metal buttons

Up until 1830, these buttons were mostly flat, suitable for military uniforms among other things. They were often decorated with the insignia of the military of affiliation, imprinted on the sheet through a rocker arm.

After that date, rounded buttons began to be produced that, in addition to being rather elegant, further brought out the engravings found on the convex surface.

Pisanello, portrait of Lionello d'Este, 1441

Painted silver, Italy, 14th century

Embroidered Italy, 14th century

Gold and coral cuff button, 1600

Afghan button, 1600

Ceramic buttons

Ceramic buttons appeared in the second half of the 18th century, becoming famous for their precious decorations - just think, for example, of those made by the ceramicist Antonibon in Nove, near Bassano, Italy. Around 1840, English company Prosser was the first to produce them on a large scale.

It was then a French industrialist, Felix Bapterosse, from Briare, to bring thoughtful changes to Prosser's techniques, creating a more refined product with lower costs. This type of button was dyed by mixing different types of metal oxides into the ceramic clay.

Fabric buttons

Considered the direct descendants of those in wood, they were formed from a wood disc that had the necessary holes for the thread that attaches them to the garment, constituting the structure of the covering fabric.

In 1844, French manufacturer Parent invented the shank of the "queue solide" button, which made sewing the garment easier and faster. Following that, a certain Clement created the machine that covers buttons in fabric.

The invention was a great success, allowing the inventor to sell 300 machines in Paris alone in a short amount of time. Its purchasers were small craft workshops, makers of a certain type of button covered in white canvas called *vestal buttons*, used in women's and children's undergarments.

Corozo buttons

The corozo nut, also known as vegetable ivory, imported from Ecuador and Panama, appeared in Europe in the second half of the 19th century. It seems that its use in the button industry arose from the suggestion of a shipowner that saw new, speculative possibilities in the exotic fruit.

In the port of Hamburg around this time, it was common to unload quantities of corozo nut stored as ballast on sail boats coming from Central America, which had previously been dumped into the sea after every voyage.

In the creation of corozo buttons, the Germans soon became the leaders, a position they held on to until Austria took up similar work. The first Italian establishments for corozo button production arose almost simultaneously between 1869-70 in Palazzolo sull'Oglio (near Brescia), thanks to Edoardo Taccini, and, in Piacenza, thanks to the efforts of Mr Vicenzo Rovera. In a short amount of time, a concentration of various factories in the two towns made products that were so perfect that they were preferred to foreign-made ones in the export market.

From their first appearance, these buttons replaced those in metal and wood as well as those with passementerie, which were much more expensive and elaborate.

Glass buttons

In the second half of the 19th century, Austria had a monopoly on these buttons. In that era, the most important factories, which produced them in all shapes and sizes, were in Gablonz, in Bohemia, a region well known since then for the button making machines they produced.

1700

Silver, France, 1800   *Engraved metal, France, 1800*

Floral ceramic and metal, 1800   *1850*

Queen helmet shell and gold, 1870

Ceramic, France, 1900   *1930*

PAPER, DOUM AND SNAP BUTTONS

Paper buttons

These buttons appeared around 1890 in France. They were used especially for canvas dresses and stockings. Made of compressed paperboard, paper buttons are waterproofed by soaking them in heated flax oil.

It isn't quite clear why in Italy, a button producing country, the military started using paper buttons in the early 1900s.

Doum nut buttons

After 1907, in addition to corozo, the Italian button-making industry found broad use for the fruit of palm trees, doum nuts, imported from Eritrea. The initial attempts to use doum nuts went back to 1902, with the honourable Mr Martini calling upon Professor Isaia Boldrati, the Director of the Eritrean Colony Entity, to work with him in Italy's African colony. Mr Boldrati, benefiting from the collaboration with an experienced colonist, brought the attention of Italian button-making companies to the nut, which had a number of manufacturing advantages over corozo, mainly less production waste.

Post snap fasteners

Post snap fasteners are made up of two sections, each divided into two parts of its own:

1) The external parts of the button, which must be affixed with a grommet.

2) The internal parts, which penetrate the fabric from the inside of the garment and which is affixed to the stud of the button with a special machine.

There are no threads that unravel or get abraded and the wide attachment base distributes the load directly on the button when being snapped and unsnapped. The two parts can be in brass or steel and the cap can feature a decorative design or logo, but it must be resistant to rust.

Once attached to the garment, they cannot be moved, so it is very important to carefully position them from the start. The fabric of the garment must be strong enough to support the stress that a similar button will be subject to (with the addition of a reinforcement if necessary).

Prong snap fasteners

Prong snap fasteners are available in a variety of shapes, but they all are made up of four elements: a cap and a socket that are combined to create the visible outer part of the fastening (called the female part), then a stud and a post that create the internal part (called the male part) of the fastening, which normally isn't seen when the garment is closed.

The cap and the post are affixed by pronged rings, meaning they can be used for lightweight fabrics for non-decorative purposes. Prong rings closures are the only ones suitable for use on knits.

These types of snaps are to be used on children's rompers and pyjamas. They are designed to make sure the fabric isn't pierced with large holes. Generally, breakages occur due to the application method instead of due to defects in the button itself. They should never be attached through a single layer of material. Instead, they need a strip of reinforcement fabric on the back, especially with knits. The size used should be suitable to the thickness and weight of the fabric.

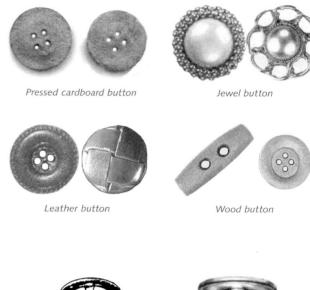

Pressed cardboard button   Jewel button

Leather button   Wood button

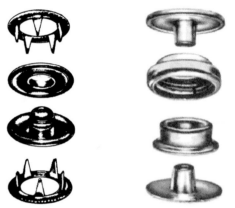

Prong and post snap fasteners

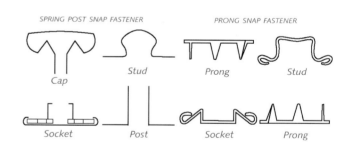

SPRING POST SNAP FASTENER   PRONG SNAP FASTENER

Cap   Stud   Prong   Stud

Socket   Post   Socket   Prong

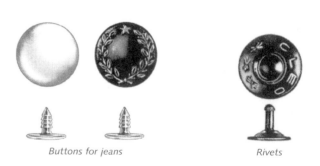

Buttons for jeans   Rivets

BUTTON SIZES AND WORKING PROCESSES

BUTTON SHAPES AND SIZES

Buttons are measured according to the diameter, using either the *decimal system* (in mm), or the *ligne system*.

Classic buttons are round and flat, with varying sizes and materials.

Other buttons can have different aspects, including geometric shapes such as square, oval, half-sphere, sphere or "creative" forms, used especially for children's garments with printed synthetic materials such as animals, flowers, dolls, etc.

Then there are *jewel buttons*, which have quite elaborate forms, enriched by gemstones, rhinestones, pearls, etc.

INDUSTRIAL BUTTON PRODUCTION

The main button production techniques, industrially speaking, are: 1) *Pressing and cutting*; 2) *Turning*.

Pressing and cutting

Pressing and cutting is a working system used for synthetics such as polyester, acrylics, phenolic resins, urea resins, etc.

These resins get to button factories in a coloured powder that is then dissolved in cold water, creating a sort of dough that is placed in a rotary press called a *blanking machine* to create the disks, called "blanks", in different sizes.

Disc cutter   Semi-automatic milling machine

LIGNE/MILLIMETRE CORRESPONDENCE CHART

LIGNE	MILLIM.	LIGNE	MILLIM.
14	9	44	28
16	10	48	30.5
18	11.4	54	34
20	12.8	60	38
22	14	65	41
24	15	70	44.5
26	16.5	75	47.5
28	18	80	51
30	19	85	54
32	20	90	58
36	23	95	60
40	25	100	63
42	27	110	70

These blanks are then placed on the flat surface of a heat press with the mould of the desired model. The buttons are pressed at a temperature of 120-200°C/248-392°F, creating their definitive shape.

These are brought to automatic machines which drill the holes, then they're shined and finished.

Turning

The turning technique is used for the majority of raw materials: mother of pearl, tortoise, vegetable ivory (corozo), wood, polyester, Plexiglas®, acrylates, acetates, galalith, etc.

Raw materials are delivered to button factories as cylinders or sheets, in a natural colour or already dyed.

To create buttons using the turning system, the following steps must be carried out: 1) cutting; 2) shaping and turning; 3) drilling of the holes; 4) polishing; 5) dying.

- *Cutting* is done with special machines called disc cutters, which can be vertical (to cut raw materials that are in the shape of a cylinder), or horizontal (to cut materials that are in sheets). With this operation, discs called "washers" are created in the desired size and thickness.

- *Shaping and turning* is an operation that is first done on the back of the washers, with a hand-operated or automatic machine, then on the front with a semi-automatic milling or turning machine (according to the outline and the design that is to be made, such as: knurls, fluting, designs in relief, filleting, concavities, etc.).

- *Drilling* is done with semi-automatic drills or with automatic machines equipped with perforating points that are programmed according to the type of button to:
1) Create 2 or 4 vertical holes; 2) Create a canal on the back of the button; 3) Apply the shank to the back of the button.

- *Polishing* is done by taking the worked buttons, mixed with abrasive powder and sawdust or pieces of wood, and putting them in special tumblers or drums, which are cylindrical or asymmetrical containers that, rotating around their central axis, continuously move the contents, producing perfectly polished buttons.

- *Dying*, done with natural or white raw materials, is done by *spraying*, with a compressed air nozzle, or with a *bath*, completely submerging the buttons into a high-temperature solution, suitable for the material, subject to washing. They then are given a final wash and dried in special electronic dryers.

BUTTON WORKING PROCESSES

CREATING MOTHER-OF-PEARL BUTTONS

Mother of pearl is the inner part of various shells, including (the most commonly used) *Trochus* and *Meleagrina* shells, which come from warm-water seas such as those near Australia, Tahiti, the Indian Ocean and the Red Sea.

Shells, which come to button factories as raw shells or even in layers, are washed with warm water then cut into disks or "washers".

Cutting takes place by diversifying the sizes, that is: first they're cut into bigger rounds, then smaller ones, then into those for men's and women's shirts.

Once they're cut, the discs are cleaned of the outer crust with special treatments, to then go on to the division of the pieces according to thickness, the turning/milling, and the finishing steps, all based on the button designed.

Artificial mother of pearl

This synthetic material, generally of polyester or in another synthesised product, is prepared in sheets of varying thickness. Before the turning, milling, and other phases, these sheets are sprayed with "essence of the East", a product made of dried and ground silver fish scales. This adds iridescence to the slabs, similar to natural mother of pearl.

WORKING VEGETABLE IVORY

Vegetable ivory is made of a hard white substance (caused by the hemicellulose in the cellular membrane) deriving from the endosperm of American palm trees in the *Phytelephas* genus, called "corozo", or from doum palm nuts, which grow in drier climates such as Eritrea, Sudan, Cyrenaica, etc.

Vegetable ivory, today mostly replaced by plastics, is worked as follows:

Mother of pearl

Polyester　　　*Leather*

Wood　　　*Metal*

Two holes　*Four holes*　*With a shank*　*For jeans*

Buffalo horn　　　*Tortoiseshell*

1) Cleaning of the dried seeds in the drums to rid them of their red shell (integument)
2) Drying and sorting of the seeds
3) Slicing and sawing of the seeds
4) Turning of the discs
5) Drilling the holes
6) Second tumbling in the drums
7) Dying
8) Third tumbling in the drums and polishing

Attaching the buttons

There are three main ways to attach buttons:
1) With holes, which can be two or four central holes on the button;
2) With a shank with a hole;
3) With a rivet-type shank, as is often seen on jeans.
These three main types come in many sub-varieties.
Buttons with two or four holes are generally flat and have holes placed at standard distances to make it possible to apply them by machine, with special tools.

The button that is eventually chosen depends in large part on the type of garment and the market, however the main necessity in terms of the creation of the garment is that the buttons can be machine-sewn.

Synthetic buttons for men's shirts　　*Mother-of-pearl buttons for women's blouses*

BUTTON MEASUREMENTS

This requires that the button can be held in a clamp while the machine sews, while for large products such as shirts, that means that the clamp must be automatically fed by a hopper system. Today, buttons are sewn on garments with continuous-cycle machines controlled and managed by a computer. These machines use a chain stitch with a single piece of thread, a knotted double stitch or a simulated hand-stitch. The latter is used generally for classic outerwear. A chain stitch with a single thread, however, doesn't guarantee the secure fastening of the button, but these types of machines are already widely in use and replacing them with a knotted stitch is slow as these machines are quite expensive.

Two or four hole buttons are attached directly. It is important that they are functional rather than just decorative, and for that reason they must be sewn with a long enough piece of thread, allowing the button to separate far enough from the garment and be turned to fit into the eyelet.

On a four-hole button, the direction of the thread in the holes doesn't matter, while for a two-hole button, the stitches that affix it must be parallel to the eyelet in order to minimise torsion and the need for a long shank or piece of thread.

Buttons with a shank have no holes on their face, but instead have a protruding portion with a hole on the back. This type of button must be clamped sideways by the equipment, so that the thread is passed through the hole of the shank, from one of its sides.

Buttons covered in fabric are generally of this type and thus follow the same rules.

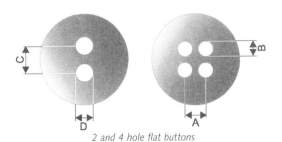

2 and 4 hole flat buttons

Buttons with a shank

Rounded buttons with a groove

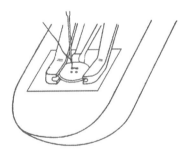

Clamp of the button-attachment machine, adjustable in accordance with the various measurements of the buttons. Its purpose is to hold the button in place while being sewn.

2 AND 4 HOLE BUTTONS				
Ligne	A	B	C	D
14"-15"	2.6	1.6	3.3	1.8
16"-18"	2.8	1.8	3.6	2.0
20"-26"	3.0	2.1	3.9	2.2
28"-36"	3.4	2.3	4.2	2.4
40"	4.1	2.5	5.2	3.0
44"	4.3	2.8	5.2	3.0
48"	4.5	3.0	5.4	3.2
54"	4.6	3.2	6.0	3.5
60"	5.1	3.5	6.0	3.5
72"-80"	5.2	3.8	7.0	4.0

2 and 4 hole button measurement chart

BUTTONS WITH A SHANK				
Ligne	A	B	C	D
14"- 20"	3.0	6.0	2.00	3.0
24"- 40"	3.5	6.5	2.25	3.5
44"- 80"	4.0	7.0	2.25	4.0

Buttons with a shank measurement chart

ROUNDED BUTTONS				
Ligne	A	B	C	D
14"- 20"	4.0	4.0	2.00	3.0
24"- 40"	4.0	5.5	2.00	3.5
44"- 80"	4.0	6.5	2.00	4.0

Domed buttons measurement chart

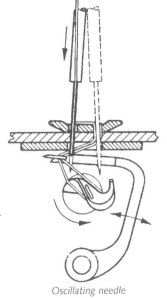

Button attachment machine with an oscillating needle, which carries out a movement similar to that of a zig-zag sewing machine, penetrating one button hole followed by the next. The width of this zig-zag movement is adjustable depending on the distance between the holes in the button. The button-holding clamp stays still for the entire sewing cycle if the button has two holes; it's shifted halfway through the cycle if it has 4 holes.

Oscillating needle

COVERED BUTTONS					
Lig.	mm.	Lig.	mm.	Lig.	mm.
18"	11.0	30"	15.0	45"	29.0
24"	15.0	36"	23.0	60"	38.0

Covered buttons measurement chart

DOG APPAREL

Main sizes 220
Fundamentals. 222
Anatomy and measurements. 223
Apparel 224
Sleeveless base coat 226
Base coat with sleeves 228
Raglan sleeve base for small dogs. 230
Coat with a motif on the back 232
Coat for large dogs. 234
Technical card and measurement
conversion table. 236
Bibliography 237
Museums and schools. 238

Main sizes

MINI/TOY

Chihuahua

Affenpinscher

Coton de Tuléar

Miniature pinscher

Pomeranian

SMALL

Shih-Tzu

Pug

Basset hound

Cavalier King Charles Spaniel

Mini/toy

Miniature or "toy" dogs are very small and weigh very little. A few examples of this type of dog are Affenpinschers, Coton de Tuléars and miniature pinschers.

In recent years, tiny dogs have become quite fashionable.

It's a trend that has led to careful genetic selection aimed at smaller and smaller dogs, leading to "toy" breeds. However, if the trend for these "mini" breeds is going strong and if we want to take a step back from the "toy" name, we need to start from a few fundamental points:

1. Avoid the use of bags to "carry" four-legged friends. Though they may be considered a sort of way to prevent all the illnesses that the animal could potentially get coming into contact with other animals and nature in general (such as parasites), or for that which may be our obsession with hygiene, letting the dog walk on its own legs is a moment of discovery and olfactory exploration (remember that smell is one of the most important senses for this animal and it's essential for them to train their nose from the time they are young), as well as a time for socialisation. Otherwise, one may create a lack of wellness for the dog without realising it.

2. Remember that, given their small size, we are dealing with rather delicate animals, meaning extra attention must be paid. Even a simple microtrauma can lead to injuries that, in relation to their size, are anything but micro.

3. Last but not least, is food.

As stated by all veterinarians specialising in nutrition, meals should be prepared according to the breed, the weight and age of the animal and his/her lifestyle (indoors or outdoors, active or sedentary).

Small

Small dogs include: Shih-Tzus, pugs, bassethounds, Cavalier Kings, Australian Terriers and so many more. They're generally from 28-35 cm/11.02-13.78" and are, out of all breeds, those that love domestic life the most. That is to say that these dogs adapt best to life in an apartment, in comparison to other breeds. Their notable ability to adapt and their love for domestic life doesn't mean, however, that these pets should stay indoors all day.

Like all other dogs, they need to go outside at least once or twice a day. Another reason that explains their ability to adapt is that, essentially, these dogs prefer peace and quiet. Generally speaking, then, all small dogs have a calm temperament, which makes them great at cuddling even though, as calm, tranquil and relaxed as they are, if they feel threatened or in a dangerous situation they will defend themselves with tooth and nail.

Medium

Both as a working dog and as a "free time companion", the first dogs were medium sized. With weights from 8 to 25 kg/17.64-55.12 lbs and heights from 43 to 60 cm/16.93-23.62", they could be defined as the ancestors of almost all other types of dogs, as they are the starting point for selective breeding. Surely, this branch of biology has given life to a large variety of mid-size dog breeds.

As far as the character of these dogs is concerned, they are quite malleable: remember that they are the most suitable for living with children because they weigh less and are a bit more delicate than large dogs and yet more robust than small dogs. This category includes: boxers, collies, poodles, bulldogs, bull terriers, chow-chows, English cocker spaniels and others.

MEDIUM

Poodles

Basenji

Boxer

Collie

LARGE

Neapolitan mastiff

Afghan hound

Saint Bernard

GIANT

Great Dane

Mastiff

Newfoundland

Large

Perhaps of all the breeds, large dogs are the most fascinating, especially in terms of their behaviour.

They weigh between 25 and 50 kg/55.12-110.23" and up to 70 cm/27.56".

Among this breed, we can count quite a few examples: Billys, Bracco Italianos, bull mastiffs, Saint Bernards, Artois hounds, Dalmatians, dobermans, huskies, greyhounds, Neapolitan mastiffs, Belgian shepherd dogs, Bergamasco shepherds, pointers, Pulis, rottweilers, Weimeraners, etc. Despite how interesting they are, it isn't always simple to be their owners and there are various problems one can come up against. The stature of these dogs doesn't make it easy for those who always want to have them by their side. These dogs, due to their size, were born to carry out specific tasks and jobs such as: hunting, guarding or personal defence, emergency search and rescue, as well as assisting the police and the blind.

Giant (Molossers)

This category includes: Great Danes, Newfoundlands, Mastiffs, Leonbergers, Landseers, and more. This type of dog can weigh over 55 kg/121 lbs and be over 75 cm/29.53" high. For giant dogs, all the inconveniences and problems that one might have in managing a large dog are, well, "enlarged". It should be mentioned, however, that the scale is balanced by the fact that they can fulfil the same roles as large dogs. They are usually calmer and calmer, but they generally don't live very long due to their notable growth and, because of their rapid development, they need special attention as they grow to ensure their bone structure isn't compromised, especially when it comes to their diet.

The coat

The coat pattern is the essential base for the creation of dog apparel with a good fit.

Plenty of different variations can be invented, based on two bases:
- classic, sleeveless, like an apron (great fit and incredibly practical);
- with sleeves/legs (less comfortable, but warmer);

Variations

All the models can be made with necklines of different shapes, with hoods, scarves, clips and ties added to two base patterns to character and style to the coat.

Don't forget that the size of the dog and the ease are important for the creation of the pattern: not all patterns are suitable for all dog sizes. Small dogs can be long and thing (like dachshunds) or short and round (like pugs), regular (like cocker spaniels and cavaliers, small bloodhounds), or minuscule (like miniature pinschers and chihuahuas).

For that reason, the measurements taken to create the coat are fundamental.

Boo Boo, a long-hair chihuahua, 10 cm/3.94" in height from the ground to the top of the shoulder and 16 cm/6.30" long is the smallest dog in the world, officially entered in the Guinness book of world records in 2010.

Giant George is the tallest dog in the world. He eats around 50 kg/110 lbs of food each month and sleeps in a real bed in the house. This enormous specimen, a grey Giant Dane born on 17 November 2005, lives with his owner David Nasser in Tucson, Arizona. His height from paw to shoulder measures 109 cm/42.91", the distance from ears to tail is a full 220 cm/86.61" and he weighs over 100 kg/220 lbs. On 15 February 2010, George was listed in the Guinness Book of World Records, earning him the title of the world's tallest dog. In addition to his notable size, Giant George is known for they way he sits on sofas and chairs as if he were a human.

Outer fabrics

Use durable performance fabrics (even better if they're waterproof), that can hold up to delicate wash cycles. Denim, Goretex, waxed cottons such as Barbour, faux leather. Wool can be used if first wet in lukewarm water.

Using materials that can only be dry-cleaned is not advisable, for obvious maintenance reasons.

Padding

Natural fibres and viscose are best. Even dogs can suffer from allergies and dermatitis! The lining should be easy to brush as the animal's fur will always be present within the coat. Cotton batting, white or dyed, fleece or wool are all perfectly good materials.

Hooks and fastenings

Choose convenient, adjustable clasps and hooks mounted on robust bands of nylon. Current products offer nice colours that easily can be combined with all types of fabric. Buttons and snaps tend to break or slacken (and thus not close as well) over time. Cotton laces are great as well, perfect for small dog coats (20-23 cm/7.87-9.06").

Customisation

Choosing a customised coat is a sign of distinction. Why should my dog have a coat that's exactly like that of another?

On the completed garment, you can embroider a design that combines the dog's name with the owner's initials.

Measurements that determine dog breed categories

If someone chooses to make a doggy garment, it means s/he really loves his/her faithful friend. This is exactly why it's useful to be aware of a few fundamental ideas about dog sizes, breeds and measurements. In addition to providing important and necessary information to better get to know one's dog, such information makes it possible to create patterns with greater skill and precision, in addition to the most suitable types of garment.

Dog sizes are divided into 5 categories:

MINI - SMALL - MEDIUM - LARGE - GIANT
- Small size dogs start at 16 cm/6.30";
- Medium size dogs start at 43 cm/16.93";
- Large size dogs start at 56 cm/22.05";
- Giant size dogs start at 72 cm/28.34";

ANATOMY AND MEASUREMENTS

The skeleton
The canine skeletal structure highlights their agility and resistance. Robust front legs, which support 60% of the animal's weight, nevertheless allow rapid, supple movements, while the hind legs, complete with powerful muscles, allow for rapid acceleration and maintain speed when running.

They allow movement to take place when the muscles attached to the bones contract: the bones move and the joints flex. It's the strength of the hind legs that allows the dog to jump and catch prey.

Even if dogs have approximately the same number of bones as people, their bones are shaped differently, developed to support their role as a predator. Strong jaws and limbs help them catch small and large prey, while their tail is important for balance and communication.

Measurements
Like with other garments, custom patterns for dogs start with taking the measurements of the "customer". Properly doing so is the most important factor for creating the best garment possible. The precautions to be aware of when measuring are:
- Measure in such a way that the dog is in a neutral yet erect position, not laying down or sitting.
- The measurements must be noted with precision on a special form, listing all the measurements to take.
- The measurements should be taken with a tailor's tape, as illustrated in the figure.
- The tailor's tape should be held snug without pinching, though be mindful that it isn't too loose either.
- The measurements should be marked down without the addition the garment's ease or margins. Those are added later, considering the type of garment to make and the fabric it is made in.

NB: *When the measurements aren't taken correctly, you may run into the issues seen in the first two pictures. The third picture on the right shows a well-fitting garment, where the measurements have been taken properly.*

How to take the measurements and choose the size.
- Chest circumference: measure at the largest part, right behind the legs;
- Neck circumference: take the measurement at the base of the neck, just below where the collar is;
- Length: measure the distance between the base of the neck (slightly above where the collar rests) and the tail;
- Other measurements: as shown;
- Abdomen circumference: measure at the narrowest point;
- Neck length: measure only if there is to be a collar;
- Front and back sleeve length: as indicated in the pattern;
- Chest width: from one shoulder to the other.

Compare the dog's measurements with those in the chart. Each measurement corresponds to a minimum and maximum size. The measurement that should take priority over the others when choosing the size is that of the chest.

NB: *The chart lists the standard garment measurements for dog apparel made by manufacturers, with reference mainly to the chest of the dogs. For custom garments, 3-5 cm/1.18-1.97" should be added as the ease.*

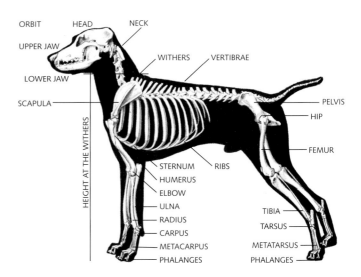

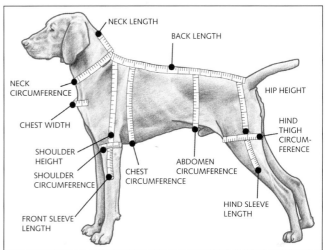

MEASUREMENT CHART (in cm/inches)

Size	Chest Cir.	Neck Cir.	Length
XS	26-28/10.24-11.02	21-22 /8.27-8.66	8-20/7.09-7.87
S	31-33/12.20-12.99	21-23/8.27-9.06	23-25/9.05-9.84
M	37-39/14.57-15.35	24-26/9.45-10.24	27-29/10.63-11.42
L	43-45/16.93-17.72	28-30/11.02-11.81	31-34/12.02-13.39
XL	50-53/19.69-20.87	33-35/12.99-13.78	36-39/14.17-15.35
2XL	58-61/22.84-24.02	37-40/14.57-15.75	41-45/16.14-17.72
3X	65-68/25.59-26.77	42-45/16.54-17.72	6-51/18.11-20.09
4XL	75-79/29.53-31.01	45-50/17.72-19.69	61-66/24.02-25.98
5XL	85-89/33.46-35.04	50-55/19.69-21.65	72-77/28.35-30.32
6XL	95-100/37.40-39.37	57-62/22.44-24.41	83-89/32.68-35.04
7XL	105-110/41.34-43.31	65-70/25.59-27.56	94-102/37.01-40.16

Dog apparel is an accessory that has been criticised by some because they consider it useless, or think it is uncomfortable or annoying to the dog. In reality, this idea isn't entirely correct. Though some animal outfits are purely for aesthetics, many also play a very important role in defending the health of the animal, which may not always be optimal.

Garment types

The most important apparel item for dogs is surely the *coat*. This garment is not, in the majority of cases, a simple whim of the animal's owner, but instead is often necessary to protect the pet's health.

When choosing this garment, it is important to evaluate a few elements before deciding if it's necessary to make it or buy it, depending on the dog. In particular:

1. **The fur.** The first element to consider is the dog's fur. In fact, long hair dogs feel the cold much less than short-hair dogs. When considering the dog's fur, however, always remember to keep the *undercoat (or down)* in mind as, when particularly thick, it protects the animal from the cold much more than long-hair, single-coated dogs.

2. **Age.** The second element to consider is the age of the animal. Very young or very old dogs are more susceptible to the cold as their body is poorly equipped to deal with drastic changes in temperature.

3. **Size.** Take the size of the dog into consideration. Lean, thin dogs often feel the cold more than a robust dog, which is why you often see small dogs, such as a poodle, instead of large dogs, such as a German shepherd, wearing coats

4. **Where they live.** Where they live, in the sense that dogs often live in the house with their owners and are used to a warm environment. When they then go outside, the change in temperature strikes them, even when they have long hair. This is why it's a good idea to cover them.

5. **Illness.** In terms of illnesses and weaknesses, the same applies for elderly or very young dogs. Their bodies are unable to provide enough warmth on their own, meaning that intense temperature swings can be particularly harmful. Again in this case we recommend a coat.

Other types of dog apparel

In addition to coats, there are various accessories available that fall under the dog apparel category, starting with simple shirts, sweaters and dresses, even caps, shoes and other similar accessories. In terms of shirts, sweaters or dresses, you will find a wide variety of models in shops today. Classic coats may be in different colours of wool or even in various materials, such as chenille, cotton, fleece, etc.

Nowadays, animals tend to be dressed increasingly like their owners, so much so that there are models of coats, dresses and sweatshirts for dogs that are entirely identical to those we could buy for ourselves. Garments in waterproof fabric are quite useful and practical because they allow the dog to be walked when it's raining, without then having the problem of a wet dog returning to the house. Of course, depending on the pattern chosen, the difficulty of execution will change as well, considering that if you choose a more sophisticated, particular version, it's execution will surely be more involving.

In addition to coats, you can make rompers, trousers and skirts. These items can also be made by choosing from among different materials and patterns. There are even outfits for dogs designed to be worn on special occasions, such as elegant suits or costumes for Halloween or Carnival. Lastly, other accessories that can be made for our dogs are, for example, scarves, caps and shoes.

The latter can give rise to rather controversial opinions about their use, but it's best to remember that they can be quite useful, especially if used when it's raining, icy or snowing as they let the dog walk easily without running into obstacles or freezing his paws.

Sleeveless base coat

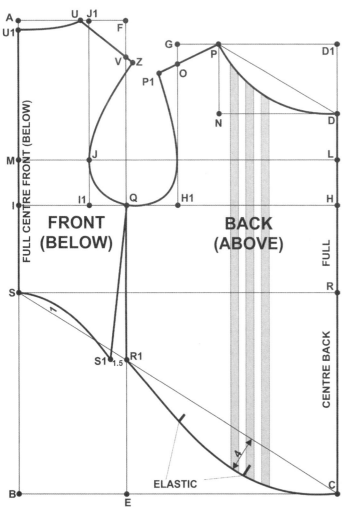

FRONT (BELOW)

BACK (ABOVE)

ELASTIC

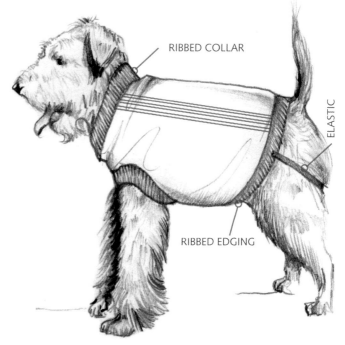

RIBBED COLLAR

ELASTIC

RIBBED EDGING

FOLD

5

32

RIBBED EDGING ON THE LEG OPENING

MEASUREMENTS
- Chest semi-circumference: 66 cm/25.94".
- Neck semi-circumference: 18 cm/7.09.
- Back length: 40 cm/15.75".

CONSTRUCTION
- Draw right angle A-B-C, with:
- A-B equal to the back length + ¼ of the same measurement
  (e.g.: 40 cm + 10 = 50/19.69")
- B-C equal to the chest circumference + garment ease
  (e.g.: 66 cm + 4 = 70 ÷ 2 = 35/13.79")
- C-D back length (e.g.: 40 cm/15.75")
- B-E ⅓ of B-C (e.g.: 35 ÷ 3 = 11.6 cm/4.57")
- A-F like B-E
- Draw E-F
- D-H ¼ of C-D (e.g.: 40 ÷ 4 = 10 cm/3.94")
- Draw H-I (Chest line)
- D-D1 like D-H-3 (e.g.: 10 - 3 = 7 cm/2.76")
- D1-G measure ½ of B-C (e.g.: 35 ÷ 2 = 17.5 cm/6.89")
- H-H1 like D-G
- Draw H1-G
- Draw H1-I18 B-C (Es.: 35 ÷ 4 = 8.75 cm/3.44")
- Draw I1-J-J1 parallel to H1-L1-G
- H-L ½ of D-H (e.g.: 10 ÷ 2 = 5 cm/1.97")
- Draw L-M - U1-S ⅔ of C-D + 1 cm/0.39"

(e.g.: 40 - 2 = 80 cm/31.50") 3 = 26.6 + 1 = 27.6 cm/10.87"
- Draw S-C

Back
- G-O 2 cm/0.79"
- D-N ¾ of D1-G (e.g.: 17.5 x 3 = 52.5 ÷ 4 = 13.1 cm/5.16")
- N-P like D-D1
- Draw D-P
- Draw P-O-P1 with the shoulder measurement (e.g.: 7 cm/2.76")
- Point Q ½ H-I
- Draw P1-Q as in the figure
- Mark point R1
- Join R1-C with a curved line

Front
- A-U ⅓ neck semi-circ. + 0.5 cm/0.20" (e.g.: 18 ÷ 3 = 6 + 0.5 = 6.5 cm/2.56").
- A-U1 1 cm/0.39"
- Draw a curved line U-U1
- F-V 4 cm/1.57"
- Draw U-Z equal to P-P1 on the back
- Draw Z-Q as in the figure
- Q-S1 like Q-R1
- Shift by 1.5 cm/0.59"
- Draw S-S1 with a curved line

226

SLEEVELESS COAT

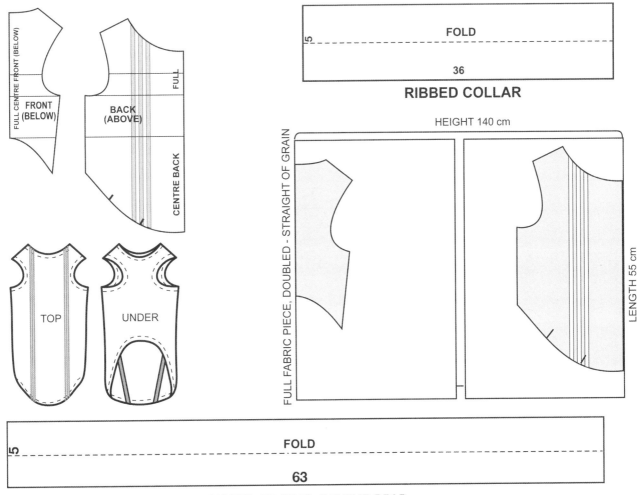

FRONT (BELOW)

FULL CENTRE FRONT (BELOW)

BACK (ABOVE)

FULL

CENTRE BACK

TOP

UNDER

FULL FABRIC PIECE, DOUBLED - STRAIGHT OF GRAIN

FOLD

36

RIBBED COLLAR

HEIGHT 140 cm

LENGTH 55 cm

5

FOLD

63

RIBBED EDGING ON THE REAR

ASSEMBLY

You'll need
- 55 cm x 140 cm (21.65 x 55.12") fleece
- 2.70 m/106.30" of phosphorescent tape, 2.5 cm/0.98" wide
- 90 cm/35.43" of ribbing, 7 cm/2.76" wide
- 1.25 m/49.21" of ribbing, 8 cm/3.15" wide
- 70 cm/27.56" of soft elastic, 2 cm/0.79" thick
- 1 heat-seal number to apply
- Tonal yarn

Laying out the pieces on the fabric
On doubled fabric, with margins towards the inside, pin down the parts of the pattern, as shown in the figure.
 Cut, adding 0.7 cm/0.28" for the sewing margins.

Assembly
(N.B. Use an overlock or flat machine to overcast the joined seam margins with a zig-zag seam)
- Bring the upper back piece to a specialised shop and have them print lettering as you desire.
- Cut six strips of tape equal to the length of the upper-back following the relative markings; onto the back, fold 5 mm/0.20" of the pieces phosphorescent tape on both of the long sides, resting the back of the piece of tape on the 'right' side of the upper part (the dog's back).
- Apply the number on the left side above the tape pieces and topstitch around the entire edge at the base of the overcasting. Sew the shoulders (join Z to P1 and P to U). Cut the collar, using the 8 cm/3.15" ribbed edging, close the collar into a ring, fold the edging in half, wrong side to wrong side, and affix the two margins with pins.

- Rest the edge on the right face of the coat, making the seam of the edge line up with the centre front below (belly point U1), tack the open sides on the neckline and sew; lift the edge and topstitch on the right side of the fabric, keeping the seam margins towards the coat, at 4 mm/0.16". Sew the sides (join Q to Q and S1 to R1). Cut the edges of the holes around the front legs in the measurement of the holes minus 2 cm/0.79", using the 8 cm/3.15" wide ribbed edging; close the edging into a ring, fold the edgings in half, wrong side to wrong side, and affix the two with pins.
- Rest the edgings on the right surface of the coat, making the seam of the edging line up with the seam of the side, tack the open sides on the leg hole and sew; lift the edging and topstitch on the right surface of the fabric, keeping the seam margins towards the coat, at 4 mm/0.16".
- Cut the lower edge of the coat in the measurements of the coat hem minus 3 cm/1.18", using the 7 cm/3.15" wide ribbed edging, close the edging into a ring, fold the edging in half, wrong side to wrong side, and affix the two margins with pins.
- Rest the edging on the right surface of the bottom of the coat, making the seam of the edging line up with the centre front below (belly point S), tack the open sides on the bottom and sew; lift the edging and topstitch on the 'right' side, keeping the seam margins towards the coat, at 4 mm/1.57".
- Cut two strips of elastic in the length necessary to affix the coat around the hind legs (not too tight); affix the ends with top stitching on the seam of the bottom edge of the upper back piece, following the relative marks.

BASE COAT WITH SLEEVES

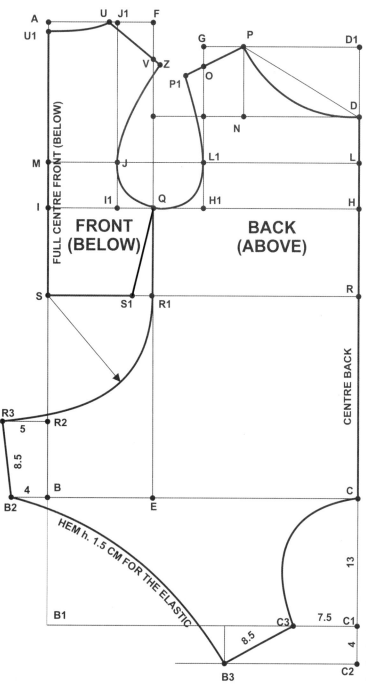

FRONT (BELOW)

BACK (ABOVE)

FULL CENTRE FRONT (BELOW)

CENTRE BACK

HEM h. 1.5 CM FOR THE ELASTIC

VELCRO®

RIBBED COLLAR

ELASTIC

- Draw I1-J-J1 parallel to H1-L1-G
- H-L ½ of D-H (e.g.: 10 ÷ 2 = 5 cm/1.97")
- Draw L-M.

Back
- G-O 2 cm/0.79"
- D-N ¾ of D1-G (e.g.: 17.5 x 3 = 52.5 ÷ 4 = 13.1 cm/5.16")
- N-P like D-D1
- Draw D-P
- Draw P-O-P1 with the shoulder measurement (e.g.: 7 cm/2.76")
- Point Q at the cross point of F-E
- Draw P1-Q as in the figure.
- C-C1 13 cm/5.12"
- Draw C1-B1
- C1-C2 4 cm/1.57"
- C1-C3 7.5 cm/2.95"
- Draw C3-B3 with the measurement ½ thigh 8.5 cm/3.35"
- B-B2 4 cm/1.57"
- Draw B2-B3 with a curved line
- B-R2 8.5 cm/3.35"
- R2-R3 5 cm/1.97"
- Draw B2-R3 and R3-R1 with a curved line.

Front
- A-U ½ of A-F-0.5/0.20" (e.g.: 11.6÷2=5.8+0.5=6.3 cm/2.48").
- Draw a curved line U-U1
- F-V 3.5 cm/1.38"
- Draw U-Z equal to P-P1 on the back
- Draw Z-Q as in the figure
- U1-S ⅔ of C-D + 0.5 cm/0.20" (e.g.: 40 x 2 = 80 ÷ 3 = 26.6 + 1 = 27.6 cm/10.87")
- Draw S-R as in the figure.
- S1-R1 2 cm/0.79"
- Draw S-S1 and S1-Q.

- Draw right angle A-B-C, with:
- A-B equal to the back length + ¼ of the same measurement (e.g.: cm 42 + 10.5 = 52.5/19.69")
- B-C equal to the chest circumference + garment ease (e.g.: 66 + 4 = 70 ÷ 2 = 35 cm/13.78")
- C-D back length (e.g.: 40 cm/15.75")
- B-E ⅓ of B-C (e.g.: 35 ÷ 3 = 11.6 cm/4.57")
- A-F like B-E
- Draw E-F
- D-H ¼ of C-D (e.g.: 40 ÷ 4 = 10 cm/3.94")
- Draw H-I (chest line)
- D-D1 like D-H-3 (e.g.: 10 - 3 = 7 cm/2.76")
- D1-G ½ of B-C (e.g.: 35 ÷ 2 = 17.5 cm/6.89")
- H-H1 like D-G
- Draw H1-G
- H1-I1 ¼ B-C (e.g.: 35 ÷ 4 = 8.75 cm/3.44")

COAT WITH SLEEVES

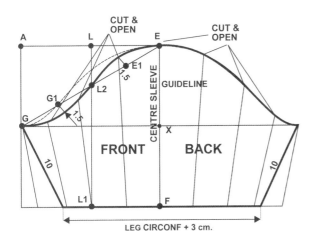

CUT & OPEN
CUT & OPEN
LEG CIRCONF + 3 cm.

SLEEVE

- Draw the sleeve as illustrated;
- Draw the lines, cut along these lines and open, as shown in the figure.

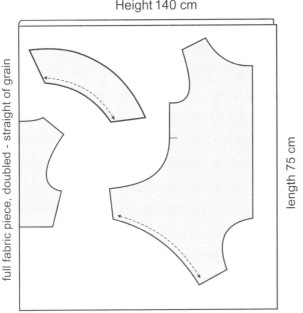

Height 140 cm

full fabric piece, doubled - straight of grain

length 75 cm

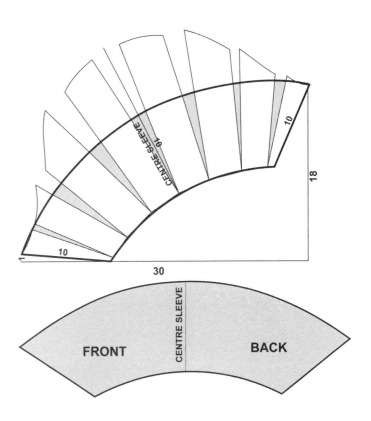

ASSEMBLY

You'll need
Lay out on the fabric:
- 75 cm x 140 cm (29.53 x 55.12") cotton
- 55 cm/21.65" of ribbing, 6 cm/2.36" wide
- 70 cm/27.56" of elastic, 1 cm/0.39" wide
- 30 cm/11.81" of Velcro®
- Tonal yarn

Laying out the pieces on the fabric
On doubled fabric, affix the pattern pieces, as shown in the layout image.
Cut, adding 1.5 cm/0.59" for the seam margins; 2 cm/0.79" for the hems on the centre back pieces; 1.5 cm/0.59" for the other hems.

Assembly
- Sew the front (belly) to the upper (back) at the sides (join S1 to R1 and Q to Q). Sew the shoulders (join P1 to Z and P to U).

- Close the sleeves of the hind legs (join R3 to C3 and B2 to B3).
- Close the edging of the collar into a ring in the measurements of the neckline minus 2 cm/0.79"; fold the edging in half, wrong side to wrong side, and affix the two margins with pins; turn the coat insdie out, add the edging, right face to right face, sew the open sides of the edging to the neckline and turn over again; topstitch on the right face of the fabric at 6 mm/0.24", keeping the seam margins towards the coat.
- Close the sleeves of the front legs (join B1 to C and F to E) and insert them in the coat.
- With an overlock or zig-zag stitch, overcast the bottom of the sleeves of the front and hind legs; fold the hem of the bottom of the sleeves of the front and hind legs onto the back side of the fabric and affix it with stitching at the base of the overcasting, leaving a small opening to insert the elastic. Insert the elastic at the bottom of the sleeves of the front and hind legs in the amount required, close it into a ring and finish the seam hems by hand stitching.
- Fold 1 cm/0.39" of the centre left rear (the back) to the wrong face of the fabric and apply the Velcro®; fold 1 cm/0.39" of the centre right back onto the right face of the fabric and apply the Velcro®.

Raglan sleeve base for small dogs

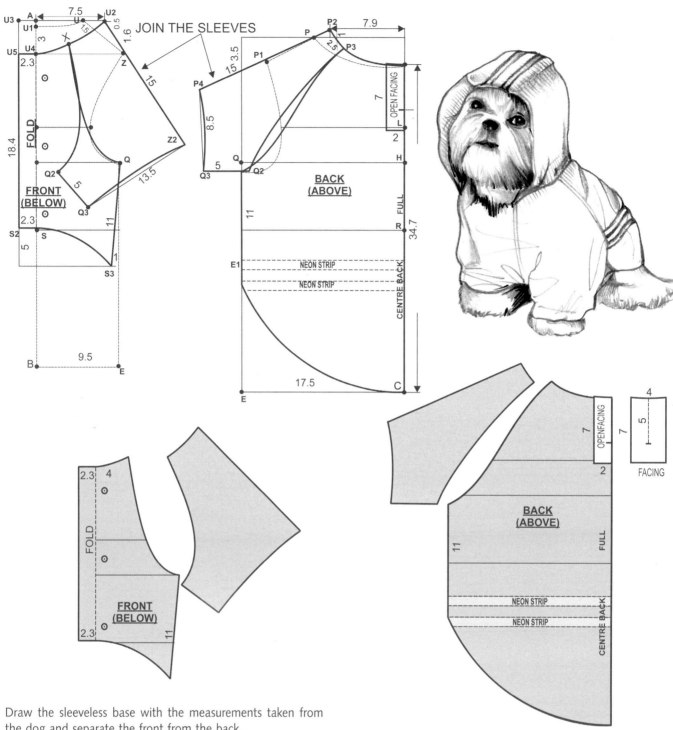

Draw the sleeveless base with the measurements taken from the dog and separate the front from the back.

Raglan sleeve patterns for dogs differ from those for people due to their clearly different conformation.

Front (below)
- U1-U4 3 cm/1.18" - Create the neckline U2-U4; - U4-X 4 cm/1.57"; Draw X-Q with a curve; - X-Q2 like X-Q; - U2-Z2 15 cm/5.91"; squared Z2-Q3 13.5 cm/5.31"; Q2-Q3 5 cm/1.97" (or the desired sleeve length).

Back (upper)
Draw the neckline as in the figure; P2-P4 like U2-Z2; P4-Q3 8.5 cm/3.35"; Q3-Q2 5 cm/1.97"; P2-P3 2.5 cm/0.98"; join P3-Q with a curve; P3-Q2 like P3-Q; Q-E1 like Q-S3 on the front; D-C back length 34.7 cm/13.66"; join E1-C with a curve.
- Draw the facing and the small flap to cover the open side as in the figure.

Sleeve
- Join the sleeve drawn on the front to that of the rear at the centre sleeve and smoothly adjust the upper part and the hemline.

Cuff
- Draw a rectangle measuring 23 x 6 cm/9.06 x 2.36" and mark the centre line with a dash for the fold.

Hood
- Draw a rectangle whose height is equal to that of the head up to the neckline - 20 cm/7.87" and whose width is equal to that of the head from eye to eye, minus the central strip - 12.3 cm/4.84".
- Shape as in the figure.

Hood strip
- Draw a rectangle measuring 23 x 6.5 cm/9.06 x 2.56" and divide to position the neon strips as in the figure.

Assembling the raglan pattern

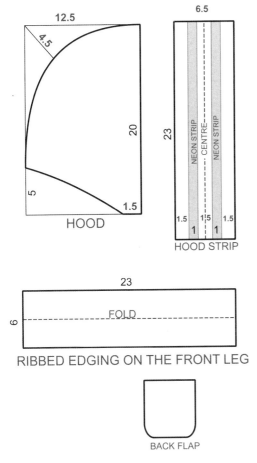

12.5
4.5
20
5
1.5
HOOD

6.5
23
NEON STRIP
CENTRE
NEON STRIP
1.5 **1.5** **1.5**
1 **1**
HOOD STRIP

23
FOLD
6
RIBBED EDGING ON THE FRONT LEG

BACK FLAP

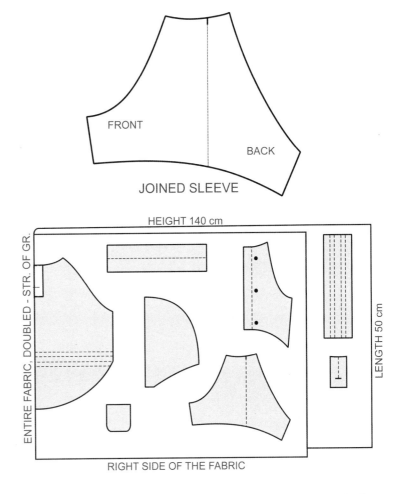

FRONT
BACK
JOINED SLEEVE

HEIGHT 140 cm
ENTIRE FABRIC, DOUBLED - STR. OF GR.
LENGTH 50 cm
RIGHT SIDE OF THE FABRIC

ASSEMBLY

You'll need
- 50 x 140 cm/19.69 x 55.12" of waterproof fabric
- 1 m/39.37" of phosphorescent tape, 2.5 cm/0.98" wide
- 3 snap fasteners
- Tonal yarn

Laying out the pieces on the fabric
On the folded fabric, pin the pattern pieces, except the hood strip and the back facing, on the 'right' side of the simple fabric, as shown in the layout image.
Cut, adding 1 cm/0.39" for the seam margins; 2 cm/0.79" for the hood hem and one short side of the hood band; 1 cm/0.39" for the other hems; neatly cut the centre front pieces.

Assembly
- Cut two strips of tape equal to the length of the rear (back); fold over to the wrong side of the fabric 5 mm/0.20" on both the long sides of the neon tape pieces, rest the back of the pieces of tape on the right face of the back, following the relative marks, and affix them with top stitching on both sides. Use the same procedure to apply the hood strip. Rest the right side of the facing on right side of the centre back, following the relative marks, create a 2 mm/0.07" seam around the opening. Cut following the relative marks, fold the lining to the wrong side and top stitch the opening at 2 mm/0.07" on the right side; fold the hem of the lining onto the wrong side and affix it with 2 mm/0.07" top stitching.
Rest the right side of a back flap on the right side of the other and sew the outline, except the high side. Discard the excess fabric, especially on the round parts and fold over again. Top stitch around the edge on the right side at 2 mm/0.07".

- Combine the back opening, without overlapping it, and affix it with hand stitching. Rest the opening flap on top, making the centre of the flap line up with the centre back and affix it with a quick seam on the neckline. Sewing the sides.
- Close the sleeves of the front legs and insert them in the waterproof fabric. With an overlocker or zig-zag stitch, overcast the hem of the waterproof fabric, fold the hem over to the wrong side of the fabric and affix it with stitches at the base of the overcasting.
 With an overlocker or a zig-zag stitch, overcast the centre front (belly). Close the edging of the front legs into a ring; fold the edges in half, wrong side to wrong side, and affix the two margins with pins.
- Turn the coat inside out, add the edging to the front legs, right side to right side, and sew the open sides of the edges on the bottom of the front leg sleeves. Turn back over, lift the edgings and top stitch on the right side of the fabric at 7 mm/0.28" keeping the seam margins towards the waterproof fabric. Join the hood and top stitch on the right side of the fabric at 2 mm/0.078", keeping the seam margins towards the hood.
With an overlocker or zig-zag stitch, overcast the opening of the hood, fold the hem over to the wrong side of the fabric and affix it with stitches at the base of the overcasting. Rest the right side of the hood on the right side of the waterproof material, fold the fastening edges of the front (belly) over the hood and sew the neckline. Turn over the fastening edges to the wrong side and overcast with an overlocker or zig-zag stitch, keeping the seam margins united. Top stitch the neckline at 7 mm/0.28" keeping the seam margins towards the waterproof fabric.
- Use top stitching to affix the front (belly) fastening edges to the base of the overcasting and apply the buttons according to the marks.

COAT WITH A MOTIF ON THE BACK

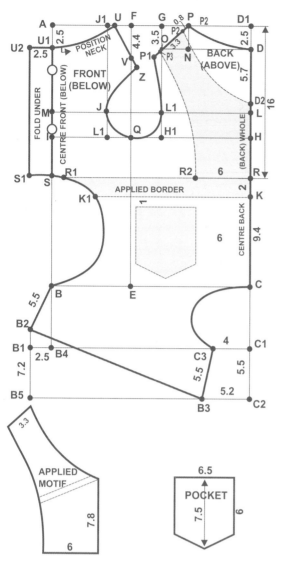

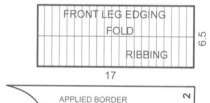

COAT
- Draw right angle A-B-C, with:
- A-B equal to the length of the back + 2.5 cm/ 0.98" (e.g.: 27.5 - 2.5 = 25 cm/9.84")
- B-C equal to the chest semi-circumference + garment ease (e.g. 21.5 cm/8.46")
- C-D back length (e.g.: 25 cm/9.84")
- B-E ⅓ of B-C + 1.5 cm/0.59" (e.g.: 21.5 ÷ 3 = 7.16 + 1.5 = 8.6 cm/3.39")
- A-F like B-E (Draw E-F)
- D-H ⅓ of C-D + 1 cm/0.39" (e.g.: 25 ÷ 3 = 8.3 + 1 = 9.3 cm/3.66")
- Draw H-I (Chest line)
- D-D1 2.5 cm/0.98"
- D1-G measure ½ of B-C + 2 cm/0.79" (e.g.: 35 ÷ 2 = 17.5 cm/6.89")
- H-H1 like D-G
- Draw H1-G
- H1-I1 ¼ B-C + 0.5 cm/0.20" (e.g.: 21.5 ÷ 5.4 + 0.5 = 5.9 cm/2.32")
- Draw I1-J-J1 parallel to H1-L1-G
- H-L ⅓ of D-H -1 cm/0.39" (Es.: 9.3 ÷ 3 = 3.1 - 0.5 = 2.6 cm/1.37").

Back
- G-O 3.5 cm/1.37"
- D-N 6.5 cm/2.56"
- N-P like D-D1
- Draw D-P
- Draw P-O-P1 with the shoulder measurement (e.g.: 5 cm/1.97")
- Point Q at the cross point of F-E
- Draw P1-Q as in the figure

- C-C1 9.4 cm/3.70"
- Draw C1-B1
- C1-C2 5.5 cm/2.17"
- C1-C3 4 cm/1.57"
- B2-B5 7.2 cm/2.83"
- C2-B3 5.2 cm/2.05"
- Draw C3-B3
- B-B2 5.5 cm/2.17"
- Draw B2-B3

Front
- A-U 6.8 cm/2.68"
- A-U1 2.5 cm/0.98"
- Draw a curved line U-U1
- F-V 4.4 cm/1.73"
- Draw U-Z equal to P-P1 on the back
- Draw Z-Q as in the figure
- U1-S 11.5 cm/4.53" (or the front measurement)
- Draw S-R as in the figure.
- U1-U2 and S-S1 2.5 cm/0.98"
- Draw U2-S1
- D1-R 16 cm/6.30"
- R-R2 6 cm/2.36"
- D-D2 5.7 cm/2.24"
- P2-P3 3.3 cm/1.30"
- Draw the application
- Draw the applied edge as in the figure.

HOOD WITH A MOTIF

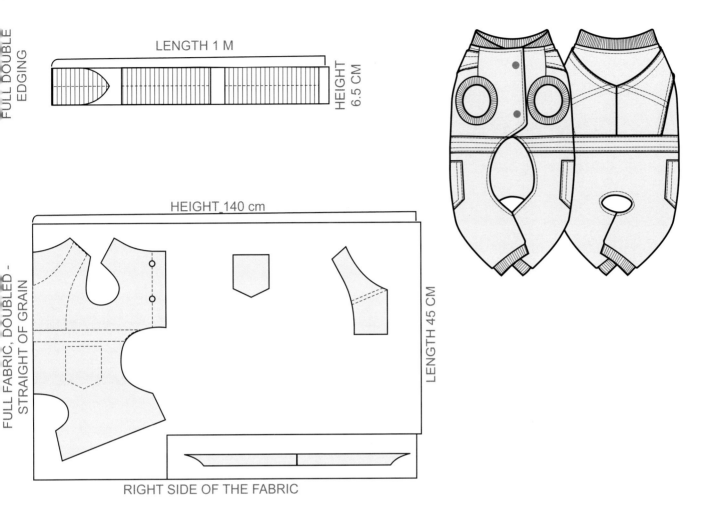

FULL DOUBLE EDGING

LENGTH 1 M

HEIGHT 6.5 CM

HEIGHT 140 cm

FULL FABRIC, DOUBLED - STRAIGHT OF GRAIN

LENGTH 45 CM

RIGHT SIDE OF THE FABRIC

ASSEMBLY

You'll need
- 45 cm x 140 cm (29.53 x 55.12") cotton
- 1 m/39.37" of ribbing, 6.5 cm/2.56" wide
- 15 x 6 cm/5.91 x 2.36" of heat-seal interfacing
- 2 snap fasteners
- Tonal yarn

Laying out the pieces on the fabric
On the folded fabric, pin the pattern pieces, except the edging applied to the right side of the open fabric, as shown in the layout image. On the folded edging, affix the pattern pieces, as shown in the layout image. Cut, adding 1 cm/0.59" for the seam margins, 1.5 cm/0.59" for the hem of the pockets; neatly cut the centre front pieces (belly), the collar and the front and hind leg sleeve edges.

Assembly
- Use an iron to fold the seam margins of the sides and the neckline of the applied motifs on the wrong side of the fabric, then affix them on the right side with a double seam. Create a double seam as a motif, following the relative marks. Place the wrong side of the motifs on the right side of the back, following the relative marks, and affix them with tacking to the base and shoulders.
- With an iron, fold the seam margins of the long sides of the applied border over to the wrong side. Place the wrong side of the edging on the right side of the back, above the motifs, following the relative marks, and affix it with tacking. Top stitch both sides on the right side with a double seam.

- Baste the hem of the pockets and affix it with a double seam; with an iron, fold the pocket seam margins onto the wrong side. Place the wrong side of the pockets on the right side of the sides, following the relative marks. Use tacking and top stitching to affix them to the right side with a double seam. Sew the shoulders (join P1 to Z and P to U).
- Reinforce the front fastening edges with heat seal interfacing and overcast using the centre front (belly) parts with an overlocker or a zig-zag stitch.
- Fold the collar in half, wrong side to wrong side, and affix the two margins with pins. Place the collar, turned downwards, on the right side of the neckline, starting from point U1 until the other and tack. Re-fold the front fastening edges (already with the heat seal fabric) over the neckline and sew the neckline. Fold the fastening edges over to the wrong side, lift the collar and top stitch on the right side at 7 mm/0.28", keeping the seam margins towards the coat.
Close the sleeves of the hind legs (join C3 to B and B3 to B2). Close the edging of the front and hind leg sleeves into a ring; fold the edges in half, wrong side to wrong side, and affix the two margins with pins.
- Turn the coat inside out, insert the hind edges into the sleeves of the hind legs, right side to right side, and sew the open sides of the edges on the bottom of the hind leg sleeves. Apply the front leg sleeve borders in the same fashion. Apply the buttons on the edges of the front (belly) fastenings, following the relative marks.

COAT FOR LARGE DOGS

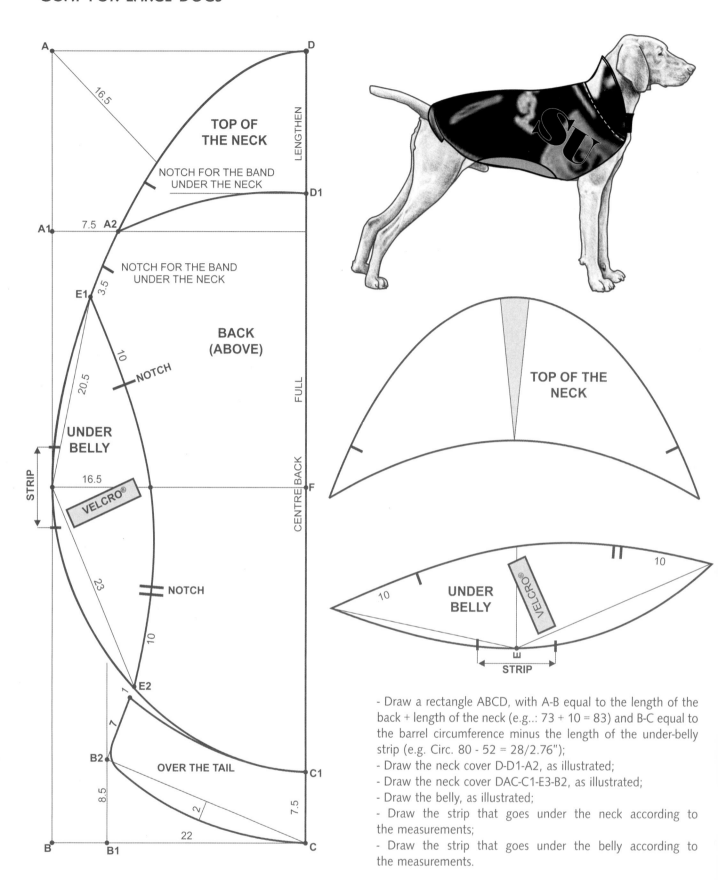

A

16.5

D

**TOP OF
THE NECK**

LENGTHEN

NOTCH FOR THE BAND
UNDER THE NECK

D1

A1 7.5 A2

NOTCH FOR THE BAND
UNDER THE NECK

E1 3.5

10

20.5

NOTCH

**BACK
(ABOVE)**

FULL

**UNDER
BELLY**

16.5

CENTRE BACK

F

STRIP

VELCRO®

23

10

NOTCH

E2

7

7

B2

8.5

OVER THE TAIL

C1

2

7.5

22

B B1 C

**TOP OF THE
NECK**

**UNDER
BELLY**

10

10

VELCRO®

E

STRIP

- Draw a rectangle ABCD, with A-B equal to the length of the back + length of the neck (e.g..: 73 + 10 = 83) and B-C equal to the barrel circumference minus the length of the under-belly strip (e.g. Circ. 80 - 52 = 28/2.76");
- Draw the neck cover D-D1-A2, as illustrated;
- Draw the neck cover DAC-C1-E3-B2, as illustrated;
- Draw the belly, as illustrated;
- Draw the strip that goes under the neck according to the measurements;
- Draw the strip that goes under the belly according to the measurements.

50/55 (check circumference)

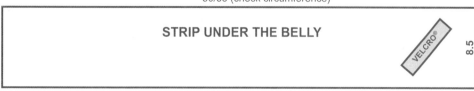

STRIP UNDER THE BELLY

VELCRO®

8.5

234

ASSEMBLING THE CAPE

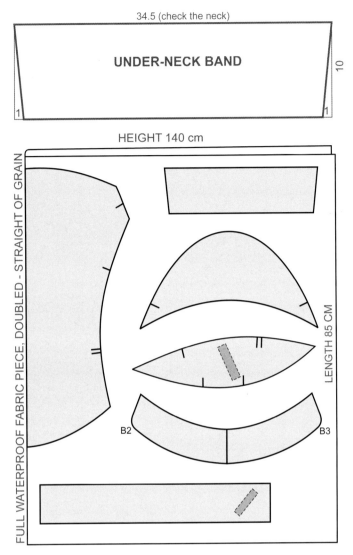

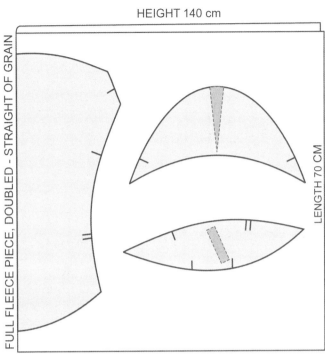

UNDER-NECK BAND

34.5 (check the neck)

HEIGHT 140 cm

HEIGHT 140 cm

FULL WATERPROOF FABRIC PIECE, DOUBLED - STRAIGHT OF GRAIN

FULL FLEECE PIECE, DOUBLED - STRAIGHT OF GRAIN

LENGTH 85 CM

LENGTH 70 CM

B2   B3

ASSEMBLY

You'll need
- 85 x 140 cm/33.46 x 55.12" of waterproof fabric
- 70 cm x 140 cm (27.56 x 55.12") fleece
- 10 cm/3.94" of Velcro®
- Tonal yarn

Laying out the pieces on the fabric
On doubled fabric, affix the pattern pieces, as shown in the layout image. Cut, adding 1 cm/0.39" for the seam margins.

Assembly
- Join the under-belly pieces to the upper (back) of both types of fabric. Turn the seam margin on to the wrong side of the entire outline of the cape in waterproof fabric and in fleece, and affix it with tacking. Place the right side of an under-belly strip on the right side of the other, tack the long sides and one of the short sides and sew; turn over.
- Place the right side of a tail flap on the right side of the other and tack around the edge (starting from E3, B2 and continue until mirrored B3), except the base, and sew. Turn over and top stitch on the right side of the base of the internal seam margins.

- Place the right side of a top collar flap on the right side of the other and tack around the edge, except the base, and sew. Turn over and top stitch on the right side of the base of the internal seam margins. Baste the tail flap on the back of the cape in waterproof fabric along the bottom, the over collar flap on the neckline, and the under-belly strip on the right-hand side, following the marks.
- Place the wrong side of one cape on the wrong side of the other, tack around the entire edge and top stitch at 5 mm/0.20", stopping contemporaneously over the tail, over the neck and the under-belly strip.
- Place the right side of an under-neck strip on the right side of the other and tack around the entire edge, leaving a small opening to turn it inside out, and sew. Turn inside out and finish the seam with hand stitches. Place the under-neck strip on the assembled cape, following the relative marks, then affix it with basting and top stitch, following the seam around the edge. Apply the velcro® to the under-belly strip and on the right side of the under-belly, following the relative marks.

TECHNICAL CARD AND MEASUREMENT CONVERSION TABLE

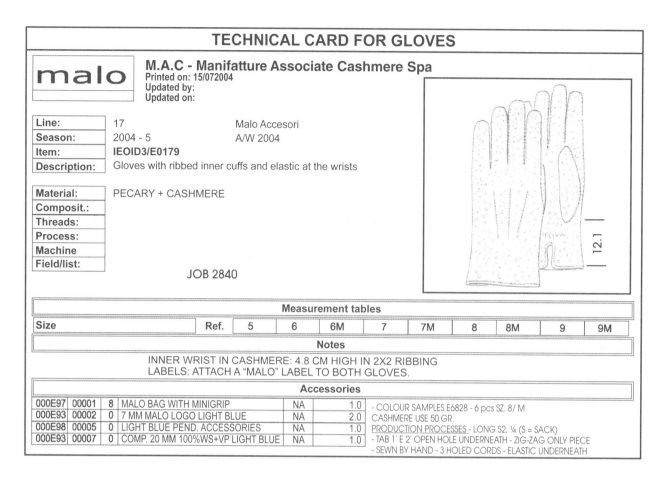

TECHNICAL CARD FOR GLOVES

malo

M.A.C - Manifatture Associate Cashmere Spa
Printed on: 15/072004
Updated by:
Updated on:

Line:	17	Malo Accesori
Season:	2004 - 5	A/W 2004
Item:	IEOID3/E0179	
Description:	Gloves with ribbed inner cuffs and elastic at the wrists	

Material:	PECARY + CASHMERE
Composit.:	
Threads:	
Process:	
Machine	
Field/list:	

JOB 2840

Measurement tables

Size		Ref.	5	6	6M	7	7M	8	8M	9	9M

Notes

INNER WRIST IN CASHMERE: 4.8 CM HIGH IN 2X2 RIBBING
LABELS: ATTACH A "MALO" LABEL TO BOTH GLOVES.

Accessories

000E97	00001	8	MALO BAG WITH MINIGRIP	NA	1.0
000E93	00002	0	7 MM MALO LOGO LIGHT BLUE	NA	2.0
000E98	00005	0	LIGHT BLUE PEND. ACCESSORIES	NA	1.0
000E93	00007	0	COMP. 20 MM 100%WS+VP LIGHT BLUE	NA	1.0

- COLOUR SAMPLES E6828 - 6 pcs SZ. 8/ M
CASHMERE USE 50 GR.
PRODUCTION PROCESSES - LONG S2, ¼ (S = SACK)
- TAB 1' E 2' OPEN HOLE UNDERNEATH - ZIG-ZAG ONLY PIECE
- SEWN BY HAND - 3 HOLED CORDS - ELASTIC UNDERNEATH

METRIC/IMPERIAL CONVERSION CHART

INCHES	CENTIMETERS	INCHES	CM	INCHES	CM
1/8	0.3	9	22.9	30	76.2
1/4	0.6	10	25.4	31	78.8
3/8	1.0	11	27.9	32	81.3
1/2	1.3	12	30.5	33	83.8
5/8	1.6	13	33.0	34	86.4
3/4	1.9	14	35.6	35	88.9
7/8	2.2	15	38.1	36	91.4
1	2.5	16	40.6	37	94.0
1 ¼	3.2	17	43.2	38	96.5
1 ½	3.8	18	45.7	39	99.1
1 ¾	4.4	19	48.3	40	101.6
2	5.1	20	50.8	41	104.1
2 ½	6.4	21	53.3	42	106.7
3	7.6	22	55.9	43	109.2
3 ½	8.9	23	58.4	44	111.8
4	10.2	24	61.0	45	114.3
4 ½	11.4	25	63.5	46	116.8
5	12.7	26	66.0	47	119.4
6	15.2	27	68.6	48	121.9
7	17.8	28	71.1	49	124.5
8	20.3	29	73.7	50	127.0

BIBLIOGRAPHY

Malabarra, I. *Signori le scarpe*, Idealibri, Milan,1985.

Tosetti, U. *Corso calzaturiero di modelleria*, Tecniche Nuove, Milan, 1988.

Girotti, E. *La calzatura, storia e costume*, Edizioni Be-Ma, Milan, 1986

Schiaffino, M. *O la borsa o la borsetta*, Idealibri, Milan, 1986

Espanet, L. *Valigia & C.*, Idealibri, Milan, 1986

Campione, A. *Il cappello da uomo*, Ed. Be-Ma, Milan 1988

Cella, C. *La mano, il guanto*, Idealibri, Milan, 1989.

Mosconi, D. and Villarosa, R. *Centottantotto nodi da collo*, Idealibri, Milan 1984

Nuvoletti, G. *Elogio della cravatta*, Idealibri, Milan 1982

Baudot, François *A Century of Fashion*, London and New York 1999

Bordignon Elestici, Letizia 1) *Borse e valigie*, Milan, 1989 2) *Ombrelli*, Milan, 1990

Bradfield, Nancy *Historical Costumes of England from the Eleventh to the Twentieth Centurx*, London 1966

Campione, Adele *Il cappello da donna*, Milan 1989

Chaille, François *The Book of Ties*, Paris 1994

Chenoune, Farid *A History of Men's Fashion*, Paris 1993

Cumming, Valerie *The Visual History of Costume Accessories*, London 1998

De Greef, John *Cravattes et accessoires*, Paris 1989

Doe, Tamasin and Cox, Patrick; *Wit Irony and Footwear* London and New York 1998

Ferragamo, Salvatore *Shoemaker of Dreams*, London 1957

Folledore, Giuliano *Il cappello da uomo*, Modena, 1989

Gibbings, Sarah *The Tie: Trends and Traditions*, London 1990

Ginsburg, Madeleine *The Hat: Trends and Traditions*, London 1990

Girotti, Eugenia *La calzatura, - Storia e costume (1945-1995)*, Milan, 1995

Leiber, Judith *The Artful Handbag*, London and New York 1995

McDowell, Colin 1) *Forties Fashion and The New Look*, London 1997; 2) *Shoes: Fashion and Fantasy*, London and New York 1994; 3) *Hats: Status, Style and Glamour*; London and New York 1997: 4) *Le Chapeau et la Mode*, Ed. Celiv, 1992

Martin, Richard *The St. James Fashion Encyclopedia*, Detroit 1997

Mercie, Marie *Voyages autour d'un chapeau*, Paris 1990

Robinson, Julian *Fashion in the Thirties*, London 1997

Worthington, Christa *Chic Aimple: Accessories*, London and New York 1996

Mazloum, C. *Come scegliere, acquistare, indossare i gioielli e le pietre preziose*, Gremese, Rome 1990.

Acerenza, F. *Gli occhiali*, Ed. Be-Ma, Milan 1988.

Bergamaschi, G. *Oro!*, Idealibri, Milan 1984.

Black, Anderson I. *Storia dei gioielli*, De Agostini, Novara 1986.

Calderini E. and T. *Acconciature antiche e moderne*, Sperling & Kupfer, Milan 1963.

Gregorietti, G. *Il gioiello nei secoli*, A. Mondadori, Milan 1969.

Mascetti Triossi, D. A. *Gli orecchini*, Longanesi, Milan 1991.

Lichtemberger, L. *Due gocce di profumo*, Idealibri, Milan 1983.

Asensio, F. *The Best Shops*, Barcelona 1990

Bally Schuhmuseum *Graphik rund um den Schuh*, in "Schriften des Bally Schuhmuseums" - Schonenwerd 1968

Baynes. K.U.K. *The Shoe Show. British Shoes since 1790*, London 1979

Blum. S. *Everyday Fashions of the Thirties as Pictured in Sears Catalogues*, New York 1986

Durain-Ress, S. *Schuhe. Vom spiiten mittelalter bis zur gegenwart*, Munich 1991

Frigeni, Renato and Tousijn, Willem *L'industria delle calzature in Italia*, Soc. Editrice Il Mulino Bologna, 1976

Giglinger, K. *Schuh und Leder*, Vienna 1990

Gillespie, C.C. *Diderot Pictorial Encyclopaedia of Trades and Industry. Manufacturing and Technical Arts in Plates*, New York 1993

Hálová-Jahodovác *Vergessene handwerkskunst*, Prague 1995

Honnef, K., Schlüter, B. and Küchels, B. *Die verlassenen Schuhe*, Bonn 1994

Mendicini, Giorgio *L'eleganza maschile. Guida pratica al perfetto guardaroba*, Mondadori Farigliano 1997

O' Keeffe, L. *Schuhe*, Cologne 1997

Roetzel, Bernhard *Il gentleman, il manuale di eleganza maschile*, Konemann 1999

The Swenters Shoes *Art Shoes or no Shoes*, Antwerp 1997

Robinson, Fred Miller *The Man in the Bowler Hat*, University of North Carolina Press, London 1993

Probert, Christina *Hats in Vogue Since 1910*, Thames and Hudson Ltd, London 1981

Demorex, Jacqueline *Le siècle en chapeaux*, Claude Saint- Cyr, Edition du May, Paris 1991

Jouvion, Philippe *Le Béret*, Editions du Rouergue, France 1998

Thaarup, Aage *Heads and Tales*, Cassell & Company Ltd London 1956

Reynolds, William and Ranch, Rich. *The Cowboy Hat*, Gibbs Smith, Layton, Utah, USA 1995

Snyder, Jeffrey B. *Stetson Hats*, Schiffer Publishing 1997

Buchet, Martine *Panama: a Legendary Hat*, Editions Assouline

Museums and schools

ITALIAN MUSEUMS

Museo dell'arte del cappello
C.so Belvedere, 279 - Ghiffa (VB)
Museo del cappello Borsalino
Via Cavour, 84 - Alessandria
Museo del cappello
Via Borgo XX Settembre - Montappone (AP)
Museo della calzatura
P.le Marconi - Sant'Egidio a Mare (AP)
Museo della Calzatura "Pietro Bertolino"
Vigevano (PV) - Istituito nel 1958
Museo dello Scarpone
V.le Zuccareda, 5 - Montebelluna (TV) - Istituito nel 1984
Museo della calzatura d'autore di Rossimoda
Via Doge Pisani, 1/2 - Stra (VE)
Museo dell'ombrello e del Parasole
Via Golf Panorama, 2 - Gignese (VB)
Museo dell'occhiale
Via degli alpini, 39 - Pieve di Cadore (BL)
Museo Ferragamo
Via de' Tornabuoni, - Florence
Museo della Seta
Via Valleggio, 3 - Como
Centro di Firenze per la Moda Italiana
Non-profit foundation est. 1954
Centro Studi Storia Tessuto e Costume
Founded in Venice in 1985
Ente Moda Italia - Florence
Non-profit foundation est. 1983
Ente Nazionale della Moda - Turin
Est. 1935
Museo del Merletto - Burano (Venice)
Museum opened in 1978

Musée du Chapeau - Route de Saint-Galmier - Chazellez-sur - Lyon (France)
Paisley Museum - High Street - Paisley Pa1 2BP, - Scotland
Silk Museum The Heritage Center
Roe Street Macclesfield Sk11 6UT - Cheshire (England)
Museu Nacional do Traje - Lisbon - Costume museum opened in 1974
Museu Textil i d'Indumentaria - Barcelona
Textile and clothing museum opened in 1982
FIT Museum - New York
The largest collection of textiles and clothing in the world, since 1967
Museum fur Kunst un Gewerbe - Hamburg
Clothing museum opened in 1877
Museum of Costume - Bath (GB) - Clothing museum, est 1963
Museum of Fine Arts - Boston
Museum on Andean Textiles, Costume and Clothing, opened in 1870
Museum of the City - New York
Museum of American Fashion, opened in 1982
Museum of Welsh Life - Cardiff (Whales)
Clothing and accessory museum opened in 1975
Musée de da Chemisiere et de l'Elegange Masculine - Argenton-sur-Creuse
(France) - Museum of mens clothing and accessories, opened in 1980
Musée de Cristian Dior - Granville (France)
Museum opened at the designer's childhood home in 1988.
Musée de la Mode - Marseille - Museum of French fashion, opened in 1993
Musée de la Mode et du Textile - Paris - Opened within the Louvre ins 1977
Musée de l'Impression sur Etoffe - Mulhouse
Local French museum of printed textiles, est in 1987
Musée des Beaux Arts et de la Dentelle - Calais (France)
Museum of hand-made and industrial lace, opened in 1930
Musée Galliera - Paris
Luxury ready-to-wear museum opened in 1977

Schools

PRIVATE ITALIAN SCHOOLS

Accademia di costume e di moda - Rome
School founded in 1964 by Rosanna Pistolese
Accademia Koefia - Rome, founded in 1952
Accademia nazionale dei sartori - Rome
Association founded in 1575
Euromode school - istituto europeo per la moda - Main campus in
Bergamo - School opened in 1939. Directed by Prof. Antonio
Donnanno - Headquarters and franchises in all of Italy and abroad
Scuola di costume e moda - Urbino
University department founded in 1998
Scuola pubblica per la moda - Milan
Regional school opened in 1999
Istituto Carlo Secoli - Milan
School founded in 1934
Istituto europeo di design - Campuses in Milan, Turin, Rome and Cagliari
School founded in 1966
Istituto Callegari - Treviso
School founded in 1937
Isttuto Marangoni - Milan
School founded in 1935
Istituto De Lazzari - Turin
School founded by Magda De Lazzari
Istituto moda design "A. Panaro" - Bari
School founded by Arduino Panaro
Istituto di moda Burgo - Milan
School founded by Fernando Burgo

PUBLIC ITALIAN SCHOOLS

Istituto tecnico industriale "G. Natta" - Padua
State school for professional garment makers

Istituto tecnico industriale - Busto Arsizio
State school for knitwear
Istituto tecnico industriale "Fauser" - Novara
State school for knitwear
Istituto professionale moda e calzaturiero
Savignano sul Rubicone (FC)
Ipsia "O. Ricci" - Fashion and footwear - Montegranaro (AP)
Ipsia "C. Scarpa" - Fashion and footwear - Montebelluna (TV)

SCHOOLS ABROAD

Royal Academy of Fine Arts - Antwerp
School founded in 1663, fashion classes launched in 1963
Ecole de la chambre syndical de la couture - Paris
School founded in 1929
Ecole superieure des arts appliquees Du-Perre - Paris
State school for textile arts and fashion design
Ecole des industries textiles de Lyon
French state school for knitwear
Royal College of Art - London
School founded in 1860, fashion classes launched in 1943
Fashlon Institute of Technology - New York
School founded in 1944
St. Gallen textilfachschulen - St. Gallen
Swiss state school for textiles
Bunka Fashion College - School founded in Tokyo in 1985
Textilfachschule Augsburg - Augsburg
State school for textiles and knitwear
Bunder-und Versuchsansatalt fur Textilindustrie
Vienna's state school for the textile industry
Escuela técnica de tejidos de punto
Fashion school in Canet de Mar (Barcelona)

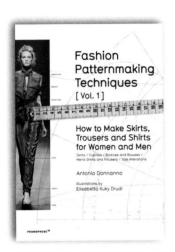

FASHION PATTERNMAKING TECHNIQUES [VOL. 1]
How to Make Skirts, Trousers and Shirts. Women / Men
Antonio Donnanno. Illustrations by Elisabetta Kuky Drudi

978-84-15967-09-5
210 x 297 mm. 256 pp.

FASHION PATTERNMAKING TECHNIQUES [VOL. 2]
How to Make Shirts, Undergarments, Dresses and Suits, Waistcoats and Jackets for Women and Men
Antonio Donnanno. Illustrations by Elisabetta Kuky Drudi

978-84-15967-68-2
210 x 297 mm. 256 pp.

FASHION PATTERNMAKING TECHNIQUES [VOL. 3]
How to Make Jackets, Coats and Cloaks for Women and Men
Antonio Donnanno. Illustrations by Elisabetta Kuky Drudi

978-84-16504-18-3
210 x 297 mm. 176 pp.

FASHION PATTERNMAKING TECHNIQUES FOR CHILDREN'S CLOTHING
Dresses, Shirts, Bodysuits, Trousers, Shorts, Jackets and Coats
Antonio Donnanno. Illustrations by Claudia Ausonia Palazio

978-84-16851-14-0
210 x 297 mm. 232 pp.

FASHION PATTERNMAKING TECHNIQUES HAUTE COUTURE [VOL. 1]
Haute Couture Models, Draping Techniques, Decorations
Antonio Donnanno

978-84-16504-66-4
210 x 297 mm. 256 pp.

FASHION PATTERNMAKING TECHNIQUES HAUTE COUTURE [VOL. 2]
Creative Darts, Draping, Frills and Flounces, Collars, Necklines and Sleeves, Trousers and Shirts
Antonio Donnanno

978-84-17412-38-8
210 x 297 mm. 200 pp.

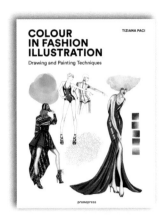

COLOUR IN FASHION ILLUSTRATION
Drawing and Painting Techniques
Tiziana Paci

978-84-16851-59-1
215 x 287 mm. 320 pp.

FASHION ILLUSTRATION & DESIGN
Methods & Techniques for Achieving Professional Results
Manuela Brambatti

978-84-16851-06-5
215 x 300 mm. 240 pp.

PALETTE PERFECT
Color Combinations Inspired by Fashion, Art & Style
Lauren Wager

978-84-15967-90-3
148 x 210 mm. 304 pp.

FASHION DETAILS
4,000 Drawings
Elisabetta Kuky Drudi

978-84-17412-68-6
195 x 285 mm. 384 pp.

Second edition in 2020

FASHION DRAPING TECHNIQUES VOL. 1
A Step by Step Course
Danilo Attardi

978-84-17656-32-4
285 x 195 mm. 192 pp.

FASHION DRAWING COURSE
From Human Figure to Fashion Illustration
Juan Baeza

978-84-15967-06-4
210 x 297 mm. 208 pp.

COLLARS & NECKLINES
Details in Fashion Design
Gianni Pucci

978-84-16504-17-6
230 x 240 mm. 224 pp.

HATS & CAPS
Fashion Accessories Design
Gianni Pucci

978-84-16851-69-0
230 x 240 mm. 224 pp.

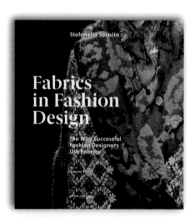

FABRICS IN FASHION DESIGN
The Way Successful Fashion Designers Use Fabrics
Stefanella Sposito.
Photos by Gianni Pucci

978-84-16851-28-7
225 x 235 mm. 336 pp.